Gospel Light's

Kids@Time ™

GOD'S KIDS GROW

IT'S BIBLE GROWN!

Reproducible!

Fruit of the Spirit

LEADER'S GUIDE

Gospel Light

How To Make Clean Copies From This Book

You may make copies of portions of this book with a clean conscience if

- you (or someone in your organization) are the original purchaser;
- you are using the copies you make for a noncommercial purpose (such as teaching or promoting your ministry) within your church or organization;
- you follow the instructions provided in this book.

However, it is ILLEGAL for you to make copies if

- you are using the material to promote, advertise or sell a product or service other than for ministry fund-raising;
- you are using the material in or on a product for sale; or
- you or your organization are not the original purchaser of this book.

By following these guidelines you help us keep our products affordable.

Thank you,
Gospel Light

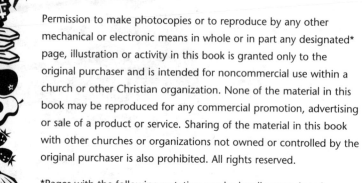

Gospel Light

Gospel Light KidsTime Curriculum

Publisher, William T. Greig • **Senior Consulting Publisher,** Dr. Elmer L. Towns • **Publisher, Research, Planning and Development,** Billie Baptiste • **Managing Editor,** Lynnette Pennings, M.A. • **Senior Consulting Editor,** Wesley Haystead, M.S.Ed. • **Senior Editor, Biblical and Theological Issues,** Bayard Taylor, M.Div. • **Senior Advisor, Biblical and Theological Issues,** Dr. Gary S. Greig • **Senior Editor,** Sheryl Haystead • **Editorial Team,** Amanda Abbas, Debbie Barber, Mary Gross, Karen McGraw • **Contributing Editors,** Linda Burlile, Mary Lou Canata, Lisa Daniel, Donna Harstine, Heather Kempton, Jean Larson, Debi Madsen, Linda Mattia, Sandy Michaud, Patty Moorehead, Willamae Myers, Noni Pendleton, Karen Perkins, Barb Platt, Sharon Short, Jay Bea Summerfield, Laura Taylor • **Illustrators,** Curtis Dawson, Chizuko Yasuda • **Designer,** Curtis Dawson

How to Use *KidsTime*

A few kids, one leader

If you teach alone, follow these simple steps to lead your class:

1. Read "*God's Kids Grow* Overview" on page 6 to get a clear view of what this course is all about.
2. Look at "Advice & Answers for Schedule Planning" on pages 8-12, choose the schedule that best fits your situation and decide which centers you will include.
3. Read the tip articles (pp. 13-26) for each center you will lead, taking note of the ways you can make each center an effective learning experience for the kids in your class.

Several kids, more than one teacher

If you teach with one or more other teachers, follow the above three steps and add one more!

Decide if each teacher will lead his or her class in all of the activities or if each teacher will lead only one activity for groups of students who rotate between the centers.

If you are the children's director or coordinator of *KidsTime*, follow the above steps and add a few more!

Lots of kids, several teachers, a director or coordinator

1. Pay special attention to "Getting & Keeping the Very Best Staff" on pages 27-28. Remember to start recruiting early—several months before *KidsTime* begins.
2. Read "Questions & Answers for a Terrific Program" on pages 29-31 for tips on how to distribute and store curriculum, special ways to involve parents, eye-catching decorating ideas and more!

Contents

How to Use *KidsTime* 3
A step-by-step *KidsTime* introduction for teachers or leaders—get a head start on a year's worth of harvesting God's fruit.

God's Kids Grow Overview. 6
Advice & Answers for Schedule Planning 8
Bible Story Center Tips. 13
Fruitful Lives Object Talk Tips. 17
Active Game Center Tips 18
Art Center Tips. 20
Worship Center Tips. 21
Bible Verse Coloring Center Tips 24
Service Project Center Tips. 25
Discipleship Activity Center Tips 26
Getting & Keeping the Very Best Staff. 27
Questions & Answers for a Terrific Program 29
Introducing Kids to Adult Worship. 32
Leading a Child to Christ 36
Lesson 1 The Fruit of the Spirit . . . . Galatians 5:22,23 37
Lesson 2 The Loving Samaritan . . . . Love 45
Lesson 3 Joy in Jail . . . . Joy. 53
Lesson 4 Abraham the Peacemaker . . . . Peace. 61
Lesson 5 The Patience of a Father . . . . Patience. 69
Lesson 6 A King's Kindness . . . . Kindness 77
Lesson 7 Daniel's Good Choice . . . . Goodness. 85
Lesson 8 Faithful in the Lions' Den . . . . Faithfulness 93
Lesson 9 Jesus, the Gentle Servant. . . . . Gentleness 101
Lesson 10 David's Self-Control . . . . Self-Control 109
Lesson 11 Jesus' Loving Acceptance. . . . . Love 117
Lesson 12 The Grateful Leper . . . . Joy. 125
Lesson 13 Solomon, Wise Peacemaker. . . . . Peace. 133
Lesson 14 Nehemiah's Patient Plan . . . . Patience. 141
Lesson 15 Abigail's Kindness . . . . Kindness 149
Lesson 16 Elisha's Good Example . . . . Goodness. 157
Lesson 17 God's Faithful Promise. . . . . Faithfulness 165
Lesson 18 A Gentle Attitude . . . . Gentleness 173
Lesson 19 Samson and Self-Control. . . . . Self-Control 181

Lesson 20 Love for a Blind Man . . . . Love 189

Lesson 21 Joyfully Found! . . . . Joy 197

Lesson 22 A Father's Trust . . . . Peace 205

Lesson 23 Abraham's Long Wait . . . . Patience 213

Lesson 24 A Boy Shares Kindness . . . . Kindness 221

Lesson 25 How Goodness Gives . . . . Goodness 229

Lesson 26 Brave and Faithful . . . . Faithfulness 237

Lesson 27 Paul's Gentle Words . . . . Gentleness 245

Lesson 28 The Greatest Love Ever . . . . Love 253

Lesson 29 Jesus Brings Great Joy! . . . . Joy 261

Lesson 30 Isaac Keeps the Peace . . . . Peace 269

Lesson 31 The Patient Prophet . . . . Patience 277

Lesson 32 Elisha's Kindness . . . . Kindness 285

Lesson 33 God's Family Listens . . . . Goodness 293

Lesson 34 Ruth's Faithfulness . . . . Faithfulness 301

Lesson 35 Joseph's Forgiveness . . . . Love 309

Lesson 36 Red Sea Celebration . . . . Joy 317

Lesson 37 Birds and Flowers . . . . Peace 325

Lesson 38 God Talks to Job . . . . Patience 333

Lesson 39 The Lame Man . . . . Kindness 341

Lesson 40 Cheerful Giving . . . . Goodness 349

Lesson 41 Noah Is Faithful . . . . Faithfulness 357

Lesson 42 Like a Forest Fire . . . . Self-Control 365

Lesson 43 Caring for Naaman . . . . Love 373

Lesson 44 Dedicated to God . . . . Joy 381

Lesson 45 Paul Keeps the Peace . . . . Peace 389

Lesson 46 Four Patient Friends . . . . Patience 397

Lesson 47 Moses in the Nile . . . . Kindness 405

Lesson 48 Esther Saves God's People . . . . Goodness 413

Lesson 49 Parable of the Talents . . . . Faithfulness 421

Lesson 50 Mary's Wise Choice . . . . Gentleness 429

Lesson 51 Solomon's Wisdom . . . . Self-Control 437

Lesson 52 A Man After God's Own Heart . . . . . Love 445

Music Resources
Word charts and lead sheets for all the music in this course 453

God's Kids Grow Overview

"The fruit of the Spirit is love, joy, peace, patience, kindness, goodness, faithfulness, gentleness and self-control. Against such things there is no law." Galatians 5:22,23

Welcome to a year's worth of good fruit!

God's Kids Grow will help you and your students discover how the fruit of God's Spirit grows in our lives. We'll explore the ways our character displays God's good fruit and learn about Christians throughout history whose lives demonstrated those character qualities. As we explore the expressions of each fruit of God's Holy Spirit in our lives, we'll learn to cultivate attitudes that will lead us to know God better and become the fruitful people He designed us to be.

Special Features

• Every lesson includes a creative play dough activity as part of the Bible story presentation. This involvement keeps kids' interest high and gives them a way to keep their hands and their minds focused on the story!

• Also included in every lesson is a Fruitful Lives Object Talk. Kids will learn about the life of a Christian whose actions exemplified the fruit that is the focus of that day's lesson.

• Because children learn in diverse ways, *God's Kids Grow* is filled with variety to appeal to kids' many learning styles. Students may participate in several learning centers involving active games, creative art activities that will help them express what they learn and a Worship Center with several options for student involvement (including a music video).

• Additionally, younger children may participate in a coloring page activity related to the Bible verse for that lesson.

• Older students will enjoy fresh ways to apply Bible truth as they participate in activities found in *The Big Book of Christian Growth*.

• For both younger and/or older students, you may choose projects from *The Big Book of Service Projects*. These activities will give students practical opportunities to demonstrate the fruit of God's Spirit in their lives.

• Because teachers are the heart of any teaching time, *God's Kids Grow* is especially easy for teachers to use. Because the Leader's Guide is reproducible, each member of the teaching team may be given his or her own page for leading any activity. Every activity emphasizes the session's Character Builder, so every team member understands the goal of the lesson. In addition, every lesson opens with a Teacher's Devotional that gives teachers insight and background about that lesson's Character Builder.

Expect a Great Harvest!

When you and your team members are full of eagerness and understanding of the lesson at hand, your students will be eager to learn and be inspired by every lesson! As you pray and organize this course to meet the needs of your group, ask God for a sense of expectancy of what He wants to do during this time and for sensitivity to ways you can be part of what He desires to accomplish. As you and your students discover how God can help us cultivate lives that express His power and presence, expect a great harvest of spiritual fruit!

Advice & Answers for Schedule Planning

Begin your planning for *KidsTime* by choosing a learning format. No matter when or where *KidsTime* takes place, there are two main format options—Self-Contained Groups and the Learning Center Plan. Read the following descriptions and select the format that fits your needs.

Self-Contained Groups

If you are confined to a single room or have a small class, Self-Contained Groups may be your best option. In this format, groups of seven or eight students are formed. Each group has a teacher who leads his or her group in the activities. (If the size of the group is larger, additional teachers or helpers are needed.)

The greatest benefit of Self-Contained Groups is that teachers are able to form meaningful relationships with the students since they remain together during the entire session. The biggest disadvantage is the difficulty in recruiting teachers who feel comfortable leading a variety of activities.

Self-Contained Groups are often the best option for small churches, house churches, or Christian schools.

Learning Center Plan

The Learning Center Plan offers an exciting recruiting and schedule variation for *KidsTime*. In this plan, each teacher prepares and leads only one activity. Guides (adults, teenagers or even responsible fifth and sixth graders) lead groups of students to rotate between the centers. In other words, each teacher specializes in only one part of the lesson. Specialization simplifies teacher preparation and often improves teaching effectiveness. The Learning Center Plan also prevents inexperienced teachers from feeling overwhelmed. And teachers who don't enjoy leading games or who are apprehensive about telling Bible stories can leave those tasks to others more skilled in those areas.

The Learning Center Plan is often the best option for medium or large churches.

What do students do and who leads them?

Students are placed in small permanent groups (12 to 16 is the best size). Each group has at least one guide who leads the group to various centers. Each group, along with its guide(s), visits each center during each session. Another idea is to place eight students in each group with one guide; then two groups participate in a center at once.

What do teachers do?

Each teacher takes responsibility for one center, remaining at the center and instructing each group as it visits the center.

What are the centers?

One room or outside area is designated for each of the *KidsTime* learning centers. Post a large sign to identify each center. Give centers fun, interesting names: The Fruit Barn (for the Bible Story Center), The Harvest Corner (for the Active Game Center), The Art Patch (for the Art Center) or The Praise Garden (for the Worship Center). Start with the centers suggested in the following diagram:

You may want to combine several groups together for one or more of the centers (for example, the Worship Center or the Bible Story Center). Other centers may be added (for example, Fruitful Lives Object Talk Center, Bible Verse Coloring Center, Service Project Center, Discipleship Activity Center).

How do I plan the time schedule?

Plan the activities in each center to last the same amount of time. The centers in *KidsTime* can be taught in any order. In a one-hour program, groups would remain in each center for 15 minutes. (Add 5 minutes to the first center each group attends to provide for a brief welcome time.) Allow 5 minutes for groups to move from center to center, following a preestablished route. With this schedule, groups would be able to participate in three centers. If you have more time for each session of the program, additional centers may be added or the time in each center may be lengthened (generally it is best to limit the time in each center to a maximum of 25 minutes in order to keep student interest high). Use the chart below as an example of how to schedule groups.

Sample one-hour schedule

	11:00-11:20	11:25-11:40	11:45-12:00
Group 1	**Welcome and Bible Story Center**	**Worship Center**	**Active Game Center**
Group 2	**Welcome and Active Game Center**	**Bible Story Center**	**Worship Center**
Group 3	**Welcome and Worship Center**	**Active Game Center**	**Bible Story Center**

How do I make the Learning Center Plan run smoothly?

• Predetermine the route each group will travel, including room and building entrances and exits. Ask guides to walk their routes in advance to become familiar with all locations.

• Establish a signal for notifying groups when it's time to move to the next center.

• Provide labeled tables or other areas where students may leave their projects and belongings during the session.

• Provide color-coded name tags to identify each group.

Schedule options

The following schedules show the use of the Basic Plan learning centers. You can adapt these sample schedules to the needs and interests of your church. Other centers can be added or substituted in order to meet the needs of younger or older students (see "Centers for Younger and Older Students" on p. 12). In addition to the centers suggested in this course, many churches include centers for such things as snacks, recreational games (soccer, baseball, volleyball), children's choir and elective classes (cooking, woodworking).

When planning your *KidsTime* schedule, remember to include a variety of activities in an order that will meet the needs of children. For example, if students have been sitting in the adult worship service before coming to *KidsTime*, plan an active center at the beginning of *KidsTime*. If students attend *KidsTime* after being in Sunday School, provide a snack at the beginning of *KidsTime*.

Basic Plan
(60-90 minutes)

Bible Story Center and Fruitful Lives Object Talk
15-30 minutes

Active Game Center
15-20 minutes

Art Center
15-20 minutes

Worship Center
15-20 minutes

Sunday Morning Option 1
(60-90 minutes)

Adult Worship Service
15-20 minutes

Active Game Center
15-20 minutes

Bible Story Center and Fruitful Lives Object Talk
15-30 minutes

Art Center
15-20 minutes

Sunday Morning Option 2
(60-90 minutes)

Bible Story Center and Fruitful Lives Object Talk
15-30 minutes

Active Game Center
15-20 minutes

Children's Choir
15-20 minutes

Art Center
15-20 minutes

Weekday Options
(75-90 minutes)

Active Game Center
15-20 minutes

Bible Story Center and Fruitful Lives Object Talk
15-20 minutes

Snack Time
15 minutes

Art Center
15-20 minutes

Worship Center
15 minutes

For help in staffing and recruiting, make a planning page to be completed on a weekly or monthly basis (see samples).

KidsTime God's Kids Grow
Date(s) __Sept. 1__
Lesson # and Title __1- The Fruit of the Spirit__
Teaching Team __Karen, Heather, Dave__

Time	Center	Teachers	Helpers
10:45	Bible Story/	Karen	Dave, Heather
	Fruitful Lives Object Talk		
11:15	Art	Heather	Karen, Dave
11:35	Active Game	Dave	Karen, Heather
11:50	Worship	Karen, Dave	Heather

KidsTime God's Kids Grow
Date(s) __Sept. 1, 8, 15, 22__
Lessons __1- 4__
Teaching Team __Linda, Mary, Jon__

Time	Center	Teachers
11:00-11:20	Active Game	Linda
11:25-11:40	Bible Story	Jon
11:45-12:00	Worship	Mary

Centers for younger and older students

If you have primarily younger or older students in your program, consider offering the Bible Verse Coloring Center (for students as young as kindergarten), the Service Project Center (for younger and/or older students) or the Discipleship Activity Center (for older students). Any of these centers can either be substituted for one of the Basic Plan centers or added to the Basic Plan.

If you would like to include preschoolers in *KidsTime*, here are some suggestions to follow:

• Preschoolers will enjoy the play dough activities that are a part of the Bible Story Center. However, expect preschoolers to make items of their own choosing or simply to play with the dough instead of making every item as older children might.

• Have preschoolers participate in the Art Center and the Worship Center.

• During the Active Game Center, either lead preschoolers in simple games such as Follow the Leader and Mother, May I? or allow preschoolers to have free play on playground equipment or with toys and puzzles indoors.

Bible Story Center Tips

Maximize a student's attention and involvement! Children will understand Bible stories in a fresh way as they keep their hands busy molding play dough during each Bible story. Even during this sitting time, you'll find it easy to keep your students' interest!

A Step-by-Step Guide to Using Play Dough

To some teachers, using play dough may be a terrific idea; for others, it may be terrifying! But with a little preparation, you'll become an expert in using dough as a Bible story teaching tool! (Note: If dough is not possible in your church, provide chenille wire, yarn or string with which children may form shapes.)

What do I need?

• Provide hand wipes or a dishpan of soapy water and paper towels for kids to use in cleaning their hands before and after dough use.

• Provide a paper plate or waxed-paper square for each student ("Waxies" are available in bulk at restaurant supply stores). Or simply cover tables with plastic tablecloths that can be folded up and then shaken outdoors. Plastic tablecloths may also be placed on the floor. Students may sit around the edges of the cloths, or cloths may be spread beneath tables where students will work.

• Provide approximately ¼ cup (2 oz.) of play dough for each student (a ball of dough about the size of a child's fist) and a resealable bag or small, clean container such as a recycled yogurt container. To prevent sharing of germs, label each container with the student's name. (Optional: At the first session of *God's Kids Grow*, you may provide ingredients, so every student makes his or her own dough, preparing extra for future visitors as well.) Periodically throughout the year, provide a fresh batch of play dough. Refrigerate dough between sessions if needed.

• Occasionally provide flat toothpicks, pencils or craft sticks as tools to vary the ways students model dough during the Bible Story Center. A variety of these tools are suggested in the Bible Story Center when appropriate.

What's the plan?

• Ask the story-related question in the box at the top of the Bible Story Center to spark student interest. As students give their answers, helpers or older students distribute labeled dough containers. (Optional: If students rotate from center to center, they may pick up their own dough as they come to the Bible Story Center.)

• Seat students so that everyone can

see a teacher, helper or older student molding the dough objects. For small groups, push tables into a V shape, so everyone can see the teacher seated at the point of the V. For larger groups, seat helpers around the circle, so a group of students can see the helper's hands clearly. Students will be more likely to follow along with you if they can see the hands of someone who is molding the next object.

• Redirect attention to the activity at hand if a student begins using play dough in disruptive ways. "John, have you made a donkey yet? Let me see yours! That's an interesting donkey! Thank you for sharing it." When students know you are interested in what they are doing, they will be more likely to be making the item for that story section and be ready to show their work.

• Conclude the Bible story. Several discussion questions are provided, along with a summary of the lesson's Character Builder. Call students' attention to the large, eye-catching poster from the *Poster Pack* that highlights the fruit of God's Spirit you have been discussing.

• Collect play dough at the end of the Bible Story Center. Students place dough in their own containers, and then helpers put the containers away. That way, the teacher is able to continue with the discussion without interrupting the flow of the Bible story.

How do I keep the lesson fresh?

• Expect that younger students will make fewer objects than older students. Even though younger students may only play with their dough while you tell the Bible story, the activity still helps them keep hands in one place and holds their attention. You may want to allow younger students time to play with their dough before giving instructions to make story objects.

• Encourage older students to make more objects or more complex objects to keep their interest high. Don't worry that older students may grow tired of dough play (we've never heard of it happening yet!). Rather, enlist them as your allies: Before class, give copies of the story to older students. Invite them to be demonstrators of the illustrated dough items.

• When it's time to replace dough, invite students to make and take home special sculptures instead of throwing old dough away.

• For variety, provide two colors of dough for students to use in making objects.

• Use other "hooks" to keep student interest high—show pictures, recruit first-person storytellers in Bible-times costumes, prepare skits, etc.

• Recruit older children to read or act out a skit of the story.

• For occasional variety, show a Bible story video during the Bible Story Center.

• You may also want to display a children's Bible time line in order to help children locate the events of each lesson.

What kind of play dough is best?

• A pliable dough that can be easily manipulated by students is best. As often as it's needed (at least every two months) make or purchase a fresh batch of dough. Keep in mind that play dough will eventually dry out, get dirty and even disappear by bits and pieces!

• Purchase commercially made play dough (some come in containers with individual portions) or make one of the recipes on pages 15-16.

• Ask older students or parents of students to make the dough as a service project.

Dough Recipes

Salt and Flour Dough

Ingredients:

2 parts flour
1 part salt
1 tablespoon alum for every 2 cups flour
Food coloring
Water

Utensils and equipment:

Mixing bowl
Large spoon
Breadboard
Resealable bags or airtight containers

Measure ingredients; mix dry ingredients well. Add coloring to water as desired. Slowly pour colored water into dry ingredients; mix and add water until dough forms a ball around spoon. Knead dough on floured board. If dough is too soft, add more flour. If dough is too stiff, slowly add more water. Divide dough into portions the size of a child's fist; package each portion in a resealable bag or container, labeling each with a student's name and leaving some unlabeled for use by visitors.

Salt, Flour and Cornstarch Dough

Ingredients:

1½ cups flour
1 cup cornstarch
1 cup salt
Food coloring
1 cup warm water

Utensils and equipment:

Mixing bowl
Large spoon
Breadboard
Resealable bags or airtight containers

Mix dry ingredients; then add food coloring to warm water. Slowly pour colored water into dry ingredients; mix and add water until dough forms a ball around spoon. Knead dough on floured board. If dough is sticky, dust with flour. If dough is stiff, slowly add water. Divide dough into portions the size of a child's fist; package each portion in a resealable bag or container, labeling each with a student's name and leaving some unlabeled for use by visitors.

Sawdust Dough

Ingredients:
2 parts fine sawdust
  (any kind except redwood)
1 part flour
Water

Utensils and equipment:
Large bowl or bucket
Wooden spoon
Breadboard
Resealable bags or airtight containers

Mix dry ingredients well. Add water a little at a time, stirring until mixture reaches a stiff but pliable consistency. Add more flour and water if dough is too crumbly. Knead dough until it becomes elastic. Divide dough into portions the size of a child's fist; package each portion in a resealable bag or container, labeling each with a student's name and leaving some unlabeled for use by visitors.

Sand Dough

Ingredients:
1 cup sand
½ cup cornstarch
1 teaspoon powdered alum
¾ cup hot water

Utensils and equipment:
Large pot
Wooden spoon
Heating element
Resealable bags or airtight containers

Mix dry ingredients in pot. Add hot water and stir vigorously. Cook over medium heat until thick, stirring constantly. After dough has cooled, divide dough into portions the size of a child's fist; package each portion in a resealable bag or container, labeling each with a student's name and leaving some unlabeled for use by visitors.

Dough Options
• Add cake coloring paste instead of food coloring to dough to create more vibrant colors.
• Add unsweetened Kool-Aid to dough to add both color and fruit scent.
• Add drops of essential oils (patchouli, peppermint) or small amounts of spice to dough to create interesting scents.

Fruitful Lives Object Talk Tips

The Fruitful Lives Object Talk can be a highlight of each lesson, drawing children in and helping them understand how the fruit of God's Spirit has been shown in the lives of Christians throughout history. These object talks can be given as part of the Bible Story Center or as a separate center.

Getting the Most Out of an Object Talk

• Preparation is the key to object talks! Read an object talk at least several days ahead of time to give ample time to gather the needed materials and to find out more about the person in question, as your interest dictates.

• If you are interested in learning more about the person whose life is featured, try the *Dictionary of American Biography*, the Internet or an encyclopedia for more information. Download photos of the person for your students to see. Libraries may also have biographies available.

• Whenever possible, invite students to participate in the object talk. Ask a different student each week to read the Bible verse aloud (highlight the verse in your Bible and mark its location with a bookmark).

• Occasionally describe situations in which learning about the person about whom you're telling or in which understanding the Character Builder has helped you. Tell students how the Bible verse presented in the center has been important to you.

• During the object talk, you may also wish to play on the *God's Kids Grow* cassette/CD or video the song related to that day's featured fruit of God's Spirit, inviting children to sing along.

• Because of the limited space available in the Fruitful Lives Object Talks for the study of the lives of various well-known Christians, set up an information station where students may learn more about each featured individual. Pictures, books, printouts of information gleaned from the Internet and objects related to the time period of that person's life can all enhance a student's understanding of what God did through that person's life.

Using a Children's Sermon During Adult Worship

If the children in your church join the first part of the adult service, consider using the Fruitful Lives Object Talk as the basis for a weekly children's sermon. Introduce the idea of the *God's Kids Grow* course to the adult audience by saying, **This year our children are learning about the fruit of God's Spirit. Today they will be studying ___. Their Bible verse to memorize is ___ and we will talk about (the character builder of the lesson).** Then give the object talk.

Active Game Center Tips

The Active Game Center can be the perfect place for your students to let off steam, work out the wiggles and be open to guided discussion that relates the Character Builder of the day's lesson to students' lives.

Creating a Playing Area

Before leading a game, give yourself ample time to set up the game area. You may have little space in your classroom for a game area, so consider alternatives: outdoors, a gymnasium or a vacant area of the church from which sound will not carry to disturb other programs.

Once you have chosen the area, plan what you will need:
• Will you need to move furniture?
• Will you need to mark boundaries? Use chalk or rope outdoors; yarn or masking tape works indoors. (Remove masking tape from carpets after each session.)
• How much space will you need? Carefully review the game procedures to plan what amount and shape of space will be needed.

From time to time, take stock of your classroom area. Is it time to remove that large table or unused bookshelf? Should the chairs be rearranged or the rug put in a different place? Small changes in arrangement can result in more usable space!

Forming Groups or Teams

To keep students' interest high and to keep cliques from forming, use a variety of ways to determine teams or groups:
• Group teams by clothing color or other clothing features (wearing a sweater, wearing tennis shoes, etc.).
• Place equal numbers of two colors of paper squares in a bag. Students shake the bag and draw out a square to determine teams.
• Group teams by birthday month (for two teams, January through June and July through December); adjust as needed to make numbers even.
• Groups teams by the alphabetical order of their first or last names.
• Group teams by telling them to stand on one foot: those standing on a right foot form one team; those standing on a left foot form the other team.

After playing a round or two of a game, announce that the person on each team who is wearing the most (red) should rotate to another team. Then play the game again. As you repeat this rotation process, vary the method of rotation so that students play with several different students each time.

Leading the Game

Explain rules clearly and simply. It's helpful to write out the rules to the game. Make sure you explain rules step-by-step.

Offer a practice round. When playing a game for the first time with your group, play it a few times just for practice. Students will learn the game's structure and rules best by actually playing the game.

Dealing with Competition

For younger children (and for some older ones) competition can make a game uncomfortable—especially for the losers. If your group is made up primarily of younger children, consider making a game more cooperative than competitive: give a special job (calling time, operating the CD player) to a child who is out; have the winning team serve a snack to the losing team; rotate players so that no one remains on the winning or losing team.

Guiding Conversation

Using guided conversation turns a game activity into discovery learning! Make use of the discussion questions provided in the curriculum all during game time. You might ask a game's winners to answer questions or to consult with each other and answer as a group. You might discuss three questions between the rounds of a game or ask a question at the beginning of the round, inviting answers when the round is over.

Art Center Tips

The Art Center is a place where children can become absorbed in a creative activity that opens their minds as you help them relate the day's lesson to their lives. Each of the art activities is related to the fruit of God's Spirit being discussed, and students are encouraged to talk about the Character Builder and fruit of the Spirit.

Before You Begin

Preparation is the key to making an art experience a joyful, creative one. No one enjoys a long stretch of waiting for the right crayon. So make sure you have the following supplies on hand: newspaper (to protect surfaces), functional scissors, usable glue bottles and sticks, working markers, usable crayons and chalk, an adequate supply of tape, paint smocks (or men's old shirts) and butcher paper.

Before Every Activity

Before students arrive at your center, cover the work tables with newspaper, securing it with masking tape, if needed. Set out materials in an orderly fashion, making sure you have enough materials for the number of children who will visit the Art Center.

If most of your students are younger, use older students as helpers (for taking dictation, stapling, etc.) during the Art Center time.

As Children Create

Ask the questions listed at the bottom of each Art Center page to help children relate the Character Builder to their daily lives. As children create, they are relaxed and eager to talk. Guided discussion will take the activity beyond art to discovery of Bible truth.

Because the goal of this activity goes beyond an artistic product, take advantage of those moments when a child says "Look at my picture!" Relate the child's work and interest to the Character Builder idea. Use "I see . . ." statements to affirm the value of the child's work while helping him or her see how his or her work relates to the Character Builder. **Jacob, I see you drew a lot of balloons on your card. The balloons remind me of a time when my friend was kind to share her balloon with me when I lost mine. Today we're going to learn more about kindness.**

Avoid making value judgments ("That's nice" or "How pretty!"). First, any child who then doesn't hear such a positive judgment will be crushed. Second and most important, focusing on the visual appeal of the artwork will not help children better understand the lesson. How a child's work *looks* is far less important than the child's *process* of creating that work. Comment on colors, lines and ideas you see represented. **Jenna, I see you made lots of orange and apple prints on your project. Tell me about your work.** As you invite children to tell you about their work, many opportunities will arise for you to ask the discussion questions printed in bold type at the bottom of the page or to make comments that will help children understand the Character Builder. **Thank you for telling me about your orange and apple prints, Jenna. Those prints show one of the ways God shows love and faithfulness to us—by giving us good things to eat.**

Worship Center Tips

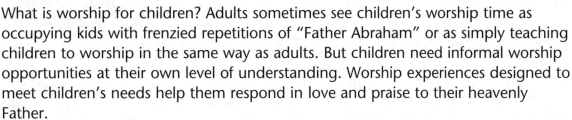

The Worship Center brings together all the other aspects of each center. It can be a fine small-group time or an excellent large-group time. Either way, the goal is to help children participate in meaningful worship. Prayer, saying or reading God's Word and lesson-related music activities are provided in the Worship Center, as well as a variety of options you can use to enrich the Worship Center or to involve older students.

A Time of Worship

What is worship for children? Adults sometimes see children's worship time as occupying kids with frenzied repetitions of "Father Abraham" or as simply teaching children to worship in the same way as adults. But children need informal worship opportunities at their own level of understanding. Worship experiences designed to meet children's needs help them respond in love and praise to their heavenly Father.

Worship is indeed a time to show reverence and respect for God, but it doesn't mean always sitting still and being quiet. The activities offered in the Worship Center involve children and help them interact with each other and with teachers in singing praise to God and hearing His Word.

A Place of Worship

Worship is also enhanced by setting apart a place especially for praising Him. To create a space in your classroom for the Worship Center, prayerfully consider the ages and abilities of the children in your group, the kind of worship experience appropriate for them and the time and space available.

Consider ideas such as displaying a contemporary picture of Jesus, spreading a rug on the floor upon which children sit, and playing a song related to that week's fruit of the Spirit at the beginning of each Worship Center time. This creates an invitation to worship. You may also want to play "The Fruit of the Spirit" or "Good Fruit" each week as children enter the Worship Center; these theme-related songs can be used as a signal to begin worship.

If taking an offering, singing a particular response or placing candles on an altar-piece are part of your church's adult worship, occasionally add those elements to the Worship Center as well. Give a simple explanation to help children understand why each of these acts is part of worship.

Keep in mind that the Worship Center is not a place for entertainment or observation; your goal is to see every child participate in a positive way that is in keeping with his or her development.

Music Just for You!

Consider making cassette copies of the *God's Kids Grow* music to help your students become familiar with the songs used during this course. A wide variety of musical styles is represented, making it easy for you to customize your worship time to include your students' favorites. Also included are two Scripture songs, so your students will understand the biblical basis for what they're learning.

There are many ways to use the *God's Kids Grow* music video. Play it as part of the Worship Center. As students enter, play a particular song to give students a clue as to the fruit of the week and to signal the opening of worship time; or play it as a way to reinforce the day's lesson as students wait for their parents.

Leading songs

Each of the up-beat songs on the *God's Kids Grow* cassette/CD and music video are designed to relate to a specific fruit of the Spirit. In addition, there are several songs that present the theme of this course. Singing the theme songs for several weeks in succession results in the songs' messages having a greater impact on the children.

Children may participate by singing, clapping, playing rhythm instruments, holding up word charts, operating the overhead projector or adjusting the cassette/CD player. Help children understand that all these activities have one goal: to honor and praise God. Your loving example sets the tone—it is the strongest teaching about worship the children will receive.

Learning new songs can be difficult for some teachers. Listen to the song on the *God's Kids Grow* cassette/CD or watch it on the music video. Then play the song again and sing along. Practice it several times (listen to it while driving in the car, while you cook, etc.). You may want to choose three or four favorite songs from the *God's Kids Grow* cassette/CD and repeat them at each session, rather than teaching a variety of new songs.

To teach a new song to children, print the words on a large chart or use the word charts in this book to make a transparency to project on an overhead projector. Project the words

on a place where they may be seen easily by all the children.

As you play the song, sing along with the song, inviting children to join in with you. It is usually a good idea to sing only one stanza and/or chorus the first time through. If you are using an overhead, cover the entire transparency with a blank sheet of paper. As you sing, move the paper to reveal words one line at a time.

Choosing additional songs

If your church chooses to lead students in additional worship songs, select songs with the same prayer and sensitivity with which you'd plan adult worship. Utilizing simple worship choruses and hymns from among your own church's favorites will prepare children for the transition to adult-level worship in a gradual, age-appropriate manner. In this way, children will become familiar with a body of songs used in adult worship.

Whatever songs you use, be sure to explain any words or concepts that are unfamiliar to children. If unfamiliar words are used, take the time to give a brief definition of the word. Use a children's Bible dictionary if needed. For example, **The word "holy" means to be chosen or set apart. When we sing that God is holy, it means that He is perfect and without sin.** If you cannot put the words or concepts of any song in terms a child can truly understand, recognize that the song is probably appropriate only for adult worship.

Bible Verse

The simple verse activity provided encourages students to hear and/or say the Scripture in a creative way reflective of a more formal order of worship. While children may often memorize the verse as part of this activity, Bible memory is not the primary goal. Instead, the goal is simply the interactive reading or hearing of God's Word.

If the reading abilities of children and the number of teachers permit, children may find and read the verse in Bibles as part of this activity.

Consider printing out each week's verse on a computer banner for easy reading.

Prayer Time

Prayer is an integral part of worship. Don't deny children this privilege because they seem unable to hold still with folded hands and bowed heads for long periods of time. Instead, involve children in prayer in ways that will help them understand that prayer is something they can do. Don't insist that students pray in a particular posture; keep prayer times short and make them times of high involvement. Remember that your prayers give the students in your class a model for prayer which they will follow. Keep your prayers brief and use simple words. Long sentences and long prayers make prayer seem boring and not something for a child.

Invite students to say sentence prayers; use a prayer journal to record requests and answers; list prayer requests on a large sheet of paper and allow children to pray with eyes open so that they are able to read and recall requests.

Bible Verse Coloring Center Tips

Coloring pages from *Bible Verse Coloring Pages #2* provide an ideal activity for the youngest students in *KidsTime*. First and second graders (or even kindergartners) will enjoy the opportunity to color in their own style a picture related to the lesson's Bible verse.

Preparation

• It's easiest to copy at one time all the pages needed for a quarter rather than photocopying on a weekly basis. Store the pages in marked folders for easy use.

• If you plan to use markers for the coloring pages, photocopy those pages onto heavier stock to avoid marker bleed-through.

• Provide a variety of art materials for coloring; besides crayons and markers, colored pencils and watercolors add interest.

Color and Talk

While students are coloring, ask the questions suggested in the curriculum. Encourage student participation by introducing each question with a statement, **I'm looking for four students wearing red to answer this question.** Another way to attract the interest of students is to say, **Someone whose name begins with the letter *J* can answer this question.**

More than Coloring!

For each coloring page, an optional enrichment idea is suggested. Additional items to draw, touch-and-feel materials to glue to the page, or fun display ideas are some of the creative add-ons to this activity.

"Give us today our daily bread."
Matthew 6:11 *(NIV)*

"Whatever your hand finds to do, do it with all your might." Ecclesiastes 9:10 *(NIV)*

Service Project Center Tips

The Big Book of Service Projects provides fresh ideas and complete instructions for activities to give students hands-on chances to grow the fruit of God's Spirit in their lives through acts of kindness and service to others.

Use the questions and conversation ideas listed to link the day's Character Builder to the project you are preparing together. Soon you'll find that asking the right questions and effectively guiding conversation become second nature!

Getting the Most Out of *The Big Book of Service Projects*

To use the project ideas you find in *The Big Book of Service Projects*, keep these tips in mind:

• If the project suggested in the lesson is not appropriate for your facility or students, choose another project from the book.

• When sending information ahead of time to the person who will lead the activity, always include the first page of the lesson. This will give the leader the Bible Verse, Bible Story Reference and Character Builder that will help him or her relate the lesson to the day's project. Also consider mailing the introductory articles from the beginning of *The Big Book of Service Projects*.

• If a wide age range of students are working together on a service project, pair younger children with older children. This helps the younger child understand the best way to do the work while giving the older student a sense of responsibility, helping to eliminate misbehavior.

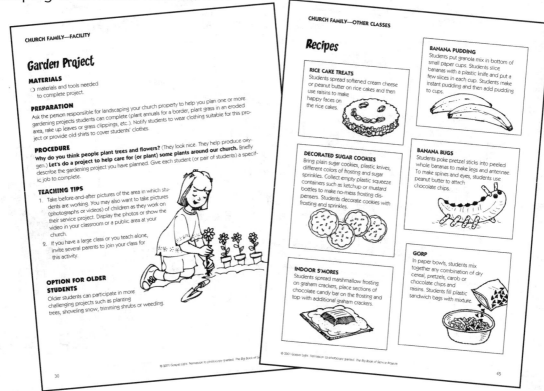

Discipleship Activity Center Tips

The Big Book of Christian Growth is filled with activities and discussion starters that will transform your students from passive listeners to kids excited about finding out what the Bible has to say about their lives! This book provides Discussion Cards related to a particular passage of Scripture and to the day's Character Builder. The Discussion Cards are used with active games, quiet games and activities and instant activities—all of which are guaranteed to get your kids thinking, talking and applying Scripture in ways meaningful to them!

In every lesson, both an active option and a quiet option are suggested from which you may choose. When older students need more activity, use the more active option. When time and space are limited, the quiet option will work best. If time permits, you may even want to provide both options for your older students.

Passages are repeated throughout the year to help older students understand and remember these clear, basic and important passages of Scripture.

Discussion Cards • Psalm 146:7-10

According to Psalm 146:9, God "sustains" orphans and widows. What does it mean to sustain someone? What are some ways that we could help sustain people who are alone?

Psalm 146:7-10

A group of kids are making fun of a developmentally disabled student by imitating his voice when they talk to you. What do you say?

Psalm 146:7-10

According to Psalm 146:9, God "watches over" people who are strangers or outsiders. How can we watch over others who are alone because they are different in some way(s)?

Psalm 146:7-10

A girl in a wheelchair has started coming to your class. One day after school you are in a hurry to get to your bus, but she is in your way. What do you do?

Psalm 146:7-10

When have you seen someone care for the kinds of people described in Psalm 146:7-10? What happened as a result?

Psalm 146:7-10

There is a blind lady who lives next door to the aunt you are visiting. You meet her standing on a busy street corner. You think you should help her across the street. What do you say or do?

Psalm 146:7-10

Active Games
Crazy Relay

Materials
- ☐ Bibles
- ☐ Discussion Cards for Bible passage you select (prepared as instructed on p. 73)
- ☐ index cards
- ☐ markers

Preparation
Write five silly instructions on separate index cards. (Count backward from 10 to 1. Shake the hands of two other people. Sing "Row, Row, Row Your Boat." Bark like a dog. Do six jumping jacks.) Add five Discussion Cards and then mix up and stack cards. Make a stack of cards for each team of four or five students.

Introduction
Guide volunteers to read aloud the Bible passage you selected. Students refer to Bible passage during the activity.

Procedure
Group students into two teams. Students line up on one side of the room. Place stacks of cards opposite each team on the other side of room. First player of each team takes an instruction from the top of the stack belonging to his or her team, returns to the team and performs the action or answers the question(s) on the card. Then the next player takes his or her turn. The first team to complete all its cards wins. Winning team chooses a Discussion Card for other team to answer. Repeat the game again as time permits.

Teaching Tips
1. If you have a small group, play the game all together.
2. To play this game quietly, have students mime their silly actions. Even if you don't need to be quiet, students will enjoy this variation.
3. You may wish to invite a parent or other adult to help supervise this activity.

Getting & Keeping the Very Best Staff

One of the most important elements in staffing a successful *KidsTime* is planning how you will recruit and organize your staff. However you do it, keep in mind that the best learning and the most fun take place when there is a teacher or helper for every six to eight children.

The optimum plan for staffing is to have the same teachers in place for six months to one year. Both teachers and children benefit from regular interaction. Having long-term teachers creates a wonderful opportunity for spiritual growth in students as they build relationships with adults who are faithful in demonstrating God's love.

While it may be easier to recruit teachers to teach one session at a time, such short-term staffing creates other problems. Many churches have found that rotating teachers frequently not only makes learning and growth difficult for children, but it also creates a heavy workload in administration (distributing curriculum, orienting a constant stream of new teachers, etc.).

Here are some options if long-term commitment is difficult in your situation.

• Ask teachers to teach for a shorter time period—three or four months at a time instead of a year.

• Find two teams of teachers and helpers who will each teach for a month. Then plan to rotate the two teams so that they alternate teaching a month at a time. Over the course of a year, teachers and children become familiar with each other and can benefit from regular interaction.

• If you must rotate teachers more frequently (weekly or biweekly), have greeters or leaders at the Worship Center and/or the Bible Story Center who are present every week.

Recruiting Tips

Recruiting teachers and helpers is one of the key tasks to making *KidsTime* an effective and fun learning experience for the children of your church and community. Keep the following tips in mind as you seek the volunteers and then match their talents to the tasks to be done:

• Pray for guidance in finding the people God wants to serve in this ministry.

• Start early!

• Keep all the leaders of your Sunday School and other children's ministries aware of and praying about staffing needs.

• Develop a written job description for each *KidsTime* staff position.

• Make a list of potential teachers and helpers. Consider a wide variety of sources for volunteers: church membership list, new members' classes, suggestions from adult teachers or leaders, lists of previous and current teachers and survey forms. Get recommendations from present teachers. Don't overlook singles, senior citizens, youth and collegians. Be sure to follow your church's established procedures for screening volunteers.

• Look for team members with interests and abilities in specific areas. For example, the teaching team for 24 children might consist of three adults: one who prepares and leads the Bible Story Center each week, one who prepares and guides the Active Game Center and a third adult who prepares and leads the Worship Center. While each team member has primary responsibility to lead only one center, all team members are involved throughout the session as helpers.

• Recruit a separate team of teachers and leaders for each center. Each team might consist of two or more adults who enjoy teaching together, or consider asking a family with teenagers to work together to form a teaching team.

• Prayerfully prioritize your prospect list. Determine which job description best fits each person's strengths and gifts.

• Personally contact the prospects. Sending a personal letter or a flyer to each prospect is a good first step. Follow up with a phone call to answer any questions or to see if the prospect has made a decision.

• Provide new volunteers with all the needed materials, forms, helpful hints and training that will help them to succeed. For all teachers and helpers, you may want to schedule one or more training meetings at which you distribute curriculum, review schedule and procedures, learn the songs together, etc.

• During the volunteer's time of service, make sure the volunteer knows who will be available to answer questions or lend a helping hand. Look for specific actions and services contributed by the volunteer and offer your thanks!

• Plan a thank-you brunch or pizza dinner or lunch for teachers and their families. Even if they don't attend, they'll be grateful for your appreciation!

Recruiting Announcements

The teachers and helpers who will be your *KidsTime* teachers and helpers will appreciate clear, concise information about the program—and a little added inspiration couldn't hurt! Here are some attention-grabbing recruiting announcements.

BECOME A GARDENING EXPERT!

Do you love to grow great things? Help us yield a harvest of good fruit! Our new *KidsTime* program, *God's Kids Grow*, has exciting songs, adaptable games, worship activities and a fun music video that help kids learn about all the ways they can grow the fruit of God's Holy Spirit! But that's not all! You'll be able to keep kids coming back for more as they use dough to shape memorable parts of the Bible story, hear object talks about the lives of godly people throughout history, make awesome art projects, and much more!

If you'd like to learn to grow good fruit every single Sunday, we're now taking applications for teachers who can show God's love to kids, use their imaginations and have fun learning more about ways to grow the good fruit of God's Spirit!

The *God's Kids Grow* course will start on _____ (date)

and continue through _____ (date) at _____ (times) .

Become a growth expert as you teach and amaze kids during this understanding-expanding course!

DO YOU LOVE A GARDEN PARTY?

Get ready to grow! Let our new *KidsTime* program, *God's Kids Grow*, help you teach our kids how to grow the fruit of God's Spirit! This course will involve kids in the Bible in a fresh way. Kids will hear amazing stories about godly believers throughout history and will learn about the spiritual fruit God gives all of us. What better way to grow your own spiritual life than to teach eager kids in this kid-friendly program!

God's Kids Grow has exciting songs, adaptable games, worship activities and a fun music video that will give kids new ways to understand and grow the fruit of God's Spirit! But that's not all! You'll be able to keep kids coming back for more through awesome art projects, fresh service opportunities and absorbing dough fun that keeps kids' attention during Bible story time. All it needs to be the best is YOU! Act now to ensure your spot as a teacher or helper in this understanding-expanding experience!

Questions & Answers for a Terrific Program

What's the Best Way to Distribute and Store *KidsTime* Curriculum?

When you first receive your curriculum, pull out the perforated pages and place them in a binder. Use dividers to separate the main sections of the book: planning pages, lesson pages, music resources.

At the beginning of the program, photocopy all the lesson pages, making multiple copies of the first page of each lesson (one for each teacher or helper). Also make multiple copies of the tips page for each activity center (one of the appropriate center for each teacher or helper).

Distribute the appropriate pages to teachers and helpers at a *KidsTime* orientation meeting, or mail them to teachers a week or so before teaching assignment begins. (If pages will be distributed periodically throughout the year, store the photocopied pages in a separate notebook.)

How Can We Build Enthusiasm for *KidsTime*?

Children of all ages will respond positively to your efforts to create interest in *KidsTime*.

• Plan theme days such as Fruit Day (everyone is served a specific fruit for a snack), Crazy Hat Day (everyone wears a funny- or silly-looking hat), Color Day (everyone wears clothes of a certain color) or Parent Day for Sunday evening or weekday programs (as many parents or grandparents as possible attend *KidsTime* with their children or grandchildren).

• Design a special name tag just for the children who attend *KidsTime*.

• Make or decorate T-shirts for *KidsTime* participants to wear.

• Create a special name or logo for your *KidsTime* program and use it on all publicity, recruiting letters, T-shirts, name tags and classroom signs.

These special attention-getting ideas can be used all year long, to kick off the beginning of *KidsTime*, as an outreach emphasis or as "shot-in-the-arm" ideas at any time during the year when you feel enthusiasm and attendance are lagging.

Brittany Smith

What Are Some Ways of Keeping Older Kids Interested in *KidsTime*?

Throughout *KidsTime*, challenging options for older students are suggested in the centers. Two of the centers are designed specifically for older students: the Service Project Center and the Discipleship Activity Center. Offer these centers while younger children are participating in another center. If your group is large enough to divide into classes, group older students in a separate class.

Involving older students in *KidsTime* can be a valuable experience for them as they explore and interact with the Bible and discover the more in-depth information clearly marked for them on most of the Fruitful Lives Object Talk pages. Because of their age, they are more than able to develop an understanding of God's Word through each Character Builder and to grasp the significance of the ways they can grow the fruit of God's Holy Spirit. Younger students will benefit as well from the presence of older children who can help them when needed. Teachers also appreciate the assistance of willing hands. Older students can be assigned to assist in specific centers:

• As you tell the story in the Bible Story Center, one or more older students can demonstrate the dough object for younger students to copy.

• At the Active Game Center, older students can be valuable assistants in demonstrating the games.

• At the Art Center, older students can help younger students with their projects.

• In the Worship Center, older students may also be able to help lead songs or lead the Bible verse activity.

How Can We Use Awards at *KidsTime?*

Many churches, especially those that desire a club-type program, like to offer awards to their children. Awards have long been a fun way to motivate children. However, to avoid having children try to defeat each other and thus create a group of losers, offer awards that ensure every child can be a winner.

• Give award tickets for specific, predetermined actions (e.g., attendance, repeating the Bible verse, bringing a Bible, or any desired positive behavior). At the end of the session (or month), award tickets can be exchanged for prizes. Distributing award tickets for positive behaviors allows the teacher to make sure everyone gets something. Avoid a public display that shows how far ahead (or behind) some students are in the number of points or awards received. Such displays often encourage attitudes or actions in kids (and adults) that are the opposite of the fruit of God's Spirit!

• Plan a cooperative contest in which the entire class or group works together to reach a goal and everyone shares in the awards. For example, a cooperative contest might set a goal for the total number of children attending on a specific day (or over a month's time) or a total number of Bible verses to be memorized. When the goal is reached, the class is given a special award—a pizza or ice cream party, inexpensive toys or gift certificates.

What Can We Do to Decorate Our *KidsTime* Room(s)?

A bit of decoration can make all the difference in creating that special, fun atmosphere that kids (and teachers) enjoy! And you'll discover that with the theme of fresh fruit and growth in mind, many natural opportunities will come to

vary the room decoration and create fresh interest—with students involved and enjoying doing most of the work!

• Create a fruit-related theme for your *KidsTime* program—an orchard, a farm or a fruit stand. It's easy to decorate with a three-dimensional effect by twisting and stapling brown grocery bags to make tree trunks in an orchard, vines in a vineyard or lumber for a fruit stand.

• The three theme posters and the Scripture poster included in the *Poster Pack* are suitable for posting throughout the course. You may wish to post the fruit of the Spirit posters one at a time as you discuss each fruit of the Spirit or arrange and display them as boxes of produce for sale.

• Create an art gallery in your room to collect and display finished work by students who have participated in the Art Center and wish to have their work displayed.

• Periodically take pictures of students participating in the various centers and use the photos to create a Good Fruit photo display.

Introducing Kids to Adult Worship

For a few moments, let's do a little pretending. Let's pretend that we are six-year-old children and that we are sitting in the adult worship service of our church. What words will we hear that we don't understand? What books are we asked to use that we don't know how to read? What happens in front that we can't see because we are small? What are we expected to do that is confusing to us? How long do we have to sit still when we are not used to sitting?

As you think through some of the things your children experience in a typical worship service, you may come to the realization that the adult worship service sometimes becomes an uncomfortable, passive experience for a child rather than an opportunity to praise and worship God.

However, you as *KidsTime* leader, as well as parents, pastor and others involved in leading the adult worship service, CAN take many specific actions to make the service more meaningful and enjoyable for children. Whether the children in your church are approaching the first time they will attend the service, attend the service only occasionally, frequently attend at least part of the service or are about to be promoted from their own *KidsTime* program into regular attendance at the adult worship service, here are some specific suggestions to help them enjoy and benefit from being with the grown-ups in "Big Church."

When Children Are in the Worship Service

Encourage parents to sit with their children near the front of the worship service. The children will not only see and hear better, but they will also have more of a sense that the person up front is speaking to them. Proximity encourages participation.

Arrange for those who are involved in leading worship to meet periodically with the children in fairly small groups. This can be done briefly at the end of Sunday School or as a part of another children's program. Use this time to explain one feature of the service the children are about to attend. If this is done every week or on some other regularly scheduled basis, the children can gradually be introduced to the entire spectrum of worship activities which occur in your services.

A significant bonus of this approach is that children will also get to know your leaders as friends who care about them, rather than viewing them as strangers who lead unfamiliar ceremonies at a distance. Perhaps of even greater significance, this brief time of interaction will alert these leaders to the presence of children in the worship service, helping the leaders become more effective in including children in the worship experiences.

HINT: If you invite someone to meet with the children and this person is not experienced in speaking at a child's level, structure the time as an interview which one of the children's teachers or leaders will conduct. Let your invited guest know ahead of time the specific questions that will be asked.

Provide parents with a sheet of tips of things to have the child do before, during and after the service (see p. 35) in order to gain maximum understanding and participation.

Tips for the *KidsTime* Leader

As the *KidsTime* leader, you can also take specific actions to make the adult worship service more meaningful for the child. Look at everything that is done through a "six-year-old's filter." Ask yourself, *What would a child understand from what we just did?* This is not a plea to conduct six-year-old-level worship services, but it will help adults become aware of the presence of children and their right to be led in meaningful worship of the Lord. The child will not understand EVERYTHING that occurs in every service, but the child deserves to understand SOMETHING in every service.

Meet with the person(s) responsible for planning the worship service and talk about ways to make the service more helpful to children. Consider these ideas:

• Choose at least one hymn or song with a repeating chorus, which makes it easier for children to learn and participate.

• Choose at least one hymn or song with fairly simple words and melody.

• Introduce at least some hymns with a brief explanation for children.

• Once or twice in the service say, "Our children are worshiping with us and we want to help them know what we are singing (talking) about." This will help raise the congregation's awareness of their responsibility to guide children and will also explain some things to adults and teenagers that they might be embarrassed to ask about.

• Provide simple explanations of special observances (baptism, the Lord's Supper, etc.).

• When inviting people to greet one another, remind them to include children in their interaction. Instructions such as "Talk to at least one person from a generation other than your own" or "Greet someone who is now attending school" are enjoyable ways to alert adults without making the children feel put on the spot.

• Find ways to involve children in some specific aspects of the service. Many churches are familiar with occasionally having a children's choir sing, but often the children feel more like outside performers than participants in family worship. Occasionally invite children to assist in receiving the offering (perhaps have parent-child teams), handing out bulletins, reading Scripture, answering a question, etc. Some churches periodically give their choir the day off and form a family choir with moms, dads and kids singing a simple song with other families after a brief rehearsal or two.

Worship Room

• If the adults in your congregation wear name tags, provide name tags for the children, too.

• Provide clipboards, paper and crayons for children to use during the service. Before the sermon, the person leading the service suggests that the children listen for a particular person or event during the sermon and draw a picture about that person or event on the paper. Children may pick up the clipboards during a hymn or some other appropriate time just before the sermon.

• Make a checklist of things for the children to listen for during the service. As the children hear one of the things listed, they check it off the list.

• Several months before children are promoted from *KidsTime* into regular attendance at the adult worship service, plan to have the children participate in a portion of each service each week or the entire service once a month.

• Ask a person with video equipment to make a recording of the entire worship service. Then, occasionally during the Worship Center, choose specific parts of the service to show and explain.

• If the order of worship is printed in your bulletin, give each child a bulletin and briefly explain the order of worship. Describe in childlike terms how each part of the service helps us worship God.

• If your congregation often sings a particular song (such as the "Doxology" or "Gloria Patri"), teach it to the children. You may also help them become familiar with the Lord's Prayer and the Apostles' Creed (if they are used in your church) by repeating them from time to time in your program.

• Help children understand that worship is anything we do that shows that we love and respect God. Use your conversation in the Worship Center to help your children understand how praise, music, prayer and learning from God's Word are all important aspects of worship.

Kids in Adult Worship

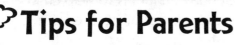

Tips for Parents

Before the service:

- Sit near the front where your child can easily see what is happening.
- If your church prints an order of service in the bulletin, help your child identify, find and mark locations of hymns and Scripture readings.
- Let your child underline all the words in the bulletin he or she can read.
- Briefly explain the meaning of any difficult words or phrases in at least the first hymn you will sing.
- Share your own feelings about the hymns or songs to be sung: "This is one of my favorites"; "I really like to sing this because it helps me tell God I love Him"; "This is one I've never learned—I hope it's easy to sing"; etc.

During the service:

- Let your child help hold the hymnal or song sheet. Run your finger beneath the words being sung to help your child follow along. If your church displays words of song on an overhead, make sure you sit where your child can see the words.
- Touch your child (not just when the wiggles are in action) to build a sense of warmth in being together.
- Provide writing and/or drawing materials. Encourage your child to write or draw about things he or she sees or hears during the service ("Draw a picture of something the pastor talks about in his sermon").
- If there is a time of greeting one another, introduce your child to those around you.
- Let your child take part in passing the offering plate, registration cards or other items distributed throughout the congregation.

After the service:

- Express your appreciation at being in church with the child.
- Commend your child for specific times when he or she was participating well ("You really did a good job singing that first hymn").
- Talk about what went on in the service. Avoid making this sound like an exam, but ask one or two questions to let the child know that you expect him or her to be listening. The following are a few good questions to use: "What is one thing you remember from the service?" "Which song did you like best?" "What Bible person did the pastor talk about?" "What was the pastor trying to teach us about?"
- Share your own answers to those questions, or let your child ask you any questions he or she desires.
- Explain one or two things that happened in the service that you think your child was interested in or could have been confused by.

Leading a Child to Christ

One of the greatest privileges of serving in Sunday School is to help children become members of God's family. Some children, especially those from Christian homes, may be ready to believe in Jesus Christ as their Savior earlier than others. Ask God to prepare the children in your class to receive the good news about Jesus and prepare you to communicate effectively with them.

Talk individually with children. Something as important as a child's personal relationship with Jesus Christ can be handled more effectively one-on-one than in a group. A child needs to respond individually to the call of God's love. This response needs to be a genuine response to God—not because the child wants to please peers, parents or you, the teacher.

Follow these basic steps in talking simply with children about how to become members of God's family. The evangelism booklet *God Loves You!* (available from Gospel Light) is an effective guide to follow. Show the child what God says in His Word. Ask the questions suggested to encourage thinking and comprehension.

1. God wants you to become His child. (See John 1:12.) **Do you know why God wants you in His family?** (See 1 John 4:8.)

2. You and all the people in the world have done wrong things. (See Romans 3:23.) **The Bible word for doing wrong is "sin." What do you think should happen to us when we sin?** (See Romans 6:23.)

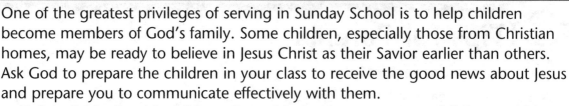

3. God loves you so much He sent His Son to die on the cross for your sins. Because Jesus never sinned, He is the only One who can take the punishment for your sins. (See 1 Corinthians 15:3; 1 John 4:14.) **The Bible tells us that God raised Jesus from the dead and that He is alive forever.**

4. Are you sorry for your sins? Do you believe Jesus died to be your Savior? If you do believe and you are sorry for your sins, God forgives all your sins. (See 1 John 1:9.) **When you talk to God, tell Him that you believe He gave His Son, Jesus Christ, to take your punishment. Also tell God you are sorry for your sins. Tell Him that He is a great and wonderful God. It is easy to talk to God. He is ready to listen. What you are going to tell Him is something He has been waiting to hear.**

5. The Bible says that when you believe in Jesus, God's Son, you receive God's gift of eternal life. This gift makes you a child of God. This means God is with you now and forever. (See John 3:16.)

Give your pastor the names of those who make decisions to become members of God's family. Encourage the child to tell his or her family about the decision. Children who make decisions need follow-up to help them grow in Christ.

NOTE: The Bible uses many terms and images to express the concept of salvation. Children often do not understand or may develop misconceptions about these terms, especially terms that are highly symbolic. (Remember the trouble Nicodemus, a respected teacher, had in trying to understand the meaning of being "born again"?) Many people talk with children about "asking Jesus into your heart." The literal-minded child is likely to develop strange ideas from the imagery of those words. The idea of being a child of God (see John 1:12) is perhaps the simplest portrayal the New Testament provides.

The Fruit of the Spirit

Bible Verse

The fruit of the Spirit is love, joy, peace, patience, kindness, goodness, faithfulness, gentleness and self-control. Against such things there is no law. Galatians 5:22,23

Bible Story Reference

Acts 8:1-3; 9:1-31; 13—15:30; Galatians 5:22,23

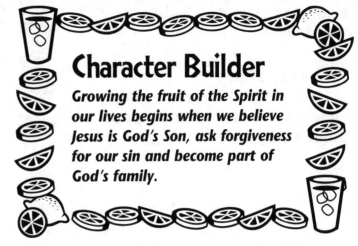

Character Builder

Growing the fruit of the Spirit in our lives begins when we believe Jesus is God's Son, ask forgiveness for our sin and become part of God's family.

Teacher's Devotional

Whether you are

- a full-time children's director or a once-a-month volunteer,

- a skilled and experienced storyteller or a novice who dreads having to stand in front of a group and keep their interest,

- a creative whirlwind who always has plenty of ideas for learning activities or a self-confessed klutz who abhors glue, scissors and markers,

your example in front of children will teach them more about the fruit of the Spirit than the words you will say.

This *God's Kids Grow* course presents the great virtues that God's Holy Spirit is ready to begin developing in the lives of each child you teach. If you will be with the children throughout the entire year or even for just a few lessons, by far the most important preparation you can do is to renew and nurture your own relationship with Jesus Christ. Your personal growth as God's child, loving and obeying Him, is more significant than your skill in presenting a lesson.

There really is no shortcut to being an effective teacher of children. Consider the opportunities you have to spend time reading God's Word. Think about what you can do to make prayer a meaningful, regular part of your daily life. When can you actively seek out opportunities to learn, to serve, to worship? Make a renewed commitment to grow God's fruit in your life.

As you experience God's love at work in your life, you will be able to reflect the qualities that the Holy Spirit wants to develop in children's lives. And that's when God can use your skills, energy and personality to help children discover God's love for themselves.

Bible Story Center

Materials

Galatians 5:22,23 poster from *Poster Pack*;
¼ cup (2 oz.) play dough and pencil for
each student.

Tell the Story

**Follow along with me to make
some faces and a word that tell
about today's story.**

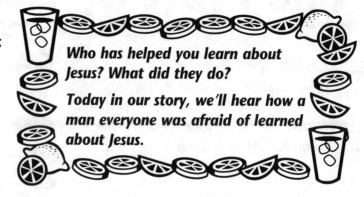

*Who has helped you learn about
Jesus? What did they do?*

*Today in our story, we'll hear how a
man everyone was afraid of learned
about Jesus.*

1. **Roll your dough into a ball.** All over Jerusalem, people were talking
about Jesus, believing that Jesus was God's Son and accepting His love
for them. God's family was getting bigger every day. That was GOOD
NEWS to many people! But to a man named Saul, it was TERRIBLE news.
Saul was an important leader in Jerusalem. He didn't believe Jesus was
God's Son. And he was ANGRY that so many people DID believe Jesus
was sent from God. Because of Saul's anger, many people were afraid of
him.

2. **Use a pencil to make an angry face on the dough ball.** Saul was so
angry, he wanted to ARREST Jesus' friends! Saul wanted to find people
who were telling about Jesus and put them into jail. That's how he
hoped to STOP this talk about Jesus! So Saul went to a city named Damascus (duh-MAS-kuhs).

3. **Make a surprised face on the other side of the ball.** As Saul and the
men traveling with him got close to Damascus, a bright light from
heaven suddenly flashed around Saul! WOW! Saul fell to the ground.
"Saul, Saul!" a voice said. "Why are you fighting against Me?" Saul wondered, *Is this JESUS talking?*

"Who . . . who are You, Lord?" asked Saul.

"I am JESUS, the One you are trying to hurt," the voice said. UH-OH!
Saul had been so SURE that Jesus was NOT God's Son. But now, even
though no one could see Him, Jesus was SPEAKING to him!

4. **Roll dough into four ropes.** Jesus told Saul that God had important work for Saul to do. He told Saul to go into the city and wait. When Saul got up, he was BLIND. For three days, Saul didn't eat or drink; he prayed and waited.

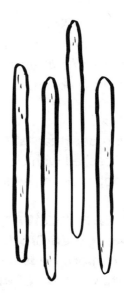

Soon, God sent a man named Ananias to talk to Saul. Even though Ananias was afraid of Saul, he obeyed God. Ananias placed his hands on Saul and said, "Saul, receive your sight!" And at that very moment, God gave Saul his sight again! Now Saul believed that Jesus is God's Son and that He is alive. Now Saul loved Jesus!

Ananias baptized Saul and brought him to meet Jesus' friends in Damascus—the very people Saul had gone there to arrest! Jesus' friends soon saw that Saul had changed COM-PLETELY! Instead of being angry toward the people who loved Jesus, now Saul wanted to show God's love and kindness to everyone. Saul began to tell people all over Damascus the good news about Jesus! When people heard Saul, they were AMAZED. But some people were UPSET that Saul now loved Jesus. They wanted to arrest HIM!

To keep Saul safe, his new friends secretly helped him escape from the city. They let him down the outside of the city wall in a big basket. And THAT was only the BEGINNING of great adventures for Saul (later called Paul)! Paul traveled to many places, telling people the good news about Jesus. For example, Paul visited many towns in an area called Galatia (guh-LAY-shuh). He told people in these towns about Jesus, and new churches began.

5. **Use each rope to make a letter of the word "Love."** Later, Paul wrote a letter to the people in these new churches in Gala-tia. Paul wrote that God gives His Holy Spirit to help each mem-ber of God's family talk and act in good ways. Paul compared the way God's Spirit helps us to grow good qualities in our lives to the way fruit grows. He wrote about nine wonderful quali-ties, or fruit, that God wants us all to grow. The first fruit is love—showing love toward God and others. God's Spirit can still help members of God's family grow that very same fruit!

● ●

Focus on the Fruit

Why was Paul angry at Jesus' friends? (He wanted them to stop telling people that Jesus is God's Son.) **What made Paul change?** (He believed that Jesus really is God's Son.) **What did Paul tell the Galatians?** (God gives the Holy Spirit to help members of God's family act in good ways, like growing good fruit.)

Show Galatians 5:22,23 poster and read verses aloud. **These are the characteristics, or fruit of the Spirit, Paul wrote about. When we love Jesus, believe He is God's Son and ask forgiveness for our sin, we can join God's family. Then God gives the Holy Spirit to help us grow God's good fruit!**

Fruitful Lives Object Talk

Bible Verse

The fruit of the Spirit is love, joy, peace, patience, kindness, goodness, faithfulness, gentleness and self-control. Against such things there is no law. Galatians 5:22,23

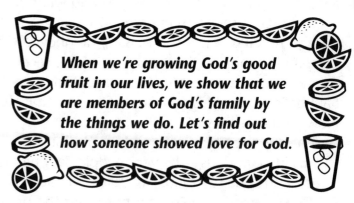

When we're growing God's good fruit in our lives, we show that we are members of God's family by the things we do. Let's find out how someone showed love for God.

Materials

Bible with bookmark at Galatians 5:22,23; suitcase packed with clothes and several Bibles; optional—hide Bibles in classroom.

Lead the Activity

1. **A man called Brother Andrew didn't grow up loving God. In fact, when he was a young man, he loved doing dangerous things and didn't care if other people got hurt because of his actions.**

   But one day Brother Andrew began to read the Bible and realized that God loved him and forgave him for his wrong actions. His love for God and others began to grow. As he learned more about loving God, Brother Andrew worked hard to show love to other people and find ways to tell them about Jesus.

2. Show suitcase. **What do you think is in this suitcase?** Invite a volunteer to look through suitcase to find Bibles. (Optional: Students find Bibles hidden in classroom.) **Brother Andrew heard of some countries where the government did not allow Bibles. So he hid Bibles in his suitcases and car and took them to Christians in these countries. If the hidden Bibles had been discovered,**  **Brother Andrew could have been put in jail. God helped Brother Andrew, and he was able to safely deliver many, many Bibles. The actions of Brother Andrew showed how much he loved God and how much he wanted others to love God.**

Conclude

Read Galatians 5:22,23 aloud. **These verses tell us the good ways in which God's Holy Spirit helps each member of His family live. Which of these characteristics have you seen someone show? How?** Pray, asking God to help students show love for God in their actions and words. Talk with interested students about becoming members of God's family (see "Leading a Child to Christ" on p. 36).

• •

Additional Information for Older Students

The name Brother Andrew was like a nickname. Because some countries didn't want Brother Andrew to bring Bibles to their people, he didn't want everyone to know his real name. Another nickname Brother Andrew had was "God's Smuggler." The name God's Smuggler was also the name of a book Brother Andrew wrote about the exciting ways God helped him show love to others.

Active Game Center: Add-a-Fruit Relay

Materials
Bibles, white paper, marker, photocopier, colored paper, butcher paper, rolls of tape, scissors, pencils.

Prepare the Game
Draw a fruit shape (apple, banana, orange, pear, lemon, etc.) on white paper. Shape should be large enough for students to write on. Photocopy onto colored paper. On a sheet of butcher paper, draw the outline of a large leafy tree. Attach the paper to the wall or place it on the floor on one side of the playing area.

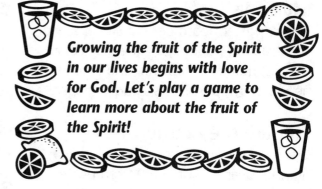

Growing the fruit of the Spirit in our lives begins with love for God. Let's play a game to learn more about the fruit of the Spirit!

Lead the Game
1. Divide group into equal teams. Each student cuts out a fruit shape. Read Galatians 5:22,23 aloud. Assign each student the name of one of the fruit of the Spirit to write on his or her shape, referring to verses in Bibles. Students then attach loops of rolled tape to the backs of their shapes.

2. Teams line up in single-file lines across the room from the tree. At your signal, students on each team take turns running to the tree, attaching shape to it, returning to team and tagging the next student in line. Play continues until each student has attached a fruit shape. Have teams sit down as they finish.

3. Ask a volunteer from the first team that finished to answer one of the Discussion Questions below or to recite Galatians 5:22,23. Repeat relay and continue discussion as time allows.

Options

1. Make tree trunk and branches by twisting brown butcher paper and attaching twists to the wall. Students stick fruit shapes onto branches.

2. To simplify preparation, each student draws a fruit on a Post-it Note and writes name of a fruit of the Spirit on the note. Students use Post-it Notes instead of fruit shapes in relay.

• •

Discussion Questions
1. *Which of the fruit of the Spirit in Galatians 5:22,23 are most needed by kids your age?*

2. *How has someone you know shown a fruit of the Spirit?*

3. *When might a kid your age show love? Patience? Joy?* Repeat with other fruit of the Spirit as time allows.

Art Center: Fruit Stuffs

Materials

Bibles, poster board or card stock, scissors, construction paper in a variety of colors, pencils, markers, stapler(s) and staples, newspaper; optional—shredded paper.

Prepare the Activity

Cut several fruit shapes (apple, banana, orange, pear, lemon, etc.) from poster board or card stock to serve as patterns. Shapes should be large enough for students to write on.

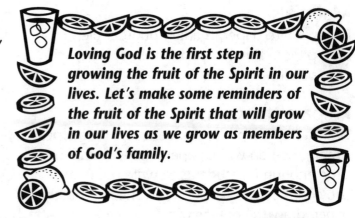

Loving God is the first step in growing the fruit of the Spirit in our lives. Let's make some reminders of the fruit of the Spirit that will grow in our lives as we grow as members of God's family.

Lead the Activity

1. Each student takes a turn to trace around a pattern on construction paper and cut out two of the same fruit shape.

2. Students read Galatians 5:22,23. On their fruit shapes, students print one of the fruit of the Spirit. Students may add decorations around each word.

3. Students staple around the edges of their shapes, leaving a few inches open. Then students tear and crumple newspaper to stuff inside their fruit shapes to create a three-dimensional effect. (Optional: Stuff with shredded paper for smoother stuffing.) When finished stuffing, students staple the opening closed.

4. As students work, ask them to describe ways they could show these fruit, or characteristics, at home, at school, with friends, etc.

Options

1. Provide real or silk leaves for students to add to their fruit shapes and/or the twisted-paper trunk or vine described on page 41 of this lesson.

2. Bring a large fruit basket. Students place their fruit shapes in it as you ask the Discussion Questions below.

3. Display fruit shapes by hanging them from ceiling with yarn or string.

• •

Discussion Questions

1. *What are some reasons to love God?* (God loves us. God made us. God sent His Son, Jesus, so that we can become members of His family.)

2. *How can others know that we are part of God's family and that we love Him?* (We can tell others about our love for God. They can see the fruit of the Spirit in our lives.)

3. *When have you seen someone showing God's love to others?* Volunteers respond.

Worship Center

Bible Verse

The fruit of the Spirit is love, joy, peace, patience, kindness, goodness, faithfulness, gentleness and self-control. Against such things there is no law. Galatians 5:22,23

Materials

Bible; *God's Kids Grow* cassette/CD or music video and player; "Fruit of the Spirit" word chart (p. 459 in this book); large sheet of paper on which you have printed Galatians 5:22,23; masking tape.

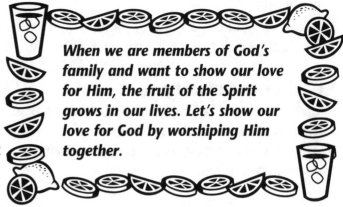

When we are members of God's family and want to show our love for Him, the fruit of the Spirit grows in our lives. Let's show our love for God by worshiping Him together.

Sing to God

Play "Fruit of the Spirit," encouraging students to sing along with the music. **Where does this song say we can learn about the fruit of the Spirit?** (In God's Word.) **What is the result of learning about God's love?** (We mirror it, or show it, to others.)

Hear and Say God's Word

Display paper on which you have printed Galatians 5:22,23. Have a volunteer read the verses aloud. **Why do you think the verse says "against such things there is no law"?** (Being kind and patient are always good ways to act.) **What is one way a kid your age could show one of these good actions?** Volunteers respond. Help students think of hand motions for each of the fruit of the Spirit. Say the verses together a few times, doing the hand motions for words as you say them.

Pray to God

Because God first loved us, we can love Him, too! And growing the fruit of the Spirit begins with accepting God's love and becoming a part of His family. Lead students in silently thanking God for loving us and sending Jesus so that we can become members of His family. Talk with students about becoming members of God's family, following the guidelines in the "Leading a Child to Christ" article on page 36.

Options

1. Sing "Galatians 5:22,23" and/or "All My Heart" (p. 461 and/or p. 453 in this book) with students.

2. In a prayer journal, record students' prayer requests and items for which they wish to thank God. Refer to the journal each week during prayer time.

3. Invite an older student to lead the prayer.

Bible Verse Coloring Center

Materials
Crayons or markers, a copy of page 161 or page 162 from *Bible Verse Coloring Pages #2* for each student.

Lead the Activity
Read Galatians 5:22,23 aloud. **What are some good attitudes and actions these verses talk about? How can you show (love, joy, etc.) to your family this week?** Students color picture.

Option
Use a paper cutter to cut construction paper into small squares and triangles. Students use glue sticks to glue paper squares and triangles to fill in the picture instead of coloring.

Service Project Center

Materials
Materials needed for "Be-Wise Bookmarks" (p. 33 from *The Big Book of Service Projects*).

Lead the Activity
Students complete "Be-Wise Bookmarks" as directed in *The Big Book of Service Projects*. **When we make these bookmarks today, we can help others remember what God's Word says. The words of Galatians 5:22,23 will help others know how to show love for God and others.**

Discipleship Activity Center

Materials
Discussion Cards for Galatians 5:22,23 (pp. 147-152 from *The Big Book of Christian Growth*); materials needed for "Candy Cups" or "Discussion Dots" (p. 10 or p. 61 from *The Big Book of Christian Growth*).

Lead the Activity
Today we're going to play a game to help us talk about ways to grow the fruit of the Spirit in our lives. Students complete activity as directed in *The Big Book of Christian Growth*.

The Loving Samaritan

Bible Verse

"Love the Lord your God with all your heart and with all your soul and with all your strength and with all your mind"; and, "Love your neighbor as yourself." Luke 10:27

Bible Story Reference

Luke 10:25-37

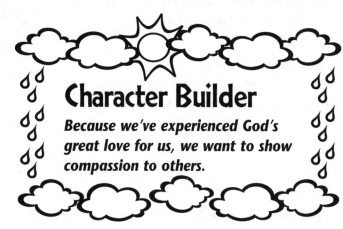

Character Builder

Because we've experienced God's great love for us, we want to show compassion to others.

Teacher's Devotional

The two greatest commands are to love: first love God and then love our neighbor. Lest anyone think that the proper response to these commands is to grit our teeth and muster our willpower, we must note that love is also the first fruit of the Spirit.

Everyone knows that love of God and of others does not always come easily. Human nature is drawn much more toward loving self and things. If the Scriptures only gave us commands, most of us would fall short most of the time. And the rest of us would miss the goal altogether.

So there is great assurance in discovering that love is not something we are required to manufacture on our own. Instead, love is nurtured within us by God's Spirit. The God of love helps us to grow in love because He knows our limits.

But don't forget those two commands. The fruit of the Spirit is not an automatic process in which God takes control and we merely go along for the ride. Jesus calls us to give our utmost effort, to love God and people with everything that is in us, even when the best we have is inadequate. That's when God's Spirit turns our weakness into strength, helping us to love beyond our capabilities, helping us to love that child who is so unlovable and, best of all, helping us to reflect His boundless, perfect love.

Bible Story Center

Materials
Love poster from *Poster Pack,* ¼ cup (2 oz.) play dough for each student.

Tell the Story
Follow along with me as we use our dough to tell today's story.

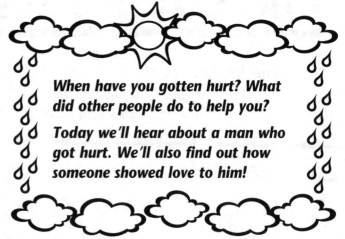

When have you gotten hurt? What did other people do to help you?

Today we'll hear about a man who got hurt. We'll also find out how someone showed love to him!

1. **Divide your dough in half. Use one half of your dough to make several hills.** One day Jesus was talking to a man about God's command "Love your neighbor as yourself." The man asked Jesus, "Who IS my neighbor?" Jesus answered the question with a story.

The story happened on the road between Jerusalem and Jericho. This road went up and down and around many hills. Sometimes robbers hid in the hills!

2. **From the other half of your dough, take off a small piece to make a man walking down a road.** There was a man traveling from Jerusalem to Jericho. As he walked down the winding road, he hurried past one hill and another hill and another hill. Then it happened: some robbers jumped out and grabbed him! They tore off his clothes and beat him and took all his money, and then they left the man lying beside the road.

The poor hurt man was so weak he couldn't get up. All he could do was hope that someone would come by and help him. And THEN he heard footsteps!

3. **Take off another small piece to make a priest walking by.** Someone was coming! The man turned his head and saw a priest. *Oh good,* thought the man. He knew that priests taught the people about God. He was sure the priest would help him. But the priest looked at the poor hurt man, crossed to the other side of the road and walked away.

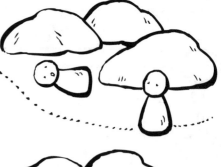

4. **Take off one more piece to make a Levite walking by.** THEN the man heard some more footsteps. Someone else was coming! The man turned his head and saw a Levite! *Oh good!* the poor hurt man thought. Levites also taught the

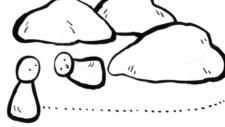

people God's laws. SURELY this Levite would help!

But the poor hurt man saw the Levite look at him, cross to the other side of the road and WALK AWAY! The poor hurt man was all alone again. He must have wondered if ANYONE would ever help him.

5. **Now use all your dough to make a donkey.** THEN he heard something! It wasn't footsteps. It sounded more like a donkey! And the hoofbeats were getting closer. The man turned his head. And sure enough, coming around the rocks was a donkey and a man.

Maybe, thought the poor hurt man, *THIS man will help me. But, oh no! The man with the donkey was a Samaritan. Samaritans did not like Jews at all. And Jews did not like Samaritans. This Samaritan would never stop to help me!* But much to the man's surprise, the man and the donkey stopped. The Samaritan walked over to the hurt man. He knelt down beside him.

Even though for hundreds of years the Jews and Samaritans had been enemies, this did not stop the Samaritan from helping the hurt man. The Samaritan put cool medicine and bandages on the hurt man. He gently helped the hurt man onto the donkey. Then the Samaritan walked beside him.

At last they came to an inn, where people who were traveling could spend the night. The Samaritan paid the owner of the inn to take care of the hurt man, and he even came back a few days later to see how the man was doing!

When Jesus finished the story, He asked, "Which of the three men was a neighbor to the hurt man?"

"The man who was kind and helped him," the man answered.

"That's right!" Jesus said. "Now you go and help people who need help, too!"

That day the man learned that a neighbor is ANYONE who needs our help!

Focus on the Fruit

Why did Jesus tell this story? (To help us know what God means when He says to love our neighbors.) **How did the Samaritan show love to the hurt man?** (Gave medicine. Gave the man a ride. Took him to an inn and paid for his stay.)

Show the Love poster. **Because we've experienced God's great love for us, it makes us want to show His love and compassion to others. That's good fruit from God's Spirit!**

Fruitful Lives Object Talk

Bible Verse

"Love the Lord your God with all your heart and with all your soul and with all your strength and with all your mind"; and, *"Love your neighbor as yourself."* Luke 10:27

Materials

Bible with bookmark at Luke 10:27, toy boat or picture of a boat.

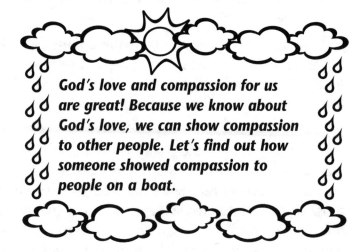

God's love and compassion for us are great! Because we know about God's love, we can show compassion to other people. Let's find out how someone showed compassion to people on a boat.

Lead the Activity

1. Show toy boat or picture of boat. **When have you sailed on a boat? What was the weather like?** Students respond. **Sailing on a boat is fun when the weather is nice, but in cold and stormy weather, boats are dangerous places to be!**

2. **One cold winter day in a sea near the country of Holland, the passengers on a boat were in big trouble. The weather was so cold that the water was beginning to freeze. The boat was getting stuck, and the people couldn't get to shore.**

To make matters worse, the rescue crew from the nearest city would not help the passengers on the boat because the passengers were all members of a church the rescue crew hated. The passengers were stranded at sea!

But one man, Menno Simons, heard about the passengers on the boat. Menno belonged to a different church from the passengers, too—but he didn't let that stop him from showing God's love. Menno and some of his friends from his church decided to help the stranded passengers. Menno and his friends risked their lives in the icy water and rescued all the passengers!

Conclude

Read Luke 10:27 aloud. **How did Menno and his friends obey the commands in Luke 10:27? What are some ways a kid your age could obey this verse?** Lead students in prayer, thanking God for His love and asking Him to help students show His love to others.

• •

Discussion Questions

1. *What does it mean to show compassion to others?* (To care about others and do what you can to help them.)

2. *How has God shown compassion to us?* (He sent Jesus so that we could be forgiven. He promised to help us and be with us.)

3. *How can you show compassion to someone in your family? At school?*

Active Game Center: Corner Questions

Materials
Bible, paper, index card, marker, masking tape, small paper bag.

Prepare the Game
Print the words "heart," "soul," "mind" and "strength" on four sheets of paper and four index cards, one word per paper and card. Post each paper in a separate corner of the room. Place index cards in small bag.

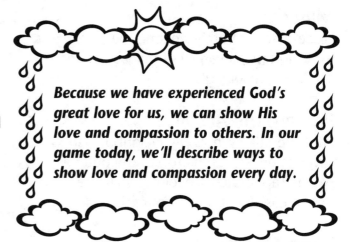

Because we have experienced God's great love for us, we can show His love and compassion to others. In our game today, we'll describe ways to show love and compassion every day.

Lead the Game

1. Volunteer reads Luke 10:27 aloud. **What does this verse describe?** (How we are to love God.) Volunteers read aloud the words on the papers in the corners of the room.

2. Students stand in a circle. Ask a volunteer to be "It." "It" stands in the middle of the circle. Students walk around the circle. After a few moments, "It" calls "Stop." Students move quickly to the nearest corners. "It" picks an index card from bag and reads card aloud before returning card to bag. Volunteer from the corner named on the index card tells one way to show love for God or compassion to others (obey God's Word, be kind to others, pray to God, be friends with people who speak a different language, etc.), recites Luke 10:27 or answers a Discussion Question below. Student who answered becomes the new "It" and game continues as time allows.

Options

1. Print Luke 10:27 on a large sheet of paper for students to refer to during the game.

2. If space is limited, use masking tape to make a large square on the floor or on a table and place one paper in each corner of the square. Students walk around the perimeter of the square and move to the nearest corner when "Stop" is called.

Discussion Questions

1. *How has God shown His love and compassion for you?* (He sent His Son, Jesus, to die on the cross to forgive my sins. He answers my prayers. He helps me do right.) *How can you show your love for God?* (Tell Him. Follow His commands. Pray to Him. Read the Bible. Tell others about Him.)

2. *What are some other words or phrases that describe ways of showing love?* (Help. Care. Encourage. Pray for. Share with.)

3. *What are some things you could do to show your love for others at home? At a park? At school?*

Art Center: Compassion Collage

Materials
Large sheet of butcher paper, markers, masking tape, a variety of magazines and catalogs, scissors, glue.

Prepare the Activity
Print the title "Who's My Neighbor?" in large letters across the top of the butcher paper. Tape butcher paper to wall at a height easy for students to reach.

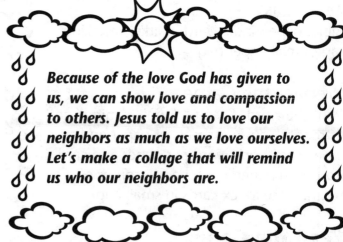

Because of the love God has given to us, we can show love and compassion to others. Jesus told us to love our neighbors as much as we love ourselves. Let's make a collage that will remind us who our neighbors are.

Lead the Activity
1. Students look through magazines and catalogs to find and cut out pictures of people of different ages and races.

2. Students glue pictures to the butcher paper to make a collage, drawing scenes around the people. Students may also use markers to add designs or borders to the collage. Ask Discussion Questions below as students add their pictures to the collage.

Options
1. Provide fabric scraps and/or construction paper. Students cut faces from magazines and create clothing out of fabric scraps and construction paper. Arms, legs and hands can be drawn or made from other magazine, fabric or construction paper pieces.

2. Older students may add conversation balloons describing ways to show compassion for others.

3. Instead of a large group collage, students make individual collages and take them home.

Discussion Questions
1. ***How does God feel about all the different kinds of people in the world?*** (He made them. He loves them. He wants us to love each other.) ***How does God show His love and compassion for people?*** (He made a beautiful world for us to live in. He gives us families who love us. He sent His Son, Jesus, to be our Savior and make us members of His family. He helps people who are hurting.)

2. ***Who do you think your neighbors are?*** (Everyone around me.) ***What are some ways you could show love to your family? Your friends? Those who are mean to you?***

3. ***What are some ways people have shown compassion to you? When are some times someone might need you to show compassion to them?*** (When they are being picked on by a bully. When they've been hurt. When they are sad or scared.)

Lesson 2

Worship Center

Bible Verse
"Love the Lord your God with all your heart and with all your soul and with all your strength and with all your mind"; and, "Love your neighbor as yourself." Luke 10:27

Materials
Bible, *God's Kids Grow* cassette/CD or music video and player, "All My Heart" word chart (p. 453 in this book), large sheet of paper on which you have printed Luke 10:27, masking tape.

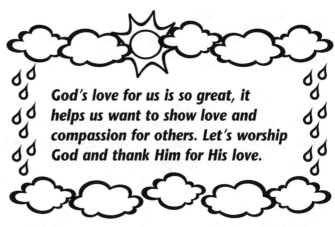

God's love for us is so great, it helps us want to show love and compassion for others. Let's worship God and thank Him for His love.

Sing to God
Play "All My Heart," encouraging students to sing along with the music. **This song reminds us to love God all the time. How could you show love for God at home? At school? When playing with friends?** (Obey parents. Work hard at school. Be fair to friends.)

Hear and Say God's Word
Display paper on which you have printed Luke 10:27. Have a volunteer read the verse aloud. **What is another way to describe how this verse says we are to love God?** (We are to love God with everything we have and in every way we can.) **What are some ways you can show God's love to your neighbor?** Volunteers respond. Students stand or sit in a circle. One student begins saying the verse up through the first "your." As the word "your" is spoken, he or she points at another student to continue the verse. Continue this procedure until the entire verse has been quoted. Student who ends verse saying the word "yourself" points to a student who will begin the verse again. Repeat until all students have had a turn and/or the verse has been repeated several times.

Pray to God
Who are people we can show compassion to? Students respond by naming categories of people (brothers and sisters, neighbors, people who are sick or lonely). Then lead volunteers to pray by completing this prayer starter using the categories they have mentioned: **Dear God, help us show Your love to . . .** Conclude by thanking God for His love and asking for His help to show compassion for others.

Options
1. During the Bible verse activity ask older students to find and read aloud these verses that talk about showing love to others: Leviticus 19:18; John 15:12,13; 1 John 4:10-12.

2. Sing "Fruit of the Spirit" (p. 459 in this book) with the students.

Bible Verse Coloring Center

Materials
Crayons or markers, a copy of page 105 or 106 from *Bible Verse Coloring Pages #2* for each student.

Lead the Activity
Read Luke 10:27 aloud. **What are the people in this picture doing? How might they show God's love to each other?** Students color picture.

Option
Students draw pictures of their houses and neighboring houses.

Service Project Center

Materials
Materials needed for "Gift Bags" (p. 89 from *The Big Book of Service Projects*).

Lead the Activity
Students complete "Gift Bags" as directed in *The Big Book of Service Projects*. **What are some other ways we can show compassion to people who have come from other countries?**
(Note: Gift bags can also be made for children at a tutoring center or for foster children or senior citizens.)

Discipleship Activity Center

Materials
Discussion Cards for Psalm 146:7-10 (pp. 93-98 from *The Big Book of Christian Growth*); materials needed for "C.H.O.I.C.E." or "Add-On Answers" (p. 12 or p. 36 from *The Big Book of Christian Growth*).

Lead the Activity
The game we're going to play today will help us think about how we can show love to the kinds of people mentioned in Psalm 146:7-10. Students complete activity as directed in *The Big Book of Christian Growth*.

Joy in Jail

Bible Verse

Sing and make music in your heart to the Lord, always giving thanks to God the Father for everything, in the name of our Lord Jesus Christ. Ephesians 5:19,20

Character Builder

God's gift of joy can help us be thankful in any situation.

Bible Story Reference

Acts 16:16-40

Teacher's Devotional

Paul and Silas were serving the Lord the day they were arrested, beaten and unfairly thrown into prison. What was their response as they endured the distress of being fastened into stocks? They prayed and sang hymns to God.

We marvel at this display of joy in the face of misery, at a time when despair seems the more likely response. The Greek word *chara* describes joy that has its foundation in God, not in situations or experiences. Although the external circumstances surrounding Paul and Silas were extremely harsh and unpleasant, the two men expressed joy that was a vivid testimony to God's control of those circumstances.

Joy that is rooted in God enables us to overcome our circumstances, even when things seem to be going from bad to worse. Because Paul and Silas turned a miserable experience into an opportunity to worship God, the jailer and his family experienced the joy of being received into God's family.

When everything around you seems depressing, be aware of God's presence with you in the midst of the trouble. Resist the temptation to complain and blame. Instead give thanks for everything, letting the spirit of joy triumph over trouble. Be ready to share with your students your joy.

Bible Story Center

Materials
Joy poster from *Poster Pack*, ¼ cup (2 oz.) play dough for each student.

Tell the Story
Follow along with me as we make some objects that are found in today's story.

Have you ever gotten into trouble and didn't get to tell your side of the story?

Today we'll hear about some men who had that problem.

1. **Make two solid rectangles from your dough.** A new church family had been started by Paul and Silas in Philippi. Things were great! But one day, when Paul and Silas went out to preach about Jesus, they got into trouble! And it was BIG trouble! Paul and Silas had helped a slave girl who had been a fortune-teller. She was happy and stopped telling fortunes. But the men who owned her and made money from her fortune-telling were FURIOUS because now they couldn't make money from her fortune-telling! The angry men dragged Paul and Silas to the leaders of the city.

"These men are upsetting our city. They are teaching things that we think are wrong!" the angry men yelled. Other people began shouting, too. Paul and Silas didn't even get to tell their side of the story. The leaders ordered the soldiers to beat Paul and Silas. Their clothes were torn off, and their backs were beaten with whips. After Paul and Silas were badly beaten, they were taken to jail. The jailer put them where he was sure they could NEVER get out!

2. **Place rectangles around two fingers to look like stocks.** Their feet were clamped into stocks—two huge blocks of wood, hinged together and locked down, with two holes cut for a person's legs. Paul and Silas were going to spend the night like that, locked in a dirty, cold jail.

Now, they could have complained. But instead, they SANG! They PRAYED! They praised God so loudly that the other prisoners could hear them! Their backs and legs must have been hurting, but Paul and Silas knew GOD was with them. And He would take care of them! Paul and Silas were JOYFUL!

The other prisoners must have been surprised at Paul and

Silas's songs. But around midnight, something else even more surprising took place. God sent an EARTHQUAKE! The ground began to tremble. It shook! Then it ROCKED!

3. **Shake fingers out of stocks.** The prison doors flew open. The stocks broke apart! The jailer woke up, terrified! He ran to see what had happened. When he saw the prison doors standing open, he was going to kill himself! He'd be KILLED if his prisoners had gotten away! But Paul shouted, "Don't hurt yourself! We're all here!"

4. **Make a rope and form a question mark.** The jailer got a torch. He ran into Paul and Silas's cell. "What must I do to be saved?" he asked them.

Paul and Silas told the jailer the answer to his question. "Believe in the Lord Jesus Christ," they said, "and you will be saved—you and everyone in your house!" The jailer took Paul and Silas to his home.

5. **Make several smiling faces.** Everyone in the house listened to Paul and Silas tell about Jesus, God's Son. They heard about God's love. They learned about things Jesus did and how He had died to take the punishment for their sins. EVERYONE in the house believed in Jesus. They were so full of joy that they wanted to be baptized RIGHT THEN!

Then they had a big celebration. They ate and they must have sung for joy. And the very next morning, the leaders of the town found out they had made a BIG mistake by arresting and beating Paul and Silas without hearing their side of the story. They politely invited Paul and Silas to leave town. Paul and Silas were free again, on their way to tell more people the good news about Jesus!

• •

Focus on the Fruit

What happened to Paul and Silas in Philippi? (They were beaten, arrested and put into stocks.) **What did Paul and Silas do?** (Praised God by singing songs of thanks.) **What question did the jailer ask Paul and Silas?** (What must I do to be saved?) **Paul and Silas told the jailer to believe in Jesus. Paul and Silas told the jailer and his family how they could become members of God's family. We can become members of God's family, too.** Talk with students about believing in Jesus. Follow the guidelines in the "Leading a Child to Christ" article on page 36.

God's gift of joy is for all the members of His family. Even when it's hard, He can help us be thankful in any situation. That's another way the fruit of His Spirit grows! Show the Joy poster. **Because we know that God is always with us and will always care for us in the ways that are best, we can be joyful.**

Lesson 3

Fruitful Lives Object Talk

Bible Verse

Sing and make music in your heart to the Lord, always giving thanks to God the Father for everything, in the name of our Lord Jesus Christ. Ephesians 5:19,20

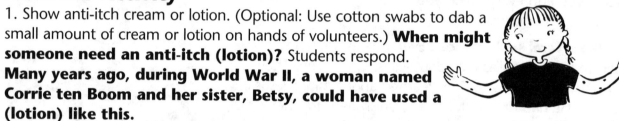

We can be thankful in any situation, because of the joy God gives to us. Let's find out about an unusual situation in which two women found that they could be thankful.

Materials

Bible with bookmark at Ephesians 5:19,20; anti-itch cream or lotion; optional—cotton swabs.

Lead the Activity

1. Show anti-itch cream or lotion. (Optional: Use cotton swabs to dab a small amount of cream or lotion on hands of volunteers.) **When might someone need an anti-itch (lotion)?** Students respond. **Many years ago, during World War II, a woman named Corrie ten Boom and her sister, Betsy, could have used a (lotion) like this.**

2. **Corrie and Betsy were living in a prison camp because they had helped Jewish people hide from the Nazis. The two sisters worked hard all day and slept in a crowded, smelly room at night. Corrie often felt like complaining—especially because the room in which they slept was full of fleas. Fleas hopped everywhere. They even lived in the straw that the women had to sleep on. The itching was awful. Things seemed terrible!**

   Betsy reminded Corrie that God could do good things in any situation. They thanked Him for the fleas. But they must have wondered how God could make something good happen in their terrible situation.

   Each night Corrie and Betsy read the Bible aloud to the other women in the room. At first, they posted lookouts to keep watch for the guards because anyone caught with a Bible would certainly be killed! But one day they found out that no guards ever came to their room—because of all the fleas! Corrie and Betsy thanked God because the fleas made it easier to read the Bible and teach others about God's love.

Conclude

Read Ephesians 5:19,20 aloud. **What do these verses say about thanking God?** Invite students to pray, telling God things they are thankful for.

• •

Discussion Questions

1. *Why do you think Ephesians 5:19,20 tells us to thank God in any situation?* (Because God promises to always be with us and help us. God gives us good things and loves us even when we are having hard times.)

2. *When are some times that it is hard to thank God? Why?*

Active Game Center: Musical Verse

Materials
Bibles, *God's Kids Grow* cassette/CD and player, one chair for each student, index cards, marker, Post-it Notes.

Prepare the Game
Place chairs in a large circle facing inward. Print "always giving thanks to God the Father for everything" on index cards, one word on each card. Mix up the cards. Make an *X* on one Post-it Note. Stick a Post-it Note, including the one with the *X*, to the back of each chair.

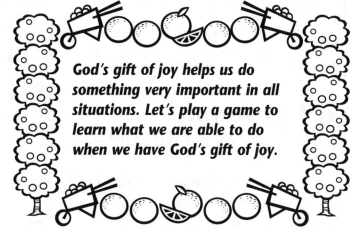

God's gift of joy helps us do something very important in all situations. Let's play a game to learn what we are able to do when we have God's gift of joy.

Lead the Game
1. As you play "Joy!" from *God's Kids Grow* cassette/CD, students walk around the inside of the circle of chairs. Stop the music after a few moments. Each student sits in a chair.

2. Students look over the backs of their chairs to locate the chair with the *X* on it. Give student sitting in the marked chair a verse card. Student places card on the floor in the middle of the circle.

3. Move Post-it Notes to different chairs so that the note with an *X* is on the back of a different chair. Then repeat play. When music stops, students sit down and check for the *X*. Student in the marked chair gets a second verse card and decides whether it should be placed before or after the first card. Continue play until all verse cards are placed in the right order. Students refer to Ephesians 5:20 for correct order if needed. Ask Discussion Questions below.

Option
Invite students to suggest a motion (hop, skip, pump fist in air, high-five a friend, etc.) to do each time they hear the word "joy" sung in the song.

• •

Discussion Questions
1. ***What is one thing we'll do when we have God's gift of joy?*** Volunteer reads verse from completed cards aloud. (Give thanks to God for everything!) ***What does Ephesians 5:19 say we'll do when we have joy?*** (Sing and make music to the Lord.)

2. ***What are some things for which you usually thank God?*** (Food. Family. Friends. Health. Safety.)

Art Center: Fingerprint Art

Materials

White construction paper, several stamp pads, disposable wipes, fine-tip markers or pens.

Lead the Activity

1. Students fold paper in half to make cards.

2. Using stamp pads, students make fingerprints or handprints to form words, or create borders or other decorations of their own choosing on the front and inside of cards. Students clean hands with wipes.

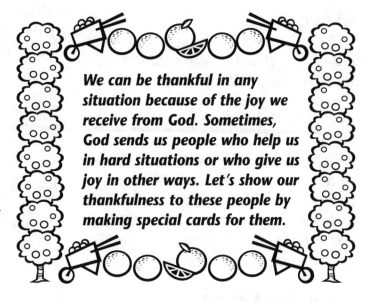

We can be thankful in any situation because of the joy we receive from God. Sometimes, God sends us people who help us in hard situations or who give us joy in other ways. Let's show our thankfulness to these people by making special cards for them.

3. Students use fine-tip markers or pens to write messages expressing thankfulness to specific people. To help students think of messages, ask, **Who has helped you when you had a problem? What did the person do? Who has helped you fix a mistake? Who has helped you learn something new? What might you say to thank the person?** Students may wish to add other drawings to their cards.

Options

1. Provide additional materials (rickrack, yarn, metallic or neon markers, stickers, rubber stamps, envelopes, etc.) for students to use in making their thank-you cards.

2. Provide Bibles and have students print a verse about thankfulness and joy on their notes. (See Psalm 28:7; 30:11,12; Isaiah 12:5,6; Ephesians 5:19,20; 1 Thessalonians 5:16-18.)

• •

Discussion Questions

1. *What are some times it might be hard to be thankful?* (When someone makes fun of you. When you feel scared.)

2. *What are some things you could do to help yourself be thankful?* (Pray to God. Remember all the good things God has given and done.)

3. *What are some ways to show God's gift of joy?* (Singing or playing an instrument in a song of praise. Telling others about God. Doing kind things for others to help them feel joyful.)

Lesson 3

Worship Center

Bible Verse

Sing and make music in your heart to the Lord, always giving thanks to God the Father for everything, in the name of our Lord Jesus Christ. Ephesians 5:19,20

Materials

Bible; *God's Kids Grow* cassette/CD or music video and player; "Joy!" word chart (p. 473 in this book); large sheet of paper on which you have printed Ephesians 5:19,20; masking tape.

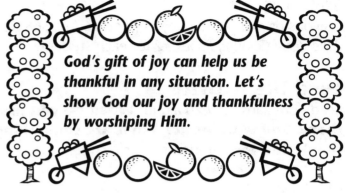

God's gift of joy can help us be thankful in any situation. Let's show God our joy and thankfulness by worshiping Him.

Sing to God

Play "Joy!" encouraging students to sing along with the music. **What did Paul and Silas do to show the joy God gave them?** (Prayed. Sang songs of joy.) **When are some times a kid your age might need God's joy?** Volunteers respond.

Hear and Say God's Word

Display paper on which you have printed Ephesians 5:19,20. Have a volunteer read the verses aloud. **What does it mean to "make music in your heart"?** (You don't have to play an instrument or sing out loud to show your joy. You can sing a song in your mind, telling God silently how glad you feel.) Students stand in a line or large circle and repeat verses, with each student saying one word of the verses in order. Student who said last word (or students who said last three words) of verses names something he or she is thankful for. (Parents. Food. Friends. Pets.) Repeat verses several times.

Pray to God

Lead students in praying aloud. Invite volunteers to tell in one word things for which they are thankful. End prayer time by thanking God for giving us His gift of joy and for helping us be thankful in any situation.

Options

1. Distribute rhythm instruments (tambourines, dried gourds, etc.) for students to use while singing song.

2. Sing "Galatians 5:22,23" and/or "Fruit of the Spirit" (p. 461 and/or p. 459 in this book) with students. Sing these theme songs frequently with students. Also consider playing them as students enter or leave classroom.

3. If students give an offering during this worship time, explain that giving money to our church is one way we can show our love and thanks to God. Describe several ways in which your church family uses the offering to help others learn about God and His love.

Lesson 3
Bible Verse Coloring Center

Materials
Crayons or markers, a copy of page 167 or 168 from
Bible Verse Coloring Pages #2 for each student.

Lead the Activity
Read Ephesians 5:19,20 aloud. **When do you praise or
thank God with music? What are some things you
thank God for?** Students color picture.

Option
Provide several collage items (aluminum foil, yarn lengths, toothpicks, etc.) for children to
glue onto their pictures.

Service Project Center

Materials
Materials needed for "Outside-In Party" (p. 39 from *The Big Book of
Service Projects*).

Lead the Activity
Students complete "Outside-In Party" as directed in *The Big Book of
Service Projects*. **What are some other ways of helping others be joyful?**

Discipleship Activity Center

Materials
Discussion Cards for Romans 8:35,37-39 (pp. 129-134 from *The Big Book
of Christian Growth*); materials needed for "Three-Ball Toss" or "Answer
Match" (p. 31 or p. 38 from *The Big Book of Christian Growth*).

Lead the Activity
**Romans 8:35:37-39 helps us discover some reasons we can have joy. Today we're
going to play a game to talk about some of those reasons.** Students complete activity as directed in *The Big Book of Christian Growth*.

Abraham the Peacemaker

 ## Bible Verse

If it is possible, as far as it depends on you, live at peace with everyone.
Romans 12:18

Bible Story Reference

Genesis 12:1-4; 13

Teacher's Devotional

If Paul had merely written the last phrase of Romans 12:18, "live at peace with everyone," there would be no end of complaints that he was simply not being realistic. *How could anyone expect me to live at peace with someone who . . . ?*

Character Builder

Putting others first can help us be peacemakers.

If Paul had merely added the first phrase to Romans 12:18, "If it is possible," there would be no end of excuses for not implementing the last phrase. *See, I knew it was impossible!*

Since Paul included that middle phrase, "as far as it depends on you," each of us must face responsibility for our own attitudes and actions. Yet each of us knows that in life's conflicts, we are often prone to stir up contention rather than to help make peace. Even children much prefer to come out on top instead of contributing to harmony.

Fortunately, peace does not depend only on us, nor on the other party. Peace is a fruit of God's Holy Spirit. As we seek to know and love God, His Spirit really does bring peace within us. And true inner peace is essential to achieving peace with others.

Bible Story Center

Materials
Peace poster from *Poster Pack*; ¼ cup (2 oz.) play dough and pencil for each student.

Tell the Story
Follow along with me as we use our dough to tell today's story.

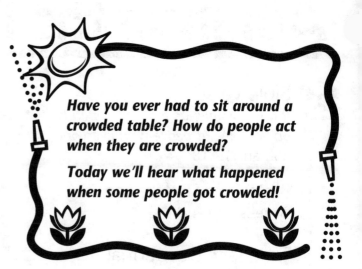

Have you ever had to sit around a crowded table? How do people act when they are crowded?

Today we'll hear what happened when some people got crowded!

1. **Use your dough to make a house with a flat roof.** Abraham was a man who lived in the city of Ur. Ur was a big city, full of fountains and trees and houses made of brick and plaster. Abraham and his wife, Sarah, had lived in Ur all their lives. They had a home and many servants. Abraham loved God. He often talked with God. And one day, God told Abraham something VERY SURPRISING. He told Abraham, "I want you to go to a new land. I will show you where to go."

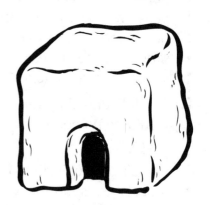

Abraham believed God and began to get ready to move. Since this move would be like a long camping trip, the people in Abraham's household packed up everything they would need for traveling—pots and pans, clothes and tents, rugs and blankets, water and food. They tied the bundles onto camels and donkeys and herded the sheep and goats. Abraham's father and his nephew Lot also went with them on this journey. Soon the whole family was off—walking to a place they knew nothing about!

2. **Roll a long rope and then flatten it to make a long path.** Abraham's family walked for weeks and months and then years! Sometimes Abraham's family must have wondered if they would ever get to the land God had promised! But Abraham trusted God. He was sure God would take care of him. He knew that, sooner or later, they were going to reach the new land where God had promised to bring them.

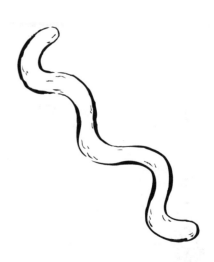

After many years of traveling and many adventures, they came to a place of hills and valleys covered with good grass that would feed many sheep and goats and cows. "This is the land I promised to you," God told Abraham. It was beautiful! The land was called Canaan.

3. **Make tiny dough balls to be herds of animals.** During all this time Abraham and his family had traveled, their flocks of sheep and herds of goats had grown and grown. There were so MANY animals, there wasn't enough water or grass for all of them. Both Abraham and his nephew Lot had HUGE flocks of animals. And in the crowded valley, the servants who took care of these animals began to fight over whose flocks should get the water and the grass.

When Abraham heard about the fighting, he said to Lot, "Let's not have any quarreling between you and me, or between your herdsmen and mine. Look around! The whole land is here for us. You may choose where you would like to go. Take your herds in that direction and I'll go the other way. Then there will be plenty for all of us."

4. **Make some flat land and some hilly land.** Lot looked and saw that the whole plain, or flat area, that went down to the sea was beautiful. He could see bright streams of flowing water and fields of green grass. So Lot chose this plain for himself and his family. He said good-bye to Abraham's family and moved down to the plain.

5. **Write "peace" or the letter _P_ on flat dough with pencil.** Because Abraham gave Lot first choice, the fighting stopped! There was peace.

After Lot had moved away, God said to Abraham, "Look around. All the land that you can see I will give to you and your family forever. Your family will grow and I will give you many grandchildren! Go, walk all through the land. I am giving it to you."

So Abraham moved his tents, his family and his herds of animals to live in the hills. Now Abraham and Lot and their servants would never have to quarrel again. God had given Abraham all the land he could see! And best of all, from Abraham's descendants would come the Savior God had promised to send.

• •

Focus on the Fruit

Why did Abraham and his family leave Ur? (God commanded him to leave.) **Why did the herdsmen fight?** (There was not enough food and water for all the animals.) **How did Abraham solve the quarrel?** (He let Lot choose where he wanted to live.)

It can be hard or even scary to try to make peace and stop a quarrel. But God will help us know what to do. Show the Peace poster. **One way to be a peacemaker is to give other people first choice. When we put others first, we treat them in ways we would like to be treated. It's a great way to grow the fruit of God's Spirit!**

Fruitful Lives Object Talk

Bible Verse

If it is possible, as far as it depends on you, live at peace with everyone. Romans 12:18

Materials

Bible with bookmark at Romans 12:18, Help Wanted section of newspaper.

Every day we have opportunities to help others live in peace. Peacemakers do what they can to put the needs and interests of others first. Let's find out what one man did to be a peacemaker.

Lead the Activity

1. Show Help Wanted section of newspaper. **What do people use this part of the newspaper for? Why might finding a job be hard?** Students tell ideas. **There are all kinds of reasons people might have a hard time finding jobs. Some people have had trouble finding good jobs just because of the color of their skin.**

2. **John Perkins was an African-American who had a hard time finding a job for fair pay. He once worked for a farmer all day and received only 15 cents as payment! Because of problems like these, many African-American people believed they needed to fight to be treated fairly.**

3. **When John Perkins grew up, he became a Christian. He wanted to help African-Americans be treated fairly without fighting. So John started telling people in Mississippi about Jesus. Sometimes he was yelled at and even beaten, but he still worked hard to help African-Americans get fair pay.**

   One time a friend of John's told him about a man and woman who were so poor that they didn't have any food or a place to live. John said he would help the man and woman. When they came for help, however, John was surprised to see that they were not African-American! John wondered if he should help them or not. But he soon realized that because God loves everyone the same, white people deserved help, too. John's hard work helped people of all races get good jobs and fair pay.

Conclude

Read Romans 12:18 aloud. **In what way was John Perkins a peacemaker?** (He helped others to get good jobs and fair pay without fighting.) Lead students in prayer, asking God to help them do what they can this week to live at peace with others.

●●

Discussion Questions

1. *When might a kid your age need help to live in peace with others?* (When someone says something mean. When someone cheats in a game.)

2. *What can you do to live at peace with others?* (Stop an argument instead of continuing it. Ask an adult for help. Pray, asking God for courage to be a peacemaker.)

Active Game Center: Red Carpet Crossing

Materials
Two sheets of red construction paper for every pair of students.

Putting others first can help us be peacemakers. Let's practice putting others first by playing a game where we must help others.

Lead the Game
1. **Red carpets are often laid down for important people to walk on as they enter buildings. When we treat someone as being important or special, we say we are giving him or her the "red-carpet treatment." In this game, we'll practice putting each other first by giving each other the red-carpet treatment with these papers.**

2. Students form pairs on one side of the classroom and decide which student in each pair will be the helper. Give each pair two sheets of red construction paper. At your signal, each helper lays down a sheet of paper for his or her partner to step on. Helper places the next paper one step away and partner moves to that sheet. Helper picks up first sheet and places it in front of his or her partner. Pairs move in this manner to the opposite side of the playing area and then race back to their starting positions. Winning pair answers one of the Discussion Questions below.

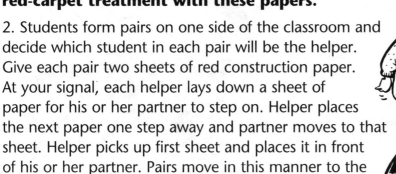

3. Students switch roles and repeat game. (Replace paper that has torn.)

Option
If there is not enough room for all pairs to play at one time, have them form teams of up to six pairs each. Teams complete game in relay fashion, one pair from each team going at a time.

• •

Discussion Questions
1. *How did you put others first in this game?* (Moved the paper for them, so they could get across the floor and finish the game.)

2. *What are some ways to put others first at home? At school?* (Stop what you are doing to help your mom when she asks. Let your sister have the last cookie. Let your classmate have the first turn at the computer.)

3. *How does putting others first help us make peace?* (Keeps fights from starting. We show we care for the other person.)

Art Center: Pieces of Peace

Materials

Large sheets of paper, markers, scissors, construction paper in a variety of colors, glue, masking tape.

Lead the Activity

1. Divide class into five groups. Assign each group a letter from the word "peace." A student in each group draws an outline of its letter on a large sheet of paper and another student cuts it out.

2. Students glue torn pieces of construction paper to fill in letters. Once letters are complete, students tape them to the wall to spell the word "peace."

Putting other people's needs and wants ahead of our own and giving them first choice can help us live at peace with others. Let's make something to remind us of the importance of being peacemakers.

Options

1. Limit size of groups to three or four. If class is very large, form enough groups to decorate the word in several lettering styles.

2. For a different look, cut letters from poster board. Students glue small pieces of colored tissue paper to the letters using paintbrushes dipped in a thin mixture of white glue and water. Brush several additional layers of glue over the tissue-paper pieces to make the colors blend together.

3. Students choose from a variety of materials (pasta shapes, grains, ribbon, yarn, fabric scraps, metallic or neon pens, etc.) to fill in letters. Point out ways students share.

4. Older students may fill in their letters with words from Romans 12:18 or with other words associated with living at peace with others.

5. Instead of tearing paper, before class cut small squares of paper using a paper cutter.

- -

Discussion Questions

1. ***Who are some peacemakers you know?*** (Police officers. People who break up fights. People who walk away from arguments.)

2. ***What are some ways to give others first choice?*** (Let a friend have the first turn when playing a game. Let a brother or sister decide what to watch on television.)

3. ***What are some things you could do this week to give others first choice?***

Worship Center

Bible Verse

If it is possible, as far as it depends on you, live at peace with everyone. Romans 12:18

Materials

Bible, *God's Kids Grow* cassette/CD or music video and player, "Peacemaker" word chart (p. 481 in this book), large sheet of paper on which you have printed Romans 12:18, masking tape, marker.

God helps us to be peacemakers by showing us how we can put others first. Let's worship God and ask for His help to be peacemakers.

Sing to God

Play "Peacemaker," encouraging students to sing along with the music. **What are some of the ways this song tells us we should treat others?** (Like they're the best. Kindly. With respect.)

Hear and Say God's Word

Display paper on which you have printed Romans 12:18. Have a volunteer read the verse aloud. **What does it mean when the verse says "as far as it depends on you"?** (It means we should try to the best of our ability.) **The more we get to know and love Jesus, the more ability we'll have to make peace. What are some ways to live at peace with others?** (Not start a fight. Be kind and generous with others. Help others. Think about another's point of view.) Mark lines on the verse paper at each of the commas to divide the verse into three phrases. Divide group into two teams. Lead one team in saying the verse one phrase at a time, stopping after each phrase to let the other team echo the phrase. Rotate which group leads and which group echoes. Repeat several times.

Pray to God

Praying for each other is a good way to live in peace. When are some times you need help being a peacemaker? List students' prayer requests on back of Romans 12:18 paper. Volunteers choose listed requests for which to pray. Allow time for students to pray silently or aloud. Close prayer time by thanking God that we can be peacemakers and by asking for help to put others first.

Options

1. Videotape the students singing "Peacemaker." Show videotape as parents arrive to pick up children.

2. Ask an older student to lead the verse activity.

3. At the beginning of this Worship Center, ask an older student to read Psalm 111:1-4 aloud as an invitation to worship.

Bible Verse Coloring Center

Materials

Crayons or markers, a copy of page 119 or page 120 from *Bible Verse Coloring Pages #2* for each student.

Lead the Activity

Read Romans 12:18. **What does this verse tell us to do? How can you obey this verse when you are with your friends?** Students color picture.

Option

Provide small fabric pieces that students may glue onto the clothing of the people in the picture.

Service Project Center

Materials

Materials needed for "First-Aid Help" (p. 78 from *The Big Book of Service Projects*).

Lead the Activity

Students complete the activity as directed in *The Big Book of Service Projects*. **How do you think this project might help someone? How might this project show that we are putting others first? What are some other ways you can put others first this week?**

Discipleship Activity Center

Materials

Discussion Cards for Matthew 5:13-16 (pp. 111-116 from *The Big Book of Christian Growth*); materials needed for "Chair Share" or "What Would You Do?" (p. 11 or p. 53 from *The Big Book of Christian Growth*).

Lead the Activity

Today we're going to play a game that will help us discover from Matthew 5:13-16 some reasons to make peace with others. Students complete activity as directed in *The Big Book of Christian Growth*.

The Patience of a Father

Bible Verse

[Love] always protects, always trusts, always hopes, always perseveres. 1 Corinthians 13:7

Bible Story Reference

Luke 15:11-31

Teacher's Devotional

Character Builder

God's patience and forgiveness show us how to be patient with others.

Most of us can reflect on our lives and say we have a measure of love, joy and/or peace. We feel good when we recognize moments in our lives when we experience those wonderful fruits of God's Spirit. But the fruit of patience can certainly seem harder to come by in our hurried society. Our efforts to maintain tight schedules often leave us drumming our fingers on the steering wheel, muttering under our breath (or sometimes out loud), urging family members to hurry up or complaining about everyone else who seems to be moving at too slow a pace.

Patience at such times is a marvelous gift of God, one that can grow in abundance within us. Look at the father in Jesus' story. He didn't run after his son, trying to fix this horrendous problem. He didn't push and prod his son to straighten up and act like a responsible adult. He simply waited and watched. God (who is, of course, the Father the story portrays) has never been impatient, late or flustered. His patience with each of us continues in spite of our repeated failures and rebellions. Not only is He patient with us, but His Spirit also gives us patience.

Our students also struggle with impatience. They live in the immediate moment, expecting instant gratification. Trying to wait for anything is often painfully difficult. Before you teach this lesson, pray for yourself and for the children you teach, asking God's help to learn patience, to always persevere and to trust that He is truly in control of all our times.

Bible Story Center

Materials
Patience poster from *Poster Pack*, ¼ cup
(2 oz.) play dough for each student.

Tell the Story
**Follow along with me to make
some of the things we'll hear
about in our story.**

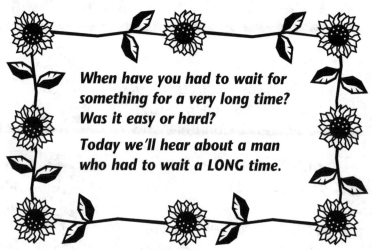

*When have you had to wait for
something for a very long time?
Was it easy or hard?*

*Today we'll hear about a man
who had to wait a LONG time.*

1. **Roll your dough into a ball.** Once Jesus was having dinner
with some people who didn't obey God. This made some
OTHER people angry at Jesus. They said Jesus should not be
friendly to these people, and they called the people sinners.
So Jesus told a story to help everyone understand how much
love God has and how patient He is, even when people do
wrong things.

Once there was a man who owned a big farm. This man
had two sons that he loved very much. The father planned to
divide his money between his sons when they were older,
according to the custom of that land. But the younger son
didn't want to WAIT for his share of the money. He just
wouldn't be patient!

"I want my money NOW, Dad," the younger son said.
He wanted to take the money and leave home. He wanted to
do whatever he wanted, even if it was wrong.

2. **Pinch the top of the ball to make a money bag.** The
father gave the younger son his part of the money. The
younger son told his dad good-bye, took his bag of money
and headed down the road to a faraway city. The father
must have been very sad. He loved his son and would miss
him.

When the younger son got to the big city, he spent his
money VERY foolishly. He didn't think about what would
happen when his money ran out. Instead, he spent money
on wild parties and fancy food and anything else he could
think of that might be fun. He had lots of friends—mainly
because they enjoyed the parties he paid for!

One day the younger son picked up his money bag. He shook it. There was no jingling of coins. It was EMPTY!

3. **Flatten the money bag.** Now that he had no money, he knew his friends wouldn't come to see him anymore. He was all alone—and in BIG trouble. He had no money to buy food or to pay for a place to live. He felt awful! On top of that, food was hard to get and jobs were scarce! So he looked for a job and finally found one.

4. **Now make a pig.** The only job he could find was taking care of pigs! And he was so HUNGRY all of the time, he began to wish he could eat the food the pigs ate! One morning the younger son thought, *I am starving to death. But the people who work for my father have plenty of food to eat. I'm going home. I'll tell my father I was wrong. I'll tell him I don't deserve to be his son anymore. But I'll ask if I can be a servant.*

Back on the farm, the father still missed his younger son very much. Day after day, the father patiently looked down the road, hoping to see his son. FINALLY, one day he saw his son walking down the road! The father was so excited that he ran to meet him! He hugged him and kissed him.

5. **Shape a ring around your finger.** When they got to the house, the father told his servants to bring his son new clothes and sandals and a beautiful ring of his own. Then the father had a BIG party to celebrate! Even though the son had done wrong things, his father was patient with him. He waited for him to come home. He had forgiven his son and was GLAD to see him!

Jesus told this story because He wanted people to know that God is like that father. God is patient and wise and loving. Even when we do wrong, like the son, God still waits for us to realize we are wrong. And when we admit to Him that we have done wrong, He will forgive us!

• •

Focus on the Fruit

Why did Jesus want people to understand that God is patient with us when we do wrong? (Because we all do wrong things and need God's forgiveness.) **How did the younger son show he was not patient?** (He had to have his money right away.) **How did the father show he was patient?** (Waited for his son to come home. Welcomed and forgave his son when he came home.)

Sometimes we don't want to wait for something. But even when it's hard to be patient, God's patience with us helps us know how to be patient with others. Show the Patience poster. **Patience is the fruit of His Spirit!**

Fruitful Lives Object Talk

Bible Verse
[Love] always protects, always trusts, always hopes, always perseveres.
1 Corinthians 13:7

Materials
Bible with bookmark at 1 Corinthians 13:7, newspaper.

God shows patience by forgiving us and loving us, even when we don't deserve it. When we realize God's patience with us, it helps us be patient with others. Let's find out how some people showed patience.

Lead the Activity

1. Give each student a sheet of newspaper. **What can you do with a newspaper?** Students demonstrate ideas. **In China, some people used newspapers in an unusual way.**

2. **Pastor Li was the leader of a church in China that met in a house. It was against the law for this church to meet and for Pastor Li to preach about Jesus. But he didn't stop. Because of his preaching, Pastor Li was arrested and severely beaten many times.**

   One day the police came to the church meeting and not only took every Bible they found, but they also took all the chairs! Still, the people didn't give up meeting together. They patiently folded up newspapers to sit on instead of chairs and kept right on meeting together and worshiping God. (Optional: Students fold newspapers, place them on the floor and sit on them.) **The people even prayed for the police and thanked God for the opportunity to talk about Jesus.**

Conclude

Read 1 Corinthians 13:7 aloud. **What word in this verse means the same thing as "patient"?** ("Perseveres.") **To persevere means to keep on doing something, even when it's hard. When we remember God's patience toward us, it helps us keep on showing patience to others.** Pray, thanking God for His patience and asking His help in showing patience toward others.

• •

Discussion Questions

1. *How did Pastor Li and the people in his church show patience?* (They kept on worshiping God and praying for others, even when the police made it hard.)

2. *When is a time you need to keep on showing patience toward others?* (When others make fun of me. When others don't keep their promises.)

3. *What can help you show patience when it's hard?* (Remembering God's love for me.)

Active Game Center: Verse Bowl

Materials
Bible, Post-it Notes, marker, 10 empty plastic soda or water bottles, paper, photocopier, pencils, tennis ball.

Prepare the Game
Print the words and reference of 1 Corinthians 13:7 on Post-it Notes, one word on each note. Stick each note on a plastic bottle. Also print the words and reference of 1 Corinthians 13:7 on a sheet of paper. Photocopy one verse paper for each student. Set plastic bottles in a bowling-pin formation on one side of the playing area.

God's patience with us shows us how to be patient with others. Let's play a game to find out a little more about patience.

Lead the Game
1. Give each student a verse paper and a pencil. Ask a volunteer to read the verse aloud. Students line up about 7 feet (2.1 m) from the verse bottles.

2. The first student in line rolls the tennis ball at the bottles. Student takes verse paper and pencil over to bottles and reads words on the knocked-over bottles. Student crosses off those words on the verse paper, returns bottles to original positions and goes to the end of the line. Next student in line repeats action. Play continues until all students have crossed off all words on their papers. The students who finish first may assist the other students by reading words on bottles and setting them back in place.

Options
1. Adjust distance from which students bowl according to their skill levels.

2. Create one bowling area for every 10 students.

• •

Discussion Questions
1. *When did you have to be patient in this game?* (Waiting for your turn. Waiting for others to finish crossing off words.) ***Which word in our verse is most like the word "patience"?*** ("Perseveres.") ***Perseverance means continuing to do something even when it is hard and patience means waiting without complaining.***

2. *How does God show patience toward us?* (He forgives us when we're sorry. He takes care of us, even when we don't thank Him.)

3. *When are some times you can be patient with your family? With your classmates?*

Art Center: To the Point

Materials

Paper, markers in a variety of colors.

Lead the Activity

Students make a simple line drawing of a nature scene or object and then color their pictures by filling in the shapes with dots, not strokes. **Some famous artists have painted large pictures with small dots of color like these. Why would this be a hard way to make a big picture? What would happen if the artist got tired and left one section with fewer dots? No dots at all? It takes a lot of patience to paint pictures this way. What are some things you do that take patience?** (Practice the piano. Clean my room. Do math problems. Rake leaves.) **It also takes a lot of patience to get along with others. When we're patient with others, we're showing them God's love. God's love is always patient and kind. He will help us show that same patience and kindness to others.** Ask the Discussion Questions below as students continue to work.

Because God shows patience with us, we can be patient with others. Artists work patiently to make their pictures the very best they can. Let's practice a technique that some artists use.

Options

1. Younger students may fill in the coloring page suggested in the Bible Verse Coloring Center for this lesson.

2. Use tempera paint and paintbrushes or chalk dipped in water instead of markers.

3. Purchase ministampers for students to use in filling in pictures.

Discussion Questions

1. *What are some ways we read in the Bible that God showed His patience and kindness?* (Saved Noah's family in the ark. Rescued Israelites from slavery in Egypt.)

2. *When has someone been patient with you?*

3. *When is it hard for you to be patient? What are some ways you could show patience with others?* (Not yelling back when someone starts yelling at you. Waiting to take a turn without complaining. Praying every day for a friend who is sick, even if he or she doesn't get well right away.)

Lesson 5
Worship Center

Bible Verse
[Love] always protects, always trusts, always hopes, always perseveres. 1 Corinthians 13:7

Materials
Bible, *God's Kids Grow* cassette/CD or music video and player, "Patient Father" word chart (p. 479 in this book), large sheet of paper on which you have printed 1 Corinthians 13:7, masking tape.

We learn to be patient with others because of the great patience and love God has shown us. As we worship God together, let's thank Him for His patience.

Sing to God
Play "Patient Father," encouraging students to sing along with the music. **According to this song, what has no end?** (God's mercy.) **What can we know about God from this song?** (God keeps His promises. God always forgives us when we ask.)

Hear and Say God's Word
Display paper on which you have printed 1 Corinthians 13:7. Have a volunteer read the verse aloud. **What four things does this verse tell us love will always do?** (Protect, trust, hope, persevere.) **What does the word "persevere" mean?** (To keep on trying even when things are hard.) Lead students in saying the verse: all boys say the first word, all girls say the second, boys say the third and so on. Have students repeat the verse in this manner several times, alternating which group says the first word.

Pray to God
Play "Patient Father" song again. Students listen to song and silently thank God for His mercy. Conclude silent prayer time by thanking God aloud for His patience and the gift of salvation. **The greatest way God showed His love to people was when He sent His Son, Jesus, to die on the cross and come back to life. God patiently waits for us to believe in Him and ask forgiveness for sin.** Arrange to meet after the session or at another convenient time with students interested in knowing more about becoming a member of God's family (see "Leading a Child to Christ" article on p. 36).

Options
1. Sing "Galatians 5:22,23" and/or "Just Like You" (p. 461 and/or p. 477 in this book) with students.

2. Ask older students to find and read aloud these verses about patience: Proverbs 16:32; 19:11; Ecclesiastes 7:9; Romans 12:12; 1 Corinthians 13:4; Colossians 3:12.

Lesson 5

Bible Verse Coloring Center

Materials
Crayons or markers, a copy of page 133 or 134 from *Bible Verse Coloring Pages #2* for each student.

Lead the Activity
Read 1 Corinthians 13:7. **Why might the children in this picture need patience? How can they be patient with each other?** Students color picture.

Option
Students add details (trees, flowers, animals, etc.) to the picture.

Service Project Center

Materials
Materials needed for "Thank-You Nameplates" (p. 60 from *The Big Book of Service Projects*).

Lead the Activity
Students complete "Thank-You Nameplates" as directed in *The Big Book of Service Projects.* **When are some times you have to be patient with people in your family? How do you think remembering things you appreciate about people in your family can help you be patient with them?**

Discipleship Activity Center

Materials
Discussion Cards for Psalm 51:1-4,10-12 (pp. 81-86 from *The Big Book of Christian Growth*), materials needed for "Circle Jump-Up" or "Guest Talk" (p. 13 or p. 44 from *The Big Book of Christian Growth*).

Lead the Activity
Today we're going to play a game to talk about Psalm 51 and learn about God's forgiveness. God's patience and forgiveness show us how to be patient with others. Students complete activity as directed in *The Big Book of Christian Growth*.

A King's Kindness

Bible Verse

May the Lord make your love increase and overflow for each other and for everyone else, just as ours does for you. 1 Thessalonians 3:12

Bible Story Reference

2 Samuel 4:4; 9

Teacher's Devotional

Character Builder

Kindness is doing good without expecting anything in return.

A bumper sticker that encourages people to "practice random acts of kindness" sounds good, at first glance. It is certainly friendlier than one that says "If you can read this bumper sticker, back off!" It is much less materialistic than "When the going gets tough, the tough go shopping." There is an obvious appeal in doing something kind for someone else when under no obligation and with no expectation of getting repaid in kind.

But when we read 1 Thessalonians 3:12, "random acts of kindness" pale by comparison. Paul's prayer for the believers in Thessalonica is a call to a life that demonstrates increasing and overflowing love. This life exhibits loving actions that reach beyond the warmth of the Christian community to touch anyone in need of kindness. And the Thessalonians knew very well what that kind of loving kindness looked like. It was the same kind of love that Paul himself felt for them (see 1 Thessalonians 3:12b).

Kindness is the spiritual fruit that helps others in practical, thoughtful, caring ways. Make 1 Thessalonians 3:12 more than a verse to recite. Make it your prayer for yourself and for the children you teach.

Bible Story Center

Materials

Kindness poster from *Poster Pack*, ¼ cup (2 oz.) play dough for each student.

Tell the Story

Follow along with me as we use our dough to tell today's story.

When have you made a promise to a friend?

Today we'll hear about someone who was glad to keep a promise he had made to his best friend!

1. **Roll two ropes from your dough.** A long time ago, in the palace at Jerusalem, there lived a little boy named Mephibosheth (Muh-FIHB-oh-shehth). He was the grandson of King Saul and the son of David's best friend, Jonathan. But in one terrible day, Mephibosheth's father, Jonathan, and his grandfather Saul were killed in a battle. Mephibosheth's nurse (the woman who took care of him) heard the sad news.

2. **Make a heart from ropes.** Mephibosheth's nurse loved him and she knew Saul's enemies would try to kill him. So she picked him up and RAN from the palace! But in her hurry, she dropped Mephibosheth. His feet were badly injured. They never healed properly, and he could never walk without help. He couldn't run or play like other little boys.

3. **Remove half of heart and add a dot to make a question mark.** Years later, David was crowned king. He was sad that his best friend, Jonathan, had died. David remembered how he and Jonathan had promised to always take care of each other's families. So now David asked his servants, "Is there anyone from Jonathan's family to whom I can show kindness for Jonathan's sake?"

One servant was a man named Ziba (ZEE-buh). He had been Saul's family servant. He told King David, "There is still a son of Jonathan's. He is crippled in both feet and lives quite a distance from here."

4. **Make a letter *M*.** David was delighted to hear about Jonathan's son named Mephibosheth! He sent servants to the house where Mephibosheth lived. They knocked on the door and told Mephibosheth that King David wanted him to come to Jerusalem!

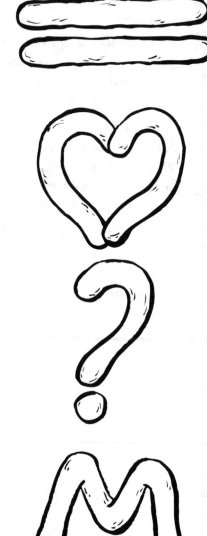

5. **Make a Bible-times crutch shaped like a *T*.** Now because Mephibosheth was crippled, he might not have been treated too kindly before this. He surely must have wondered if King David was bringing him to Jerusalem to lock him in prison or even KILL him! When he arrived at the palace, he probably shook with fear.

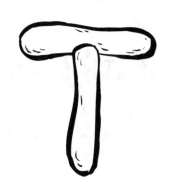

"Mephibosheth!" King David called out excitedly.

"I am your servant," said Mephibosheth, too afraid to look up.

David could see that Mephibosheth was frightened. He said, "Don't be afraid. I will be kind to you for Jonathan's sake. I will give you all the land that belonged to your grandfather Saul. And I want you to stay here in the palace and eat at the royal table every day!"

6. **Make a bowl.** WELL! Mephibosheth must have been VERY surprised—and relieved, too! He probably could hardly believe what he had heard! The KING had invited him to eat with him every day! Mephibosheth bowed down and said, "Why would you notice me and treat me so well? I am not important at all!"

7. **Make a heart.** "Your father Jonathan was my best friend. I promised to care for you years ago!" King David explained.

King David had spoken. Now Ziba and all the people who had been the servants of King Saul became Mephibosheth's servants. They farmed his land for him and took care of his animals. He now had a great deal of land, many servants and, best of all, he was treated as part of David's family! King David was as kind to Mephibosheth as if he were his own son. Mephibosheth lived in Jerusalem and ate at King David's table every day. King David showed him great kindness because of the loving promises he had made to Jonathan.

. . . .

Focus on the Fruit

How did Mephibosheth become crippled? (He was dropped when his nurse ran away with him.) **Why did King David want to help Mephibosheth?** (Because David had promised to care for members of Jonathan's family.) **How did King David help Mephibosheth?** (Gave him back his family's land. Gave him servants. Treated him as a son.)

Sometimes it isn't easy to be kind without expecting anything back. But that is what King David did. And God can help us grow the fruit of kindness in our lives, too! Show the Kindness poster.

Lesson 6
Fruitful Lives Object Talk

Bible Verse
May the Lord make your love increase and overflow for each other and for everyone else, just as ours does for you. 1 Thessalonians 3:12

Materials
Bible with bookmark at 1 Thessalonians 3:12, hammer and/or other construction tools.

When we do good without expecting anything in return, we are showing kindness. Let's look at a way some people work hard to show kindness even though they don't get paid any money for it.

Lead the Activity
1. Show hammer and/or other construction tools. **What do people use these tools for?** Volunteers tell ideas. **Carpenters who build furniture and houses usually get paid for their work. But some people who work as carpenters don't get paid at all! These people work for an organization called Habitat for Humanity. "Habitat" is a word that means the place where someone lives. "Humanity" is a word that means people. What do you think people who work for Habitat for Humanity might do?** (Build homes for people who don't have a good place to live.)

2. **One man who works for Habitat for Humanity used to be the president of the United States. His name is Jimmy Carter. After a new president was elected, President Carter could have looked for a job to earn lots of money. But instead, because he loved God and wanted to show God's love to others, he decided to spend some of his time working for Habitat for Humanity.**

   Jimmy Carter and the other people who help Habitat for Humanity don't get any pay in return for building houses for poor people. They build houses because they want to show kindness to others in need.

Conclude
Read 1 Thessalonians 3:12 aloud. **How does this verse describe showing kindness? What are some ways to show kindness to others without expecting anything in return?** (Help a younger brother or sister. Donate items to a homeless shelter.) Pray, asking God to help your students find ways to be kind to others.

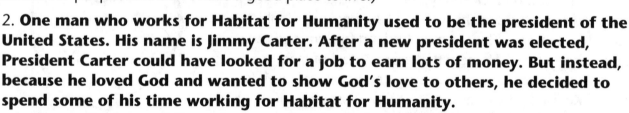

Discussion Questions
1. *What are some other ways to be kind to others and obey 1 Thessalonians 3:12?*

2. *When has someone been kind to you? What did that person do? Why do you think that person chose to be kind?*

3. *When have you been kind to another person? What happened as a result of your kindness?*

Lesson 6

Active Game Center: Overflowing Beans

Materials
Bible; dried beans; measuring cup; two of each of the following: large plastic bowls, spoons, large paper cups, shallow baking pans or boxes.

Prepare the Game
Pour at least three cups of beans into each plastic bowl. Place plastic bowls and spoons on one side of the playing area. Put paper cups in shallow pans or boxes and place them on the opposite side of the playing area.

Being kind means doing good things for others without expecting anything in return. Let's play a game about a Bible verse that tells us how God helps us to be kind.

Lead the Game
1. Divide class into two teams. Teams line up in single-file lines next to spoons. Read 1 Thessalonians 3:12 aloud. **What does this verse ask God to do?** ("Make your love increase and overflow.") **You'll know your love is overflowing when you show love and kindness to others without even thinking about what they might give you in return.**

2. **In this game, see how long it takes to make your team's cup overflow with beans.** At your signal, the first student on each team takes a spoonful of beans, walks quickly to his or her team's cup, drops in the beans, returns to his or her team and hands the spoon to the next player. Any spilled beans need to be picked up. Next student in line repeats action. Relay continues until both teams have made their cups overflow with beans, and the beans spill into the pan or box. Repeat as time allows, asking the Discussion Questions below between rounds.

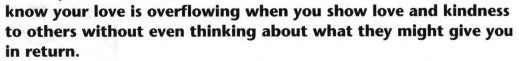

Discussion Questions
1. *When are some times it's easy to show kindness to others?* (When others have been kind to us.) *When might it be hard?* (When we're angry.)

2. *What can we do when we don't feel like being kind?* (Ask God's help. Remember God's kindness to us.)

3. *What are some ways you could let kindness overflow with your family? Your friends at school? Someone you dislike?* Students respond. *What good things might happen?*

Art Center: Marks of Kindness

Materials
Bible, a variety of colored construction paper or poster board, ruler, scissors, markers, glitter or confetti, a variety of stickers, clear Con-Tact paper.

Prepare the Activity
Cut construction paper or poster board into 2x5-inch (5x12.5-cm) strips, one for each student. Cut clear Con-Tact paper into 3x6-inch (7.5x15-cm) strips, two for each student. Make arrangements for your students to distribute bookmarks to another class.

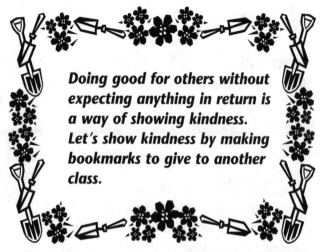

Doing good for others without expecting anything in return is a way of showing kindness. Let's show kindness by making bookmarks to give to another class.

Lead the Activity
1. Using markers, students decorate their construction-paper or poster-board strips with words or pictures about kindness. Students sprinkle glitter or confetti and put stickers on the decorated strips and then cover both sides with clear Con-Tact paper. Students trim paper close to the edges of the construction paper or poster board.

2. When students present bookmarks to the other class, ask a volunteer to read 1 Thessalonians 3:12. Students explain the words or pictures on their bookmarks as they distribute them, if appropriate.

Options
1. Provide decorative-edged scissors for students to trim edges of bookmarks.

2. Students punch a hole at the tops of bookmarks and thread yarn, ribbon or embroidery floss through holes. Tie off ends to form a tassel, adding craft beads if desired.

3. Older students cut their own construction paper or poster board and clear Con-Tact paper.

• •

Discussion Questions
1. *How would you feel if no one gave you a reward or said "Thank-you" when you did something good?* Volunteers respond. *Not expecting something in return means you wouldn't be upset if no one gave you a reward or even said "Thank-you." Why might this be hard to do?* (Everyone likes to be appreciated.)

2. *What are some good things you could do to show kindness to others?* (Help someone who's hurt. Give someone more than is asked for. Do extra chores.)

Worship Center

Bible Verse

May the Lord make your love increase and over-flow for each other and everyone else, just as ours does for you. 1 Thessalonians 3:12

Materials

Bible, *God's Kids Grow* cassette/CD or music video and player, "Be So Kind" word chart (p. 455 in this book), large sheet of paper on which you have printed 1 Thessalonians 3:12, masking tape, marker.

God will help us be kind to others without expecting anything in return. Let's thank God for His kindness to us and ask His help in being kind to others.

Sing to God

Play "Be So Kind," encouraging students to sing along with the music. **What examples of kindness does the song describe?** (Giving someone more than is expected. Sharing. Being generous.) **When can you be kind in these ways?**

Hear and Say God's Word

Display paper on which you have printed 1 Thessalonians 3:12. Have a volunteer read the verse aloud. **According to this verse, whom should we love?** (Each other and every-one else.) **Who is the verse talking about when it says "everyone else"? What are some different groups of people?** (Third graders, teachers, people who live in Africa, senior citizens, etc.) List students' ideas at the bottom of the verse paper. Then invite volun-teers to say the verse again, this time replacing the words "each other and everyone else" with one of the groups of people listed. For example, "May the Lord make your love increase and overflow for (third graders) just as mine does for you." Continue as time per-mits.

Pray to God

Write the following prayer on the back of the Bible verse paper: "God, please help us to show love to You by showing kindness to others. In Jesus' name, amen." Lead students in saying the prayer in unison.

Options

1. Older students make up motions to use while singing "Be So Kind" and teach them to the class.

2. During the Bible verse activity, lead students to make up a rhythmic pattern (such as three claps and a snap) to use when saying 1 Thessalonians 3:12.

3. Invite an older student to write a prayer for class to pray in unison.

Lesson 6

Bible Verse Coloring Center

Materials
Crayons or markers, a copy of page 189 or page 190 from *Bible Verse Coloring Pages #2* for each student.

Lead the Activity
Read 1 Thessalonians 3:12. **How are the kids in this picture obeying this verse? What are some ways you can be kind to others this week?** Students color picture.

Option
Students color picture with fruit-scented markers.

Service Project Center

Materials
Materials needed for "Welcome Box" (p. 20 from *The Big Book of Service Projects*).

Lead the Activity
Students complete "Welcome Box" activity as directed in *The Big Book of Service Projects*. **How does this project show kindness to people who are new in the community? What are some other ways to be kind to new people in your neighborhood? At school? At church?**

Discipleship Activity Center

Materials
Discussion Cards for 1 Corinthians 13:4-8a (pp. 141-146 from *The Big Book of Christian Growth*), materials needed for "Group and Regroup" or "Match Up" (p. 62 or p. 45 from *The Big Book of Christian Growth*).

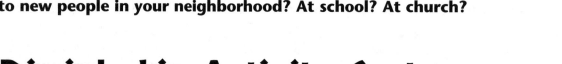

Lead the Activity
Today we're going to play a game to talk about ways to show kindness by obeying the instructions in 1 Corinthians 13:4-8a. Students complete activity as directed in *The Big Book of Christian Growth*.

Daniel's Good Choice

Bible Verse
We must obey God rather than men! Acts 5:29

Bible Story Reference
Daniel 1

Teacher's Devotional
One of the most overworked and least defined instructions that parents give their children is "Be good!" As the kids head off to school, camp or a birthday party, they hear it. But what is it parents are expecting with this directive? What do the children see as their commitment when they promise, "We will!"?

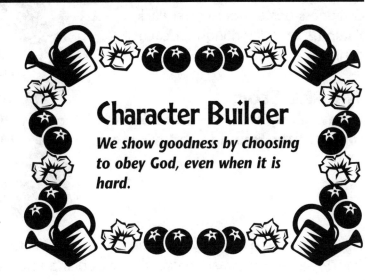

Character Builder

We show goodness by choosing to obey God, even when it is hard.

Often, the best any parent hopes for is the absence of anything bad. The child is deemed to have been good if he or she has not done anything particularly wrong or destructive. But goodness is far more than just the avoidance of misbehavior. Goodness goes beyond staying out of trouble.

Goodness involves doing things that are right, actively seeking to do what God has already defined as worthwhile. Daniel and his friends earned a good reputation in Babylon, not just by refusing to go against Jewish dietary rules and not just by taking a stand against food and drink that had first been offered to idols. They were recognized by the king as being 10 times better than all others because they excelled in their work. The lives of Daniel and his friends reflected the knowledge and understanding God had given them (see Daniel 1:17). Doing things God's way, instead of the way everyone else does them, is the definition of real goodness.

Bible Story Center

Materials
Goodness poster from Poster Pack, ¼ cup (2 oz.) play dough for each student.

Tell the Story
Follow along with me to make some things found in today's story.

What food would you probably NEVER eat? Why?

Today we'll meet some people who chose what to eat because they wanted to obey God!

1. **Make a crown out of your dough.** Many years after King David was king of Israel, the country was being attacked! The King of Babylon had come to Jerusalem with his army, tearing down the city walls and taking many people as captives. Among the people captured were four boys, who were probably about 14 years old. These boys had to walk for days and days, probably tied together like slaves. Finally, they arrived at the city of Babylon over 800 miles from home.

Soon after the captives came into the city, the king's officer, Ashpenaz (ASH-puh-nahz), came to look them over. He chose some young men from among the captives to be trained to serve the king. The four friends from Jerusalem—Daniel and three others—were chosen, too. Being trained to serve the king meant that they would not be treated like slaves. BUT there were some problems!

First, all the young men being trained were given new names, names that honored the false gods of Babylon! Then, the king ordered that everyone in his training program had to eat ONLY food from his table!

2. **Make a big plate and some pieces of meat to put on the plate.** The king may have thought this was an honor. But for Daniel and his friends, it was TROUBLE! God had commanded His people not to eat certain foods as a way to show that they wanted to obey Him. Besides, the king's meat would have first been offered to the idols of Babylon. Eating the king's meat would be like worshiping idols—and not honoring God.

If we obey the king and DO eat the king's meat, we will disobey God, Daniel and his friends thought. *But if we DON'T*

eat his meat, we will disobey the king and he may have us killed.

Daniel and his friends must have thought about all the good-tasting food the king offered them. *Why not go ahead and eat the king's food?* After all, their parents weren't with them. No one would ever know. But Daniel and his friends decided to make a good choice—to obey God's rules, no matter WHAT!

"It's against the laws of our God for us to eat this food," Daniel explained to Ashpenaz. "Please ask the king if we can just have vegetables to eat and water to drink."

But Ashpenaz was afraid he'd get into BIG trouble if he agreed to do such a thing. He wasn't willing to disobey the king!

Daniel, however, was determined to obey God. So he went to the guard whom Ashpenaz had put in charge. He told him the same idea. The guard agreed to the experiment.

3. **Remove meat and make vegetables and fruit.** For 10 days, Daniel and his friends ate nothing but vegetables and drank only water. The rest of the young men ate the food from the king's table. What do you think happened? At the end of the 10 days, Daniel and his friends looked better and stronger than the others! So the guard continued to let the four friends eat only vegetables and drink only water.

At the end of their three years of training, Ashpenaz took all the young men to the king. The king looked at them all and talked with each one. But his favorites were Daniel and his friends. God had given these four young men more wisdom than the king's own advisors.

Daniel and his friends made good choices. Even though they were away from their parents and even though they could have gone along with something that was wrong, they chose to obey God. They obeyed God, no matter what!

Focus on the Fruit

What happened to Daniel and his friends in Babylon? (Chosen to serve the king. Given the king's food to eat.) **What did Daniel and his friends choose to do?** (To obey God's rules, no matter what.) **What happened?** (After eating only vegetables, they looked stronger than the others.)

Show the Goodness poster. **Sometimes it's hard to make a good choice. We might be afraid that others will make fun of us, or we might not be sure about how to talk and act. But if we ask, God will help us do what is good and help us obey Him. That's how His fruit of goodness grows!**

Lesson 7

Fruitful Lives Object Talk

Bible Verse
We must obey God rather than men!
Acts 5:29

Materials
Bible with bookmark at Acts 5:29, sports medal or trophy.

We show goodness by choosing to obey God. Let's find out about one man who chose to obey God, even when it was hard.

Lead the Activity

1. Show sports medal or trophy. **How do you think I got this award?** Volunteers tell ideas. Briefly explain to students where the item came from. **Many athletes dream of the chance to win Olympic medals.**

2. **Eric Liddell (lih-DEHL)was an athlete in England who could run very fast! In 1924, he hoped to win a gold medal at the Olympics. But when the race schedules were announced, Eric discovered that he was supposed to run in a race on a Sunday. Years before, Eric had said that he would not work or play sports on Sundays. He made this choice to show his love and obedience to God. Eric wanted to spend time worshiping God on Sundays, not running races. So Eric said he would not run in the Sunday race.**

When people in England heard about Eric's decision, they were furious! They thought that Eric didn't care about his country. But Eric started training for a different race that did not take place on Sunday. No one thought he could win this race, however, because it was longer. On the day of the race, much to everyone's surprise, Eric not only won the race and the gold medal, but he also ran this race faster than anyone else in the world had ever run it!

Conclude

Read Acts 5:29 aloud. **How did Eric Liddell show that he wanted to obey God? Why might it have been hard for him to show goodness in this way?** Students respond. Pray, asking God to help students choose to obey Him, even when it is hard.

• •

Additional Information for Older Students
Eric made choices that showed goodness throughout his life. Just one year after winning the Olympic gold medal, Eric went to the country of China as a missionary. For 20 years, Eric Liddell helped people in China learn about Jesus. The story of Eric Liddell's life and his good choices was told in the movie *Chariots of Fire*.

Active Game Center: Shuffle Fun

Materials

Bible, index cards, marker, two paper bags, four empty shoe boxes or large tissue boxes.

Prepare the Game

Print the following commands on separate index cards: "Do three jumping jacks," "Smile and say hello to your teacher," "Clap seven times," "Wink at your team," "Turn around twice." Make two sets of cards. Place one set in each bag. Remove lids or tops of boxes.

One way we can show goodness is by choosing to obey God, even when it is hard. Let's play a game to obey some instructions, even if they are hard to do!

Lead the Game

1. Divide group into two teams. Teams line up on one side of the playing area. Place one bag of index cards on the opposite side of the playing area from each team.

2. Give the first student on each team two boxes. At your signal, the first student on each team steps into his or her boxes and shuffles to his or her team's bag. Student takes out an index card, reads card and returns it to the bag and then performs the action on the card, stepping out of the boxes if necessary. Student steps back into boxes, shuffles back to his or her team and steps out of boxes for the next student to begin the relay. Game continues until all students have had a turn.

Options

1. Draw a picture of the command instead of writing it, or have someone read the cards for any nonreaders in your class.

2. If playing surface is slippery, do not have students walk with feet in boxes. Instead, students walk to team's bag while holding on to their ankles.

● ●

Discussion Questions

1. ***What was hard about this relay?*** (Moving quickly or completing a command with the boxes on our feet.)

2. ***What are some of God's commands from the Bible?*** (Love others. Don't lie. Care for people who are different from you.) ***When are some times it is hard to obey God's commands?*** (When everyone else is disobeying God's commands. When we don't feel like being kind or loving.)

3. Read Acts 5:29 aloud. ***Why is it most important to obey God?*** (His laws are the best, even when they are hard. He loves us. He is God, the maker of everything. His laws tell us how to follow God's plans.)

Art Center: Veggie People

Materials

Bibles, two or three kinds of vegetables (broccoli, cauliflower, carrot, celery, cucumber, bell pepper, radish, etc.), kitchen knife, paper plates, plastic knives, toothpicks, napkins, vegetable dip.

Prepare the Activity

Cut vegetables into strips and chunks. Place on separate plates in the center of the work area. Make a sample vegetable person (see sketch below for ideas).

Lead the Activity

1. Show students your sample person and suggest a few other construction ideas using the vegetables you have provided.

2. On a paper plate, each student constructs a person using vegetables. As students work, ask them to tell ways kids their age could show goodness by obeying God, even in a hard situation. Ask the Discussion Questions below to expand the conversation.

3. Distribute napkins and serve vegetable dip. Students eat leftover vegetables and/or vegetable people.

Option

Post a note alerting parents to the use of food in this activity. Also check registration forms for possible food allergies.

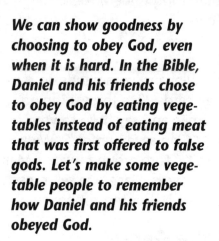

We can show goodness by choosing to obey God, even when it is hard. In the Bible, Daniel and his friends chose to obey God by eating vegetables instead of eating meat that was first offered to false gods. Let's make some vegetable people to remember how Daniel and his friends obeyed God.

radish · cauliflower · bell pepper · carrot · celery · broccoli · toothpick

Discussion Questions

1. ***How do we know what God wants us to do?*** (He tells us in His Word, the Bible. By listening to our parents.) ***What are some things God's Word tells us to do?*** Volunteers respond. Invite older students to read one or more of the following verses aloud: Exodus 20:12, Galatians 5:14, 1 Thessalonians 5:16-18, James 1:19, 1 John 3:11.

2. ***When are some times it is hard to obey God's commands?*** (When you feel tired or angry. When you don't know God's commands. When everyone else is disobeying God's commands.) ***Why do you think it's important to obey God, even in those hard times?***

3. ***Name one way you can show goodness by obeying God's commands this week.***

Lesson 7

Worship Center

Bible Verse
We must obey God rather than men!
Acts 5:29

Materials
Bible, *God's Kids Grow* cassette/CD or music video and player, "Goodness!" word chart (p. 469 in this book), large sheet of paper on which you have printed Acts 5:29 with each word scrambled, masking tape.

We show goodness by choosing to obey God, even when it is hard. Let's worship God to show that we want to love and obey Him!

Sing to God
Play "Goodness!" encouraging students to sing along with the music. **What is one way you could act to show goodness?** (Keep my promises. Tell the truth. Make choices that show I want to obey God.)

Hear and Say God's Word
Display paper on which you have printed the scrambled words of Acts 5:29. As students identify each of the scrambled words, print them on the paper. Then ask a volunteer to read the verse aloud. **This verse reminds us that when others tempt us to do wrong, we need to obey God and show our love for Him. Why is it so important to obey God?** (Because God loves us so much, He knows what is best for us.)

Pray to God
When we obey God, we are showing goodness and our love for Him. Silently think of a time when you need help obeying God's commands. Lead students in prayer, asking for His help to obey Him, even when it's hard.

Options
1. Play "Fruit of the Spirit" and/or "Just Ask Him" (p. 459 and/or p. 475 in this book), encouraging students to sing along with the music.

2. Before leading students in prayer, briefly tell about an age-appropriate example of a time you obeyed God in a difficult situation.

3. Ask an older student to read Psalm 150 aloud as a prayer of praise to God.

Lesson 7

Bible Verse Coloring Center

Materials
Crayons or markers, a copy of page 113 or page 114 from *Bible Verse Coloring Pages #2* for each student.

Lead the Activity
Read Acts 5:29. **How is someone in this picture obeying God? What are some situations in which you can obey God this week?** Students color picture.

Option
Students make borders for their pictures by gluing pictures to sheets of construction paper.

Service Project Center

Materials
Materials needed for "Breakfast in Bed" (p. 14 from *The Big Book of Service Projects*).

Lead the Activity
Students complete "Breakfast in Bed" activity as directed in *The Big Book of Service Projects*. **Doing something special for others is a way to show goodness. What are some other ways we can show goodness by obeying God this week?**

Discipleship Activity Center

Materials
Discussion Cards for James 1:22-25 (pp. 165-170 from *The Big Book of Christian Growth*), materials needed for "Post-it Pandemonium" or "Coin Cups" (p. 24 or p. 59 from *The Big Book of Christian Growth*).

Lead the Activity
James 1:22-25 tells us how to show goodness in the way we speak to others. Today we're going to play a game to talk about how to obey these verses. Students complete activity as directed in *The Big Book of Christian Growth*.

Faithful in the Lions' Den

Bible Verse

Let love and faithfulness never leave you; bind them around your neck, write them on the tablet of your heart. Proverbs 3:3

Bible Story Reference

Daniel 6

Teacher's Devotional

Kids are notorious for forgetting important things. At least they easily seem to forget the things their parents and teachers feel are important. If it were not so, why else would parents and teachers continually remind children of those things: "Don't forget your jacket!" "Remember to brush your teeth." "Don't forget your lunch!"

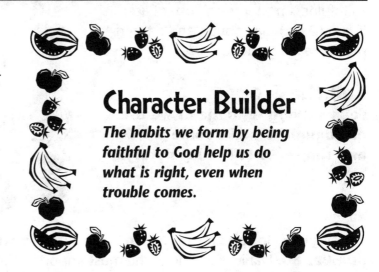

Character Builder

The habits we form by being faithful to God help us do what is right, even when trouble comes.

This is not a new phenomenon. Children, being immature, have always needed adults to remind them of things they tend to take lightly. Even King Solomon recognized a young person's tendency to overlook the truly important things in life, so the book of Proverbs (most likely compiled by Solomon, even if he did not write all of it) is filled with vivid images that capture the attention and jog the memory. Proverbs 3:3 uses this type of imagery to emphasize the need to always remember two important character qualities: love and faithfulness.

No one needed this reminder more than Solomon himself, the king who loved often (700 wives, etc.) but not faithfully (see 1 Kings 11:1-4). Even with all his wisdom, he neglected to persevere in doing right, with unfortunate results for himself and his kingdom. Had he been faithful like Daniel, how different his story would have been.

Our daily actions and words form the story of our lives, too. Take time this week to evaluate your story. Consider ways in which your love for God is seen through your faithful words and actions. Ask God's help in writing your life story to carry out the command of Proverbs 3:3.

Bible Story Center

Materials
Faithfulness poster from Poster Pack;
¼ cup (2 oz.) play dough and a toothpick for each student.

Tell the Story
**Follow along with me as we use
our dough to make some words
and shapes to tell today's story.**

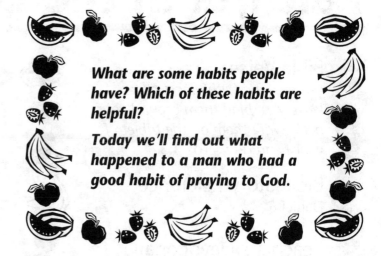

*What are some habits people
have? Which of these habits are
helpful?*

*Today we'll find out what
happened to a man who had a
good habit of praying to God.*

1. **Use your dough to make two ropes and form the
number 80.** Daniel was one of the most important leaders
in the country of Babylon. Daniel had lived in Babylon ever
since he was just a young man. During all those years he had
served as an advisor to several kings. Now he was over 80
years old and serving King Darius (duh-RI-uhs).

Because Daniel was so wise and honest, King Darius
made Daniel the governor of the whole kingdom. THAT decision made some of the other governors VERY jealous! They
searched and searched to find something Daniel might have
done wrong in his job as governor, so they could point it out
to King Darius. But it was no use! Daniel never did anything
wrong or dishonest in his work.

Since they couldn't think of any other way to stop
Daniel, the jealous governors decided to use Daniel's faithfulness to God to get him into trouble!

2. **Form the number 30.** First, some governors went to see
King Darius. They told him that ALL the governors and leaders of the kingdom had agreed that he should make a new
law: For 30 days, no one was to pray to ANYONE except
HIM! Those who disobeyed would be thrown into a den of
hungry lions!

3. **Make four ropes and form the word "pray."** Now
the governors had said that ALL the leaders liked this law;
that wasn't quite true. Daniel hadn't seen this law, of course!
But King Darius signed it, just as the leaders suggested. As
the leaders walked away, they must have thought, *Now we've
got Daniel right where we want him*!

94

Daniel soon heard about the new law. Of course he would not obey it. For many years, Daniel had openly prayed three times every day. Daniel knew that disobeying the law meant he would be thrown into a lions' den. But no law would stop him from being faithful in praying to God.

Daniel's enemies watched Daniel's house. Would he come to the window and pray, as he always did? Yes! There he was—kneeling down! They ran as fast as they could—STRAIGHT to King Darius. They told the king, "Daniel prays to his God three times a day! We saw him break your law!"

King Darius realized he had been tricked. He realized that the leaders wanted to KILL Daniel. The king worked all day to find a way to change the law, but the law could NOT be changed!

4. **Make a lion. Use a toothpick to draw details on the lion's face.** The king had to obey his own law. He sadly watched as Daniel was thrown into the den full of lions.

King Darius was up all night. He couldn't sleep, worrying about Daniel. When the king got to the lions' den early the next morning, he called out, "Daniel, servant of the living God! Was your God able to save you from the lions?"

"Yes, your Majesty!" Daniel answered. "God sent His angel to shut the mouths of the lions, so they could not hurt me. He knew I did nothing against you!"

King Darius was DELIGHTED! The king remembered the leaders who had tricked him into writing the law and said, "Arrest those men and throw THEM into the lions' den!"

Then King Darius wrote a special law to tell everyone in Babylon to respect and worship the God of Daniel. Daniel continued to serve as governor over all of Babylon. He still prayed to God three times a day—no matter what. It was a habit he wasn't going to change for anyone—not even the king!

- -

Focus on the Fruit

How would you describe Daniel? (Faithful. Loved God. Honest.) **How did the jealous men get Daniel into trouble?** (They tricked the king into making a law against praying to God.) **Why did Daniel disobey the king's new law?** (Daniel prayed only to God.) **What were some of Daniel's habits?** (Prayed to God every day. Obeyed God.)

God loves to help us grow the fruit of His Spirit! Show the Faithfulness poster. **God will help us be faithful to Him when we ask His help. One of the ways we can be faithful is by practicing good habits—praying to God, reading His Word and obeying Him—every day!**

Lesson 8
Fruitful Lives Object Talk

Bible Verse

Let love and faithfulness never leave you; bind them around your neck, write them on the tablet of your heart. Proverbs 3:3

Materials

Bible with bookmark at Proverbs 3:3, clock with hour and minute hands.

The habits we form by being faithful to God help us do what is right at all times. Let's look at some different things we can do with our time.

Lead the Activity

1. Show clock. **How long does it take for the short hand to move from one number to another?** Students respond. **What are some things you can do in an hour?** (Watch [two] cartoon shows. Drive to [a location approximately 60 miles away]. Attend soccer practice.)

2. **One person who lived a long time ago had a habit of doing something for two hours every day. Susanna Wesley, a woman who lived in England in the 1700s, prayed for two hours every day. Even though Susanna had many children to take care of** and was very busy with all kinds of work, every day she stopped whatever she was doing to pray and think about God's Word for one hour in the morning and one hour in the evening. Susanna began this habit of showing love and obedience to God when her children were young, and she faithfully continued the habit throughout her life. She had two sons who not only became famous preachers and songwriters but also were people God used to tell the good news of Jesus all over England!

Conclude

Read Proverbs 3:3 aloud. **What are some habits Proverbs 3:3 talks about?** (Showing love and being faithful to God.) **How did Susanna Wesley obey this verse?** (She prayed and thought about God's Word every day.) **What are some other habits that show love and faithfulness to God?** Lead students in prayer, thanking God for His love and asking for His help in showing love and faithfulness to Him.

- -

Additional Information for Older Students

Charles Wesley, one of Susanna's sons, wrote many songs called hymns that are still sung in churches today. (Optional: Students look through church hymnals to find and read some of Charles Wesley's hymns: "Love Divine, All Loves Excelling," "Hark! the Herald Angels Sing," "Jesus, Lover of My Soul," "O for a Thousand Tongues to Sing" and "Christ the Lord Is Risen Today." **After reading these hymns, what do you think was important to Charles Wesley? Why?)**

Active Game Center: Balloon Bop

Materials
Balloons.

Lead the Game

1. Students form pairs. Give each pair a balloon. Students inflate and tie balloons and practice hitting them back and forth to each other.

2. **Now that you've practiced hitting the balloon, count how many times you can hit the balloon back and forth before it touches the floor.** Pairs complete task. **Imagine how much easier hitting the balloon would be if you had a habit of doing it every day.** Pairs continue activity, challenging themselves to increase the number each time.

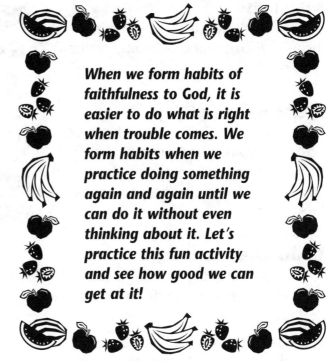

When we form habits of faithfulness to God, it is easier to do what is right when trouble comes. We form habits when we practice doing something again and again until we can do it without even thinking about it. Let's practice this fun activity and see how good we can get at it!

Options

1. Inflate and tie off balloons ahead of time.

2. Students may vary distance between themselves and their partners and try different hitting techniques to discover what works best for them.

3. Challenge older students to use their heads, knees or elbows instead of their hands to hit balloon back and forth.

4. If you have a small group of students, play the game all together in a circle instead of breaking off into pairs.

Discussion Questions

1. ***What are some things kids your age try to get in the habit of doing?*** (Making bed every morning. Putting bike in garage. Brushing teeth. Washing hands before eating. Playing an instrument.)

2. ***What kinds of habits could you form that would show your faithfulness to God?*** (Reading the Bible to learn more about God. Praying to God every day. Obeying God's commands in the ways you treat others.)

3. ***How can these habits help you when things are hard?*** (Knowing God's Word will help you know the right thing to do even in difficult situations. Praying to God will comfort you when you are scared or sad.)

Art Center: Balloon Buddies

Materials

Poster board, pencil, ruler, scissors, 9-inch (22.5-cm) round balloons, permanent markers.

Prepare the Activity

For each student, cut a heart shape from poster board (about 6 inches [15 cm] from point to top of curve). Cut a ½-inch (1.25-cm) slit up from the point of each heart.

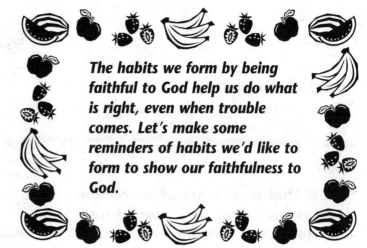

The habits we form by being faithful to God help us do what is right, even when trouble comes. Let's make some reminders of habits we'd like to form to show our faithfulness to God.

Lead the Activity

1. Give each student a balloon. Student inflates balloon and uses marker to draw a face and a body on balloon.

2. Students think of habits they want to form that will help develop their faithfulness to God (reading the Bible each day, praying each day, memorizing a Bible verse each week, writing a letter to God each week, etc.). Students write

cut ½"
(1.25 cm)
slit
6" (15 cm)

Read Bible at night.

Thank God for 2 things every day.

habits on poster-board bases and draw around their writing to create feet or shoes. Students slip the tied end of the balloons into the slits on the bases.

3. Students take home balloon buddies to remind themselves to form habits of faithfulness to God.

Options

1. Instead of drawing a heart shape, trace an oval-shaped sponge twice, one slightly overlapping the other, to create feet for the poster-board base.

2. Provide yarn, construction paper, tape and scissors for students to use in adding hair, hats or other accessories (bows, ties, etc.) to their Balloon Buddies.

• •

Discussion Questions

1. **What does it mean to be faithful to God?** (To love Him with all your heart, soul, mind and strength. To obey God's commands no matter what.)

2. **Who is someone you think is faithful to God? What is that person like?**

3. **When are some times kids your age need to remember to show faithfulness to God by obeying His commands?** (At school when others start to argue. At home when brothers or sisters are teasing.)

Lesson 8

Worship Center

Bible Verse

Let love and faithfulness never leave you; bind them around your neck, write them on the tablet of your heart. Proverbs 3:3

Materials

Bible, *God's Kids Grow* cassette/CD or music video and player, "Good Habits" word chart (p. 467 in this book), large sheet of paper on which you have printed Proverbs 3:3, masking tape.

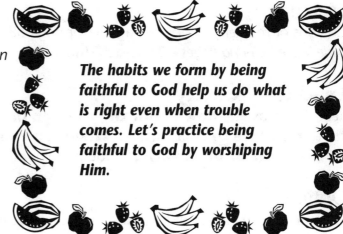

The habits we form by being faithful to God help us do what is right even when trouble comes. Let's practice being faithful to God by worshiping Him.

Sing to God

Play "Good Habits," encouraging students to sing along with the music. **What are some good habits to form?** (Praying to God every day. Reading the Bible. Playing fair. Telling the truth. Helping others.) **When we form good habits, it makes it easier to do what is right and obey God when we have hard times.**

Hear and Say God's Word

Display paper on which you have printed Proverbs 3:3. Have a volunteer read the verse aloud. **When you bind something around your neck or write it on your heart (know it by heart), it means you are trying to keep that thing close to you so that you will never lose it. What is Proverbs 3:3 telling us not to lose?** (Love and faithfulness to God.) Lead students in saying the verse in this manner: Divide students into three groups. Assign each group one phrase of the verse. When you point to each group, that group stands up and says its phrase aloud. Repeat verse several times, reassigning phrases for each repetition.

Pray to God

Let's pray and ask God for His help to show our love and faithfulness to Him. Students repeat each word or phrase of this prayer after you: **Dear God, You are the One who can help us to form good habits. We want to show our faithfulness to You and obey You, even when trouble comes. Please help us. In Jesus' name, amen.**

Options

1. When discussing the song, ask each student to think of a specific habit to work on during the week. Give each student a pencil or a sticker. **Use this (pencil) as a reminder of the habit you want to form and practice that action!**

2. Ask an older student to find the definition of "faithfulness" in a dictionary and read it to the class.

3. Give an older student a copy of the prayer. Student leads the group in prayer.

Bible Verse Coloring Center

Materials
Crayons or markers, a copy of page 57 or page 58 from *Bible Verse Coloring Pages #2* for each student.

Lead the Activity
Read Proverbs 3:3. **How might the children in this picture show love to each other? When can you show love in some of these ways?** Students color picture.

Option
Students cut hearts out of large sheets of construction paper and write one or more words from Proverbs 3:3 on the hearts.

Service Project Center

Materials
Materials needed for "Good-for-Something Coupon" (p. 16 from *The Big Book of Service Projects*).

Lead the Activity
Students complete "Good-for-Something Coupon" activity as directed in *The Big Book of Service Projects*. **How will making these coupons help you show faithfulness? What are some habits you have that help you do what is right in your family?**

Discipleship Activity Center

Materials
Discussion Cards for Proverbs 3:3-6 (pp. 99-104 from *The Big Book of Christian Growth*), materials needed for "Container Bounce" or "Advice Column" (p. 60 or p. 37 from *The Big Book of Christian Growth*).

Lead the Activity
Today we're going to play a game and answer questions about Proverbs 3:3-6 to help us discover ways to show faithfulness to God. Students complete activity as directed in *The Big Book of Christian Growth*.

Jesus, the Gentle Servant

Bible Verse
Serve one another in love.
Galatians 5:13

Bible Story Reference
John 13:1-17

Teacher's Devotional
If you read Galatians 5:23 in several different translations, you will notice that the first word of the verse is translated "gentleness," "meekness" or "humility." Gener-

Character Builder
Be ready to serve others with a gentle attitude.

ally, meekness or humility describes a person's inner attitude while gentleness is the outward action produced by that internal disposition.

By whatever name, humility, meekness and gentleness are a distinctive of the Christian gospel. The memory verse for this lesson, Galatians 5:13, presents this concept in simple, clearly understood words. However, the idea of humbly, gently serving others isn't always clearly understood and is often foreign to our culture. Gentleness is given little, if any, honor. Typically, the gentle, humble person who puts others ahead of self is seen as a naive idealist or an incompetent weakling.

In God's economy, however, gentle humility IS a virtue. Humility is not the result of a damaged self-concept but is the grateful realization of complete dependence upon God. Once a person recognizes God as the source for life, sustenance and salvation, pride diminishes and humility flourishes.

Jesus' disciples were stunned when their master knelt to wash their feet. People today often react similarly when Jesus' followers volunteer to serve rather than to be served, to nurture rather than to be nurtured, to love rather than to be loved. Be ready this week to look for opportunities to give service. Let your example of service in the classroom be a hands-on demonstration of Galatians 5:13.

Bible Story Center

Materials
Gentleness poster from *Poster Pack*, ¼ cup (2 oz.) play dough for each student.

Tell the Story
Follow along with me to make objects that are part of today's story.

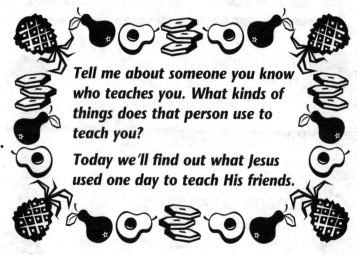

Tell me about someone you know who teaches you. What kinds of things does that person use to teach you?

Today we'll find out what Jesus used one day to teach His friends.

1. **Divide your dough into two parts.** It was Passover, the biggest celebration of the year in Israel. Big crowds of people were coming to Jerusalem to worship at the Temple, eat special meals with relatives and visit with friends. The streets were full of people!

2. **Make a shallow bowl from one part of the dough.** Jesus' disciples came together to eat a Passover meal as well. They all gathered in a room where Jesus had told them to go. But when they came into the room, all dressed and ready for the feast, no one came with a bowl and towel to wash their feet.

You see, usually when anyone came in from the outdoors, that person's feet were washed immediately because the roads were dirty, dusty and filled with animal droppings. In wealthy houses, a servant removed the person's sandals and washed and dried the person's feet.

Since no servant was there to wash their feet, Jesus' friends just sat down around the table with their feet still dirty. Perhaps they all thought that they were too good for a messy job like washing someone's feet. Whatever the reason, Jesus wanted to teach them how to show love to each other.

3. **From the remaining dough, make two feet to go in the bowl.** Jesus got up from the table where they were all ready to begin eating. He wrapped a towel around His waist and poured water into a shallow bowl. He began to wash the feet of the nearest disciple.

He finished washing His first friend's feet and dried them with the towel He had around His waist. Then He moved to the next pair of dirty feet. When Jesus came to Peter, Peter tried to stop Him.

"Lord," Peter said, "are You going to wash MY feet?" It must have seemed very strange to Peter that Jesus was doing a SERVANT'S job! It was embarrassing!

Jesus answered Peter, "You don't fully understand what I'm doing now, but you'll understand later on."

Peter said, "No! You will never wash MY feet!"

Jesus must have smiled on the inside. Peter wanted Jesus to act important, to act like the person in charge, not the lowly servant who washed feet! But Jesus did wash Peter's feet. He washed the feet of each of His friends—even the feet of Judas, who would later walk out with his clean feet and then help Jesus' enemies arrest Him.

Finally, Jesus put away the bowl and towel and sat down at the table. He looked around at His friends. "Do you understand what I have done? You all call Me teacher and Lord. But if your Lord and teacher washes your feet, you also should be willing to wash each other's feet. I did this for an example. Treat each other the way I have treated you."

Jesus' friends must have looked at each other and felt a little embarrassed. Jesus had been a gentle servant. Without saying a word, He had taught them how to treat each other. They realized they needed to treat each other as if the other person was more important. It was all right to be a servant. In fact, it was what Jesus wanted them to be!

Focus on the Fruit

What did people usually do when they came into a house in Bible times? (Had their feet washed.) **Why do you think the disciples hadn't washed their feet?** (Didn't want to act like a servant.) **How did Jesus teach His friends?** (He washed their feet.) **What did Jesus want His friends to learn?** (To serve and care for each other.)

It's not easy to treat people the way Jesus treated His friends. It takes God's help to show gentleness. Show the Gentleness poster. **But Jesus said that if we want to be great in His kingdom, we need to be gentle servants like He was. Following Jesus' example is one way to grow the fruit of the Spirit!**

Lesson 9
Fruitful Lives Object Talk

Bible Verse
Serve one another in love. Galatians 5:13

Materials
Bible with bookmark at Galatians 5:13, scrub brush, bucket.

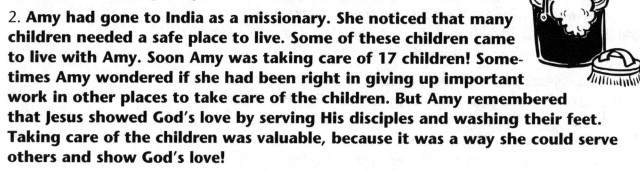

Being ready to serve others with a gentle attitude helps us show God's love. Let's find out how someone showed God's love with a scrub brush.

Lead the Activity
1. Show scrub brush and bucket. **When have you used a scrub brush or bucket?** Volunteers tell. **Some people don't like to wash floors or cars, because they think it's not very important work. In 1895 a woman named Amy Carmichael had to scrub something dirty to show what it meant to serve others.**

2. **Amy had gone to India as a missionary. She noticed that many children needed a safe place to live. Some of these children came to live with Amy. Soon Amy was taking care of 17 children! Sometimes Amy wondered if she had been right in giving up important work in other places to take care of the children. But Amy remembered that Jesus showed God's love by serving His disciples and washing their feet. Taking care of the children was valuable, because it was a way she could serve others and show God's love!**

3. **One day a new woman came to help care for the children. Amy asked the woman to serve by washing the nursery floor. The woman refused, because she wanted an easier, better job. So Amy took the bucket of soapy water and got down on her hands and knees and scrubbed the dirty floor. Because Amy was willing to do this hard work, she gently helped the woman learn how important it is to show God's love by serving others in whatever way is needed.**

Conclude
Read Galatians 5:13 aloud. **What are some ways you can show God's love by serving others at home? At school?** Students respond. **Let's ask God to help us serve others with gentle attitudes.** Lead students in prayer.

• •

Additional Information for Older Students
Amy Carmichael broke her leg when she was older. Her leg didn't heal correctly, so she couldn't walk for the rest of her life. Instead of being angry that she couldn't do the things she had done before, Amy still served others by writing many books that helped people learn more about missionaries and about God's love for people all over the world.

Active Game Center: Snack Service

Materials

Bible, individually wrapped snacks (at least one per student), paper plates.

Prepare the Game

For each group of five to seven students, place five to seven snacks on a paper plate.

Because we love God, it's important to be ready to serve others with a gentle attitude. Let's play a game to practice serving others.

Lead the Game

1. Group students into teams of five to seven students each. Teams line up on one side of the classroom. Set an empty paper plate next to the first student on each team. Place a plate of snacks across the playing area from each team.

2. At your signal, the first student on each team walks quickly to the other side of the room, retrieves a snack from the team's plate and brings it back, placing it on the team's empty plate. The next student in line repeats the action, leaving as the first student places the snack on the plate. Play continues until all members of the team have collected a snack.

3. Each student takes a snack from the team's plate and gives it someone else on the team. Students chew and swallow the snacks, and then begin to whistle. First team to have all its students whistle wins.

Options

1. Use individually wrapped single-serving packages of crackers from a restaurant or salad bar.

2. Vary manner in which students move to collect a snack, directing students to hop on one foot, skip, jump or crawl.

3. Post a note alerting parents to the use of food in this activity. Also check registration forms for possible food allergies.

4. If students are unable to whistle, suggest an alternative action: do five jumping jacks, run around a chair, etc.

• •

Discussion Questions

1. *How did we serve one another in this game?* (Gave each other snacks.)

2. *How can we serve others at school? At home? On the playground?*

3. Read Galatians 5:13 aloud. ***What do you think it means to serve someone with love?*** (Be kind and gentle when we help. Don't have a bossy or proud attitude. Pay attention to the needs of others.)

Art Center: Colorful Service

Materials
Bibles, paper towels, 8½x11-inch (21.5x27.5-cm) sheets of paper, colored chalk or pastels, dark-colored crayons, ballpoint pens, scissors.

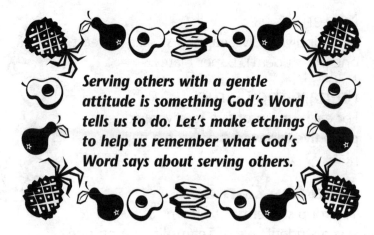

Serving others with a gentle attitude is something God's Word tells us to do. Let's make etchings to help us remember what God's Word says about serving others.

Lead the Activity
1. Give each student a paper towel and a sheet of paper. Students fold papers in half widthwise. Students place papers on top of paper towel and completely color bottom half of paper with bright colored chalk or pastels. Suggest students make blocks of color as shown in sketch a.

2. Students completely color over chalk with dark-colored crayons, using the flat side of crayons to lay as much color on the paper as possible.

3. Students refold papers. Students look up Galatians 5:13 and write the words "Serve one another in love" on outside of folded papers, pressing firmly with ballpoint pens (see sketch b). (Hint: Thick, large letters will provide the best result.)

4. Students cut off top half of papers, revealing the etchings on the colored papers underneath (see sketch c). Use paper towels to clean up extra crayon wax or chalk from table surfaces.

Options
1. In addition to paper towels, provide premoistened towelettes for cleanup.

2. Print Galatians 5:13 on large sheet of paper for students to refer to during the activity.

3. Simplify activity by providing colored paper for students to cover with dark crayons instead of using chalk.

• •

Discussion Questions
1. ***What are some ways to serve others?*** (Get a glass of water for someone who is sitting down resting. Set the table without being asked. Help your mom by taking care of younger brothers or sisters while she cooks dinner. Make a card for someone who is sick.)

2. ***How does Galatians 5:13 tell us we should serve others?*** (Serve others with love.)

3. ***How can you serve others with a loving and gentle attitude?*** (Be patient and kind to others when you are serving them. Learn what would help the other person most and give it to that person.)

Lesson 9
Worship Center

Bible Verse
Serve one another in love. Galatians 5:13

Materials
Bible, *God's Kids Grow* cassette/CD or music video and player, "Gentle Servant" word chart (p. 463 in this book), large sheet of paper on which you have printed Galatians 5:13, masking tape, marker.

When we love God and realize how much He loves us, it helps us be ready to serve others with gentle attitudes. Let's praise Jesus and thank Him for His example of how to serve others!

Sing to God
Play "Gentle Servant," encouraging students to sing along with the music. **What three questions does this song say we can ask to find ways to serve others?** ("What can I do to make things better?" "What can I do to help you out?" "What can I do to make you happy?")

Hear and Say God's Word
Display paper on which you have printed Galatians 5:13. Have a volunteer read the verse aloud. **What does this verse command us to do?** (Serve one another in love.) **What are some other words we could use to describe ways to serve?** ("Help." "Encourage." "Give first choice to." "Give food to.") List students' ideas on large sheet of paper below Galatians 5:13. Repeat the verse together several times, each time substituting one of the words or phrases students have suggested for "serve." Repeat Galatians 5:13 correctly the last time.

Pray to God
How did Jesus give us examples of ways to serve others? (Helped sick people. Talked to lonely people. Showed love to children.) **Let's thank Jesus for His example of serving others and for showing love to everyone by dying on the cross for our sins.** Students thank Jesus for specific examples of service. End the prayer time by asking Jesus for help in serving others with a gentle attitude.

Options
1. Sing "Galatians 5:22,23" and/or "Circle of Love" (p. 461 and/or p. 457 in this book) with students.

2. In the verse activity, students add motions, pantomiming the different ways of service they mention with each verse repetition.

Lesson 9

Bible Verse Coloring Center

Materials
Crayons or markers, a copy of page 141 or page 142 from *Bible Verse Coloring Pages #2* for each student.

Lead the Activity
Read Galatians 5:13. **Who in this picture is obeying Galatians 5:13? How? What are some other ways you can do what this verse says?** Students color picture.

Option
Students glue dried parsley or other herbs to picture for leaves.

Service Project Center

Materials
Materials needed for "Secret Service" (p. 18 from *The Big Book of Service Projects*).

Lead the Activity
Students complete "Secret Service" activity as directed in *The Big Book of Service Projects*. **How do you think the things you are planning to do might help or encourage the people for whom you do them? What are some other ways you can serve others in love this week?**

Discipleship Activity Center

Materials
Discussion Cards for 1 John 3:16-18 (pp. 171-176 from *The Big Book of Christian Growth*), materials needed for "Seek 'n' Find" or "Take Aim!" (p. 25 or p. 29 from *The Big Book of Christian Growth*).

Lead the Activity
The commands in 1 John 3:16-18 give us good ideas about ways to show the fruit of gentleness. Today we're going to play a game to talk about these verses. Students complete activity as directed in *The Big Book of Christian Growth*.

David's Self-Control

Bible Verse

A fool gives full vent to his anger, but a wise man keeps himself under control. Proverbs 29:11

Bible Story Reference

1 Samuel 24

Character Builder

God can help us control angry feelings so that we can treat others in ways that please Him.

Teacher's Devotional

Everybody is in favor of self-control—for everybody else. It's so easy to see when other people are unable to restrain themselves. We have a veritable arsenal of advice ready to drop on people whose willful emotions have gotten them in trouble:

"Get a grip."

"Get a hold of yourself."

"Settle down."

"Calm down."

"Take it easy."

"Cool off."

The list goes on and on. Our language would never have come up with so many ways to encourage people to regain control if there weren't frequent situations when self-control was in danger. And so far, we are only talking about adults.

Usually when adults talk to children about self-control, we have in mind a cessation of wiggles and noise. But the fruit of self-control is not focused on the ability to sit still and listen. (Maturation of nerve endings will take care of that in a few years.) The self-control that the Holy Spirit grows within us is the strength to resist temptation and to avoid excess in our enjoyment of life. It's the strength to interact with others in ways that show our love and obedience to God. Even a child can learn to exercise limits instead of indulgence. In your discussion of self-control, help your students think of specific actions or words they can put into practice in situations that tempt them to lose their self-control. Be ready to tell an example or two of ways you have exercised self-control in order to show your love for God and others. Most important, guide students to a knowledge of the ultimate source of self-control: God's Spirit living in us.

Bible Story Center

Materials
Self-Control poster from *Poster Pack*, ¼ cup (2 oz.) play dough for each student.

Tell the Story
Follow along with me as we use our dough to tell today's story.

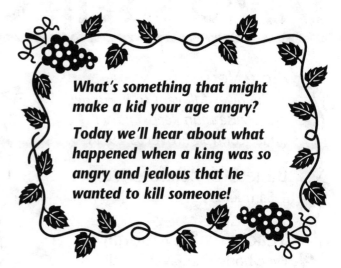

What's something that might make a kid your age angry?

Today we'll hear about what happened when a king was so angry and jealous that he wanted to kill someone!

1. **Roll your dough into a ball.** In the years before David became the king of Israel, he spent a lot of his time running for his life. He was being chased by King Saul. You see, King Saul wanted to KILL David!

2. **Make an angry face on the ball.** Saul wanted to kill David because he was so jealous of David and angry with him. The people in Saul's kingdom seemed to love David better than Saul. Saul's son Jonathan was David's best friend. AND Saul's daughter Michal was married to David! Besides that, Saul knew that God had planned for David to be the king one day.

3. **Change face into a hill with a cave in it.** Now King Saul had just heard that David was hiding with some of his friends out in the desert hills. So Saul chose 3,000 of his best fighting men to help him capture David. He set out to look for David and his friends with this huge army.

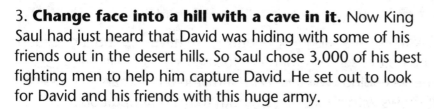

David and his friends could see Saul's army coming in the distance, so they hid in the back of a cave. They were probably hoping that Saul and his men would pass right by. But guess who came right into the cave? It was SAUL! He came in without his soldiers. David and his friends must have stared in amazement! They could clearly see him—King Saul was all alone at the opening of the cave.

David's friends whispered, "Look! It's Saul! God has put him here, so you can GET him!"

4. **Now use your dough to make a robe shaped like a cape.** Now, David had the chance to KILL Saul if he wanted. He could even take Saul as a prisoner. But David decided to keep control of his feelings about the mean way Saul was treating him.

Quiet as a shadow, David unsheathed his knife and slipped to the front of the cave. Saul's outer robe was lying behind him on the cave floor. Quietly, quickly, David held his breath and sliced a corner from Saul's robe.

5. **Pinch a corner from the robe.** Saul picked up his robe, left the cave and began walking down the hillside, never knowing anyone had been near him. Suddenly, Saul heard a VERY familiar voice from behind him!

"My lord, the king!" David shouted. Saul whirled around. Standing in the opening of the cave was David. David said, "Why do you listen to people who tell you I want to hurt you? Do you realize what just happened? While you were in the cave, my men and I were right there! They wanted me to kill you; but I said, 'I can't hurt Saul. He is God's chosen king.'

"Do you see what I have in my hand? It's the corner of your robe! I was that close to you, with my knife in my hand. But I only cut the corner from your robe. I will not hurt you, no matter what you do to me."

6. **Roll dough into a ball and make a sad face.** Saul felt VERY sad and ashamed! He said, "David, you treated me well, but I have treated you badly. May God reward you for the way you treated me."

Saul went on his way then, and David and his friends went back up into a safe place in the mountains. Even when Saul kept trying to hurt him, David was wise. David knew that it was up to God to decide when Saul should stop being king. Later when David did become king, he was glad God had helped him treat Saul in ways that showed self-control.

• •

Focus on the Fruit

Why was Saul trying to kill David? (Saul was jealous.) **What did David do when Saul was in the cave?** (Cut off the corner of Saul's robe.) **Why didn't David kill or hurt Saul?** (He did not want to hurt the king God had chosen.)

God tells us that if we ask Him, He will help us have self-control, like David did. Then we will treat others as God wants us to, no matter what they do to us. That's growing the fruit of self-control in our lives! Show the Self-Control poster.

Lesson 10
Fruitful Lives Object Talk

Bible Verse

A fool gives full vent to his anger, but a wise man keeps himself under control.
Proverbs 29:11

Materials

Bible with bookmark at Proverbs 29:11, month-by-month calendar; optional—copy of "I Have a Dream" speech by Dr. Martin Luther King, Jr. (available from library or on the Internet).

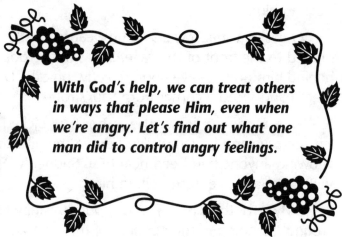

With God's help, we can treat others in ways that please Him, even when we're angry. Let's find out what one man did to control angry feelings.

Lead the Activity

1. Show calendar. Invite several volunteers to find favorite holidays listed on the calendar. **What or whom do these holidays help us to remember?** Students tell. **Martin Luther King, Jr., is a man whose actions are remembered each year by many people.**

2. **Martin Luther King, Jr., Day is celebrated each year on the third Monday of January. What do you know about Dr. King?** Volunteers respond. Supplement students' information as needed with the following information: **In 1954, Dr. King became the pastor of a church in Alabama. At this time many African-American people felt very angry, because they weren't being treated fairly. Dr. King was angry, too. Dr. King believed that because God loves everyone the same, all people should be treated fairly.**

   Even though he was angry, Martin Luther King, Jr., didn't let his angry feelings cause him to treat others in unkind ways. Instead, he led marches to call attention to unfairness. He gave speeches and preached sermons, telling people to treat each other fairly. Dr. King asked government leaders to pass laws so that African-Americans would be treated fairly. He also warned people to do what was right at all times and to treat others in ways that pleased God.
(Optional: Read aloud part of Dr. King's "I Have a Dream" speech.)

Conclude

Read Proverbs 29:11 aloud. **What does Proverbs 29:11 say a wise man does?** Volunteer answers. **When we keep our words and actions under control, it means we think about and plan our words and actions so that they show love and obedience to God.** Lead students in prayer, asking God to help them show self-control.

• •

Discussion Questions

1. *When are some times it is hard for kids your age to control their anger?*

2. *What are some things people do to help control their anger?* (Count to 10. Take a deep breath. Walk away. Tell God about their anger. Ask God's help in being kind.)

3. *Why do you think it is wise to control your anger?*

Active Game Center: Ball Toss

Materials
Large sheet of paper, marker, masking tape, large container, soft ball or beanbag.

Prepare the Game
Print the word "self-control" across the top of a large sheet of paper. Draw a line down the center of the paper. Print "Team 1" on one side of the line and "Team 2" on the other. Display in classroom. Place container on the floor on one side of the playing area.

God can help us control our angry feelings so that we can treat others in ways that please Him. Let's play a game to help us remember the name of this fruit of the Spirit.

Lead the Game

1. Divide class into two teams. Play a ball-tossing game similar to H-O-R-S-E. Students stand about 5 feet (1.5 m) from the container and take turns attempting to toss the ball or beanbag into it. Each time the ball lands in the container, the tossing team writes one letter of the word "self-control" on its side of the paper. First team to complete the word wins.

2. Ask a volunteer from the winning team to answer one of the Discussion Questions below. Repeat game as time allows.

Options
1. Adjust distance from which students toss ball according to skill level.

2. Use different methods to divide class into teams: Have students line up alphabetically according to their first names or numerically according to the last digit of their phone numbers; divide the line equally. Or have students group themselves by the color of clothes or the kind of shoes they are wearing; combine various groups as needed to make two evenly numbered teams.

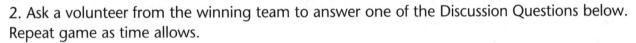

Discussion Questions
1. *When are some of the times angry feelings are hard to control?* (When someone is continually mean or rude to you. When someone makes you feel bad.)

2. *How can we control our angry feelings?* (Pray and ask God for His help. Walk away. Take a deep breath and wait before speaking.)

3. *When God helps us have self-control, how will we act toward others?* (We won't act angrily. We will treat them in ways that please God, being kind to them instead of treating them in the way they treated us.)

Art Center: Poster Playground

Materials

Tape, large sheets of poster board, markers, building materials (recyclables, aluminum foil, paper towel tubes, scissors, string, glue, construction paper, drinking straws, clay, etc.).

God helps us control our angry feelings so that we can treat others in ways that please Him. Let's make a big model of a place we sometimes need God to help us control our anger—the playground!

Lead the Activity

1. Tape together several large sheets of poster board for students to work on (allow one poster-board rectangle for every three students). Students create a model of a playground using the materials provided. Students may draw items directly on the poster board or construct playground items and tape or glue them onto the board. If students need ideas, suggest they make a tetherball from a straw, string and aluminum foil; slides, swings and monkey bars from straws and paper towel tubes covered with aluminum foil; a merry-go-round from construction paper and straws; and a basketball hoop from construction paper, string and straw.

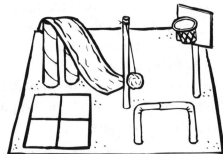

2. Use the Discussion Questions below to ask students about situations that might happen in the area of the playground they are constructing.

Options

1. Pairs or small groups of students work on separate sheets of poster board to create designated areas of the playground. Tape all sheets together to show complete playground.

2. Play "Self-Control" song from *God's Kids Grow* cassette/CD as students work.

3. Older students write answers to Discussion Questions as captions and attach to different areas of the playground. For example, students attach to the slide area a caption which says "We can have self-control by not pushing someone who first pushed us down the slide."

• •

Discussion Questions

1. ***What might happen (playing tetherball) that would make a kid your age angry?*** (Get hit in the face with the ball. Someone cuts in line in front of him or her.)

2. ***How might that kid react to the situation in a way that would please God?*** (Not yell at the person who hit the ball in his or her face or who cut in line.)

3. ***What can a kid your age do if he or she feels unable to control his or her feelings and react positively?*** (Walk away from the situation before speaking or acting rudely. Take time out to pray to God. Talk about the situation with a person who loves God.)

Worship Center

Bible Verse

A fool gives full vent to his anger, but a wise man keeps himself under control. Proverbs 29:11

Materials

Bible, *God's Kids Grow* cassette/CD or music video and player, "Self-Control" word chart (p. 485 in this book), large sheet of paper on which you have printed Proverbs 29:11, masking tape.

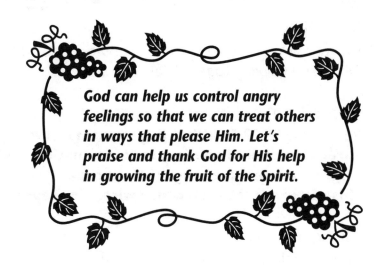

God can help us control angry feelings so that we can treat others in ways that please Him. Let's praise and thank God for His help in growing the fruit of the Spirit.

Sing to God

Play "Self-Control," encouraging students to sing along with the music. **What are some of the ways this song suggests to help us have self-control?** (Take things slowly, so we have time to think before we act. Pray to God, telling Him how you feel and asking Him to teach you to have love and self-control.)

Hear and Say God's Word

Display paper on which you have printed Proverbs 29:11. Have a volunteer read the verse aloud. **To give vent to your anger means to let your anger out by saying or acting in unkind, mean ways. Who does Proverbs 29:11 say gives vent to his anger?** (A fool.) **Who keeps himself under control?** (Someone who is wise.) Lead all the boys to say the first half of the verse and all the girls to say the second half of the verse. Repeat verse in this manner several times, naming a different group of students to say each half of the verse each time. (For example, everyone older than nine says the first half and everyone younger than nine says the second half; or everyone wearing blue says the first half and everyone wearing white says the second half; etc.)

Pray to God

Praying for others is something that pleases God. Let's pray for each other, asking God's help in controlling our angry feelings. Students form pairs and pray aloud for each other, filling in this sentence prayer with their partners' names: **"God, please help (Jill) have self-control, especially when she is angry. In Jesus' name, amen."**

Option

If students give an offering during this worship time, explain that it takes self-control to save money for the offering instead of using the money only for ourselves. Describe several ways your church uses the offering to help other people learn about God.

Bible Verse Coloring Center

Materials
Crayons or markers, a copy of page 69 or page 70 from *Bible Verse Coloring Pages #2* for each student.

Lead the Activity
Read Proverbs 29:11. **What is happening in this picture? How would you feel in this situation? Why might someone feel anger? How could the kids in this picture treat each other wisely in ways that please God?** Students color picture.

Option
After completing coloring, students cut pages into five or six puzzle pieces. Students put their own puzzles together or trade with other students to complete puzzles. Provide envelopes for students to take puzzle pieces home.

Service Project Center

Materials
Materials needed for "Boxed Help" (p. 69 from *The Big Book of Service Projects*).

Lead the Activity
Students complete "Boxed Help" activity as directed in *The Big Book of Service Projects*. **What are some actions, or ways to treat people, that would show self-control or please God? How do you think our project today might please God?**

Discipleship Activity Center

Materials
Discussion Cards for Romans 12:9-14,17-21 (pp. 135-140 from *The Big Book of Christian Growth*), materials needed for "Chair Trade" or "Cartoon Creations" (p. 58 or p. 40 from *The Big Book of Christian Growth*).

Lead the Activity
Today we're going to play a game about Romans 12:9-14,17-21 to discover some ways of growing the fruit of self-control in our lives. Students complete activity as directed in *The Big Book of Christian Growth*.

Jesus' Loving Acceptance

Bible Verse

Accept one another, then, just as Christ accepted you, in order to bring praise to God. Romans 15:7

Bible Story Reference

John 4:1-42

Teacher's Devotional

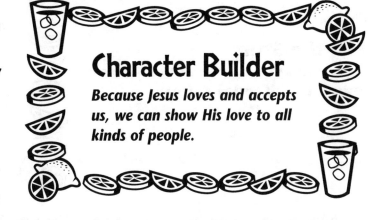

Character Builder

Because Jesus loves and accepts us, we can show His love to all kinds of people.

Before Jesus surprised the Samaritan woman at the well with His insights into her life, He had already amazed her with His simple willingness to talk with her (see John 4). It would have been so easy for Him to follow the custom of the day and avoid eye contact or even to get up and stroll away from the well when she came to draw water. But Jesus saw this outcast as someone with a need. So He reached out to her and transformed her life.

There will be children in your group who feel like outcasts, who ache for someone to love them or to accept them. It is not at all unlikely that at least some children will demonstrate this need in less than desirable ways. They are not unlike this Samaritan woman at the well, for she had sought satisfaction in a series of immoral relationships. Compounding the problem with these children is that their misbehaviors often make it more difficult for others to love and accept them, again like the Samaritan woman who had to draw water when her neighbors were not around.

Focus your prayers this week on asking God's help to love those children who may be the hardest to love. Pray that through you, God's love will draw those children to Himself. Just as with that woman, a personal encounter with a loving Jesus can transform a life.

Bible Story Center

Materials

Love poster from *Poster Pack*, ¼ cup (2 oz.) play dough for each student.

Tell the Story

Follow along with me as we use our dough to tell today's story.

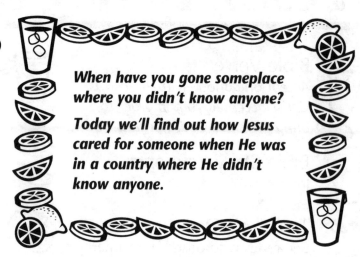

When have you gone someplace where you didn't know anyone?

Today we'll find out how Jesus cared for someone when He was in a country where He didn't know anyone.

1. **Divide your dough into three balls.** When Jesus lived on the earth, He traveled with His disciples to many places to tell people about God's love. One day Jesus and His disciples were getting ready to go to Galilee, where Jesus grew up. Jesus decided they would travel through the country of Samaria. Now MOST Jewish people in Jesus' time would not go NEAR Samaria. They would travel AROUND Samaria to get to Galilee! That made the trip a lot longer, but the Jews and Samaritans had disliked each other for HUNDREDS of years. But Jesus had a reason for walking through Samaria!

2. **From one ball, make several rocks and put them in a circle to form a well.** Jesus and His friends walked until it was nearly noon. They were getting tired and hot and hungry; so when they came to a town in Samaria, Jesus' disciples went into town to buy food and Jesus stopped to rest by a well. The well was a deep hole dug in the ground to reach water. It usually had a wall of rocks built in a circle around it.

As Jesus rested by the well, He saw a Samaritan woman walking toward Him. She carried a jug on her shoulder and was coming to get water at the well. This was strange, because women usually came to get water for the day early in the morning when it was cool, not at noon when it was hot!

3. **Make a water pot from a ball of dough.** When the woman got to the well, Jesus asked her for a drink of water.

"What?" the woman asked in surprise. "How can YOU ask ME for a drink?!" You see, in Bible times a man and woman did NOT speak to each other in public. And besides that, Jews and Samaritans hardly EVER talked to each other.

Jesus said to the amazed woman, "If you knew who I am, you would ask ME for LIVING water!"

The woman didn't understand. "How can You give me LIVING water?" she asked. "You don't have a bucket or a rope for this well. Where would You get this living water?"

"Anyone who drinks this water will become thirsty again," Jesus told her. "But whoever drinks the water I give will never be thirsty again. The water I give will be like a flowing stream inside the person. It will last forever!"

"Give me some of this water!" the woman said. "Then I'll never be thirsty again, and I won't have to come to the well every day to get water." The woman thought Jesus was talking about water she could drink. She didn't know that Jesus meant He could give her life from God that would last forever.

4. **Use remaining dough to make figures of people to place around the well.** As Jesus and the woman kept talking, she found out that Jesus knew EVERYTHING about her! And Jesus told her that He was the Messiah, the Savior God had promised to send. WOW! The Bible tells us the woman was so excited to hear this news that she left her water jug at the well and hurried back to town.

"Come and see a man who told me everything I have ever done!" the woman told the people in the town. "Could He be the Messiah?"

People from the town hurried to the well to see Jesus. If the Messiah had come, they wanted to see Him! On that day many of these people believed that Jesus was the Messiah because of what the woman told them. Others came to learn more about who Jesus was. One thing was certain: this town would never be the same—all because Jesus cared about, accepted and talked to a woman—a Samaritan whom most people would ignore!

∙ ∙

Focus on the Fruit

How did Jesus show His care for the Samaritan woman? (Jesus talked to her. Jesus offered her living water—life from God that never ends.) **Jesus offered her salvation. He offers us salvation, too.** Talk with children about becoming members of God's family, following the guidelines in the "Leading a Child to Christ" article on page 36.

When we are members of God's family, we can show God's love and acceptance to other people. Accepting others means showing love and care to others whether or not they are our friends. Show the Love poster. **Caring for and loving others, even if they are different from us, is a way to grow the fruit of love!**

Fruitful Lives Object Talk

Bible Verse

Accept one another, then, just as Christ accepted you, in order to bring praise to God. Romans 15:7

Materials

Bible with bookmark at Romans 15:7, one or more Hawaiian items (lei, shirt, pictures of Hawaii, etc.).

Because of Jesus' love for and acceptance of us, we can show His love to other people, no matter who they are or where they live. Let's find out about some people who were difficult to accept and care for.

Lead the Activity

1. Show Hawaiian items. **What do you think of when you hear someone talk about Hawaii?** Students tell ideas. **We usually think that because Hawaii is so beautiful, everyone who lives there must be happy! But a long time ago, in the 1800s, there were some people living in Hawaii who weren't happy because they were sick with leprosy (a disease now called Hansen's disease).**

2. **At that time there was no treatment for leprosy, so everyone in Hawaii with leprosy was sent away to live on the Hawaiian island of Molokai** (MOH-loh-ki). **Ships came to bring food and medicine, but no healthy person lived on Molokai to help the sick people living there.**

   Then a man named Father Damien heard about the people who were sick with leprosy. Even though Father Damien lived far away from Hawaii in the country of Belgium and even though he knew that he could get sick, too, he moved to Molokai.

   Father Damien was a friend to the people with leprosy. He taught them to grow crops and take better care of themselves. He gave the people medicine and helped them bandage their sores. Father Damien stayed with the people he cared about until he got sick and died from leprosy himself.

Conclude

Read Romans 15:7 aloud. **How did Father Damien show that he accepted others?** Volunteers respond. Pray, asking God to help students accept and care for others.

Discussion Questions

1. *When are some times that it is hard to accept others or treat them like friends?*

2. *What are some good reasons to accept others?* (Christ accepts us and loves us.)

3. *How can you show friendship and acceptance this week to someone who hasn't been a friend before?*

Active Game Center: Quick Pass

Materials
Bible with bookmark at Romans 15:7, index cards, marker.

Prepare the Game
Print the words of Romans 15:7 on index cards, one word on each card.

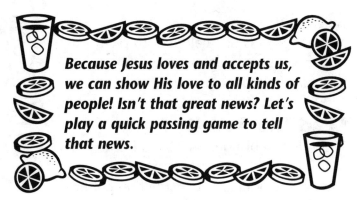

Because Jesus loves and accepts us, we can show His love to all kinds of people! Isn't that great news? Let's play a quick passing game to tell that news.

Lead the Game

1. Students sit in a circle. Ask a volunteer to read Romans 15:7 aloud. **According to this verse, why should we accept others?** (Because Christ accepted us. To bring praise to God.) Read verse to students one more time as a review.

2. Give one word card each to two students who are seated at opposite sides of the circle. At your signal, students start passing cards, one student passing to the left and one student passing to the right. Students continue passing cards around the circle until one student gets both cards at the same time.

3. Student places cards in the middle of the circle, arranging them in verse order. Repeat play by giving two more verse cards to two different students in the circle. Continue play until all cards have been passed and arranged in verse order.

Options
1. Keep Bible open to Romans 15:7 for reference during game.

2. Play with four cards each round to decrease time it takes for someone to receive two cards simultaneously. Add two more cards to the circle each time two are placed in verse order.

• •

Discussion Questions

1. *Romans 15:7 tells us to love and accept one another. What does it mean to accept someone?* (Be friendly and treat that person kindly, no matter what that person acts, looks or sounds like.)

2. *How does it make you feel to know that Jesus Christ loves and accepts you?*

3. *What are some ways to accept and show love to a grandma? A younger brother or sister? A person in another country? A person from another country who now lives by you?*

Art Center: Stand-Up People

Materials
Magazines, ads or catalogs with pictures of people; scissors; glue sticks; construction paper; large paper clips.

Lead the Activity

1. Students cut figures or faces from magazines, ads or catalogs. Students lightly glue figures to construction paper and then cut around them.

2. Each student straightens one loop of a large paper clip, leaving the other loop to serve as the base of the holder (see sketch a). Student inserts the straightened end of the paper clip between the picture and the construction-paper backing, firmly pressing picture and backing together around the paper clip. Student stands figure, adjusting the curve of the base loop until the figure is balanced (see sketch b). As students work, ask the Discussion Questions below.

3. Display figures in classroom as reminders to show love to others.

Because Jesus loves and accepts us, we can show His love to all kinds of people. Let's make a crowd of different kinds of people and think about ways to show love.

Options

1. Make a sample to show students and to become familiar with adjusting paper clips. Too much twisting may break the paper clip.

2. Challenge students to find a variety of people or faces to include in their crowd. Figures should be smaller than 5 inches (12.5 cm) to balance well on paper clips.

3. Students may draw figures on construction paper instead of cutting out figures. Provide books that show a variety of people for students to illustrate in drawings. Students tape figures to paper-clip stands.

4. If students find it difficult to make figures stand up, they may tape paper clips to the table.

• •

Discussion Questions

1. *What are some of the ways these people are different from each other?*

2. *Why might kids your age have trouble getting along with each other?*

3. *What are some ways to show love to people who are older than you? Kids who go to a different school from yours? Kids who are younger than you? Brothers and sisters?*

Lesson 11
Worship Center

Bible Verse

Accept one another, then, just as Christ accepted you, in order to bring praise to God. Romans 15:7

Materials

Bible, *God's Kids Grow* cassette/CD or music video and player, "All My Heart" word chart (p. 453 in this book), large sheet of paper on which you have printed Romans 15:7, masking tape, beanbag.

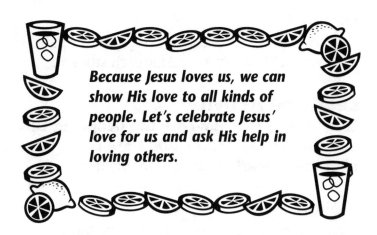

Because Jesus loves us, we can show His love to all kinds of people. Let's celebrate Jesus' love for us and ask His help in loving others.

Sing to God

Play "All My Heart," encouraging students to sing along with the music. **According to this song, what does it mean to love the Lord with all your heart?** (Love God all the time with all my heart, soul and mind.) **One way to show our love for God is to show His love to others.**

Hear and Say God's Word

Display paper on which you have printed Romans 15:7. Have a volunteer read the verse aloud. **What does it mean to accept someone?** (To treat someone as a friend. To show love and care to others, no matter what they are like.) **This verse says that when we love and accept others we show how great God is.**

Students sit in a circle. Hand the beanbag to a student, saying the first word of the verse as you hand it off. Student who receives the beanbag says the second word of the verse as he or she passes it to the student next to him or her. Students continue passing beanbag around the circle, each student saying the next word of the verse as the beanbag is passed. Continue until verse has been said several times.

Pray to God

Let's rewrite the words of Romans 15:7 to make it a prayer. On the Bible-verse paper, change the words of Romans 15:7 to read "Jesus, help us accept one another, then, just as You accepted us, in order to bring praise to You." Read the sentence together as a prayer.

Options

1. If you have mostly older students, expand the verse activity by having the first student say the first and second words of the verse; the second student say the first, second and third word of the verse; and so on, until the entire verse has been quoted.

2. Sing "Hear, O Israel" (p. 471 in this book) with students.

Bible Verse Coloring Center

Materials
Crayons or markers, a copy of page 125 or page 126 from *Bible Verse Coloring Pages #2* for each student.

Lead the Activity
Read Romans 15:7. **How are the people in this picture obeying Romans 15:7? What are some other ways to obey this verse?** Students color picture.

Option
Students use glitter crayons to color picture.

Service Project Center

Materials
Materials needed for "Breakfast in a Bag" (p. 70 from *The Big Book of Service Projects*).

Lead the Activity
Students complete "Breakfast in a Bag" activity as directed in *The Big Book of Service Projects*. **Knowing Jesus loves and accepts us makes us want to love and accept others. How do you think this project will help people in our community? What are some other ways to show Jesus' love to people around us?**

Discipleship Activity Center

Materials
Discussion Cards for Ephesians 4:1-6 (pp. 153-158 from *The Big Book of Christian Growth*), materials needed for "Hopscotch Rocks" or "Pass and Switch" (p. 18 or p. 47 from *The Big Book of Christian Growth*).

Lead the Activity
Showing love and acceptance to others is an important part of being in God's family. Today we're going to play a game about Ephesians 4:1-6 to discover more about what God's family is like. Students complete activity as directed in *The Big Book of Christian Growth*.

The Grateful Leper

Bible Verse

The Lord is my strength and my shield; my heart trusts in him, and I am helped. My heart leaps for joy and I will give thanks to him in song. Psalm 28:7

Bible Story Reference

Luke 17:11-19

Teacher's Devotional

Character Builder

God's gifts to us bring joy and cause our thankfulness to overflow.

Joy is not usually a dignified, quiet virtue. When the psalmist wrote about joy, no mere basking in a warm glow or smiling contentedly was mentioned or intended. No, the psalmist talks about leaping and singing, an exuberant response to God's provision. Similarly, the tenth leper, "when he saw that he was healed, came back praising God in a loud voice" (Luke 17:15).

In neither case was the celebrant seeking to be noticed. These were spontaneous displays of powerful emotion—deep, resonating joy that had to be expressed.

Reading these and many similar incidents in Scripture, we see an obvious but often neglected connection between joy and thanksgiving. Repeatedly we see that giving thanks and experiencing joy go hand in hand. Is it any surprise that recognizing and affirming God's great goodness releases deep, joyful feelings?

Everyone desires the euphoria of joyous emotion, but not everyone wants to give thanks. When we fail to give thanks to God, choosing instead to complain about what we don't like or to claim credit for what we do, is it any surprise that joy seems to elude us? This week, focus on giving thanks often. Encourage your students to do the same. And perhaps practice a little singing, shouting and leaping, just to be ready.

Bible Story Center

Materials

Joy poster from *Poster Pack*; ¼ cup (2 oz.) play dough and several 3-inch (7.5-cm) lengths of yarn for each student.

Tell the Story

Follow along with me to use our dough to tell today's story.

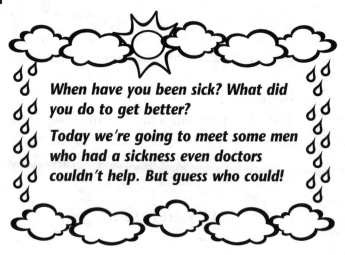

When have you been sick? What did you do to get better?

Today we're going to meet some men who had a sickness even doctors couldn't help. But guess who could!

1. **Divide your dough in half. From one half, roll two ropes. Make the number 10.** Once there were 10 men who had a sickness called leprosy. Leprosy caused terrible sores. In Bible times, doctors couldn't help people with leprosy. The sickness got worse and worse until eventually people with leprosy died. And there was another reason it was awful, too—the law said that people with leprosy couldn't even go NEAR other people. They had to stay far away from healthy people for fear of making them sick, too.

More than anything else in the whole world, those 10 sick men wanted to get WELL! They must have been very sad to have to live outside the city and stay far away from their families and friends. But these men had heard that Jesus could make people well.

2. **From the other half of your dough, make a heart. Use yarn to decorate your heart.** One day, these men heard that Jesus was coming past the place where they lived. So they went out to meet Him. When they saw Jesus, they stayed a distance away from Him, as the law required. They must have wondered if Jesus would walk past and ignore them the way other people did.

When they saw Jesus coming, the men with leprosy called, "JESUS, have pity on us! Jesus, please HELP us!"

Jesus saw these men. He didn't ignore them. He loved them and wanted to make them well!

He called to them, "Go and show yourselves to the priests." That sounds like a strange thing to say. But in those days, the law said any person who had been cured of leprosy had to be examined by a priest. That meant Jesus was saying they were CURED!

The 10 men hurried off in amazement. *Show themselves to the priests? They sure would. WOW!* As they jogged along, they looked at each other. Their sores were GONE. Their leprosy was HEALED! They COULD go to the priest. He would say they could go HOME. They could live with their families again!

3. **Take away the one from the number 10. Add eyes and mouth to the zero to make a happy face.** The Bible doesn't tell us what nine of these men did next, but it DOES tell what one man did. When this man saw that he was healed, he didn't keep jogging on his way to see the priest. He stopped. He turned around and ran back to Jesus. He threw himself down on the ground at Jesus' feet. And he said, "Jesus, wonderful teacher, THANK YOU! You have made me WELL!"

Jesus looked down at this happy, grateful man. He asked, "Weren't all 10 of you made well?"

"Yes, we were all HEALED!" the man answered.

"Where are the other nine?" Jesus asked. "Didn't they come with you to thank God for being healed?"

This man must have looked around in surprise. NONE of the others had come back to thank Jesus for healing him.

Jesus looked kindly at the man and said, "Get up now. You may go. Your faith in Me has made you well!"

Jesus was glad to see how thankful the man was. God's gift of making him well had filled him with joy! His thankfulness was OVERFLOWING! He was so grateful to Jesus for loving him and healing him that he had to come back and say thank-You. He didn't care what anyone else did. He was filled with JOY!

• •

Focus on the Fruit

Why were the 10 men waiting for Jesus? (They wanted Jesus to make them well.) **What did Jesus tell the men? What did it mean?** (Jesus told them to show themselves to the priest. That meant they were cured.) **What did one man do?** (Came back to thank Jesus.) **Why do you think the others didn't?**

God has given us wonderful gifts, too. That's because He wants us to be filled with joy. When we are grateful to God for all He has done, it gives us so much joy we can't help showing it to others! Show the Joy poster. **Being grateful to God grows joy in our lives!**

Fruitful Lives Object Talk

Bible Verse

The Lord is my strength and my shield; my heart trusts in him, and I am helped. My heart leaps for joy and I will give thanks to him in song.
Psalm 28:7

Materials

Bible with bookmark at Psalm 28:7, hymnal.

Remembering God's gifts to us helps us be joyful and want to thank God. Let's look at a book written by people whose thankfulness to God couldn't help but show.

Lead the Activity

1. Open hymnal and show it to students. **What is in this book? How are books like this used?** Volunteers respond. **Hymnals are books of songs about God. These songs were written by many different people who loved God and wanted others to love Him, too. One hymn writer's name was Francis Crosby.** (She is often called by the nickname "Fanny.")

2. **Francis Crosby was born in New York in 1820. When Francis was only six weeks old, she became sick and eventually became blind. Then shortly after Francis became blind, her father died and her family became very poor.**

   In spite of the bad things that happened to her, Francis Crosby didn't feel sorry for herself. When she grew up, Francis became a teacher at a school for the blind. She also was a concert singer and played the piano and the harp. And Francis wrote songs, thousands of them! During her lifetime, Francis Crosby wrote over 8,000 songs and poems—and many of them were written to show her love and thankfulness to God.

Conclude

Read Psalm 28:7 aloud. **Why does this verse say we can thank God? What are some other good things God does for us?** Lead students in prayer, thanking God for His gifts to them.

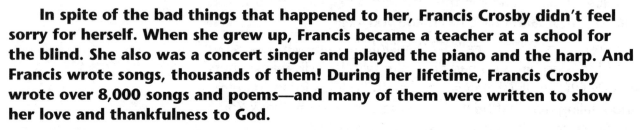

Additional Information for Older Students

Use Post-it Notes to mark several hymns written by Francis Crosby. Her hymns include "To God Be the Glory," "Blessed Assurance," "I Am Thine, O Lord," "Praise Him! Praise Him!" and "Redeemed." Volunteers find and read or sing hymns written by Francis Crosby. **What do these hymns talk about? After reading these hymns, what do you think was important to Francis Crosby? Why? What did she want to thank God for?**

Active Game Center: Praise Phrases

Materials

Index cards, marker, a cardboard box for every group of four to six students, paper, pencils.

Prepare the Game

On the index cards, print individual words that can be used in giving praise to God: "I," "we," "give," "thanks," "for," "God," "love," "gifts," "help," "sing," "joy," "your," "Son," "food," etc. Prepare at least three cards for each student, repeating words as needed. Place cardboard boxes around the playing area.

God's gifts to us bring us joy and cause our thankfulness to overflow! Let's play a game to give God thanks and praise for all His good gifts.

Lead the Game

1. Give each student at least three cards. Students form groups of four to six.

2. Each group stands around a cardboard box, 3 to 5 feet (.9 to 1.5 m) from the box. Students take turns tossing cards like Frisbees into the box, tossing each card only once.

3. When all students have finished tossing, students in each group collect cards that landed in their box and use the words to write sentences praising God. Encourage groups to tell their favorite praise sentences to the rest of the students. Continue discussion using questions below.

Options

1. For older students, brainstorm words to use in sentences giving praise to God. Students print words on separate index cards, making a large number of cards. Make a string or yarn circle about 4 feet (1.2 m) around the cardboard box. Students throw cards into the box for 30 seconds, rethrowing any cards that land outside of the circle. Students may reach over but not step over string circle to retrieve cards and throw them again. When 30 seconds have passed, call time. Students continue as above.

2. If you have mostly younger students or fewer than eight students, play the game as one group.

• •

Discussion Questions

1. ***What are some good gifts God gives us?*** (People who love us. Food. Clothing. Forgiveness of sins. Talents.)

2. ***What can you do to thank God for these gifts?*** (Tell Him words of praise and thanks. Tell other people how great He is. Sing songs of thankfulness to Him. Use the gifts He has given us to praise Him.)

3. ***When are some times you can thank God?*** (Before bed. Walking to school. Riding bike. At church.)

Art Center: Pencil Praises

Materials

Chenille wires, scissors, ruler, unsharpened pencils, small jingle bells, plastic or metallic beads in a variety of shapes and colors.

Prepare the Activity

Cut chenille wires into 4-inch (10-cm) lengths. Make a sample pencil following directions below.

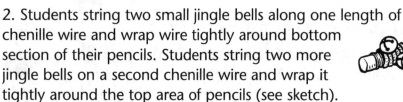

Thinking about God's gifts to us helps us be joyful and thankful. Let's make some pencils we can use to help express our joy about God's good gifts.

Lead the Activity

1. Show students your sample. Give each student one unsharpened pencil, three chenille wires, four jingle bells, eight to ten beads and a scissors.

2. Students string two small jingle bells along one length of chenille wire and wrap wire tightly around bottom section of their pencils. Students string two more jingle bells on a second chenille wire and wrap it tightly around the top area of pencils (see sketch).

3. Students cut third chenille wire in half and string four or five beads on each half. Students loosely wrap each beaded wire around the middle section of pencils, twisting the ends of each wire together to form a circle. Beaded wire circles should be able to slide up and down and slap together in between the jingle-bell wires.

4. Students shake pencils up and down or tap pencils against the palms of their hands to use them as rhythm sticks.

Options

1. Play "Good Fruit" song from *God's Kids Grow* cassette/CD. Students sing and shake pencils along with music.

2. Provide a pencil sharpener and paper. Students sharpen and use pencils to write out Psalm 28:7, trying to make as much jingling with pencils as possible. **When you use your pencils at home or at school, remember the joy that comes from God's good gifts to us and thank Him!**

• •

Discussion Questions

1. ***What kinds of good gifts has God given you for which you can thank Him?*** (Forgiveness through Christ's death on the cross. Eyes to see. Ears to hear. Hands to make things.)

2. ***What does it mean for something to overflow?*** (To spill out or run over the edges of a cup, for example, because there is so much extra.)

3. ***How can your thankfulness to God overflow?*** (Say thanks to God often. Tell it to others.)

Lesson 12

Worship Center

Bible Verse
The Lord is my strength and my shield; my heart trusts in him, and I am helped. My heart leaps for joy and I will give thanks to him in song.
Psalm 28:7

Materials
Bible, *God's Kids Grow* cassette/CD or music video and player, "Joy!" word chart (p. 473 in this book), large sheet of paper on which you have printed Psalm 28:7, masking tape, index cards, markers.

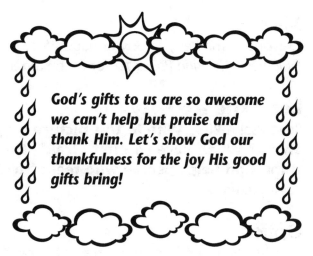

God's gifts to us are so awesome we can't help but praise and thank Him. Let's show God our thankfulness for the joy His good gifts bring!

Sing to God
Play "Joy!" encouraging students to sing along with the music. **How does this song say we can be joyful?** (Look at what God's given us. Think of His love for us.)

Hear and Say God's Word
Display paper on which you have printed Psalm 28:7. Have a volunteer read the verse aloud. **How does this verse describe God?** (Our strength and our shield.) **What are some other things you know about God that you want to thank Him for?** After volunteers answer, ask students to suggest and demonstrate motions for the words of Psalm 28:7. Lead students in doing the motions and saying the verse several times.

Pray to God
Let's thank God for His good gifts that bring us joy. Distribute an index card and marker to each student. Students quickly draw a picture reminding themselves of a gift God has given them. (Family. Friends. Jesus' love.) Lead students in prayer, praying **God, our thankfulness overflows because You have given us . . .** Volunteers name gifts they have drawn on cards. End prayer by thanking God for the joy His gifts give us.

Options
1. If you have a large number of students, divide students into small groups during the verse activity and assign each group a phrase of the verse for which to create motions. Students teach each other motions and then do motions and say verse several times.

2. If students participated in this lesson's Fruitful Lives Object Talk, make copies of Francis Crosby's hymn "To God Be the Glory" and sing it with students.

3. Ask an older student to read aloud Psalm 100 as an invitation to students to worship.

Lesson 12

Bible Verse Coloring Center

Materials
Crayons or markers, a copy of page 25 or page 26 from *Bible Verse Coloring Pages #2* for each student.

Lead the Activity
Read Psalm 28:7. **Who in this picture might feel afraid? When have you felt afraid? How do you think God helps people who feel afraid?** Students color picture.

Option
Each student begins coloring his or her own page. After several minutes, each student signs name on page and trades page with another student. Repeat trading several times until all pages are colored.

Service Project Center

Materials
Materials needed for "We've Got Rhythm" (p. 49 from *The Big Book of Service Projects*).

Lead the Activity
Students complete "We've Got Rhythm" activity as directed in *The Big Book of Service Projects*. **What are some ways people use musical instruments to express joy or thankfulness? How do you think our gifts of musical instruments might bring joy to the children who receive them? What are some gifts you have received that brought you joy?**

Discipleship Activity Center

Materials
Discussion Cards for Psalm 23 (pp. 75-80 from *The Big Book of Christian Growth*), materials needed for "Team Bowling" or "Sentence Connections" (p. 30 or p. 49 from *The Big Book of Christian Growth*).

Lead the Activity
Psalm 23 tells us some reasons to have joy. Today we're going to play a game to talk about Psalm 23. Students complete activity as directed in *The Big Book of Christian Growth*.

Solomon, Wise Peacemaker

Bible Verse

Let us therefore make every effort to do what leads to peace. Romans 14:19

Bible Story Reference

1 Kings 3:4-28

Teacher's Devotional

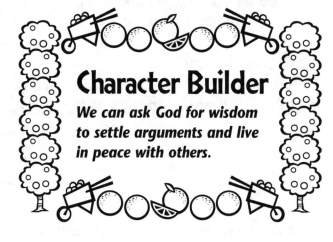

Character Builder

We can ask God for wisdom to settle arguments and live in peace with others.

People certainly talk about peace a great deal! Christmas cards announce "Peace on earth." Rock stars join together to sing, "Give peace a chance." Newspapers announce one peace conference after another. Yet from the international level to the personal level, peace seems to elude us. We feel helpless to effect peace in the world; and our personal lives often reflect worry, tension and stress.

Still, genuine peace is within our grasp—even in times of friction, even when outward circumstances or inner attitudes are filled with turmoil, even when we are unable to see any possible way that our conflicts can be resolved.

Jesus is our source of lasting peace (see Ephesians 2:14). A living relationship with Him brings true peace, a peace that goes far beyond the mere absence of strife, a peace that brings more than a cease-fire from open hostility. His peace comes to us—and can flow through us—in the middle of life's worries and tensions. His calming presence helps us to see our situations in a new light and respond to them in new ways.

Bible Story Center

Materials
Peace poster from *Poster Pack*, ¼ cup
(2 oz.) play dough for each student.

Tell the Story
**Follow along with me as we use our
dough to tell about today's story.**

*What's something kids your
age might argue about?*

*Today we'll find out how
someone stopped a big
argument in a very wise way!*

1. **Make a crown from your dough.** King David had
grown to be a very old man. He knew he was going to die
soon. So he declared that his son Solomon should be king in
his place. Solomon became the new king. He loved God and
wanted to be a good king.

One day after Solomon had gone to a special place to
worship God, he stayed there for the night. As Solomon lay
sleeping, God came to him in a dream. He said, "Ask for
whatever you want Me to give you."

Solomon could have asked for more money. He could
have asked for power. He could have asked for all of his enemies to disappear!

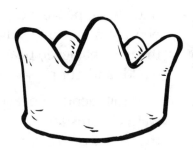

2. **Make a *W* for wisdom.** But instead Solomon told God,
"O Lord God, You have made me king. But I am like a little
child. I don't know how to do this great work You have given
me to do. I need wisdom to rule Your people and to know
what is right and wrong. How else can I do this great work?"

God was pleased that Solomon had asked for wisdom
instead of money or power or something else. God said, "I
will do what you have asked. I will give you wisdom. You will
be wiser than anyone who ever lived or will live! Besides that,
I will give you riches and honor and if you always obey me, a
long life!"

Solomon woke up. WOW! What a wonderful promise
from God! Solomon didn't know it, but he would soon have
a chance to depend on God's wisdom.

3. **Make a baby from your dough.** Soon after Solomon returned home to Jerusalem, two women came to see him. They were having a TERRIBLE argument, and they wanted HIM to settle it! The first woman told Solomon, "We live in the same house. We both had babies at the same time. And last night, this other woman rolled over in her sleep and SMOTHERED her baby. Then she came and took MY baby and put her dead baby in my baby's place!"

"That's not TRUE!" the other woman interrupted. "It's true that we live in the same house and that we both had babies at about the same time. But I did NOT roll over on my son or take HER son!"

The women argued and argued in front of the king, both insisting, "The living baby is MINE!"

4. **Make five ropes. Use the ropes to spell out the word "Peace."** Solomon must have thanked God for His promise to give him wisdom! He said, "Both of you say this baby belongs to you. I have a solution."

He called a servant. "Bring me a sword, " King Solomon said. "I will cut the baby in two. Half goes to each of you!"

One woman said, "FINE! That's fair. NEITHER of us will have the baby!"

But the woman who was the REAL mother said, "Please, my king! Give the other woman the baby! Don't kill him!"

"Give the baby to the woman who doesn't want the baby killed. She is his mother," Solomon ordered.

Everyone in Israel heard about Solomon's decision. The king wasn't really going to hurt the baby because he knew that his plan would prove who the real mother was. The REAL mother wouldn't let such a thing happen to her child! God had given him great wisdom, and as a result, Solomon made peace in a very wise way.

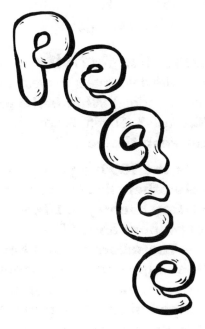

● ●

Focus on the Fruit
What did Solomon ask God to give him? Why? (Wisdom. Because he had a big job to do and knew he couldn't do it without God's wisdom.) **How did Solomon show God's wisdom?** (Gave a wise test to settle a big argument. Made peace between the two women.)

God promises to give us wisdom, too! Our Bible tells us that if we ask God for wisdom and trust Him, He will help us be wise in any situation (see James 1:5). Show the Peace poster. **That's one way He helps us be peacemakers, like Solomon! We can ask Him to help us be wise and live in peace as we grow the fruit of His Holy Spirit!**

Fruitful Lives Object Talk

Bible Verse
Let us therefore make every effort to do what leads to peace. Romans 14:19

Materials
Bible with bookmark at Romans 14:19, sheriff's badge; optional—construction paper, marker, scissors, straight pin.

Prepare the Activity
(Optional: Make badge from construction paper [see sketch].)

> God will help us live in peace with others when we ask Him for help and wisdom to settle arguments. Let's find out about a man who had to be very brave to live in peace.

Lead the Activity

1. Invite a volunteer to wear sheriff's badge. (Optional: Volunteer wears paper badge.) **What is the job of someone who wears a badge like this?** (Sheriff. Police officer.) **How does a sheriff or police officer keep the peace?**

2. **In the 1800s a young man named Samuel Morris had a chance to help others live in peace. Samuel was sailing on a ship from the African country of Liberia to America, because he wanted to go to school to learn more about God.**

   The sailors on the ship, however, didn't like Samuel because he was African. One angry sailor even threatened to kill him! One day, that sailor thought others were making fun of him, so he swung his sword to attack them. Samuel jumped in the way, putting his own life in danger, and shouted, "Don't kill!" The angry sailor surprised everyone by putting down his sword and walking away. Everyone was amazed! After that, whenever there was a fight, Samuel helped to stop it and kept peace by praying for the men. Samuel Morris showed that he was willing to do whatever he could to help people live peacefully together.

Conclude
Read Romans 14:19 aloud. **What are some actions we can do to help others live in peace?** Invite volunteers to pray, asking God to help them do actions that will help friends and family members live in peace.

• •

Additional Information for Older Students
Samuel Morris attended Taylor University in America for only one year before he died from injuries he had received as a teenager. But during that year, Samuel helped many people learn to trust and obey God. Many people at Taylor University decided to become missionaries because of Samuel's actions.

Active Game Center: Bucket Brigade

Materials
Bible, large disposable cups, two tennis or Ping-Pong balls.

Lead the Game

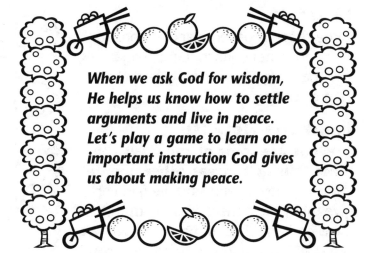

When we ask God for wisdom, He helps us know how to settle arguments and live in peace. Let's play a game to learn one important instruction God gives us about making peace.

1. Divide class into two equal teams. Each team forms two parallel lines facing each other.

2. Give each student a cup. Give a tennis or Ping-Pong ball to the student at the end of one line of each team. Students put balls in cups.

3. At your signal, the students roll (for mostly younger students) or toss (for mostly older students) the balls to the students across from them in line. Those students catch balls in cups and roll or toss balls to the next students opposite them. Students continue tossing or rolling the balls in zigzag fashion down the lines (see sketch) and back to the students who began the brigade.

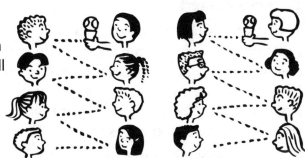

4. Student from the first team to finish answers one of the questions below or repeats Romans 14:19. Students repeat game as time allows.

Options

1. Ask for a donation of large cups at a local fast-food restaurant or convenience store.

2. If you have fewer than 10 students, play as one team. Time each round, challenging students to beat their time in each succeeding round.

3. Allow teams to have a practice round, rolling or tossing the ball from cup to cup.

• •

Discussion Questions

1. Ask a volunteer to read Romans 14:19 aloud. **What is God's instruction to us in this verse?** ("Make every effort to do what leads to peace.") **What does it mean to "make every effort"?** (To try as hard as you can. To do something to the best of your ability.)

2. What did we make every effort to do in our game? (Catch the ball in our cups. Pass it to the other players.)

3. How can you make every effort to do what leads to peace at home? At school? (Let your brother or sister be first or borrow something when he or she asks. Ask God for wisdom about how to treat the person who is bothering you at school. Be kind to a person who treats you badly again and again. Don't argue. Don't tease.)

Art Center: Peace Mobile

Materials

Large sheet of paper, markers, construction paper, hole punch, tape, magazines, newspaper flyers, scissors, glue sticks, yarn or curling ribbon.

Lead the Activity

1. **What are some of the ways the Bible tells us to treat other people?** (Share. Be loving and kind. Be fair. Forgive them. Help them. Tell the truth.) List ideas on large sheet of paper. **When we treat others in these ways, we can be peacemakers.**

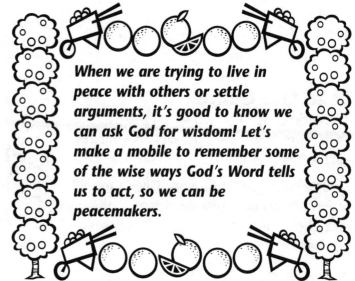

When we are trying to live in peace with others or settle arguments, it's good to know we can ask God for wisdom! Let's make a mobile to remember some of the wise ways God's Word tells us to act, so we can be peacemakers.

2. Give each student a sheet of colored construction paper and a marker. Students fold papers lengthwise in thirds and on the middle third of papers print "Peacemaker" or another phrase about peace. Keeping the papers folded, students punch four holes along the bottom of the folded papers, below their writing, and punch two holes above their writing. Students unfold papers and tape the two long edges together to create a triangular shape.

3. Students look through magazines and newspaper flyers to find words or letters of words from peacemaker list. Students cut out no more than eight construction-paper shapes and glue words to shapes. (Students may also write words on shapes.) Students punch a hole in the top of each shape and tie a length of yarn (or curling ribbon) between each shape and the triangular base. Students hang an equal number of shapes from each side to balance the mobile and tie one long length of yarn to the holes at the top of the mobile to hang it up.

Options

1. If you have mostly younger students, prefold papers.

2. Students draw a picture of the peacemaking action on the back of each shape before attaching shapes to mobile.

3. Bring decorating materials (stickers, glitter glue, etc.) for students to use on mobiles.

• •

Discussion Questions

1. *When have you been a peacemaker or settled an argument while playing with friends? With your family?* Tell students an age-appropriate example about God giving you wisdom to be a peacemaker.

2. *What is your favorite way to be a peacemaker?*

3. *What is one of the hardest times for you to remember to be a peacemaker?*

Lesson 13

Worship Center

Bible Verse
Let us therefore make every effort to do what leads to peace. Romans 14:19

Materials
Bible, *God's Kids Grow* cassette/CD or music video and player, "Peacemaker" word chart (p. 481 in this book), large sheet of paper on which you have printed Romans 14:19, masking tape.

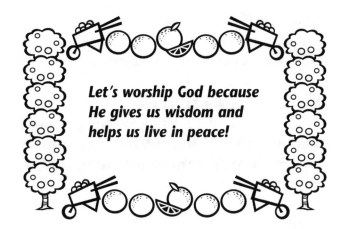

Let's worship God because He gives us wisdom and helps us live in peace!

Sing to God
Play "Peacemaker," encouraging students to sing along with the music. **What does it mean to be a peacemaker?** (To help people live in peace with each other.) **What are some ways you can live in peace?** (Tell the truth. Be kind even when feeling angry.)

Hear and Say God's Word
Display paper on which you have printed Romans 14:19. Have a volunteer read the verse aloud. **What are some of the actions we can do which lead to peace?** (Be kind. Let others be first. Be considerate. Forgive others. Pray to God for wisdom.) List students' ideas on Bible-verse paper. Lead students in saying verse, each time adding one of the ways suggested to the end of the verse. (For example, "Let us therefore make every effort to do what leads to peace by being kind.")

Pray to God
Lead students in prayer, students repeating each phrase of this prayer after you: **Dear God, please give us wisdom to live in peace with others.** End prayer by thanking God that He promises in the Bible to give us wisdom when we ask for it.

Options
1. During the verse activity, ask an older student to read James 3:17,18 aloud as a description of the kind of wisdom God gives us to help us live in peace together. **How does being (considerate) help us make peace?**

2. As part of the prayer activity, ask an older student to read James 1:5 aloud. **What promise does God make in this verse?**

3. Sing "Just Ask Him" and/or "Fruit of the Spirit" (p. 475 and/or p. 459 in this book) with students.

Lesson 13

Bible Verse Coloring Center

Materials

Crayons or markers, a copy of page 121 or page 122 from *Bible Verse Coloring Pages #2* for each student.

Lead the Activity

Read Romans 14:19. **Who in this picture is obeying Romans 14:19? How? What are some other things we can do to help others get along and have peace?** Students color picture.

Option

Students glue completed pictures onto large sheets of construction paper and then draw conversation balloons for the people in the picture. Students write (or dictate) what they think the people are saying.

Service Project Center

Materials

Materials needed for "Absentee Cards" (p. 23 from *The Big Book of Service Projects*).

Lead the Activity

Students complete "Absentee Cards" activity as directed in *The Big Book of Service Projects*. **Why do you think it is important to let people who are absent know that we miss them? What can you tell people who weren't here today about what we learned about living in peace with others?**

Discipleship Activity Center

Materials

Discussion Cards for Ephesians 4:29—5:1 (pp. 159-164 from *The Big Book of Christian Growth*), materials needed for "Mark the Spot" or "Family Talk" (p. 22 or p. 42 from *The Big Book of Christian Growth*).

Lead the Activity

Today we're going to talk about Ephesians 4:29—5:1 and play a game to discover ways of living in peace with others. Students complete activity as directed in *The Big Book of Christian Growth*.

140

Nehemiah's Patient Plan

Bible Verse

Stand firm. Let nothing move you.
Always give yourselves fully to the work
of the Lord. 1 Corinthians 15:58

Bible Story Reference

Nehemiah 1—8:12

Teacher's Devotional

Character Builder

Patiently continue to do what
is right in all situations.

It is not always easy to be patient with other people, especially when those others do not support our efforts to do what is right. The difficulty of persevering only increases when other people come right out in opposition!

How, then, did Nehemiah manage to persist in rebuilding the city wall in the face of the open ridicule from Sanballat or the taunting remarks from Tobiah? When ridicule turned to anger and threats, how could Nehemiah patiently continue to oversee the work day after day? Then when the people working with him began to complain that the job was too much for them, what kept Nehemiah going? And when others saw only the huge piles of rubble and the slow pace of progress and feared for their safety, how did Nehemiah keep from being discouraged by these attitudes or by the low, exposed places along the wall?

The answer is sprinkled throughout Nehemiah 4: Nehemiah answered ridicule with prayer, and "so we rebuilt the wall till all of it reached half its height" (vv. 4-6). Nehemiah responded to angry threats with more prayer and "posted a guard day and night to meet this threat" (v. 9). Nehemiah met complaints, more threats and the obvious difficulty of the task before them by reminding himself and his coworkers to "remember the Lord, who is great and awesome" (v. 14).

Patiently continuing to do what is right is not merely a matter of plodding along or following a habitual pattern. Patience is continuing to do what is right, because we know that almighty God is with us. Help your students understand that there is nothing they can't talk to God about. With a strong foundation of prayer, patience is built, stone by stone.

Bible Story Center

Materials
Patience poster from *Poster Pack;* ¼ cup (2 oz.) play dough and a plastic knife for each student.

Tell the Story
Follow along with me as we make some items found in today's story.

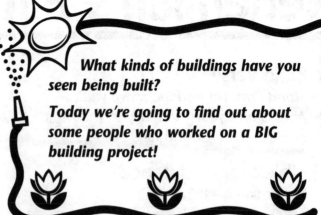

What kinds of buildings have you seen being built?

Today we're going to find out about some people who worked on a BIG building project!

1. **Make a Bible-times cup from your dough.** About 100 years after God's people had been taken to Babylon, a man from Israel named Nehemiah lived in the king's palace in Persia. Nehemiah had an important job. Nehemiah worked as the king's cupbearer. The cupbearer brought the king's drinks to him and often talked with the king about important decisions the king had to make.

   One day Nehemiah's brother came to visit him from Jerusalem. The brothers talked and talked. When Nehemiah asked how things were in Jerusalem, his brother sadly told him that the wall around Jerusalem was broken down and the houses were falling down, too. Without a strong wall, the city couldn't be protected! The people were in danger!

2. **Make a big block and then cut as many small blocks as you can.** After he heard this bad news, Nehemiah was very sad for many days. He didn't even eat. But he DID do one thing—he prayed! He asked God to help him get the king's permission to go and help rebuild the wall and the houses in Jerusalem.

   When Nehemiah came to bring the king his cup, even though as the king's servant he was expected to always be happy, his face showed the king that something was very wrong. The king asked, "Why are you so sad?"

   "Oh king," Nehemiah said, "my brother told me that the wall in Jerusalem is broken."

   "What do you want?" the king asked. Nehemiah silently asked God to help him say the right words. "I want VERY much to help the people rebuild the wall," Nehemiah answered.

The king thought about Nehemiah's request. He told Nehemiah he could go, AND the king promised to give Nehemiah supplies and people to help do the job! Nehemiah excitedly thanked the king. Soon he was on his way to Jerusalem!

Nehemiah called the people in Jerusalem together and announced that the king had sent him to help rebuild the city wall. Soon people were volunteering to repair sections of the wall. People hammered and chiseled to cut stone and sawed wood to make gates. Everyone worked! It took a lot of patience for everyone to work together.

But some ENEMIES of the Jews were angry that Jerusalem would be strong and safe again. They wanted to stop the workers. First, they made FUN of the wall. They said it would fall right down again! Next, the enemies tried to SCARE the Jews. They said they would kill the workers! THEN they tried to make trouble with the king who had sent Nehemiah! The people building the wall were worried and afraid.

But Nehemiah told the people not to be afraid. He patiently worked out a plan. Workers took turns guarding while others were working. It took a longer time to finish, but finally the wall was DONE!

3. **Put your blocks together with a neighbor to make a big wall.** Everyone was glad to see the wall high and strong! The people came together to celebrate. Ezra the priest read the scroll of God's Law aloud to them. Then Nehemiah told them to celebrate! They had heard God's laws. The city had a STRONG wall. They had worked together patiently, even when trouble came. And NOW, a GREAT thing had been done!

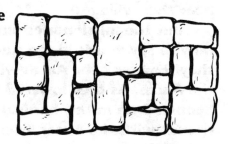

• •

Focus on the Fruit

When Nehemiah heard about the wall, what did he do first? (Prayed.) **How did God help Nehemiah?** (Made the king want to help him. Helped him be patient when enemies came. Gave him wisdom to make a plan.) **Why did Nehemiah tell the people to celebrate?** (Wall was finished. They heard God's laws.)

   Sometimes we have to be patient during hard times, too. Show the Patience poster. **The Bible promises God will be with us and help us have patience. He promises to use the hard times in our lives for a GOOD thing—to help us grow the fruit of patience!**

Fruitful Lives Object Talk

Bible Verse
Stand firm. Let nothing move you. Always give yourselves fully to the work of the Lord.
1 Corinthians 15:58

Materials
Bible with bookmark at 1 Corinthians 15:58, bucket, rope, small prize for each student.

Prepare the Activity
Tie rope onto bucket's handle. Place prizes in bucket.

Doing what's right, even in difficult situations, is a way to show patience. Let's find out how a man showed patience in a hard situation.

Lead the Activity
1. **What kind of gift would you give a friend?** Volunteers respond. **I'm going to give you a gift in an unusual way today.** Hold bucket by the rope and invite each student to take a prize from the bucket. **Usually when people exchange gifts, it shows that they are friends. Let's find out how a man named Jim Elliot gave gifts in a bucket to try to make friends with some dangerous people.**

2. **Jim Elliot and four other missionaries lived in the country of Ecuador in South America. The missionaries wanted to tell a group of people called the Aucas (OW-kuhs) about Jesus. But there was a BIG problem. The Aucas were not friendly people. In fact, they usually killed anyone who came near their villages!**

   But the missionaries didn't give up. First, they patiently learned how to say words in the Aucan language. Then, for several months, they flew over the Aucas' villages, lowering buckets filled with gifts for the Aucas. As they lowered the buckets, they called out greetings to the people. Even in this hard situation, Jim Elliot patiently kept trying to make friends with the Aucas. Eventually, the missionaries were able to meet the Aucas face-to-face.

Conclude
Read 1 Corinthians 15:58. **To stand firm means to keep doing what is right and trust in God.** Pray, asking God to help students patiently do what is right.

• •

Additional Information for Older Students
Shortly after Jim Elliot and his friends met the Aucas, they were killed by the Aucas. Some people thought that all of Jim Elliot's efforts to make friends had been wasted. But several years later, Jim's wife and another woman became friends with the Aucas and lived in their village. Because the missionaries patiently kept doing what was right, many Aucas became Christians.

Active Game Center: Human Foosball

Materials
Bible, masking tape, chairs, tennis ball or soft foam ball.

Prepare the Game
Tear off masking-tape strips (two for each student). Position chairs as shown in sketch.

Lead the Game
1. Divide group into two teams. Position students as shown in sketch, both teams facing away from their respective goalie. Students should stand at least an arm's length from each other. Give each student two strips of masking tape. Students on one team make masking-tape *X*s on floor to mark their positions. Students on other team make masking-tape *L*s on floor.

2. Gently roll the ball toward the middle of the playing area. Students try to kick the ball toward their team's goal, each student keeping at least one foot on his or her masking-tape mark at all times and not touching the ball with his or her hands.

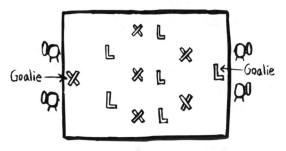

3. Students continue kicking ball until a goal is scored. (Note: Goalies only use their feet to defend goal.) After each goal, ask a volunteer from the team that scored the goal to answer a question below. Begin again by giving ball to a player from the team that did not score.

Options
1. Play outside with a soccer or playground ball, and use chalk to mark students' positions.

2. Players may be seated on chairs instead of standing on masking-tape marks.

3. If you have mostly younger students, all players may be on the same team, trying to get the ball into one goal.

• •

Discussion Questions
1. ***During this game, you stood firm by not moving off the tape. Listen to what the Bible says about standing firm.*** Ask a volunteer to read 1 Corinthians 15:58 aloud. ***What does it mean to "stand firm" and "let nothing move you"?*** (Keep on doing what is right, even when other people around you are doing wrong things.)

2. ***What is "the work of the Lord"?*** (Loving others. Obeying God's commands.)

3. ***Name one time (at school) that it is hard to do what is right. How can you patiently keep doing right in that situation?*** Repeat question, substituting other places or situations for the words "at school."

Art Center: Creative Construction

Materials
Newspaper, masking tape, scissors, staplers.

Lead the Activity

1. Demonstrate how to make a newspaper tube. Open four sheets of newspaper and place them in a stack. Roll the newspapers diagonally to form a tube. Secure the tube with tape and trim ends to even out tube.

2. Guide students to form groups of three to four. Distribute newspaper for students to begin making tubes. While students make tubes, groups plan what they will construct (tent, fort, cave, bridge across two chairs or tables, letters, flower garden, swing set, etc.).

3. Students build three-dimensional structures by stapling or taping tubes together. Unrolled newspapers can be draped over tube shapes to form walls or roofs.

Options

1. Students use paper towel tubes as guides when making newspaper tubes, rolling the newspapers around the paper towel tubes. Slide the paper towel tubes out of the newspapers before securing them with tape.

2. Students use newspaper tubes to spell the word "patience."

3. If you have a smaller class, work as one group instead of forming separate groups.

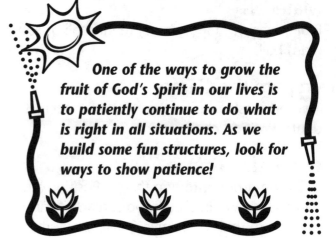

One of the ways to grow the fruit of God's Spirit in our lives is to patiently continue to do what is right in all situations. As we build some fun structures, look for ways to show patience!

Discussion Questions

1. **What is patience?** (Doing something that takes a long time without complaining. Treating others with kindness, even when they keep bothering you.) **What part of this activity took patience?** (Rolling the tubes. Experimenting with ways to make the structure.)

2. **What are some situations in which it is hard to have patience and do what is right?** (Your brother or sister keeps bothering you. Someone is yelling at you. You are tired and don't want to do what is right.)

3. **What is one right action you can take (when your younger brother keeps taking your markers)?** Repeat question, substituting other situations in which patience might be needed.

Lesson 14

Worship Center

Bible Verse

Stand firm. Let nothing move you. Always give yourselves fully to the work of the Lord.
1 Corinthians 15:58

Materials

Bible, *God's Kids Grow* cassette/CD or music video and player, "Patient Father" word chart (p. 479 in this book), large sheet of paper on which you have printed 1 Corinthians 15:58, masking tape.

Let's thank God that when God's Spirit lives in us, we can patiently continue to do what is right in all situations.

Sing to God

Play "Patient Father," encouraging students to sing along with the music. **This song reminds us that God always keeps His promises. What does this song say we can ask God to help us do to show patience?** (Forgive others. Be kind. Be slow to get mad.)

Hear and Say God's Word

Display paper on which you have printed 1 Corinthians 15:58. Have a volunteer read the verse aloud. **What three things does this verse tell us to do?** (Stand firm. Don't let anything move you. Do your best to obey God all the time.) **To stand firm and not let anything move you means to keep doing what is right and trust in God, no matter what is happening around you.** Students form three groups. Assign each group a sentence of the verse. Students say verse, standing up to say their sentence of the verse. Lead the group in reciting the verse in this manner several times. (Optional: Older students may create motions for the words in their sentence.)

Pray to God

Lead students in prayer, pausing to let students repeat each phrase after you: **Dear God, thank You for Your promise that You are always with us and will help us. Please help us to be patient as we learn to do what's right in all situations. In Jesus' name, amen.**

Options

1. Before you pray, ask several older students to read aloud the following promises of God's presence with us: Joshua 1:9 and Isaiah 41:10.

2. Lead students in singing "All My Heart" and/or "You Promised!" (p. 453 and/or p. 487 in this book).

3. Lead students in a prayer of thanks after singing "Patient Father."

Lesson 14

Bible Verse Coloring Center

Materials

Crayons or markers, a copy of page 135 or page 136 from *Bible Verse Coloring Pages #2* for each student.

Lead the Activity

Read 1 Corinthians 15:58. **How are people in this picture obeying 1 Corinthians 15:58? When can you obey 1 Corinthians 15:58 by doing something right?** Students color picture.

Option

Students draw before and after pictures, first drawing family members in car on the way to serve food and then drawing family members talking with people they met while serving food.

Service Project Center

Materials

Materials needed for "Play Dough Fun" (p. 40 from *The Big Book of Service Projects*).

Lead the Activity

Students complete "Play Dough Fun" activity as directed in *The Big Book of Service Projects*. **What are some ways to show patience while we work on this project? When are some other times you need patience to continue to do what is right?**

Discipleship Activity Center

Materials

Discussion Cards for Matthew 6:9-13 (pp. 117-122 from *The Big Book of Christian Growth*), materials needed for "Crazy Relay" or "Circle Count" (p. 15 or p. 58 from *The Big Book of Christian Growth*).

Lead the Activity

Jesus' prayer in Matthew 6:9-13 tells us to ask God's help in doing right. Today we're going to play a game to talk about this prayer. Students complete activity as directed in *The Big Book of Christian Growth*.

Abigail's Kindness

Bible Verse

Command them to do good, to be rich in good deeds, and to be generous and willing to share.
1 Timothy 6:18

Bible Story Reference

1 Samuel 25

Teacher's Devotional

Paul's words to Timothy in this lesson's Bible verse sound as though they might have been intended for teachers or parents

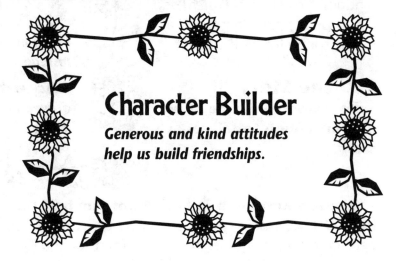

Character Builder

Generous and kind attitudes help us build friendships.

of preschoolers. Doing good and sharing generously are high on the list of actions that people want to see young children develop. Even an older child may need reminders to carry out a good deed or to share with someone else.

But Paul did not have children in mind when he penned this instruction. The preceding verse shows that he was thinking about adults—grown-ups, people who should have developed these qualities in their formative years, people who should have already known better.

Paul was not even thinking about adults in general. He had a very specific group in mind: "those who are rich in this present world" (1 Timothy 6:17). He was thinking about successful adults, well-to-do adults, influential adults. He was thinking about those who have achieved positions of status in the community. He was thinking of those of us who may have gotten so absorbed in the quest for success that we are prone to forget what is really important.

Nabal, the Old Testament character we read about in 1 Samuel 25, was certainly a fellow who had lost sight of these virtues. He was a bottom-line type of guy. However, he was focused on the wrong bottom line. While his hardheaded approach to business earned him money and perhaps even the respect of some, it also cost him his life. What a difference faith in God, some good deeds, some sharing and some kindness would have made!

If Nabal had been able to read Paul's words, would he have changed his ways? Would he then have enjoyed the benefits of generosity that Paul describes: the kind of treasure that is a firm foundation for true life (see 1 Timothy 6:19)? Having read Paul's words ourselves, will it make a difference to us?

Bible Story Center

Materials

Kindness poster from *Poster Pack;*
¼ cup (2 oz.) play dough and a
plastic spoon for each student.

Tell the Story

**Follow along with me as we
use our dough to tell today's
story.**

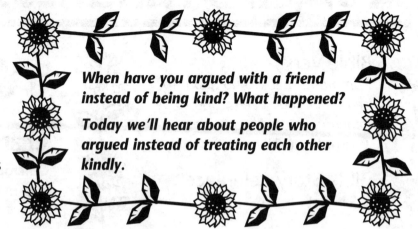

*When have you argued with a friend
instead of being kind? What happened?*

*Today we'll hear about people who
argued instead of treating each other
kindly.*

1. **Divide your dough in half. From one half make some
hills. Use a plastic spoon to shape hills.** Before David
became the king of Israel, he and his men spent a lot of time
living out in the hills. For one thing, they were trying to stay
away from King Saul. King Saul wanted to KILL David because
he knew David would one day become the king. But because
David did not want to hurt Saul AND because he wanted to
stay safe, he and his men stayed far from the palace and
camped out in places where there were very few people.

2. **From the other half of your dough, roll tiny balls to
make a flock of sheep.** But out in the hills there were robbers who would raid the flocks belonging to others. So while
David and his men were living out in the hills, they often protected flocks of sheep and the shepherds who took care of the
sheep. One year, David and his men protected the sheep and
shepherds of a man whose name was Nabal.

　　Later that year, David and his men were still living out in
the hills. And they were very HUNGRY! They needed food and
water. So David sent some of his men to the place where Nabal
was shearing his sheep. They greeted Nabal and politely
reminded Nabal that while his shepherds and sheep were out in
the hills, David and his men had protected them.

　　David's men then asked if Nabal might please give them
whatever food and drink he could spare. Now MOST people
would have gladly given David and his men whatever they
asked for, because David was a hero in that country!

　　But no matter what ANYONE else might have done,
NABAL wasn't about to share anything! The Bible says he was
mean and selfish in the way he treated people. The name
"Nabal" meant "fool," and this was one time he lived up to his
name!

"Who IS this David?" Nabal asked, as if he had never HEARD of David! He went on to insult David. Then Nabal finished up by saying he saw no reason to share his food and water with some stranger! Nabal probably thought he had really shown David who was boss!

3. **Make a sword.** David's men returned and told him everything Nabal had done and said. David then instructed his men to put on their swords. They were going to have to TAKE food and water from this selfish, foolish man who would not share.

But in the meantime, one of Nabal's workers ran home and told Nabal's wife, Abigail, what had happened!

"See what you can do," the worker told Abigail. "I think we're going to have trouble with David, because our master is such a wicked man. No one can talk to him!"

4. **Make a donkey. Add bundles to its back.** Abigail was a wise woman and immediately made plans to stop the quarrel her husband had started with David. Abigail quickly had her servants pack many pounds of bread, figs, raisins, grain and good things to drink on donkeys. She told her servants to go on ahead of her.

Soon Abigail, herself, came riding up to David's camp. She greeted David humbly and said, "Sir, let me take the blame for Nabal's meanness. Ignore him—he is a fool, just as his name says. Please accept these gifts I bring and forgive Nabal's actions."

David was impressed with this wise and kind woman. He thanked God that she had come and stopped the trouble between him and Nabal. David told Abigail to go in peace; he would not hurt Nabal. Soon after this, however, Nabal died. When David heard that Nabal died, he remembered Abigail. He remembered her generosity and kindness. David sent his servants to ask Abigail to become his wife! And kind and generous Abigail married David, who later became king of Israel!

• •

Focus on the Fruit

What made Nabal a foolish man? (He didn't listen to others. He was mean and would not share.) **Why did David ask him for help?** (David and his men had been kind and had protected Nabal's sheep.) **How did Abigail show she was kind and wise?** (Brought food to David and his men. Apologized for her husband's actions.) **Abigail's kindness made a big difference by helping to keep peace between David and Nabal.**

Being generous and kind can make a difference in our lives, too. Show the Kindness poster. **Growing the fruit of kindness in our lives pleases God. It also helps us make and keep good friends!**

Fruitful Lives Object Talk

Bible Verse

Command them to do good, to be rich in good deeds, and to be generous and willing to share. 1 Timothy 6:18

Materials

Bible with bookmark at 1 Timothy 6:18, kerosene lantern or a flashlight.

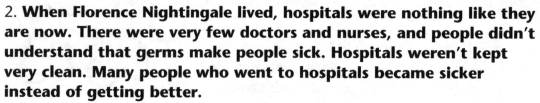

We can build friendships by being generous and kind in our attitudes and actions. Let's find out what one lady did because she was so kind.

Lead the Activity

1. Show lantern or flashlight. **When do people use lights like these? How might a light like this help when you are afraid in the dark?** Students respond. **In England during the 1800s, a woman named Florence Nightingale became known as "the Lady with the Lamp."**

2. **When Florence Nightingale lived, hospitals were nothing like they are now. There were very few doctors and nurses, and people didn't understand that germs make people sick. Hospitals weren't kept very clean. Many people who went to hospitals became sicker instead of getting better.**

   When Florence became a nurse, she believed God wanted her to change things! She used her own money to buy clean clothes for patients. She hired people to wash sheets and blankets. Florence often worked until late at night, carrying a lamp through the hospital as she checked on her patients. She was never too tired to help someone.

   As Florence worked, she also talked to people about Jesus. Florence—"the Lady with the Lamp"—helped people learn about Jesus' love and saved the lives of many sick or injured people because of her kindness and generosity.

Conclude

Read 1 Timothy 6:18 aloud. **How was Florence Nightingale kind and willing to share? How can you be kind and share?** Students tell ideas. **Let's ask God to help us build friendships by being generous and kind this week.** Lead students in prayer.

• •

Discussion Questions

1. *What are some generous or kind actions kids your age can do? How might these actions help to build friendships?*

2. *Read 1 Timothy 6:18. How can we "be rich in good deeds"?* (Do good things often.)

3. *How would obeying 1 Timothy 6:18 help the kids in your school?*

Active Game Center: Bounce It!

Materials
Bible, large rubber ball or tennis ball.

Lead the Game
1. Students stand in a circle and practice bouncing the ball to each other.

Remembering to be kind and generous helps us make and keep friends. Let's play a game to help us think of some generous and kind attitudes.

2. Ask a volunteer to read 1 Timothy 6:18 aloud. **What does this verse command us to do?** (Do good deeds. Be generous. Be willing to share.) **What are some ways to follow these commands?** Volunteers tell ideas.

3. At your signal, students begin bouncing the ball to each other. When you signal stop, the student with the ball tells a way to obey 1 Timothy 6:18 or says the verse aloud. Continue play as time allows.

Options
1. Play music from *God's Kids Grow* cassette/CD as students bounce the ball.

2. Use two balls. Write "2" on one ball and "3" on the other (numbers may be formed with masking tape if needed). When you signal stop, students holding balls name that many ways to obey 1 Timothy 6:18.

3. Play a few rounds in which student holding the ball names a Bible character, a fruit of the Spirit or a book of the Bible.

4. As students bounce ball, they say the words of 1 Timothy 6:18, continuing until the entire verse has been quoted.

Discussion Questions
1. *What are some ways to be generous at school? With friends? With people you don't know?* (Share scissors or pencils. Share toys when you are playing together. Give offering.)

2. *Why are kind attitudes the best ones for building friendships?*

3. *What actions does the Bible tells us to do?* (Love others. Honor your parents. Tell others about God's love.)

Lesson 15

Art Center: Share-a-Stamp

Materials
Sturdy cardboard, scissors, several stamp pads, Fun Foam and/or yarn, glue sticks, paper.

Prepare the Activity
Cut the cardboard into rectangles no larger than the surfaces of the stamp pads, cutting at least one rectangle for each student. Make a sample of the type(s) of stamp(s) your students will make.

Lead the Activity
1. Show students your sample stamp. Give each student a cardboard rectangle. Students bend up about ½ inch (1.25 cm) of cardboard on each end, creating handles for stamp (see sketch a).

Showing Jesus' love by being kind and generous to others is a good way to show friendship. Let's do a fun art project in which we practice being kind and generous by sharing. Our sharing will make everyone's art project better!

2. Students create stamps following one of these methods: (*a*) Students cut shapes or designs from Fun Foam, and then glue Fun Foam shapes to cardboard rectangles (see sketch b); (*b*) Students draw simple designs on cardboard rectangle with glue sticks. Students place yarn lengths on glue, cutting off any excess yarn (see sketch c). (Note: Use glue sticks, so glue will dry quickly.)

3. Students firmly press stamps onto stamp pads and then onto sheets of paper, creating their own designs and sharing stamps with each other. Ask Discussion Questions below as students create stamp designs.

Options
1. Students make alphabet stamps and then use stamps to spell key words of 1 Timothy 6:18.

2. Provide plastic bags in which students can take stamps home.

3. Students share their finished stamp designs by giving them to friends.

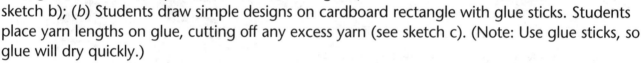

Discussion Questions
1. ***What does it mean to have a generous attitude?*** (Being willing to share or give more than what is usual or expected.)

2. ***What are some things we can share to show that we have a generous or kind attitude?*** (Food with people who are happy. Time to help someone who is hurt.)

3. ***How does sharing help build friendships?*** (People like to be around others who are generous and kind. People are often more willing to share when you have been generous with them.)

Lesson 15

Worship Center

Bible Verse

Command them to do good, to be rich in good deeds, and to be generous and willing to share. 1 Timothy 6:18

Materials

Bible, *God's Kids Grow* cassette/CD or music video and player, "Be So Kind" word chart (p. 455 in this book), paper, marker, large sheet of paper, masking tape.

Generous and kind attitudes help us build friendships and share God's love with others. Let's thank God that He is generous and kind to us!

Prepare the Activity

Scramble the letters of the words "good," "deeds," "share" (if you have older children also scramble "generous"); print each scrambled word on a separate sheet of paper. Print the words of 1 Timothy 6:18 on the large sheet of paper, leaving blanks for each of the scrambled words.

Sing to God

Play "Be So Kind," encouraging students to sing along with the music. **What are some of the ways this song suggests that we can be kind and generous?** (Give others more than they are looking for. Share what you have. Put others first.)

Hear and Say God's Word

Display paper on which you have printed 1 Timothy 6:18. Show a paper on which you have printed the scrambled letters of one of the words of the verse. Students identify the scrambled word. Print word in correct place on verse paper. Recite verse together; then hold up another scrambled word. Repeat until all words have been unscrambled. **We usually think that a rich person is one who has a lot of money. What does 1 Timothy 6:18 tell us to be rich with?** (Good deeds.) **What would a person who is rich with good deeds act like?** (Help others. Treat others fairly.)

Pray to God

Tell students one way God has been kind and generous to you. Invite students to complete this sentence in prayer: **Thank You, God, for being kind and generous by . . .** End prayer time by asking for God's help to show His love by being kind and generous.

Option

If students give an offering during this worship time, explain that giving money to God is one way to obey 1 Timothy 6:18. Tell an example of how your church has been generous in giving to others.

Bible Verse Coloring Center

Materials

Crayons or markers, a copy of page 195 or page 196 from *Bible Verse Coloring Pages #2* for each student.

Lead the Activity

Read 1 Timothy 6:18. **What good thing is someone in this picture doing? What are some good things you can do at school this week? What good things can you do at home?** Students color picture.

Option

Also provide a copy of "Draw a picture of a time someone was kind to you or to a friend" page (p. 229 from *Bible Verse Coloring Pages #2)*. Students draw and color pictures.

Service Project Center

Materials

Materials needed for "Story Time" (p. 86 from *The Big Book of Service Projects*).

Lead the Activity

Students complete "Story Time" activity as directed in *The Big Book of Service Projects*. **Working on this service project is a way for us to be generous and kind. To whom can you be generous and kind this week? What are some ways you can be generous and kind to each of these people?**

Discipleship Activity Center

Materials

Discussion Cards for Galatians 5:22,23 (pp. 147-152 from *The Big Book of Christian Growth*), materials needed for "Foiled Juggling" or "Card Toss" (p. 17 or p. 57 from *The Big Book of Christian Growth*).

Lead the Activity

Today we're going to play a game to talk about ways obeying Galatians 5:22,23 can help us show kindness. Students complete activity as directed in *The Big Book of Christian Growth*.

Elisha's Good Example

Bible Verse

Don't let anyone look down on you because you are young, but set an example for the believers in speech, in life, in love, in faith and in purity. 1 Timothy 4:12

Bible Story Reference

2 Kings 6:8-23

Teacher's Devotional

Often the word "good" is used in a vague, general sense—people are labeled as either good or bad or indifferent. And if a person is good at entertaining us or at playing a sport we like or if a person votes on issues the way we want, we tend to be indifferent toward a lot of bad actions.

Character Builder

Our right actions can help others do what is good.

However, to discover the essence of the goodness that the Holy Spirit produces in the life of the believer, we must go to the source of all goodness—God. Good means first and foremost what God is. Whatever He does and whatever He encourages in the lives of His creatures is good. In other words, God is good, and good is from God. We humans are good just so far as we conform to the will of God. And it is the will of God that His children show His goodness by doing good works (see Ephesians 2:10).

God's goodness is to be reflected in every area of our lives: our conversations, our actions, our relationships, our devotion to God and our morality (see 1 Timothy 4:12). Never are good works to be viewed as obligations we must fulfill to earn God's favor or to offset the times when we have done wrong. Children tend to focus on outward actions, often missing the essential inner motivations for doing good: love and gratitude to God and a desire to please Him.

Today as you lead children to explore Elisha's remarkable good deeds toward his enemies, encourage your students to keep in mind the true source of goodness—Jesus Christ. Help them understand that the better they know God, the better they will be at doing good. And be sure to point out the result of Elisha's good example: "the bands from Aram stopped raiding Israel's territory" (2 Kings 6:23).

Lesson 16 • 2 Kings 6:8-23

Bible Story Center

Materials
Goodness poster from *Poster Pack;* ¼ cup (2 oz.) play dough and toothpick for each student.

Tell the Story
Follow along with me as we use our dough to tell today's story.

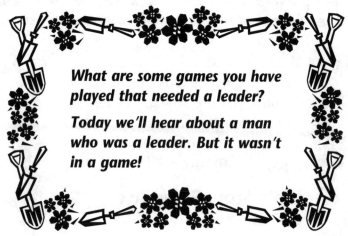

What are some games you have played that needed a leader?

Today we'll hear about a man who was a leader. But it wasn't in a game!

1. **From your dough, make two crowns for two kings in this story. Use a toothpick to draw jewels in the crowns.** Elisha was a prophet of God who lived in Israel. Elisha told God's messages to the people of Israel and their king. God also gave Elisha power to do amazing things.

At this time, some people called the Arameans were at war with Israel. But the king of the Arameans was getting very upset. The Israelite army always KNEW what he was going to do before he did it! Was there a spy in his army? No. It was just that God kept telling Elisha all of the Arameans' battle plans! And Elisha told the king of Israel everything God said!

Finally, one officer in the Aramean army told the king that Elisha the prophet was the one who was finding out and telling all the king's plans. "Elisha even tells the king of Israel what you say in your bedroom!" he added.

2. **Make several spears like the ones soldiers used to carry.** The king of the Arameans was FURIOUS! He sent out spies to find out where Elisha was. When he found out that Elisha was at a city called Dothan, the king sent soldiers to CAP-TURE Elisha.

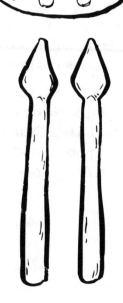

When Elisha's servant got up early the next morning, there were Aramean soldiers all around the city! Elisha's servant was AFRAID! But Elisha knew God had armies of His own! Elisha asked God to show his servant that the hills all around them were full of soldiers and horses and chariots of FIRE! God's army was ready to protect them!

3. **Roll a rope. Lay your rope in a circle with an opening to make a city wall.** As the enemy soldiers came to capture him, Elisha asked God to make them blind. Suddenly, the whole army of Aramean soldiers couldn't see! Elisha came to the leader and told him that the army was on the wrong road. He invited them to follow him. What else could the soldiers DO? They had to trust this man they couldn't see! So the whole Aramean army followed Elisha. He led them on a long walk, all the way into the Israelite city of Samaria!

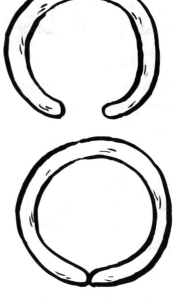

4. **Close the gates to your wall.** Once the soldiers were inside and the city gates were closed, Elisha asked God to take away the soldiers' blindness. God did! NOW the Arameans looked around. They could see they were in big trouble—shut inside an Israelite city! There was no way to escape! *Will we all be KILLED?* they wondered.

Even the king of Israel thought this was the perfect time to get rid of these enemies. He was ready to kill the Aramean soldiers! But Elisha told the king God's very SURPRISING plan: they were to feed the soldiers and send them safely HOME!

5. **Make a big banquet table.** So the people of Samaria prepared a big feast for the enemy soldiers. The soldiers may have wondered why the Israelites were being so kind! But they were hungry, so they ate. When they were full, the whole army was allowed to go home unharmed. No one had hurt them. Instead, the Israelites had been very GOOD to them! And for a very long time, the Arameans didn't fight with the Israelites at all!

Elisha had been good to people who didn't deserve it. His actions helped the people of Israel do what was good! And their goodness made their enemies go away and not bother them for a long time!

• •

Focus on the Fruit

Why did the king of the Arameans want to capture Elisha? (Elisha knew the king's plans.) **What did Elisha's servant see on the hills?** (Soldiers, horses and chariots of fire.) **Where did Elisha lead the blind soldiers?** (To the city of Samaria.) **What good thing did Elisha tell the Israelite king to do?** (Feed the soldiers and send them home safely.)

When one person does what is good, it helps others do what is good, too. Show the Goodness poster. **Depending on God's help in doing what's good is a great way to grow the fruit of goodness. And when we do good, it helps others to grow in goodness, too!**

Fruitful Lives Object Talk

Bible Verse

Don't let anyone look down on you because you are young, but set an example for the believers in speech, in life, in love, in faith and in purity. 1 Timothy 4:12

Materials

Bible with bookmark at 1 Timothy 4:12, one or more old eyeglasses or sunglasses with petroleum jelly smeared on the lenses.

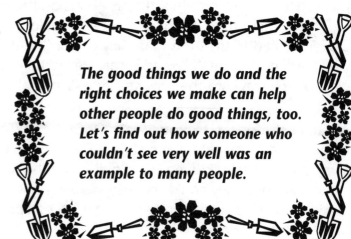

The good things we do and the right choices we make can help other people do good things, too. Let's find out how someone who couldn't see very well was an example to many people.

Lead the Activity

1. Volunteers try on the glasses you prepared. **What are some things it would be hard to do if this is how you could see?** Students tell ideas. **A woman named Henrietta Mears had very poor eyesight, but that didn't stop her from doing great things.**

2. **When Henrietta Mears was a child, her doctor said that she would probably become blind. So as she grew up, Henrietta decided to study hard, read a lot and memorize large portions of the Bible in case she later lost her eyesight. Henrietta's eyes were a problem for her throughout her life, but the doctor's prediction never did come true. She was never completely blind.**

   When Henrietta grew up, she became a high-school teacher in a small town. She was determined to help her students learn to do good things. When Henrietta discovered that her school didn't have a football team, she hired a coach and helped to organize the team. Henrietta went to every game to cheer for her students. Soon the football players started coming to Henrietta's Sunday School class where she taught them about the Bible. By the end of one year, many young people had decided to believe in Jesus and had learned to love and obey God because of Henrietta's teaching.

Conclude

Read 1 Timothy 4:12 aloud. **How was Henrietta Mears an example to others? Who has set a good example for you to follow? Who do you think might follow your example to do good?** Students tell ideas. **Let's ask God to help us do what is right so that other people can learn about Him.** Lead students in prayer.

• •

Additional Information for Older Students

Henrietta Mears was an example to many well-known Christian leaders, including Billy Graham. Henrietta started a publishing company that produces Sunday School curriculum. She also started a Christian camp that many children and adults attend every year. Her poor eyesight did not stop her from doing good!

Lesson 16

Active Game Center: Lead Me On

Materials
Chair, table.

Prepare the Game
In the middle of the playing area, place a chair and table where students can easily walk around them.

When we do what's right, we can help others do good, too. In the game we're going to play, your words and actions will help lead others on a safe path.

Lead the Game

1. Have three volunteers line up behind you and place their right hands on the waist of the people in front of them (see sketch). Volunteers close their eyes. Give verbal directions for students to follow as you lead students on a walk around room, between the chair and the table and back to your starting position.

2. Repeat activity, with a student acting as the leader and six to eight students lined up behind the leader. Each time the activity is repeated, choose a different leader and rearrange chair and table if possible.

Walk straight and then turn left.

Options

1. For younger students, have each student lead only one or two other students.

2. Create additional obstacles: step over a book or box of crayons, walk in and out of a doorway or walk a certain number of times around a chair.

3. If you have a large number of students, form several groups. Each group's leader guides his or her group on a different route around the room.

• •

Discussion Questions

1. ***How did the right actions of the leaders in this game help others?*** (Helped others walk safely around the room.)

2. ***Whose good example have you followed? Who might follow your good example? How?*** (Younger brother might help someone who is hurt after he sees you help someone who is hurt.)

Art Center: Good Views

Materials
Large sheet of butcher paper, markers, ruler, cardboard, craft knife, paper, pencils, tape.

Prepare the Activity
Draw a large house on the butcher paper. Cut slits to make windows at least 3-inches (7.5-cm) square, placing cardboard under each window as you cut it. Make at least one window for each student.

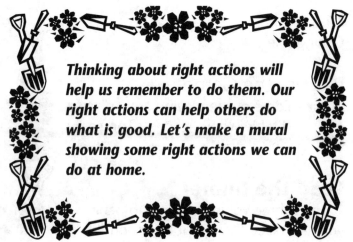

Thinking about right actions will help us remember to do them. Our right actions can help others do what is good. Let's make a mural showing some right actions we can do at home.

Lead the Activity
1. Distribute a sheet of paper to each student. Invite each student to open one window on the house. Student places paper behind the window and lightly draws the outline of the window on his or her sheet of paper.

2. Within the outline, each student draws a picture showing a right action he or she might do at home. Ask the first Discussion Question below to help students think of ideas. Continue asking other questions as students draw pictures.

3. Students tape completed pictures behind their windows so that the pictures can be seen through the windows. If time allows, students use markers to add details to outside of house.

Options
1. Draw a school building instead of a house and make windows in classrooms. Students illustrate right actions that can help others do what is good at school.

2. If you have a large number of students or limited time, draw window outlines before class.

· ·

Discussion Questions
1. ***What kinds of good actions might happen in a living room? In a kitchen? In a bedroom?*** (Helping a child with his or her homework. Clearing the dishes from the table. Reading a story to a younger brother or sister on a bed. Sharing the computer.)

2. ***How might our right actions help another family member do good?*** (Reading a story to a younger brother might help him fall asleep. Clearing a table might help a parent have time to call a lonely friend.)

3. ***What is one right action from our mural that you will do this week to help others do something good?***

Worship Center

Bible Verse

Don't let anyone look down on you because you are young, but set an example for the believers in speech, in life, in love, in faith and in purity.
1 Timothy 4:12

Materials

Bible; *God's Kids Grow* cassette/CD or music video and player; "Goodness!" word chart (p. 469 in this book); large sheet of paper on which you have printed 1 Timothy 4:12; masking tape;

God will help us do what's right and good. Our right actions can help others do good. Let's thank God that He helps us do what is good.

five index cards on which you have printed the following words or phrases, one word or phrase per card: "in speech," "in life," "in love," "in faith," "in purity."

Sing to God

Play "Goodness!" encouraging students to sing along with the music. **This song tells us that "obeying God makes goodness grow." When we obey God, we can also help others do what is right. How might a kid your age who tells the truth help others do what is right?** (Other kids might follow the example of telling the truth.)

Hear and Say God's Word

Display paper on which you have printed 1 Timothy 4:12. **How does 1 Timothy 4:12 say we can set an example for others?** (By the way that we talk and act.) Give index cards to volunteers. Say the word or phrase on the card as you hand it to each volunteer. **As I read 1 Timothy 4:12, listen for the words on your card. The rest of us will echo the words as you hold up your card.** Say verse, pausing for volunteers to hold up cards and students to echo the words. Repeat as time allows, with different students holding the cards each time.

Pray to God

When are some times you can do right actions and be good examples for the people around you? Students respond. Lead students in prayer, thanking God that we can be examples for others and asking for His help to be an example in the situations students mentioned.

Option

Give each student a sheet of paper on which to write a short prayer to God. Invite volunteers to read their prayers aloud. Younger children may dictate their prayers.

Bible Verse Coloring Center

Materials

Crayons or markers, a copy of page 193 or page 194 from *Bible Verse Coloring Pages #2* for each student.

Lead the Activity

Read 1 Timothy 4:12. **How are these children being an example to others? What are some ways you can be a good example for others this week?** Students color picture.

Option

After pages are completed, each student cuts his or her picture into four irregular pieces. Several students mix their pieces together and then see how quickly they can find their own pieces and put pages back together again.

Service Project Center

Materials

Materials needed for "Appreciation Party" (p. 58 from *The Big Book of Service Projects*).

Lead the Activity

Students complete "Appreciation Party" activity as directed in *The Big Book of Service Projects*. **What are some other ways to encourage others to do what is good?** Gifts may also be prepared for community workers (police officers, fire fighters, etc.). Deliver thank-you notes with gifts.

Discipleship Activity Center

Materials

Discussion Cards for Matthew 5:13-16 (pp. 111-116 from *The Big Book of Christian Growth*), materials needed for "Behind-the-Back Toss" or "Spin the Light" (p. 56 or p. 50 from *The Big Book of Christian Growth*).

Lead the Activity

Today we're going to play a game to discover how following the instructions in Matthew 5:13-16 can help us show goodness. Students complete activity as directed in *The Big Book of Christian Growth*.

Lesson 17

God's Faithful Promise

Bible Verse

Praise the Lord, all you nations; extol him, all you peoples. For great is his love toward us, and the faithfulness of the Lord endures forever.
Psalm 117:1,2

Bible Story Reference

Isaiah 9:6,7; Micah 5:2; Luke 2

Teacher's Devotional

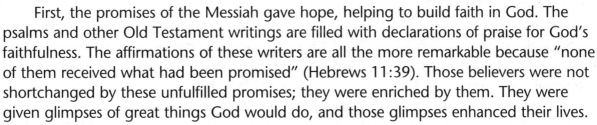

Character Builder

God showed His faithfulness in keeping His promise to send the Savior.

Why do you suppose God made all those promises about the Messiah many hundreds of years before they were fulfilled? Think of all those people over the centuries who read the prophetic writings but died long before the blessed event. Why get their hopes up for something that they would never live to see? Why not hold off on the good news until closer to the event? There are four reasons.

First, the promises of the Messiah gave hope, helping to build faith in God. The psalms and other Old Testament writings are filled with declarations of praise for God's faithfulness. The affirmations of these writers are all the more remarkable because "none of them received what had been promised" (Hebrews 11:39). Those believers were not shortchanged by these unfulfilled promises; they were enriched by them. They were given glimpses of great things God would do, and those glimpses enhanced their lives.

Second, the promises of the Messiah gave proof that Jesus truly was who He claimed to be. The Gospels and Epistles repeatedly point out ways in which Jesus was the fulfillment of the prophecies, showing that He was far more than a gifted teacher or spiritual leader.

Third, the time between the promises and their fulfillment instruct us about God's greater purpose. We tend to view God in light of our most recent experiences or our present circumstances. Reading of God's plan of the ages gives us perspective, an awareness that God is doing something in this world far bigger than our immediate concerns.

Fourth, God's faithfulness in fulfilling His promises encourages us to nurture faithfulness in our own lives. The better we know God and His character, the more we can allow His Spirit to shape His character within us. What a security it is to know that we have the promise "Faithful is He who called you, who will also do it" (see 1 Thessalonians 5:24).

Bible Story Center

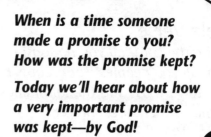

Materials
Faithfulness poster from *Poster Pack,* ¼ cup (2 oz.) play dough for each student.

Tell the Story
Follow along with me as we use our dough to tell today's story.

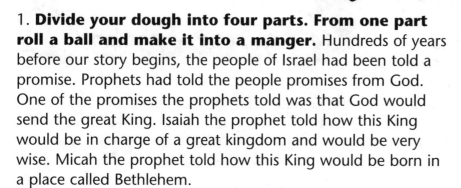

When is a time someone made a promise to you? How was the promise kept?

Today we'll hear about how a very important promise was kept—by God!

1. **Divide your dough into four parts. From one part roll a ball and make it into a manger.** Hundreds of years before our story begins, the people of Israel had been told a promise. Prophets had told the people promises from God. One of the promises the prophets told was that God would send the great King. Isaiah the prophet told how this King would be in charge of a great kingdom and would be very wise. Micah the prophet told how this King would be born in a place called Bethlehem.

   Now hundreds of years had passed since any prophet in Israel told God's words to the people. But the people still read the scrolls written by the prophets many years earlier. These scrolls still told of God's promise to send the great King.

   A young lady named Mary especially remembered God's promise when an ANGEL came to talk with her! The angel told her that she was going to be the mother of God's very special Son, the King whom God had promised. An angel also came to Joseph, the man Mary was going to marry. The angel told Joseph about this special child who was to be born.

2. **From the second part of your dough, make a baby and lay it in the manger.** Not long after the angels' visits, the ruler of all the countries in that part of the world wanted to count everyone to keep track of the people from whom he could collect money. All the men had to return to the towns from which their families came. Joseph and Mary went to Bethlehem, because Joseph belonged to the family of David— the very same David who had been the famous king of Israel long, long ago.

3. **From the third part of your dough, make Mary and Joseph.** It was terribly crowded in Bethlehem when Joseph and Mary arrived! Mary's baby was ready to be born soon. So Joseph looked for a place where they could stay. But no one in that crowded town had any room for them. The only place Mary and Joseph could find to stay was a stable for animals. But there was clean hay in the manger, and it was out of the wind. It wasn't very fancy, but it was warm and better than being outside.

That night God's special Son was born. Mary fed Him, and Joseph and Mary wrapped Him to keep Him warm. They named Him Jesus, just as the angels had told them to do. Baby Jesus slept on the hay in the manger.

4. **Set your figures together to make a manger scene. Add a shepherd.** That very same night, some shepherds were nearby, watching their sheep in the fields. SUDDENLY an angel came to them and a bright light shone all around! The shepherds were afraid, but the angel said not to be afraid. There was good news: the Savior, Christ the Lord, was born! After the angel spoke, many, MANY angels appeared in the sky, praising God!

After the angels went back to heaven, the shepherds hurried off to find this baby! They found Jesus and knew that here was the King whom God had promised to send! God had been faithful and had kept His promise! The shepherds were so excited that they told everyone they met about the wonderful baby! They returned to their sheep, praising God for all they had seen and heard that night.

• •

Focus on the Fruit
What are some things the prophets said about Jesus? (He would be the great King. He would be born in Bethlehem.) **What did the angels tell the shepherds?** (Good news. Don't be afraid. The Savior is born.)

God showed His faithfulness when He sent Jesus to live here on the earth as He had promised to do. Show the Faithfulness poster. **God is faithful. He always keeps His promises! He wants us to keep our promises, too. It's a way to show you are growing the fruit of faithfulness!**

Fruitful Lives Object Talk

Bible Verse

Praise the Lord, all you nations; extol him, all you peoples. For great is his love toward us, and the faithfulness of the Lord endures forever. Psalm 117:1,2

Materials

Bible with bookmark at Psalm 117:1,2; one or more items security guards use (flashlight, keys, billy club, walkie talkie, handcuffs, etc.).

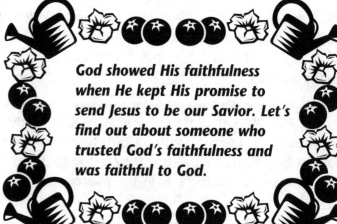

God showed His faithfulness when He kept His promise to send Jesus to be our Savior. Let's find out about someone who trusted God's faithfulness and was faithful to God.

Lead the Activity

1. Show items you brought. **Watchmen, or security guards, use things like these to help them protect buildings and people and make sure that they are safe. Just like watchmen watch for problems and tell people what they need to know to be safe, preachers pray for people and tell them what they need to know to become members of God's family and be saved from sin's punishment.**

2. **In the early 1920s, a man in China changed his name from Ni Shu-tsu to Watchman Nee. He chose this name because his mother had prayed for him to be born while she listened to the night watchman make his rounds. When Ni Shu-tsu heard that his mother promised God that her son would love and obey Him, Ni Shu-tsu decided that the name Watchman would remind him and others of his plan to serve God.**

   For the rest of his life, Watchman did his best to be faithful in obeying God. One day Watchman got a letter asking him to preach in the city of Chien-O. He wanted to go, but the boat trip to Chien-O cost 80 dollars and Watchman only had 10 dollars. Watchman asked for God's help and then went to the river. There was a small boat going to Chien-O for only seven dollars! Watchman Nee's faithful dependence on God meant others could hear about God.

Conclude

Read Psalm 117:1,2 aloud. **What do these verses tell us about God?** Students respond. Lead students in prayer, thanking God for His faithfulness.

• •

Discussion Questions

1. *How has God shown faithfulness to us?* (He kept His promise to send Jesus. He makes us part of His family when we trust in Him. He keeps His promises to love and be with us.)

2. *When might people today have a hard time trusting God's faithfulness? What could you say or do to encourage someone in a situation like this?*

3. *How does knowing about God's faithfulness help us?* (We can depend on Him.)

Lesson 17

Active Game Center: Coin Toss

Materials
Large sheet of paper, marker, coins, paper, pencils.

Prepare the Game
Draw, divide and number a large star on the sheet of paper (see sketch). Place paper on the floor in the middle of the playing area.

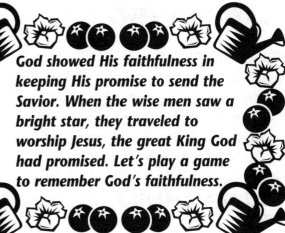

God showed His faithfulness in keeping His promise to send the Savior. When the wise men saw a bright star, they traveled to worship Jesus, the great King God had promised. Let's play a game to remember God's faithfulness.

Lead the Game
1. Group students into teams of three to four. Teams gather around the paper, standing at least 4 feet (1.2 m) from the paper. Give each group a coin, a paper and a pencil.

2. Silently choose a number over 30. Teams take turns tossing coins onto the paper, one student at a time. One student on each team keeps track of team's points, adding them up and announcing the point total after each toss.

3. Call stop when a team gets close to or scores the exact number you chose. Announce what your number was. Volunteer from the team who got closest or scored the exact number you chose tells a way God shows His faithfulness. Continue discussion by asking questions below. Repeat game as time allows, choosing a new number for each round.

Options
1. Provide stuffed fabric Christmas ornaments for students to toss onto star.

2. For older students, instead of using numbers, print one letter of the word "faithfulness" in each section of the star. First team to toss a coin into each of the sections and collect all the letters of the word tells a way God shows His faithfulness. Repeat game as time allows.

3. For mostly younger students, make a simple star shape and use fewer numbers. Choose a number between 10 and 20.

Discussion Questions
1. **What have you heard or read about in the Bible that shows God's faithfulness?** (God kept His promise to send Jesus, the Savior. God kept His promise to Noah that a flood wouldn't destroy the earth. God rescued the Israelites from slavery in Egypt.)

2. **How does God show His faithfulness to people today?** (Answers prayers. Forgives us.)

3. **Why is it important to know God kept His promise to send us a Savior?** Talk with interested students about becoming a member of God's family. Refer to guidelines in "Leading a Child to Christ" on page 36.

Art Center: Waxed-Paper Ornaments

Materials

Waxed paper, ruler, scissors, colored cellophane or tissue paper in a variety of colors, towel, iron, permanent markers, seasonal cookie cutters (stars, bells, etc.), hole punch, yarn or ribbon.

By keeping His promise to send the Savior, God showed His faithfulness. Making ornaments to celebrate Jesus' birth helps us remember God's faithfulness.

Lead the Activity

1. Distribute two 12-inch (30-cm) squares of waxed paper to each student. Each student cuts colored cellophane or tissue paper into small pieces and arranges on waxed-paper square. When satisfied with the arrangement, student covers with second piece of waxed paper.

2. Using a low temperature setting on the iron, cover each student's work with a towel and iron until waxed-paper squares fuse together. (Caution: Do not allow young children to use iron. Closely supervise use of iron by older students.) Allow a moment for waxed paper to cool before returning it to student.

3. Students use markers to trace cookie cutter shapes on fused waxed paper and then cut out the shapes. (Optional: Students draw details on shapes.) Students use hole punch to make a hole at the top of each shape and thread yarn or ribbon through the holes and knot for hangers. Students take ornaments home or use them to decorate classroom.

Options

1. Between pieces of waxed paper, students may place words torn from magazines, pieces of yarn, confetti, glitter or crayon shavings.

2. Instead of ornament shapes, students cut large letters to spell phrases such as "God is faithful," "Merry Christmas," "God sent the Savior." String letters in order with yarn or ribbon to form a garland.

Discussion Questions

1. ***What are some of the ways God has shown His faithfulness?*** (He keeps His promises. He is always with us.)

2. ***What are some ways you can show your faithfulness to other people?*** (Do chores and homework. Always help friends when needed.)

3. ***What are some ways you can show your faithfulness to God?*** (Pray to God. Read His Word each day. Go to church on Sundays. Act in ways that show you love Him.)

Worship Center

Bible Verse

Praise the Lord, all you nations; extol him, all you peoples. For great is his love toward us, and the faithfulness of the Lord endures forever. Psalm 117:1,2

Materials

Bible; *God's Kids Grow* cassette/CD or music video and player; "Just Ask Him" word chart (p. 475 in this book); large sheet of paper on which you have printed Psalm 117:1,2; masking tape, marker.

Let's thank God for His faithfulness in keeping His promise to send a Savior, baby Jesus.

Sing to God

Play "Just Ask Him," encouraging students to sing along with the music. **What does this song tell us about the ways God is faithful?** (He will help us when we pray. He always cares for us and loves us.)

Hear and Say God's Word

Display paper on which you have printed Psalm 117:1,2. Have a volunteer read the verses aloud. **According to this psalm, who should praise God?** (All nations. All people.) **For what can all these people give praise to God?** (God shows great love toward all people. The Lord is always faithful and keeps His promises.) Mark lines on the paper to divide the verses into six phrases, making marks at every comma and period. Lead students in saying the verses alternately, with boys saying the first phrase and girls saying the second phrase, etc.

Pray to God

What are some of the ways God has shown His faithfulness? (Sent His Son, Jesus, to be born and to save us. Keeps the promise He made to Noah about no flood ever again destroying everything on the whole earth.) Lead students in prayer, students repeating each phrase of this prayer after you: **Thank You, God, for Your faithfulness. Help us to trust You, because You always keep Your promises. Thank You for sending Jesus to us. Amen.**

Options

1. Have an older student read aloud God's promise in Isaiah 9:6 about sending a Savior.

2. During the Bible verse activity, discuss what it means to endure forever. Ask students to name things they think last a long time. Explain that God's faithfulness lasts longer than anything we can imagine, and He is always going to care for us and do the things He said He would do. An older student may read Psalm 48:14 aloud as an example of God's eternal faithfulness.

Lesson 17

Bible Verse Coloring Center

Materials

Crayons or markers, a copy of page 45 or page 46 from *Bible Verse Coloring Pages #2* for each student.

Lead the Activity

Read Psalm 117:1,2. **What are the kids in this picture doing? Why is Christmas a good time to thank God?** Students color picture.

Option

Provide students with a variety of markers (glitter pens, metallic pens, neon pens, etc.) to use in coloring picture.

Service Project Center

Materials

Materials needed for "Surprise Packages" (p. 87 from *The Big Book of Service Projects*).

Lead the Activity

Students complete "Surprise Packages" activity as directed in *The Big Book of Service Projects*. **How might this project help someone remember God's faithfulness? What are some things you remember that God has promised us? How do you know God will keep His promises?** (Optional: Instead of writing messages about Jesus, students write promises of God: Joshua 1:9; Psalm 23:1; 1 John 4:9.)

Discipleship Activity Center

Materials

Discussion Cards for Romans 8:35,37-39 (pp. 129-134 from *The Big Book of Christian Growth*), materials needed for "Clean-Sweep Relay" or "Celebrity Interviews" (p. 14 or p. 41 from *The Big Book of Christian Growth*).

Lead the Activity

Romans 8:35:37-39 tells us about God's faithfulness. Today we're going to play a game to talk about times we need to remember God's constant love. Students complete activity as directed in *The Big Book of Christian Growth*.

A Gentle Attitude

Bible Verse

Do nothing out of selfish ambition or vain conceit, but in humility consider others better than yourselves. Philippians 2:3

Bible Story Reference

Luke 18:9-14

Teacher's Devotional

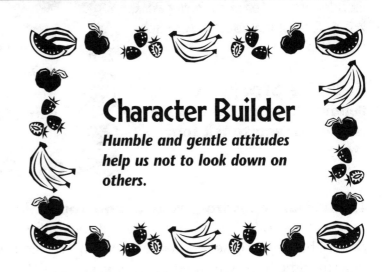

Character Builder

Humble and gentle attitudes help us not to look down on others.

When most children hear the story of the tax collector and the Pharisee, they tend to be very impressed by the Pharisee's prayer. Anyone who was thankful to not be like "robbers, evildoers, [and] adulterers" (Luke 18:11) sounds like the kind of person parents and teachers are always holding up as a positive example. Plus, this fellow went without food twice a week and gave away 10 percent of his income.

Of course children might assume that the Pharisee is the one whose prayer was answered. After all, the other fellow was a tax collector, and every child who has heard the story of Zacchaeus knows that tax collectors in the Roman Empire were dishonest and greedy. The tax collector in Luke 18 even admitted that he was a sinner. He had probably been the type of child good parents warn their nice children not to play with. Of course God would listen to the Pharisee instead of the tax collector!

As a result of this common perspective, Jesus' words that the tax collector and NOT the Pharisee was the one who pleased God (see Luke 18:14) are like a bolt out of the blue. For God to accept the tax collector rather than the Pharisee flies in the teeth of all the good moral instruction children have heard since infancy. And suddenly, as they try to make sense of this strange turn of events, children begin to get a glimpse of the essence of the Gospel. They begin to understand that we can never impress God with our list of accomplishments. Only a gentle, humble attitude enables us to admit our weaknesses and thus receive God's grace. And only a gentle, humble attitude helps us reflect God's acceptance to others.

Bible Story Center

Materials
Gentleness poster from *Poster Pack*,
¼ cup (2 oz.) play dough for each
student.

When have you heard a grown-up pray?

Today we'll hear about two grown-ups who were both praying, but their prayers were VERY different!

Tell the Story
Follow along with me as we use our dough to tell today's story.

1. **Roll four ropes from your dough and make the word "LAWS."** One day, Jesus was talking with some men called Pharisees. These men were important religious leaders in Jesus' time. Pharisees tried to obey every one of the Old Testament laws. They even obeyed MORE laws than were IN the Old Testament. They thought their obedience caused God to love them more than He loved anyone else. They were proud of all the things they did to make God love them.

But these men were WRONG—wrong about God's love and wrong about being proud. Jesus wanted these men to learn the truth, so He told them a story.

2. **Now make the word "PRAY."** Jesus' story was about two men who went to the Temple to pray. The first man Jesus talked about was a Pharisee. This Pharisee stood up in the Temple. He lifted his arms, so everyone could see him. He began to pray so loudly that everyone could hear him. He was proud of all he had done.

"God," he said, "I thank You that I am not like other men. I am not a thief or a bad person." The Pharisee paused for a moment and looked around. He spotted the second man in Jesus' story—a tax collector. "I'm also not like that evil tax collector! I even go without eating two days a week. I give to God part of all the money I get!"

Perhaps everyone in the Temple who heard this Pharisee might have been impressed. After all, he not only followed the rules, but he also did MORE than the rules said to do. He fasted (did not eat) twice a week, even though the Old Testament law said that everyone needed to fast only on one special day each year.

3. **Make the word "HATE."** Now in his prayer, the Pharisee mentioned he was glad he wasn't like the tax collector whom he saw in the Temple while he was praying. The Pharisee probably thought that a person like the tax collector should never even be allowed INTO the Temple!

Tax collectors were hated by the people of Israel. You see, when the Romans took control of the cities of Israel, they hired Jewish men to be tax collectors. The Romans allowed them to gather MORE money than Roman law said they should take for taxes. Tax collectors kept the extra money for themselves! The Pharisee was sure everyone hated the tax collector as much as he did.

4. **Make the word "SINS."** That tax collector also may have felt like he wasn't good enough to come into the Temple. But he hadn't come to impress people with his goodness. His prayer was very different from the prayer of the Pharisee. The tax collector stood by himself. He couldn't even look up.

Beating himself on the chest and sobbing, he prayed, "God, have mercy on me! I am a sinner." The tax collector remembered his sins—he knew he had disobeyed God. He understood that he didn't deserve anything good from God. He was humble, not proud. To be humble means we don't think we are better than others. The tax collector knew that the only way he could receive God's forgiveness was if God had mercy on him. He hadn't done ANYTHING good to try to make God love him!

5. **Make the word "LOVE."** Jesus said to the men listening, "God forgave the tax collector but NOT the Pharisee." He looked around at these people who were so proud of themselves. He wanted them to know the truth about God: God loves EVERYONE. And everyone should come to God with a humble attitude like the tax collector had. The Bible says God listens to people who have a humble spirit!

● ●

Focus on the Fruit

Who were the men who went to the Temple to pray in Jesus' story? (Pharisee. Tax collector.) **Why did the Pharisee come to pray?** (To brag.) **Why did the tax collector come to pray?** (To ask mercy and forgiveness.) **Why did God forgive the tax collector?** (He was humble and knew he needed forgiveness.)

Show the Gentleness poster. **Being gentle is not something people talk much about. But gentleness helps us to be humble and not to look down on anyone else. And as God helps our gentleness and humility grow, we treat others in ways that show God's love!**

Lesson 18
Fruitful Lives Object Talk

Bible Verse

Do nothing out of selfish ambition or vain conceit, but in humility consider others better than yourselves. Philippians 2:3

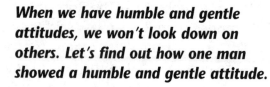

When we have humble and gentle attitudes, we won't look down on others. Let's find out how one man showed a humble and gentle attitude.

Materials

Bible with bookmark at Philippians 2:3, several dollar bills.

Lead the Activity

1. Show dollar bills. **What are some ways people get money? Why do you think some people want to have lots of money?** Students tell ideas. **When do you think someone might NOT want to have lots of money? In the country of Japan, a man by the name of Kagawa (kah-GAH-wah) chose not to be paid a lot of money for his hard work.**

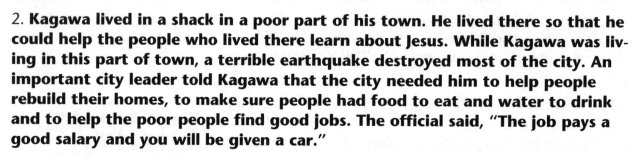

2. **Kagawa lived in a shack in a poor part of his town. He lived there so that he could help the people who lived there learn about Jesus. While Kagawa was living in this part of town, a terrible earthquake destroyed most of the city. An important city leader told Kagawa that the city needed him to help people rebuild their homes, to make sure people had food to eat and water to drink and to help the poor people find good jobs. The official said, "The job pays a good salary and you will be given a car."**

   Kagawa surprised the official when he said that he would be glad to do the job, but he would not take money or a car. Instead, Kagawa asked that his salary be used to help poor people. Kagawa's actions showed that he was humble. He believed that the needs of poor people were just as important as his own needs.

Conclude

Read Philippians 2:3 aloud. **How can kids today be humble in the way they treat others?** (Think about other people's feelings and needs. Listen to others.) Lead students in prayer, asking God to help students have humble and gentle attitudes.

• •

Discussion Questions

1. *What are some ways to describe a person who is humble?* (Cares about others. Remembers that other people are important. Wants to do what is best for other people.)

2. *How do you feel when someone acts like he or she is better than you? How would you want to be treated instead?*

Lesson 18

Active Game Center: "After You"

Materials

Bible, one tube sock for each pair of students.

Lead the Game

1. Students form pairs. Pairs stand on one side of the playing area.

2. Give each pair a tube sock. Partners hold sock between them, each with one hand on the sock. Pairs practice stepping over the sock, one foot at a time, without letting go of the sock.

When we care about others, we remember God's love for them, and our humble and gentle attitudes help us not look down on them. Let's each practice a humble attitude by putting others first in our game today.

3. To begin game, students stand at one side of the playing area. At your signal, one student in the pair says "After you," and his or her partner takes a step, putting one foot and then the other over the sock. Then the partner who stepped says "After you," and the other partner takes a turn. Students continue in this manner, moving across the playing area and back.

4. After all pairs have returned to the starting area, ask the pair who finished first to answer one of the Discussion Questions below, or play several more rounds and then lead the discussion.

Options

1. Instead of a tube sock, pairs use a kitchen towel, a scarf, a fabric strip or a 1-foot (.3-m) length of thick yarn or string.

2. For a challenge for older students, give each pair a paper plate to use. If partners let go of the paper plate while moving across the playing area, players must go back and start again.

3. If you have mostly younger students, students play without competing against each other, simply saying "After you" as they move across the room and back.

• •

Discussion Questions

1. ***What are some examples of a humble and gentle attitude?*** (Letting others go first. Not thinking you are better than anyone else. Listening carefully when others speak.)

2. Ask an older student to read Philippians 2:3 aloud. ***What does this verse say about having a humble attitude?*** (Don't do things because you are trying to get something for yourself or because you think you are better than other people. Don't spend too much time thinking about yourself.)

3. ***When we have humble attitudes, we don't spend our time comparing ourselves to others. What should we think about instead?*** (Ways to love God and others. How we can help others.)

Art Center: Fuzzy Folks

Materials

Markers, small slips of paper, two small paper bags, a variety of chenille wires, pencils, scissors, construction paper, glue, markers; optional—tape.

Prepare the Activity

Print names of a variety of age groups (grandparent, teenager, parent, child your age, toddler, baby, etc.) on separate slips of paper—at least two for each student. Place in a paper bag labeled "People." Print names of a variety of places (school, park, church, soccer field, mall, etc.) on separate slips of paper—one for each student; place slips in paper bag labeled "Places."

Being humble and gentle helps us not think of ourselves as better than other people. Let's make scenes of ways we can serve each other to remind us of ways to show humility and gentleness.

Lead the Activity

1. Each student selects two slips of paper from "People" bag and one slip of paper from "Places" bag. Invite volunteers to tell ways in which the people named on their papers could serve others at the places named on their papers. (For example, a teenager could push a toddler on a swing at the park.)

2. Students make figures from chenille wires. To form the torsos of the people, students form coils by wrapping chenille wires around pencils and then removing pencils (see sketch a). Students cut and attach additional chenille wires to torsos to form arms and legs (see sketch b), posing arms and legs to show actions.

3. Students glue completed figures to construction paper and draw details to complete their scenes. (Optional: Tape figures to paper.)

Option

To make stand-up scenes (see sketch c), students stand figures in tiny balls of clay or play dough. Clay or dough may also be used to create items such as rocks, chairs, walls, etc.

Discussion Questions

1. *Who is someone you think is humble and gentle? What are some things they do to show these attitudes?* (They are patient. They care about the needs of others. They find ways to help others.)

2. *How should we treat others instead of looking down on them?* (Always show love and acceptance. Be willing to serve and help others.)

3. *Who is someone you can treat in a gentle way? How?*

Worship Center

Bible Verse

Do nothing out of selfish ambition or vain conceit, but in humility consider others better than yourselves. Philippians 2:3

Materials

Bible, *God's Kids Grow* cassette/CD or music video and player, "Gentle Servant" word chart (p. 463 in this book), large sheet of paper on which you have printed Philippians 2:3, masking tape.

Let's practice having humble and gentle attitudes while we worship God today!

Sing to God

Play "Gentle Servant," encouraging students to sing along with the music. **What are some of the ways you think Jesus wants us to serve others?** (Speaking kindly. Helping others, even when we don't feel like it. Caring about the feelings of others.)

Hear and Say God's Word

Display paper on which you have printed Philippians 2:3. Have a volunteer read the verse aloud. **What does this verse say we should do to act with humility and gentleness?** (Don't do things out of selfishness or conceit. Consider other people better than ourselves.) Invite volunteers to suggest sound effects (clap hands, snap fingers, stamp feet, cheer, etc.) for five or six words of the verse. Practice the sound effects with all students. Then divide group in half. As one half of the group says the verse aloud, the other half does the sound effects. Trade assignments and repeat.

Pray to God

Invite volunteers to suggest words or phrases which describe gentleness and humility ("patience," "kindness," "listening," "sharing," "taking turns," etc.). Then lead students in prayer, asking God's help to show gentleness and humility. In your prayer, mention the words or phrases suggested by volunteers.

Options

1. Sing "Circle of Love" and/or "Good Fruit" (p. 457 and/or p. 465 in this book) with students.

2. If giving an offering is a regular part of your worship center, explain to students that giving our money to help people who need it more than we do is a good example of acting with a humble and gentle attitude, without conceit or selfishness.

Lesson 18

Bible Verse Coloring Center

Materials
Crayons or markers, a copy of page 173 or page 174 from *Bible Verse Coloring Pages #2* for each student.

Lead the Activity
Read Philippians 2:3. **Humility means we think about the needs of others and try to help them. How are the children in this picture showing humility?** Students color picture.

Option
Provide water color paints, brushes and paint smocks. Students paint pictures instead of coloring.

Service Project Center

Materials
Materials needed for "Cheer Mail" (p. 94 from *The Big Book of Service Projects*).

Lead the Activity
Students complete "Cheer Mail" activity as directed in *The Big Book of Service Projects*. **How do you feel when you receive mail? How do you think your letters will help the people who receive them? How can your letters show that you have gentle and humble attitudes?**

Discipleship Activity Center

Materials
Discussion Cards for 1 Corinthians 13:4-8a (pp. 141-146 from *The Big Book of Christian Growth*), materials needed for "Sticky Ball" or "Penny Pass" (p. 27 or p. 48 from *The Big Book of Christian Growth*).

Lead the Activity
When we show love in the ways described in 1 Corinthians 13:4-8a, we are also showing the fruit of gentleness. Today we're playing a game to talk about ways to obey 1 Corinthians 13:4-8a. Students complete activity as directed in *The Big Book of Christian Growth*.

Samson and Self-Control

Bible Verse

Be on your guard; stand firm in the faith; be men of courage; be strong.
1 Corinthians 16:13

Bible Story Reference

Judges 13—16

Teacher's Devotional

Character Builder

Depending on God for self-control helps us make good choices.

Self-control, put very simply, is just controlling yourself. But self-control is never simple. Samson may be the best (or worst!) example in Scripture of just how difficult self-control really is. Samson was a man of great strength, great gifts and great blessings. However, his tragic end was the culmination of a long-standing pattern of indulging, not controlling, his desires.

Today we are familiar with athletes who have disciplined their bodies and minds to excel at the rigors of their sport but whose personal lives show a great lack of simple self-control. We read of entertainers, politicians and even ministers who have practiced at great length to cultivate their gifts but who have failed to govern themselves. As a result, their gifts were squandered.

As Christians, we must allow God's Holy Spirit to develop His discipline in our daily lives. The Holy Spirit not only assists us in controlling our actions, but He can also change those desires and attitudes that seem appealing but which will bring us to failure.

Not a day passes without the opportunity to rely on the Holy Spirit to help us exercise self-control. The Holy Spirit's presence in our lives gives us the strength we need to face life's challenges with steady perseverance and commitment to do what is right.

At first glance, many of us would probably like to have the Holy Spirit serve as our personal deflector shield, keeping away all threats to our self-control, even to the extent of taking control for us. Instead, God's Spirit strengthens us, equipping us to live victoriously, developing our self-control from His abundant resources. In this way we experience firsthand the amazing miracle of God at work in our lives in the most practical of ways.

Bible Story Center

Materials
Self-Control poster from *Poster Pack;*
¼ cup (2 oz.) play dough and pencil
for each student.

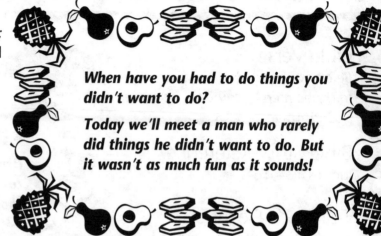

When have you had to do things you didn't want to do?

Today we'll meet a man who rarely did things he didn't want to do. But it wasn't as much fun as it sounds!

Tell the Story
Follow along with me as we use our dough to tell today's story.

1. **Divide your dough in half. Roll a ball from half your dough. Use a pencil to add a face.** After God's people had moved into the land God had promised them, they forgot to obey God's instructions. As a result, the Philistines began to attack them. But God had a plan to help His people. God sent His angel to an Israelite woman who had no children. He told her that she would have a son who would help the Israelites defeat the Philistines.

2. **Make seven small ropes from the second half of your dough. Put the ropes on the head for hair.** The angel said that her son was to follow some special rules: not to eat any grapes or drink any wine, not to touch anything dead and never, EVER to cut his hair. When this special baby was born, his parents named him Samson. Samson grew up to be VERY strong. Because he never cut his hair, it was very long. Samson wore his hair in seven braids. Although Samson was strong, he didn't always obey the laws God had made. God had given good gifts to Samson, but Samson didn't always use God's gifts to do right.

For instance, God had told the Israelites never to marry Philistines, because the Philistines worshiped false gods. But Samson wanted to marry a Philistine girl! Samson's disobedience led to lots of trouble with the Philistines. When the Philistines fought with Samson, he destroyed their fields. When their army came to kill him, he killed them all. He pulled down the gates of a town! No one could stop him! When Samson did what HE wanted, there was often lots of trouble!

All this trouble didn't keep Samson from continuing to disobey God. Samson soon fell in love with another Philistine woman named Delilah. The Philistines paid her to find out how to make Samson as weak as other men. Delilah asked and asked, but Samson told her one false story after another.

3. **Take the seven ropes from the head and make the face look sad.** Well, finally Delilah nagged and nagged Samson so much that he told her the TRUE story: If she were to cut his hair, he'd become as weak as other men. Delilah told the Philistine officials all about what Samson had said. And as soon as Samson was asleep, Delilah called a man to SHAVE Samson's head! Now he didn't have any hair at ALL.

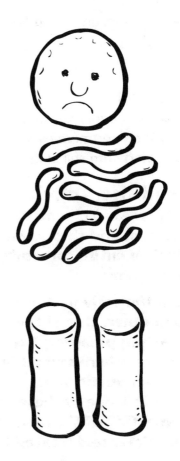

Because Samson did not have the self-control to stay away from Delilah and to keep his hair from being cut, God's power left him. He became as weak as other men. The Philistines tied him up and made him a slave. They even blinded him and forced him to grind grain every day in prison. But slowly, Samson's hair began to grow back.

4. **Use all your dough to make two pillars.** One day, many Philistines had a big party at their temple to honor their idol. They brought Samson into the temple and tied him between the two main pillars that held up the roof. The Philistines wanted to make fun of their once-great enemy. But Samson wanted to STOP the Philistines one more time.

Samson prayed, "God, let me be strong once more, so I can knock down this temple full of Philistines." He began to push on the pillars! Soon, WHAM! the whole BUILDING fell down! Samson died, too, but the Philistines left Israel alone for a long time.

• •

Focus on the Fruit

What were some things Samson was not supposed to do? (Eat grapes, drink wine. Touch anything dead. Cut his hair. Marry a Philistine.) **What happened when Samson didn't show self-control and disobeyed God's rules?** (Trouble came.) **What do you think might have happened if Samson had more self-control, acting and speaking in wise ways?** (Wouldn't have had so much trouble. Wouldn't have lost his strength.)

Samson shows us that self-control is not always easy to have. Show the Self-Control poster. **But God will help us have self-control if we ask Him. Asking God for help is a way to grow good fruit!**

Lesson 19
Fruitful Lives Object Talk

Bible Verse
Be on your guard; stand firm in the faith; be men of courage; be strong. 1 Corinthians 16:13

Materials
Bible with bookmark at 1 Corinthians 16:13, one or more ears of corn (if possible, bring corn still in its husk).

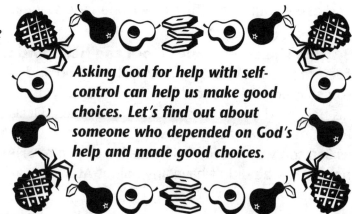

Asking God for help with self-control can help us make good choices. Let's find out about someone who depended on God's help and made good choices.

Lead the Activity

1. Show ear(s) of corn. **We usually eat the corn and throw the husk and the cob away. One man, Peter Cartwright, used an entire cornstalk to show self-control and to help another person do the same thing.**

2. **In the early part of the 1800s, many families in America lived far away from each other. One of the few times these families would get together was when a traveling preacher, like Peter Cartwright, came to visit. Each time Peter came to an area where several families lived, he led church meetings and talked with the families about God.**

   After one of these church meetings, Peter was invited to dinner at a nearby home. One of the men at the dinner was angry with Peter, because he thought that Peter had treated the man's son unfairly. The man challenged Peter to a duel to the death!

   Peter could have gotten angry with the man. Instead he just said, "According to the rules of honor, I have the right to choose the weapon. Isn't that right?" The man nodded. Peter smiled and said, "Let's go outside and grab a couple of cornstalks to fight with. I think that ought to settle things. Don't you?" The other man started to laugh and realized that he didn't need to be so angry. Soon the argument ended. At the next church meeting, the man became a member of God's family.

Conclude

Read 1 Corinthians 16:13 aloud. **How did Peter Cartwright obey this verse?** (Peter didn't get angry. He helped the other man do what was right.) **How did his self-control help to avoid trouble?** Students respond. **Let's ask God to help us have self-control and make choices to obey 1 Corinthians 16:13.** Lead students in prayer.

• •

Discussion Questions

1. *When do you think a kid your age needs self-control?*

2. *When were some times you needed to have self-control? How did your self-control help the situation? What might have happened if you didn't have self-control?*

Lesson 19

Active Game Center: On Guard!

Materials
Masking tape, measuring stick, cardboard box, scrap paper in two or three different colors.

Prepare the Game
Use masking tape to make a 5-foot (1.5-m) square in the middle of the playing area. Place the box in the middle of the masking-tape square.

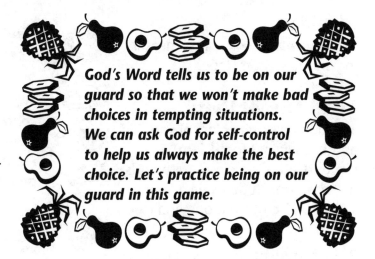

God's Word tells us to be on our guard so that we won't make bad choices in tempting situations. We can ask God for self-control to help us always make the best choice. Let's practice being on our guard in this game.

Lead the Game
1. Students form two or three teams. Teams stand on different sides of the playing area. Give each team one color of scrap paper. Students wad paper into balls. Invite one volunteer from each team to be a guard. Guards stand inside the masking-tape square in front of any team except their own.

2. At your signal, students attempt to throw their paper balls past the guard and into the box, making sure to stay behind the masking-tape line at all times. The guards try to block the paper balls.

3. After a short time, signal students to stop throwing the paper balls. Ask another volunteer from each team to collect their paper balls from the box, counting how many balls of their team's color are in the box. A volunteer from the team with the most balls in the box answers one of the Discussion Questions below. Students collect paper balls and play game again, choosing new volunteers as guards for the teams.

Options
1. If you have more than 20 students, divide group into four teams.

2. If it becomes too difficult for students to throw balls into box, use only one guard.

• •

Discussion Questions
1. *When might you find it hard to show self-control and need to remember to be on guard? Why?* Volunteers respond.

2. *What might result if you don't have self-control when you are tempted to (copy someone's homework)?* Volunteers respond.

3. *What kinds of good choices might you make when you depend on God for self-control?* (You can control your temper. You can obey God's Word by treating others kindly and not lying or stealing.)

Art Center: Reminder Bands

Materials

Yarn in a variety of colors, measuring sticks, scissors, tape.

Lead the Activity

1. Students select colors of yarn and cut seven 3-foot (.9-m) pieces. Gathering pieces with ends matched up, students tie a knot 1 inch (2.5 cm) from one end (see sketch a).

2. Each student tapes the knotted end of the yarn strands to a table or asks a friend to hold it. Holding on to the other end, student twists yarn in one direction until tight (see sketch b). Then, holding the center in one hand, student brings together and holds the ends of the twisted yarn. Student releases center, and the strands will twist together.

3. To finish the wristband, each student threads the ends of the strands through the loop formed at the center and knots the other end (see sketch c).

We can depend on God to give us self-control and help us make good choices. Let's make wristbands to remind us to ask God for self-control and help in making good choices.

Options

1. Demonstrate how to make a wristband before giving materials to students.

2. Use three strands of embroidery floss instead of yarn and braid strands instead of twisting them.

3. Thread beads onto yarn before twisting yarn. Beads with alphabet characters can be strung to spell words or phrases from the memory verse: "On your guard," "Stand firm," "Courage," "Be strong," etc.

• •

Discussion Questions

1. **What is something that might get a kid your age in trouble at school? At home? At the park?** (Cheating on a test. Fighting with a brother or sister. Not waiting for a turn on the swings.)

2. **What are some good choices a kid could make instead of (cheating on a test)?** (Studying for the test. Doing his or her best work. Asking the teacher for help.)

3. **What can you do when you need self-control and the ability to make good choices?** (Pray to God and ask for His help. Remember Bible verses that tell about God's help.)

Lesson 19

Worship Center

Bible Verse

Be on your guard; stand firm in the faith; be men of courage; be strong.
1 Corinthians 16:13

Materials

Bible, *God's Kids Grow* cassette/CD or music video and player, "Self-Control" word chart (p. 485 in this book), large sheet of paper on which you have printed 1 Corinthians 16:13, masking tape.

Let's worship God because He loves us and gives us self-control to make good choices.

Sing to God

Play "Self-Control," encouraging students to sing along with the music. **What examples of self-control are in this song?** (Not fighting. Saying what God wants us to say instead of saying bad things.)

Hear and Say God's Word

Display paper on which you have printed 1 Corinthians 16:13. Have a volunteer read the verse aloud. **What is this verse saying to guard against?** (People or things which might encourage you to disobey God and make bad choices.) **How does this verse tell us to be on our guard?** (Keep a strong faith, believing God will help you. Be courageous and strong about following God's ways.) Guide students to form four groups. Assign each group one phrase of the verse. Lead students in reciting verse, pointing to each group in turn to stand and say its phrase. Continue several times, varying the speed at which you point to each group.

Pray to God

When are some times kids your age need self-control to make good choices? Students respond. Volunteers pray aloud, completing this sentence: **God, help me have self-control to make good choices when . . .**

Options

1. Ask an older student to lead the verse activity.

2. Lead students in singing the "Self-Control" song again during the prayer time, explaining to students that some songs are prayers to God set to music. **This song asks God for His help in having self-control.**

3. As part of the prayer activity, ask an older student to read Psalm 119:9-11 aloud.

Bible Verse Coloring Center

FOR **YOUNGER** CHILDREN

Materials
Crayons or markers, a copy of page 137 or page 138 from *Bible Verse Coloring Pages #2* for each student.

Lead the Activity
Read 1 Corinthians 16:13. **This verse reminds us that we should guard against doing what's wrong. Who is like a guard in this picture?** Students color picture.

Option
Students add gummed star stickers to the sky.

Service Project Center

FOR **YOUNGER** CHILDREN AND **OLDER** CHILDREN

Materials
Materials needed for "Dexterity Balls" (p. 104 from *The Big Book of Service Projects*).

Lead the Activity
Students complete "Dexterity Balls" activity as directed in *The Big Book of Service Projects*. **What are some ways this project can help people be strong? What are some ways we can be strong and use self-control when we are trying to obey God?**

Discipleship Activity Center

FOR **OLDER** CHILDREN

Materials
Discussion Cards for Matthew 6:19-21,24 (pp. 123-128 from *The Big Book of Christian Growth*), materials needed for "Determination Squares" or "You Blew It!" (p. 16 or p. 54 from *The Big Book of Christian Growth*).

Lead the Activity
Matthew 6:19-21,24 tells us that our actions show what's really important to us. Today as we play a game about these verses, we'll find out ways to show self-control by making choices that please God. Students complete activity as directed in *The Big Book of Christian Growth*.

Lesson **20**

Love for a Blind Man

Bible Verse
My command is this: Love each other as I have loved you. John 15:12

Bible Story Reference
Mark 10:46-52

Teacher's Devotional
God loves us so much that He gave His only Son to take the punishment for our sin. God sees in us something so precious that, in spite of our unworthiness, He made the ultimate sacrifice for us. Only God incarnate, who is sinless, could demonstrate this perfect love.

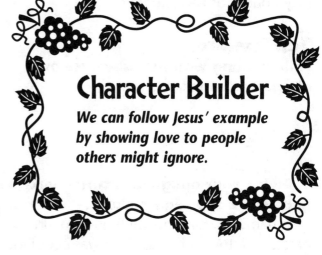

Character Builder
We can follow Jesus' example by showing love to people others might ignore.

It is solely out of God's perfect love for us that our love is born—both for God and for others. There is no doubt that God is precious and worthy of our love. But what about the imperfect humans with whom we interact each day? How can we love them when they so often seem to be unlovable?

Bartimaeus of Jericho was not very easy to love. His blindness made him a liability in most people's view. His poverty made him unattractive, even suspect for having done something deserving of this handicap. And then there was his mouth! Bartimaeus was loud—obnoxiously loud! Even when a noted rabbi was entering the city, Bartimaeus did not hesitate to begin bellowing about his unhappy state in life. Who could love a fellow like this, especially when the best efforts of the people around him could not get him to quiet down? Who could love him? Jesus could. While others were concerned about respectability and saw Bartimaeus as a nuisance, Jesus was attuned to hear a blind beggar's cry.

Long before Jesus made that ultimate demonstration of His love for us, He was making repeated smaller demonstrations of His love for individuals. How do we know the way to show love to others? Watching Jesus respond to Bartimaeus is a great place to begin.

Lesson 20 • Mark 10:46-52

Bible Story Center

Materials
Love poster from *Poster Pack,* ¼ cup (2 oz.) play dough for each student.

Tell the Story
Follow along with me as we use our dough to tell today's story.

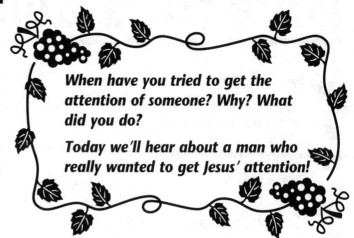

When have you tried to get the attention of someone? Why? What did you do?

Today we'll hear about a man who really wanted to get Jesus' attention!

1. **Divide your dough into three parts. With the first part, roll a rope and make the letter B.** One day a blind man named Bartimaeus (BAR-tih-MAY-uhs) was sitting at the gate of the town of Jericho. He was begging. Bartimaeus couldn't see to plant seeds and take care of plants like a farmer. He couldn't see to cut wood and build like a carpenter. In Bible times, the only way that a blind person got the money he needed was to beg. Beggars called out to people walking nearby, asking them for money or food. So Bartimaeus sat along the busy road and begged. Day after day all the people around would hear Bartimaeus calling out for people to help him.

2. **Turn the B sideways to look like blind eyes.** One day Bartimaeus heard many people walking together along the road. Bartimaeus called out to the crowd, "What's going on?"

"Jesus of Nazareth is coming!" someone shouted back.

3. **With the second part of your dough, roll a rope. Make an open mouth under the blind eyes.** "JESUS! Son of David, have mercy on me," Bartimaeus shouted. (Son of David was a name used for the Savior that God had promised to send. To have mercy means to care about and be kind to a person.)

Bartimaeus was making a LOT of noise! The people around Bartimaeus told him, "BE QUIET!" These people had seen Bartimaeus begging every day. Perhaps they thought he was making too much noise. Or maybe they wanted to see what Jesus was going to do and didn't want Jesus to be interrupted.

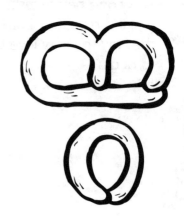

But Bartimaeus didn't listen to the people who told him to be quiet. He wanted Jesus to HEAR him! So he shouted out louder still, "JESUS, HAVE MERCY ON ME!" Bartimaeus hoped that Jesus would hear him and care about him.

Jesus could have passed right on by this noisy man. He could have said, "Not now, Bartimaeus." But Jesus didn't ignore him. He didn't keep walking down the road. No, Jesus cared. He STOPPED! He said, "Bring Me that man who is shouting out My name."

Several people quickly came to Bartimaeus. "Cheer up! Get on your feet. JESUS is calling you!" they said. They pulled Bartimaeus up by the arms and guided him to Jesus.

When Bartimaeus came up to Jesus, Jesus asked, "What do you want Me to do for you?"

Bartimaeus said, "Wonderful Teacher, I want to SEE!"

4. **Add the third part of your dough to the *B* eyes so that they look open.** Jesus must have smiled when He heard what Bartimaeus wanted. This man was VERY sure Jesus could help him! Bartimaeus wouldn't be stopped, even though other people hadn't cared about him. He wouldn't be stopped, although they had said unkind words to him.

Jesus said to him, "Then open your eyes. Your faith in Me has healed you!"

5. **Change the open mouth to a smiling mouth.** Instantly Bartimaeus could SEE! Jesus' face was probably the first thing Bartimaeus ever saw! He was so happy that he began praising God for giving him sight!

Bartimaeus could SEE the crowd following Jesus. Now he could WALK by himself without bumping into things. He wanted to stay with Jesus, who had loved him and healed him. So Bartimaeus came right along with the crowd and followed Jesus, too! The crowd was AMAZED! They joined Bartimaeus in praising God. They had seen a MIRACLE—something only God can do. And it only happened because Jesus cared about this noisy blind man when others just wanted him to be quiet!

Focus on the Fruit

Why did Bartimaeus beg for a living? (He was blind and couldn't earn money.) **What did people tell him to do when he began to call to Jesus?** (Be quiet.) **How did Jesus treat Bartimaeus?** (Paid attention to him. Helped him.)

Sometimes we see people to whom others don't pay much attention. Show the Love poster. **Jesus cared about all people, including people others didn't care much about. He wants us to act like that, too. It's one way to pass on His love to other people. Showing God's love to others helps us grow the fruit of His Spirit in our lives!**

Fruitful Lives Object Talk

Bible Verse

My command is this: Love each other as I have loved you. John 15:12

Materials

Bible with bookmark at John 15:12, bag containing six to eight school supplies (pencil, notebook, eraser, ruler, pencil sharpener, crayons, folder, book, etc.).

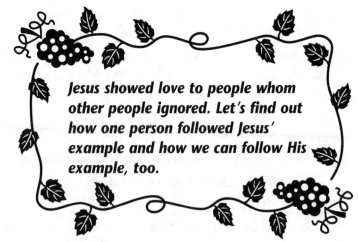

Jesus showed love to people whom other people ignored. Let's find out how one person followed Jesus' example and how we can follow His example, too.

Lead the Activity

1. Show bag. **This bag is full of things you might need for school.** Invite volunteers to guess items in the bag. Show items that students correctly guess and then identify items not guessed. **A long time ago in England, some children didn't have any of these things. They didn't even have a school to go to, because they lived with their mothers in a prison. The children hadn't done anything wrong; but at that time, children had to go to prison with their mothers if they didn't have other family members to care for them.**

2. **Even though most people didn't care about prisoners, a woman named Elizabeth Fry visited this prison. She was shocked by the horrible conditions in which the women and their children lived. Within a few years, Elizabeth helped to organize a school for the children and collected the school supplies they needed. Then she set up a room where the women prisoners could learn to sew.**

   Elizabeth also wanted the prisoners to know about Jesus' love for them. She talked about Jesus to the women and children and read from her Bible about Jesus' love and forgiveness. Elizabeth's work to help women and children in prison became so well known that people in the English government and even the queen of England, Queen Victoria, gave money to support her work.

Conclude

Read John 15:12 aloud. **How did Elizabeth Fry obey this verse?** Students respond. **Let's thank God for Jesus' example and ask Him to help us show His love to others.** Lead students in prayer.

• •

Discussion Questions

1. *When have you felt ignored? How did another person help you?*

2. *Who are some people kids your age often ignore or don't pay any attention to?* (Younger children. Kids they don't like.)

3. *What are some things you could do to care for someone who doesn't seem to have any friends?*

Active Game Center: Memory Moves

Materials
Bible, large sheet of paper, marker, tape.

Prepare the Game
Print John 15:12 on large sheet of paper and display paper where students can read it.

Lead the Game
1. Ask a volunteer to read John 15:12 aloud. **These words were spoken by Jesus. What did Jesus command in this verse?** (To love others like Jesus has loved us.) Students say verse together.

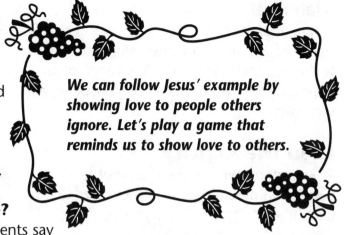

We can follow Jesus' example by showing love to people others ignore. Let's play a game that reminds us to show love to others.

2. Students stand in a circle. In order around the circle, assign each student a word of the verse for which to create a motion. Each student thinks of and practices a simple motion for his or her word.

3. To begin, the student with the first word of the verse says word while doing motion. The next student says the first word while doing the first student's motion and then says his or her own word while doing his or her motion. Continue around the circle, each student saying and doing the previous words and motions and adding his or her own word and motion until the entire verse is recited with motions. Invite volunteers to try saying the entire verse with motions.

Options
1. If there are more than 12 students in your class, divide group into two to play game or have students work in pairs to create a motion. If there are fewer than 12 students in your class, assign some students more than one word or assign each student a phrase of the verse.

2. To provide more action, students take turns to run to designated spot, say word(s) and perform motion(s) and then return to the group. Note the time it takes for the whole verse to be recited, and then have students repeat to try to beat that time.

• •

Discussion Questions
1. *What kinds of people does Jesus love?* (All people, even people whom others ignore.)

2. *In what ways did Jesus show love to people when He was on Earth?* (Talked to them. Helped them with their problems. Cared for them. Fed them.) *What can we do to follow Jesus' examples of loving people?*

3. *When are some times kids your age get ignored?* (At school on the playground. At a friend's house.) *What are some ways to show love to these kids?* (Talk to them. Invite them to play a game with you. Share school supplies with them.)

Art Center: Texture-Talk Posters

Materials

A variety of textured materials (fabric, corrugated paper, felt, sandpaper, aluminum foil, textured paper, etc.), pencils, scissors, glue sticks, large sheets of paper, large paper grocery bag.

Lead the Activity

1. Brainstorm with students a list of short words that describe ways to show love to others ("share," "give," "care," "help," "fair," "good," "kind," etc.).

Jesus gave us a great example to follow when He showed love to people others ignore. Let's figure out some ways to follow Jesus' example and show those ways on posters!

2. Assign each student or pair of students a word. Students create posters by drawing and then cutting large letters out of textured materials. Students glue letters in order to sheets of paper.

3. When students have finished creating words, collect all posters. Mix up posters. Secretly place one poster into bag. Invite a volunteer to close eyes and put hand in bag to feel letters and guess the word on the poster. Repeat with other posters and new volunteers as time allows. Ask Discussion Questions as each word is guessed.

Options

1. Students create posters for the words of John 15:12.

2. If posters will not easily fit into paper bag, cover poster with large towel. Students place hands under towel to feel and identify letters.

• •

Discussion Questions

1. ***When is a time kids your age might feel ignored?*** (On the playground. When parents or brothers and sisters are busy doing other things. In the classroom.)

2. ***What is one way to (share) with someone other people often ignore?*** Repeat question, using other words from list students used for posters.

3. ***What are the good results of following Jesus' example and showing love to people who are often ignored?*** (Those people will feel loved. We are obeying God. People can learn about God's love.)

Lesson 20

Worship Center

Bible Verse
My command is this: Love each other as I have loved you. John 15:12

Materials
Bible, *God's Kids Grow* cassette/CD or music video and player, "All My Heart" word chart (p. 453 in this book), large sheet of paper on which you have printed John 15:12, masking tape.

Let's thank Jesus for His example of loving others!

Sing to God
Play "All My Heart," encouraging students to sing along with the music. **According to this song, how can we learn to show love to God and others?** (Read God's Word. Ask God's help.) **What are some other ways to learn to show love?** (Learn from people like Sunday School teachers and parents who teach us about God's love.)

Hear and Say God's Word
Display paper on which you have printed John 15:12. Have a volunteer read the verse aloud. **What is Jesus' command in this verse?** (Love others in the same way He loves us.) **What are some ways to show Jesus' love to others?** (Be kind and care for the people around you. Tell others about God's love and forgiveness.) Lead all the students wearing (white) to say the first half of the verse and all the students wearing (blue) to say the second half of the verse. Repeat verse in this manner several times, naming a different group of students to say each half of the verse. (For example, everyone younger than eight says the first half and everyone older than eight says the second half; everyone who plays the piano says the first half and everyone who plays soccer says the second half, etc.)

Pray to God
Let's pray for each other. Let's ask God to help us show Jesus' love to those around us, especially people others ignore. Students take turns praying aloud for the person next to him or her, using this prayer: **Jesus, please help (Sam) show love to others like You did.** End prayer time by thanking Jesus for His example of love.

Options
1. If you have more than 10 students, students form circles of four to complete the prayer activity.

2. Ask students for any specific prayer requests and pray for students' requests, or ask an older student to pray for them. Record the prayer requests in your class prayer journal.

Bible Verse Coloring Center

Materials
Crayons or markers, a copy of page 111 or page 112 from *Bible Verse Coloring Pages #2* for each student.

Lead the Activity
Read John 15:12. **Who in this picture do you think is obeying this verse? How can you show love to the people in your family? To your neighbors?** Students color picture.

Option
Also provide a copy of "Draw a picture of a way to show God's love to others" page (p. 223 from *Bible Verse Coloring Pages #2).* Students draw and color pictures.

Service Project Center

Materials
Materials needed for "Tray Brighteners" (p. 103 from *The Big Book of Service Projects*).

Lead the Activity
Students complete "Tray Brighteners" activity as directed in *The Big Book of Service Projects.* **How do you think people in nursing homes or hospitals might feel? How might our project help these people? What are some other ways we could show love to people who have to stay in nursing homes or hospitals?**

Discipleship Activity Center

Materials
Discussion Cards for 1 John 3:16-18 (pp. 171-176 from *The Big Book of Christian Growth*), materials needed for "Human Tic-Tac-Toe" or "Partner Concentration" (p. 19 or p. 46 from *The Big Book of Christian Growth*).

Lead the Activity
Today we're going to play a game to discover ways 1 John 3:16-18 says to show love to others. Students complete activity as directed in *The Big Book of Christian Growth.*

Joyfully Found!

Bible Verse

I will rejoice in the Lord, I will be joyful in God my Savior. Habakkuk 3:18

Bible Story Reference

Luke 15:1-10

Teacher's Devotional

What does joy look like, sound like, feel like? How about the sound of un-self-conscious singing, the warmth of an exuberant hug, the grin on the face of someone who has just been freed from a terrible burden?

Character Builder

God's gift of salvation brings great joy.

While joy is not something we can hold in our hand, it is something very real, something we all recognize when we meet it.

Jesus told several parables about joy. In His stories about the lost sheep and the lost coin, Jesus described God's deep love and His concern about finding and saving each one who is lost. Then the final point of the stories was reached as Jesus told about God's great joy when just one person turns to Him. Jesus painted vivid scenes of spontaneous celebration, jubilant parties to which everyone in the vicinity was drawn.

We can share in this joy, too. When we reach out to God for help, we have the joy of discovering that He is ready to receive us. As we share this good news with children and their families, we discover the great joy of helping others to enjoy God's goodness. The joy of the Lord truly is contagious.

The intriguing thing about all this joy is that it is precisely what God desires for us to experience. He wants our joy to be full, and that is certainly more than reason enough for us to rejoice in the Lord!

Bible Story Center

Materials
Joy poster from *Poster Pack;* ¼ cup (2 oz.) play dough and coin for each student.

Tell the Story
Follow along with me as we use our dough to tell today's story.

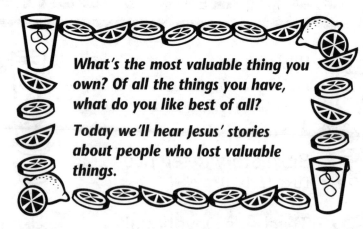

What's the most valuable thing you own? Of all the things you have, what do you like best of all?

Today we'll hear Jesus' stories about people who lost valuable things.

1. **Make four ropes from your dough.** Jesus told many stories while He was living on earth. Some people were glad to hear what Jesus said. But other people, especially the religious leaders called the Pharisees, were NOT. They muttered, "This Jesus WELCOMES sinners—people who do bad things!" They thought Jesus should spend time only with good people like themselves. Jesus knew the Pharisees didn't understand that God had sent Him to show love to all people, so Jesus told two stories to help them understand why He had come to Earth.

2. **Make a sheep pen from one rope.** The first story Jesus told was about a shepherd who had 100 sheep. The shepherd took good care of each sheep. Every day he took his sheep to places where they could find good things to eat and water to drink. Every night he gathered his sheep together and took them to a place where they would be safe. And each night he counted his sheep to make sure that all of them were safe.

3. **Make the number "99" from two ropes.** One night, the shepherd was counting his sheep; and everything was going fine until he got to the end, "95, 96, 97, 98, 99." There were ONLY 99 sheep! The shepherd started over and counted again, but there were still only 99. One sheep was MISSING! Now some shepherds might have said, "Oh well, too bad," and gone to sleep. But not THIS shepherd! He left the 99 sheep in a safe place, and then he went out to find his one missing sheep. That one sheep was important!

The shepherd looked down cliffs and into creek beds, where the sheep might have fallen. He searched behind big rocks, up hills and along roads. He searched EVERYWHERE for his lost sheep. Every few minutes, he paused to listen, hoping he would hear his lost sheep bleating.

4. **Turn your "9"s into "0"s. Add a "1" to make "100."** Finally, the shepherd found the lost and frightened sheep, picked it up and gently laid it across his shoulders. He carried it all the way back to the safe place where his other sheep were. He was DELIGHTED!

The shepherd called to his friends and neighbors, "Come and see! Come and see! My lost sheep has been FOUND!" And all his friends and neighbors celebrated.

5. **From all your dough, make 10 pieces. Press a coin onto each piece to form a shape like a coin.** The second story Jesus told was about a woman who had 10 silver coins. These coins were worth a lot. One day the woman saw that one coin was MISSING!

Oh no, she probably thought. *What will I do?* First, she lit a lamp, so she could see into every corner. Then she took her broom and swept the floor of her small house. She looked under the beds, inside all the jars and into every dish and pot.

The woman looked and looked. Where WAS that coin? SUDDENLY there, glinting in the lamplight, was her COIN! She was SO happy!

She ran to tell her friends, "I found my coin! I found my coin! Please, come help me CELEBRATE!"

And all her friends and neighbors came to see her coin, hear her story and celebrate with her.

It was very obvious to the religious leaders what Jesus' stories meant. Jesus wanted them to see that God is like the shepherd and the woman. Before people become members of God's family, they are lost like the sheep or the coin. God sent Jesus to show His love to people and to make it possible for them to be part of God's family. When we ask God to forgive us and we join God's family, God is DELIGHTED! He is SO happy that each one of us has come to Him that God—and everyone in heaven—CELEBRATES!

● ●

Focus on the Fruit

How many sheep did the shepherd in Jesus' story have? (100.) **Why did the shepherd search for the lost sheep?** (He cared about each of his sheep.) **How did the shepherd feel when he had found the sheep?** (Glad. Joyful.) **What did the woman do when she had found her valuable coin?** (Invited friends and neighbors to celebrate.)

Show the Joy poster. **God loves us VERY much. When we become part of His family, God is joyful! And His gift of salvation makes us joyful, too! That's the first step to growing the fruit of joy in our lives!** Talk with children about accepting God's gift of salvation. Follow the guidelines in the "Leading a Child to Christ" article on page 36.

Lesson 21
Fruitful Lives Object Talk

Bible Verse
I will rejoice in the Lord, I will be joyful in God my Savior. Habakkuk 3:18

Materials
Bible with bookmark at Habakkuk 3:18, shoe box with shoes inside.

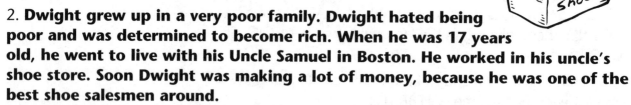

When we accept God's gift of salvation, it brings us great joy. Let's find out how one person learned about the joy that comes with God's gift of salvation.

Lead the Activity
1. Show shoe box. **When have you gone to a store to buy new shoes? How did a sales person help you?** Students respond. **Dwight Moody was a successful shoe salesman in Boston, but one day his shoe sales didn't go as planned.**

2. **Dwight grew up in a very poor family. Dwight hated being poor and was determined to become rich. When he was 17 years old, he went to live with his Uncle Samuel in Boston. He worked in his uncle's shoe store. Soon Dwight was making a lot of money, because he was one of the best shoe salesmen around.**

   Uncle Samuel insisted that Dwight go to Sunday School. One day the Sunday School teacher, Mr. Kimball, visited Dwight at the shoe store. Dwight thought that his teacher had come to buy shoes. But Mr. Kimball did more than that—right there in the store he invited Dwight to become a member of God's family! Dwight did. He said he felt a new kind of happiness and that he "never loved the bright sun shining over the earth so much before. . . . Everything was different." Now Dwight knew that true joy came from being a part of God's family! Dwight didn't want to keep his joy a secret. He went back home to visit his family to tell them about Jesus, too. And for the rest of his life, Dwight spent most of his time telling people about Jesus and the joy that comes from being a Christian.

Conclude
Read Habakkuk 3:18 aloud. **What are some reasons we have to be joyful in God? What are some reasons we have for being thankful to God?** Students respond. **Let's thank God for His gift of salvation.** Lead students in prayer.

• •

Additional Information for Older Students
Dwight Moody became known as a man who tried to honor and obey God in all his actions. Dwight Moody traveled all over America and England to preach about Jesus. Many people learned about Jesus through Dwight Moody's preaching. People today still learn about Jesus from organizations Dwight Moody helped to form, such as the Moody Bible Institute and Moody Press in Chicago.

Lesson 21

Active Game Center: Shoe Search

Materials
None.

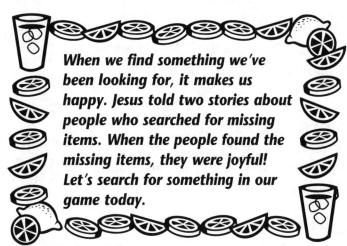

When we find something we've been looking for, it makes us happy. Jesus told two stories about people who searched for missing items. When the people found the missing items, they were joyful! Let's search for something in our game today.

Lead the Game

1. Students form two teams. Students on each team take off shoes and place them in a team pile on one side of the playing area. Students line up in single-file lines on other side of playing area, across from their team's shoe pile. Mix up shoes within each pile.

2. At your signal, the first student on each team skips to shoe pile, finds one of his or her shoes, puts it on and skips back to his or her team. The next student in line repeats the action. Students continue, taking turns until everyone on team has collected and put on both shoes.

Option
Review Habakkuk 3:18 with students. Stand by one pile of shoes and have a helper do the same by the other pile. When a student comes to shoe pile, begin reading the verse. Stop at any point. Student finishes saying the verse, takes a shoe from the pile and returns to team.

Discussion Questions

1. *What are some of the ways people hear about God's gift of salvation and the joy it brings?* (Friends tell them. They go to church. They read the Bible.)

2. *When we hear about God and accept God's gift of salvation by becoming members of God's family, we experience joy. Why?* (Our sins are forgiven by God. We can have eternal life. We know God loves us.) Talk with interested students about becoming members of God's family (refer to "Leading a Child to Christ" article on p. 36).

3. *The Bible tells us that God is joyful when we become a part of His family. Why?* (He loves us and wants us to be part of His family.)

Art Center: Peanut Pals

Materials

God's Kids Grow cassette/CD and player, paper, fine-tip markers, paper plates, unshelled peanuts, chenille wires, scissors.

Prepare the Activity

Post a note alerting parents about the use of peanuts in this activity in case children are allergic to peanuts.

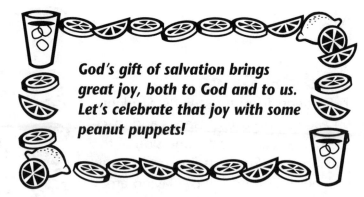

God's gift of salvation brings great joy, both to God and to us. Let's celebrate that joy with some peanut puppets!

Lead the Activity

1. Give each student a paper plate and several unshelled peanuts. Students create Peanut Pals in one or both of the ways described below.

2. Play "Joy" song from *God's Kids Grow* cassette/CD. Students put peanuts on fingers or hold peanut figures and move peanuts to the music, singing along with the words.

Peanut Finger Puppet

Crack off small section of bottom half of the back of a peanut shell and remove nut. Draw a face and hair on the top front of the peanut. Insert finger into cracked back to use as a finger puppet. Make finger puppets for several fingers if time permits (see sketch a).

Pose-able Peanut Figure

Draw a face, hair and other body details on peanut shell. Cut short sections of chenille wire for arms and legs. Gently poke wire into peanut shell between ridges. Pose chenille wire arms in any position and bend bottom of legs into feet, so figure can stand (see sketch b).

Options

1. Bring enough peanuts to allow students to eat some as they work on their figures.

2. If you have students with peanut allergies, students make puppets from tongue depressors or wooden spoons.

• •

Discussion Questions

1. ***When are some times kids your age feel joyful or truly happy and thankful?*** Volunteers respond.

2. ***Why does accepting God's gift of salvation and becoming a member of His family bring great joy?*** (You know God loves you and has forgiven your sins. You know you will have eternal life and be with Jesus now and forever.) Talk with interested students about becoming members of God's family, referring to the "Leading a Child to Christ" article on page 36.

Lesson 21

Worship Center

Bible Verse

I will rejoice in the Lord, I will be joyful in God my Savior. Habakkuk 3:18

Materials

Bible, *God's Kids Grow* cassette/CD or music video and player, "Joy" word chart (p. 473 in this book), large sheet of paper on which you have printed Habakkuk 3:18, masking tape.

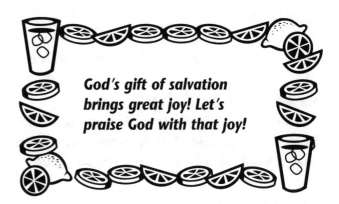

God's gift of salvation brings great joy! Let's praise God with that joy!

Sing to God

Play "Joy," encouraging students to sing along with the music. **What are some of the reasons we can have joy?** (God loves us and cares about us. He showed His love for us by sending His Son to die for us and allowing our sins to be forgiven.) Repeat the third stanza of the song if time allows.

Hear and Say God's Word

Display paper on which you have printed Habakkuk 3:18. **What does it mean to "rejoice" or "be joyful in God"?** (Be very glad and thankful for what God has done and who God is.) Lead students in repeating the verse in unison while standing up. Tell students to kneel and repeat the verse together again. Repeat the verse together a few more times, directing students to move to another position (sit, lift arms, look up, etc.) each time they recite the verse.

Pray to God

What can we say to tell God we are joyful because of Him? (Thank Him for the things He has done, like forgiving our sins. Tell Him that we are so glad He saved us and that He loves us.) Volunteers pray aloud. End prayer time by thanking God that He is so great we can always thank and praise Him, no matter what is happening.

Options

1. At the beginning of this center, ask an older student to read aloud Psalm 66:1,2 as an invitation to worship.

2. During the verse activity, students may clap as they say each word of the verse, or provide rhythm instruments for students to use.

3. As you are discussing the joy that comes from God's gift of salvation, be aware of any students who might not know about this joy or who may have questions about salvation. Talk with any interested students about becoming members of God's family, referring to the "Leading a Child to Christ" article on page 36.

4. Ask an older student to find the definition of "rejoice" in a dictionary. Student reads definition aloud during the verse activity.

Bible Verse Coloring Center

Materials

Crayons or markers, a copy of page 79 or page 80 from *Bible Verse Coloring Pages #2* for each student.

Lead the Activity

Read Habakkuk 3:18. **Knowing about God's love for us helps us feel joyful. What are some other things that make you joyful?** Students color picture.

Option

Each student begins coloring his or her own page. After several minutes, each student signs name on page and trades page with another student. Repeat trading several times until all pages are colored.

Service Project Center

Materials

Materials needed for "Invitation to Church" (p. 118 from *The Big Book of Service Projects*).

Lead the Activity

Students complete "Invitation to Church" activity as directed in *The Big Book of Service Projects*. **Why do we want other people to learn about Jesus? How might you tell your friends about Jesus? How do you think knowing Jesus might help other people have more joy?**

Discipleship Activity Center

Materials

Discussion Cards for Psalm 139:1-3,13-16 (pp. 87-92 from *The Big Book of Christian Growth*), materials needed for "Keep It Moving!" or "Calendar Toss" (p. 20 or p. 39 from *The Big Book of Christian Growth*).

Lead the Activity

Psalm 139:1-3,13-16 tells us some reasons we can be joyful and praise God. Today we're going to play a game to talk about these verses. Students complete activity as directed in *The Big Book of Christian Growth*.

A Father's Trust

Bible Verse

The Lord gives strength to his people; the Lord blesses his people with peace. Psalm 29:11

Bible Story Reference

John 4:43-54

Teacher's Devotional

The frantic father had left his dying son at home in Capernaum and traveled through the rugged hills to Cana. The plight of his ill child drove this man of high position to desperation. He had heard stories of Jesus' miracles and of His recent return to Galilee. When he found Jesus after his hurried journey, the father begged for Jesus' help.

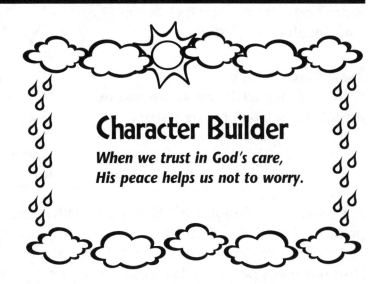

Character Builder

When we trust in God's care, His peace helps us not to worry.

A few gentle words from Jesus changed everything. The worry and fear and turmoil in the father's soul ended with Jesus' declaration that the boy would live. The outer circumstances had not changed in any way that anyone could see. Jesus and the father were still standing in the dusty street of Cana. The boy was out of sight, hours away. Yet "the man took Jesus at his word" (John 4:50), and that was more than enough to create peace where there had been worry.

Jesus wants to give you peace in exchange for your every fear and worry. The circumstances may truly look frightening. Things may be far from serene. But Jesus, our peace, has promised to care for us, His children.

Take Him at His word. Trust Him. You will find that as you trust, while you are still on the way, dealing with situations that have been the source of upset and stress, His peace—true and lasting—will grow in you!

Bible Story Center

Materials
Peace poster from *Poster Pack*, ¼ cup (2 oz.)
play dough for each student.

Tell the Story
**Follow along with me as we use our
dough to act out today's story.**

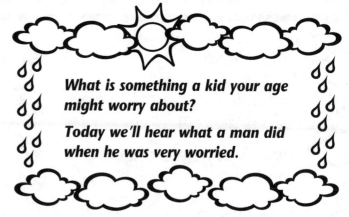

*What is something a kid your age
might worry about?*

*Today we'll hear what a man did
when he was very worried.*

1. **Divide your dough into five parts. With the first
part, make a little bed.** Jesus had been busy helping people
in the big city of Jerusalem. Besides teaching them about God,
Jesus made sick people well and made blind people see. He
made lame people walk and deaf people hear. He helped sad
people to be happy, too. Many people heard about this wonderful man who could do these special miracles. So when Jesus
came back to the area where He had grown up, all the people
crowded around Him to welcome Him.

2. **With the second part of your dough, make a person
to lay on your bed.** In the meantime, an important official
had a problem. It was a problem that his important position
could not help. This man's little boy was terribly sick. In fact,
the little boy was SO sick that he was about to die! The official
must have been VERY worried about his little son.

So when this official heard that Jesus was in a town nearby
and heard that Jesus made sick people well, what do you think
he did? He hurried off to find Jesus!

3. **Use the rest of the dough to make three people: the
father, Jesus and servant. Act out the story.** The father
walked and walked. The journey must have seemed even longer
than usual because he was so worried! When he got to the
town where Jesus was, he walked and WALKED and looked and
LOOKED until he found Jesus. There was Jesus, in the middle of
a crowd! The father pushed his way through the crowd until
finally, he was face-to-face with Jesus.

"Jesus, PLEASE come to my house," the official begged.
"My son is dying. Only You can help him. He needs You!"

Jesus looked at the whole crowd and said, "Won't any of
you believe in Me unless I do more and more miracles?"

The official DID believe that Jesus could help his son. He said to Jesus, "Please hurry to my home right away before my boy dies!"

Jesus looked at the official and said, "You may go home. Your son is HEALED!"

Even though the official couldn't see his son, he believed what Jesus said to him. So the official immediately began his long journey home. But he wasn't worried anymore. After talking to Jesus, the official was SURE his son was healed!

It was a long journey to get back home, but now the man's worry was gone. Jesus' words had given him peace. The next day while the official was still traveling home, some of his servants came running toward him, very excited and out of breath!

"Sir, sir!" they called.

"What is it?" the official asked.

"Your son. Your son is WELL!" they called out to him.

"I know—I know!" laughed the father. He hurried to join his servants. "When did my son begin to feel better?"

"Yesterday afternoon, at about one o'clock, his fever just disappeared!" a servant answered.

Then the official knew that his son was healed at the EXACT time that Jesus had said to him, "Your son will be well."

"Jesus made my boy well!" the official exclaimed.

When the official reached his home, who do you think came running out to meet him? There was his boy, healthy and happy again! The father must have told his family the story of finding Jesus and everything that Jesus had said. Everyone in the household knew that Jesus had healed the boy. And from that time on, this official and his whole family believed that Jesus is the Son of God. Jesus had given peace to the official when He told him his boy would be well. And now everyone in the official's household knew God's gift of peace.

• •

Focus on the Fruit

What did this official want Jesus to do? (Come to his house. Heal his son.) **Why do you think Jesus did not go with the man?** (Didn't need to go there to heal the boy.) **How did the official react to Jesus' words?** (Believed Jesus had healed his son. Had peace.)

Sometimes when we are worried, it is hard to have peace. Show the Peace poster. **But God asks us to trust Him and believe He will keep His promises. When we trust Him, He gives us His peace. That's one way to grow the fruit of His Spirit!**

Lesson 22

Fruitful Lives Object Talk

Bible Verse

The Lord gives strength to his people; the Lord blesses his people with peace. Psalm 29:11

Materials

Bible with bookmark at Psalm 29:11, one or more items people use for home security (warning sign, lock, keys, light, etc.).

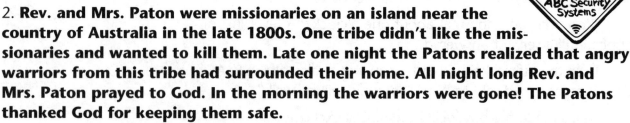

When we trust in God's care, the peace He gives will help us not to worry. Let's find out how some people trusted in God and how God helped them in a very scary situation.

Lead the Activity

1. Show items you brought. **What do people use these items for? What are some other things people depend on to protect them?** Students respond. **Two missionaries, Rev. Paton and his wife, knew one night that they needed protection.**

2. **Rev. and Mrs. Paton were missionaries on an island near the country of Australia in the late 1800s. One tribe didn't like the missionaries and wanted to kill them. Late one night the Patons realized that angry warriors from this tribe had surrounded their home. All night long Rev. and Mrs. Paton prayed to God. In the morning the warriors were gone! The Patons thanked God for keeping them safe.**

   About a year later, the tribal chief who had planned the attack became a Christian. The chief asked Rev. Paton who the men were the chief had seen guarding the missionary home the night of the attack. Rev. Paton told the chief that he and his wife were the only people there. Both men then realized that the warriors had seen angels God sent to protect the missionaries.

Conclude

Read Psalm 29:11 aloud. **What does this verse say that God does? How did Reverend and Mrs. Paton show that they believed this about God?** Students respond. **God cares for us, too. When are some times that kids your age need to remember God's care and depend on Him for peace? Let's thank God for helping us have peace.** Lead students in prayer.

• •

Discussion Questions

1. *What are some scary situations kids your age often face? What do you know about God that might help someone in a situation like this to have peace?*

2. *What are some ways God has cared for you or for someone you know?* Describe one or more ways God has cared for you before asking students to respond.

3. *How can you remember to trust God's care when you are worried or afraid?* (Pray. Read a Bible verse. Talk to someone who loves God.)

Active Game Center: Peace Hop

Materials

Butcher paper, measuring stick, markers, masking tape.

Prepare the Game

Draw a large grid on butcher paper, forming at least 20 10-inch (25-cm) squares. Print one letter of the word "PEACE" in each square, as shown in sketch. Tape grid to floor in center of playing area.

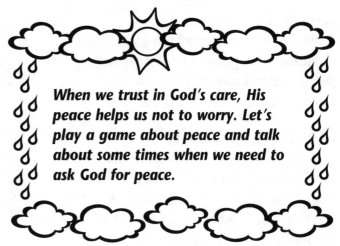

When we trust in God's care, His peace helps us not to worry. Let's play a game about peace and talk about some times when we need to ask God for peace.

Lead the Game

1. To play game, students stand around edges of the grid. Starting at any *P* square on the grid, first student hops on squares to spell "PEACE," and then he or she thinks of a time when kids his or her age might worry or not have peace. Student writes that situation in any square with a *P* in it. To finish this round of the game, repeat activity with four other students, instructing them to write situations in squares with *E, A, C* and *E.*

2. Play several rounds of the game, until all squares have situations written in them or until time is up. As students suggest situations, ask the Discussion Questions below.

Options

1. Prepare a grid for each group of six to eight students.

2. To make the game more challenging, students may not hop in any square that has a situation written in it.

3. Instead of writing situations, students say Psalm 29:11 aloud (or find and read it in a Bible) and then write their names in squares.

● ●

Discussion Questions

1. ***What does it mean to say that we have God's peace?*** (We can depend on God's love and care for us. We know He will help us in any situation.)

2. ***When have you seen someone have God's peace because he or she remembered God's promise of care?*** Share your own example before students answer.

3. ***What might a kid do instead of worrying if he prayed and trusted God about (lost homework)?*** (Do his homework again. Have courage to talk to teacher.) Repeat question with other situations students wrote in grid.

4. ***When is a time you need to ask God to give you peace?***

Art Center: Magnetic Bookmarks

Materials

Bibles, adhesive-backed magnetic strips, scissors, small paper clips, construction paper, ruler, tape, markers, decorative-edged scissors, stencils, stickers.

Prepare the Activity

Cut the magnetic strips into rectangles the size of small paper clips. Cut construction paper into 8x2-inch (20x5-cm) rectangles. Prepare one magnet and one paper for each student.

God has promised to care for us, no matter what happens. When we trust in God's care, His peace helps us not to worry. Let's make some bookmarks to help us remember God's gift of peace!

Lead the Activity

1. Give a magnet, a paper clip and a paper rectangle to each student.

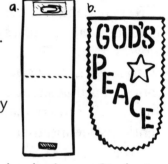

2. Students peel the adhesive backing from the magnet and stick it about 1 inch (2.5 cm) in from one end of the paper rectangle (see sketch a). Students fold paper in half with the magnet inside, and they mark with a finger where magnet hits other half of paper. Students tape a paper clip to that spot.

3. Students trim around edges of folded bookmark using decorative-edged scissors. Students decorate the bookmark using stencils, stickers and markers, writing phrases about God's peace and trusting in God instead of worrying (see sketch b). Ask Discussion Questions as students work.

Options

1. Use heavier weight paper, such as card stock or wallpaper samples, for bookmarks.

2. If students brought their own Bibles to class, suggest students use bookmark to mark and read a verse (Psalm 28:7; 29:11; 117:1,2; or Philippians 4:6,7) that will help them remember that they can trust in God's care instead of worrying.

Discussion Questions

1. ***What can you do when you are worried about something?*** (Pray to God and ask Him for His peace and help. Remember that God promises to love and care for you, no matter what. Read about God's promises to care for you.) Ask an older student to read Psalm 29:11 and/or Philippians 4:6,7 aloud.

2. ***What might happen if you trusted God instead of worrying about (playing in your piano recital)?*** (You might be able to concentrate better and enjoy the recital.) Repeat with other situations in which your students might worry.

3. ***What can you do to help other people when they are worried?*** (Pray that God will give them peace. Help them with what they are doing. Tell them promises God makes to care for them, be with them and give them peace.)

Worship Center

Bible Verse

The Lord gives strength to his people;
the Lord blesses his people with peace.
Psalm 29:11

God's care is something we can always depend on. When we trust in God's care, His peace helps us not to worry! Let's thank God for the peace He gives His people!

Materials

Bible, *God's Kids Grow* cassette/CD or music video and player, "Peacemaker" word chart (p. 481 in this book), large sheet of paper on which you have printed Psalm 29:11, masking tape, foam ball, paper, pencils.

Sing to God

Play "Peacemaker," encouraging students to sing along with the music. **What does this song talk about doing?** (Being a peacemaker.) **When we pray to God and trust Him to care for us, He helps us to have peace.**

Hear and Say God's Word

Display paper on which you have printed Psalm 29:11. Have a volunteer read the verse aloud. **What does this verse tell us that God gives to His people?** (Strength. Peace.) **How might you act at school if you have God's peace?** (Won't argue. Will stay calm when you take a test or turn in an assignment. Won't say mean things to others.)

Students sit in a circle. Throw the ball to a student, saying the first word of the verse as you throw it. Student who catches the ball says the second word of the verse as he or she throws the ball to another student. Continue until the entire verse has been said several times.

Pray to God

Give each student a sheet of paper and a pencil. **Write about or draw a picture of a time when you worry.** When students have finished, volunteers pray aloud, asking God for His help in the situations they described in their papers. End prayer time by thanking God that we can trust His care for us and that His peace helps us not to worry.

Options

1. Use a bean bag, a tennis ball or a balloon instead of a foam ball during the verse activity.

2. Sing "Good Fruit" and/or "Read All About" (p. 465 and/or p. 483 in this book) with students.

3. Invite older students to read aloud the following verses about God's peace: Psalms 28:7; 29:11; 117:1,2; Philippians 4:6,7.

4. For younger students, roll the ball instead of throwing it.

Lesson 22

Bible Verse Coloring Center

FOR **YOUNGER** CHILDREN

Materials
Crayons or markers, a copy of page 27 or page 28 from *Bible Verse Coloring Pages #2* for each student.

Lead the Activity
Read Psalm 29:11. **What do you think these people are praying about? What are some things that you want to pray about?** Students color picture.

Option
Provide yellow tissue paper. Students tear small pieces of paper, crumple them and glue to ducks in the picture.

Service Project Center

FOR **YOUNGER** CHILDREN AND **OLDER** CHILDREN

Materials
Materials needed for "Trustworthy Posters" (p. 47 from *The Big Book of Service Projects*).

Lead the Activity
Students complete "Trustworthy Posters" activity as directed in *The Big Book of Service Projects*. **When are some times people need to remember that God cares for them? How might our posters help others to trust God's care?**

Discipleship Activity Center

FOR **OLDER** CHILDREN

Materials
Discussion Cards for Psalm 23 (pp. 75-80 from *The Big Book of Christian Growth*), materials needed for "Active Alphabet" or "Match Up" (p. 56 or p. 45 from *The Big Book of Christian Growth*).

Lead the Activity
Today we're going to play a game to discover ways Psalm 23 can help us have God's gift of peace when we are worried. Students complete activity as directed in *The Big Book of Christian Growth*.

Lesson 23

Abraham's Long Wait

Bible Verse
We wait in hope for the Lord; he is our help and our shield.
Psalm 33:20

Bible Story Reference
Genesis 12:1-9; 15:1-6; 18:1-15; 21:1-7

Teacher's Devotional
Twenty-five years is a long time to wait for anything. Waiting 25 years for something must seem even longer when all the evidence indicates that the desired something can never happen.

Character Builder
Wait patiently and depend on God to keep His promises.

Yet that is what Abraham did. He waited and trusted and trusted and waited. He had been 75 years old when he left his lifelong home to head for some other place. God had promised, "I will make you into a great nation" (Genesis 12:2), and Abraham trusted that it would be so.

Upon arriving in Canaan, God announced to Abraham, "To your offspring I will give this land" (Genesis 12:7). Abraham patiently trusted. When conflicts arose between his servants and those of his nephew Lot, Abraham gave Lot first choice of the available land, still trusting that God would fulfill His promise. God responded by expanding on that promise: "All the land that you see I will give to you and your offspring forever. I will make your offspring like the dust of the earth, so that if anyone could count the dust, then your offspring could be counted" (Genesis 13:15,16).

Still, Abraham was getting older, and he had no offspring at all. As the years went by, even though there were times when Abraham questioned, the dominant pattern of those 25 years was one of patience, a firm dependence that God would do what He had said.

The next time you wonder why God hasn't answered a particular prayer, remember Abraham and his years of patient waiting. And then remember how marvelously God kept His promise.

Bible Story Center

Materials
Patience poster from *Poster Pack,* ¼ cup (2 oz.) play dough for each student; optional—several star-shaped cookie cutters.

When have you had to wait a long time for something?

Today we'll hear about a man and a woman who waited a long, LONG time for something!

Tell the Story
Follow along with me as we use our dough to act out today's story.

1. **Make a tent from your dough.** Abraham had lived in a city called Ur for many years. Abraham loved God and God loved him. One day, God told Abraham to leave Ur. God promised to lead Abraham to a new country. So Abraham packed up his family and followed where God led him. For many years, he and his family lived in tents as they traveled.

Many years passed, and during that time God made a promise to Abraham: Abraham would be a father. God said that Abraham would have many grandchildren and great-grandchildren. But Abraham and his wife, Sarah, were old—even OLDER than most grandparents. And they didn't have ANY children yet!

2. **Make as many stars as you can.** (Optional: Students take turns using cookie cutters.) But God hadn't forgotten His promise. He told Abraham again, "You WILL have a baby boy. From that baby will come more grandchildren and great-grandchildren than you can imagine!"

Out under the night sky, God said, "Look at the stars, Abraham. Can you count them? You'll have more grand-children than there are stars in the sky!" Abraham believed God. He trusted that God would keep His promise.

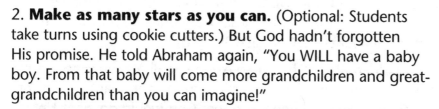

More years went by and Abraham grew even older. But STILL he and Sarah did not have a baby. Surely it was too late for Abraham and Sarah to become parents. But God hadn't forgotten His promise about a son. Abraham still believed God would give them a son, even though by this time Abraham was 100 years old and Sarah was 90!

3. **Shape a rope into a "3."** More time went by, and still there was no baby. Then one day, three visitors came to Abraham's tent home. And even though the visitors looked like men, one of them was really GOD! Abraham invited his guests to eat and rest. He asked Sarah and a helper to get some food ready. Abraham served a good meal to these important guests.

As the visitors ate out under a tree, Sarah stood at the opening of the tent. She was listening to the things God and Abraham were talking about. Guess what she heard? She heard God say that within a year she and Abraham would have a SON!

4. **Shape your "3" into a smile.** Now what do you think Sarah did? Sarah LAUGHED to herself! *What an impossible thing!* she thought to herself. *I'm so OLD! Will I really have a child NOW?*

God knew what Sarah had said to herself. He said to Abraham, "Why did Sarah laugh? Don't you know? NOTHING is too hard for the Lord! When I come back here next year, Sarah really WILL have a son!"

5. **Make a baby.** Later, at the EXACT time God had promised, Abraham and Sarah DID have their own baby boy! They named him Isaac. The name means "laughter"!

Sarah looked down at the beautiful baby in her arms. She said, "God has made me laugh! Everyone who hears about this baby will laugh, too. Who would have BELIEVED that old Abraham and Sarah would have a baby?"

Abraham and Sarah were VERY happy to have little Isaac. He must have made them laugh many, many times. And every time they laughed, Abraham and Sarah must have remembered that God NEVER forgets His promises!

● ●

Focus on the Fruit

What did God promise to give Abraham and Sarah? (A new place to live. A son.) **How old were Abraham and Sarah when they had a son?** (Abraham was 100. Sarah was 90.) **What did Isaac's name mean?** (Laughter.) **Why did his parents name him this?** (Because God had made them laugh by giving them a son when they were so old.)

Sometimes it's VERY hard to wait patiently. Show the Patience poster. **But when God makes us a promise, He will always keep it. So while we wait and trust His promises, it helps us grow the fruit of patience in our lives!**

Lesson 23

Fruitful Lives Object Talk

Bible Verse

We wait in hope for the Lord; he is our help and our shield. Psalm 33:20

Materials

Bible with bookmark at Psalm 33:20, an item from your home you would want to save in the event of a house fire; optional—copy of "Upon the Burning of Our House" by Anne Bradstreet (available on the Internet and in most American literature anthologies).

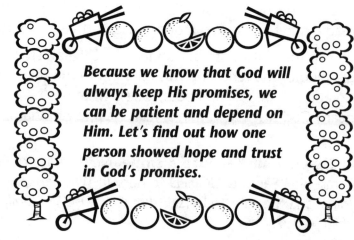

Because we know that God will always keep His promises, we can be patient and depend on Him. Let's find out how one person showed hope and trust in God's promises.

Lead the Activity

1. **What would you try to save if your house caught on fire?** Show item you brought. **This is something I would not want to lose in a fire.** Explain why the item is important to you. **Anne Bradstreet realized that something else was important when her house burned down.**

2. **Anne Bradstreet, her husband and her parents sailed on a boat from England to America in 1630. They made their home in the Massachusetts Bay Colony. One night, Anne woke up to the sounds of a fire. Anne and her family were able to escape the blaze, but they couldn't save anything at all in their house. The entire house and everything in it were destroyed!**

     Anne wrote a poem about her feelings when her home burned. In the poem, Anne said that she would miss the many things that were destroyed, but the things most important to her—God's promises—could not be burned. Anne believed that God's promises were her most important treasures. Through her poem, Anne showed that she trusted God to care for her family and that she chose to hope and trust in God's promises. (Optional: Read "Upon the Burning of Our House" aloud.)

Conclude

Read Psalm 33:20 aloud. **How did Anne Bradstreet show hope in God? Why do you think Anne chose to respond the way she did?** Students respond. **Let's ask God to help us remember to depend on His promises and be patient.** Lead students in prayer.

• •

Discussion Questions

1. *What are some promises you know God has made? What do you know about God that would make you trust Him to keep His promises?*

2. *How might someone show his or her belief in God's promises?*

Active Game Center: Tunnel Ball

Materials

Bibles, at least three shoe boxes or other cardboard boxes, scissors, measuring stick, marker, masking tape, foam balls or tennis balls.

Prepare the Game

Cut both ends out of boxes to form tunnels. Set up tunnels at least 7 feet (2.1 m) from each other, arranging them in a circular course (see sketch). Number each tunnel. Use masking tape to make a start/finish line.

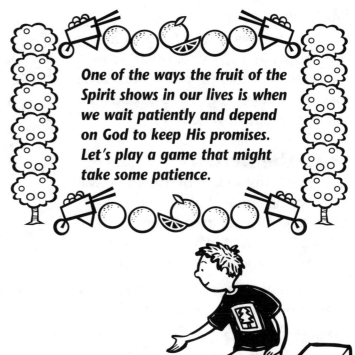

One of the ways the fruit of the Spirit shows in our lives is when we wait patiently and depend on God to keep His promises. Let's play a game that might take some patience.

Lead the Game

1. Group students into two teams. Give each team a ball.

2. Students on each team take turns rolling the ball cooperatively around the course from start to finish, with each student allowed one roll at a time. Each student begins his or her turn from where the ball stopped rolling. The ball must pass through each tunnel in order. Volunteer from team that finishes first answers one of the Discussion Questions below.

Options

1. Print each of the following verse references on three index cards, one reference per card: Joshua 1:9; Psalm 29:11; 136:26. Tape one index card on each tunnel. As students roll the balls through the tunnels, a team member finds the verse and reads God's promise aloud.

2. Instead of rolling the balls, each student taps the balls with a toy plastic golf club or a mallet made by taping a dry kitchen sponge to one end of a yardstick.

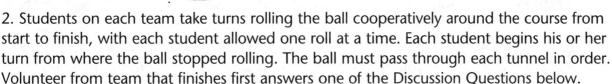

Discussion Questions

1. ***What are some of the promises God has given us in the Bible?*** (He will always love us. He will always be with us. He will answer our prayers.)

2. ***When might you need to wait patiently for God to keep a promise?*** (When praying about a problem. When you need God's help to know what to do.)

3. ***What might help us wait patiently for God to keep His promises?*** (Remember the times He has helped us in the past. Thank Him for His love for us. Pray and ask Him for patience.)

Art Center: Patience Plants

Materials

Bibles, a clear plastic cup for each student, paper in a variety of colors, scissors, markers, tape, yarn or ribbon, small rocks or pebbles, large spoons, potting soil, parsley seeds, water.

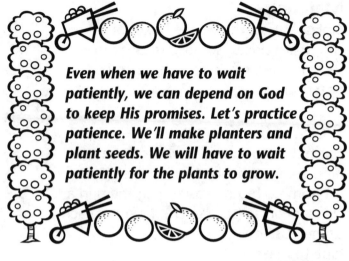

Even when we have to wait patiently, we can depend on God to keep His promises. Let's practice patience. We'll make planters and plant seeds. We will have to wait patiently for the plants to grow.

Lead the Activity

1. Student cuts a piece of paper that will fit along the inside of plastic cup. Student writes phrases from Psalm 33:20 on the paper. Student may also draw pictures and designs to decorate paper.

2. Student puts the paper into cup and tapes to secure (see sketch). Trim with a bow made from yarn or ribbon.

3. Student places a few rocks or pebbles in cup and uses spoon to add potting soil. When potting soil is about 1 inch (2.5 cm) below rim, add seeds, cover with a thin layer of potting soil and sprinkle with water. Planters should be kept in a sunny window and watered every day or two.

Options

1. Instead of parsley seeds or if you do not have potting soil, use grass seeds or mustard seeds; they do not need soil to sprout. Students place dampened cotton balls in their planters and sprinkle seeds on top. Keep in a warm, dark place, watering often, so the cotton doesn't dry out. When the plants are about 2 inches (5 cm) high, they can be moved to a sunny spot.

2. Students make planters out of egg carton sections. Using markers, faces are drawn on the egg carton sections. As plants grow, they will look like green hair.

3. Instead of placing paper inside cups, students use permanent markers to write words and draw pictures on colored cups.

4. If you have mostly younger students, cut papers before class.

• •

Discussion Questions

1. *What are some of God's promises for which you never have to wait?* (God's promise to always be with us. God's promise to give us courage.)

2. Read Psalm 33:20. *What does it mean when the verse says that God "is our help and our shield"?* (That God will give us the help we need and keep us from danger.)

3. *When is a time it would be good for a kid your age to remember that God "is our help and our shield"?*

Lesson 23

Worship Center

Bible Verse

We wait in hope for the Lord; he is our help and our shield. Psalm 33:20

Materials

Bible, *God's Kids Grow* cassette/CD or music video and player, "Patient Father" word chart (p. 479 in this book), large sheet of paper on which you have printed Psalm 33:20, masking tape, large Post-it Notes, marker.

Because God always keeps His promises, we can wait patiently on Him. Let's thank and praise God that we can depend on Him to help us and protect us at all times.

Sing to God

Play "Patient Father," encouraging students to sing along with the music. **In this song, what are some of the things we ask God to help us do?** (Be more like God. Trust in God. Keep promises. Be kind.)

Hear and Say God's Word

Display paper on which you have printed Psalm 33:20. Have a volunteer read the verse aloud. **What does the verse mean when it says that God is our shield?** (God will always protect us.) **What are some other promises God has given us?** (He will always love us. God is always ready to forgive us. God hears and answers our prayers.) Ask a volunteer to use a Post-it Note to cover one word from the verse. Students repeat the verse, filling in the missing word. With different volunteers, continue covering words and repeating the verse until all the words are covered. Repeat as time allows.

Pray to God

When are times that kids your age might need God's help? (When a bully is picking on them. When they have to move to a new town.) Write the following prayer on the back of the verse paper: "God, please help us to wait patiently for Your help. We know we can depend on You always to keep Your promises. In Jesus' name, amen." Lead students in saying the prayer in unison.

Options

1. Sing "You Promised!" and/or "Fruit of the Spirit" (p. 487 and/or p. 459 in this book) with students.

2. During the verse activity, older students find the following verses describing some of God's promises and read the verses aloud: Exodus 15:13; Joshua 1:9; Psalm 18:2,3; Isaiah 58:11.

3. Videotape students singing and doing the motions for the song(s).

Lesson 23

Bible Verse Coloring Center

Materials

Crayons or markers, a copy of page 29 or page 30 from *Bible Verse Coloring Pages #2* for each student.

Lead the Activity

Read Psalm 33:20. **What are some things for which you have to wait? How do you feel when you are waiting? This verse tells us that we can wait and trust God to keep His promises.** Students color picture.

Option

Students draw other fish and animals in the picture.

Service Project Center

Materials

Materials needed for "Bearing Fruit" (p. 50 from *The Big Book of Service Projects*).

Lead the Activity

Students complete "Bearing Fruit" activity as directed in *The Big Book of Service Projects*. **How can we encourage others to depend on God to keep His promises? What are some reasons you have for depending on God?**

Discipleship Activity Center

Materials

Discussion Cards for Proverbs 3:3-6 (pp. 99-104 from *The Big Book of Christian Growth*), materials needed for "Straw Relay" or "This Is a Fish" (p. 28 or p. 51 from *The Big Book of Christian Growth*).

Lead the Activity

Today we're going to play a game to help us discover ways of patiently trusting in God. Students complete activity as directed in *The Big Book of Christian Growth*.

A Boy Shares Kindness

Bible Verse

*Share with God's people who
are in need. Practice hospitality.*
Romans 12:13

Bible Story Reference

John 6:1-15

Teacher's Devotional

Often we have a tendency to equate
kindness with politeness. We commend ourselves, because we don't
cut in front of others in line. We
usually put our trash in cans, rather than litter. We say "Thank you" and "Please." This
is considered polite behavior. But it doesn't scratch the surface of what kindness is really
all about.

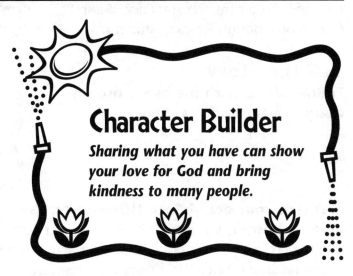

Character Builder

*Sharing what you have can show
your love for God and bring
kindness to many people.*

While the miracle of Jesus multiplying loaves and fish to feed a multitude is truly
awe inspiring, there was another miracle worth noting in the story: the miracle of kindness when a boy gave his lunch to help others who were hungry. (Parents of growing
boys claim there was a third miracle: the boy hadn't already eaten his lunch. Perhaps
his excitement at seeing Jesus held off his hunger pangs for a while!)

Because we know what Jesus was about to do with that lunch, the boy's sharing
may not seem all that remarkable. After all, three of the four Gospels do not even mention the boy as they present the story. But keep in mind that the boy had no idea what
Jesus was about to do. All the boy knew was that he had something that other people
needed. It would have been so easy to claim that all those other people should have
planned ahead and brought their own lunch. Instead, the boy shared what he had.

We can get by with simply being nice and polite. It's safe. But God calls us to be
kind, to be compassionate toward those in need, even toward those we may not particularly like. Extend kindness to the children in your class, even to those who aren't your
favorites. Your actions will be a living example of obedience to God's Word.

Bible Story Center

Materials
Kindness poster from *Poster Pack,* ¼ cup
(2 oz.) play dough for each student.

Tell the Story
**Follow along with me as we use our
dough to tell today's story.**

*When have you been really glad
someone shared with you?*

*Today we'll find out when
thousands of people were glad
someone shared!*

1. **Divide your dough into three parts. Use one part to
make a basket.** Jesus and His disciples had gotten into a boat
and rowed from the city of Capernaum across the Sea of Galilee
to the far shore. Since there were no large towns nearby, the
disciples thought they could be alone, away from the crowds.
They were ready for a rest!

But when they got to the far shore, the disciples got a
surprise! THOUSANDS of people were waiting for them! Some
people had seen them leave Capernaum. Word had spread
quickly. Now more than 5,000 people from towns near and far
had come to see Jesus! When the tired disciples saw the crowds
of people, they must have wondered if they would ever rest
again!

Even though Jesus needed some time to rest, He had compassion for the people when He saw the crowd. "Compassion"
means to care about another person's needs and to want to
help that person. Jesus cared about these people, so He took
time to teach them and heal them.

2. **Use the second part of your dough to make five
small loaves of bread.** Soon the day had almost ended. It
was nearly supper time, but the people weren't ready to go
home. Nobody wanted to miss ANYTHING Jesus was going
to say or do! But Jesus' disciples were hungry. They knew Jesus
and all the people were hungry, too. But it would be IMPOSSI-
BLE for all these people to find food to buy for supper! There
were no towns nearby. And even a BIG town wouldn't have
enough food to feed such a crowd.

Jesus was concerned about the needs of the hungry crowd.
He looked at His disciples and asked, "Where will we buy bread
for these people to eat?"

"It would take a fortune to feed these people!" Philip cried.

3. **Use the last part of your dough to make two small fish. Put the bread and fish in your basket.** Jesus understood what the problem was, but He had a plan. Andrew had met a boy with a small basket that held five small barley loaves and two small fish—just a small lunch! Andrew took the boy to Jesus. He said, "Here is a boy with five small loaves and two small fish, but how far will they go among this many people?"

Jesus simply smiled. "Have the people sit down in groups on the grass," He said.

The disciples hurried away to seat the people. Jesus took the food in His hands. He thanked God for the food. Then Jesus began to break the bread and fish into pieces. The boy who gave his lunch to Jesus must have gasped. He probably rubbed his eyes and looked again, for his little lunch of five loaves and two fish had GROWN—there were hundreds and HUNDREDS of pieces of bread and fish. Right before his eyes, Jesus was making MORE of everything!

Jesus gave food to each disciple to pass out to the hungry people. No matter HOW much Jesus gave away, there was always MORE!

The disciples gave food to every single hungry person. When they finished, many people had food left over. So the disciples passed baskets around to gather up the extra food. They filled 12 baskets with the leftover bread and fish! Jesus had made enough for everyone to eat their fill—and more besides!

Everyone was full—and amazed! The boy had been willing to share his lunch. Jesus had taken that small lunch willingly shared by the boy and made it into enough food to feed thousands and THOUSANDS of people! Because the boy was kind, he shared. And because the boy shared, Jesus fed every hungry person—and showed that He cared about their needs.

• •

Focus on the Fruit

Where did Jesus and His friends go? Why? (To the far side of the Sea of Galilee. To be alone.) **What did the people who followed them need?** (To hear Jesus teach. Food.) **What did the boy share?** (The food he had.) **What did Jesus do with that food?** (Fed everyone, with food left over.)

The Bible tells us to share like the boy did. Show the Kindness poster. **Even though we may not always feel like sharing, it's not only a way to show kindness, but it is also a way to show our love for God. When we are kind, we can grow the fruit of God's Holy Spirit!**

Fruitful Lives Object Talk

Bible Verse

Share with God's people who are in need.
Practice hospitality. Romans 12:13

Materials

Bible with bookmark at Romans 12:13,
food wrapper or bag from a fast-food
restaurant.

*We can bring kindness to many
people when we share what we have. As
we learn about one person who shared,
think about how you can show God's
love by sharing and bringing kindness to
others.*

Lead the Activity

1. Show food wrapper or bag. **What do
you know about the place I got this (wrapper)?** Students respond.
S. Truett Cathy is one person who started a fast-food restaurant.

2. **When he was a young man, Truett Cathy had a dream of own-
ing a restaurant. He worked hard and saved his money. In 1946,
Truett and his brother opened their first restaurant. Eventually,
Truett started a chain of fast-food restaurants called Chick-fil-A.
Chick-fil-A restaurants became very popular and soon Truett
was rich.**

   **Some rich people spend their money on big houses or new
cars. But Truett loved God and believed the Bible verse that says that it
is better "to give than to receive"** (Acts 20:35). **Truett chose to spend his money
helping children in foster care—children who have to live away from their parents, because their parents can't take good care of them.**

   **Many times children in foster care don't even get to keep living with their
brothers and sisters. Truett felt sorry for these children, so he used his money to
build foster homes where brothers and sisters could live together. Foster parents
also live in the homes, so the children have a safe place to live and grow. Foster
children in these homes are loved and cared for.**

Conclude

Read Romans 12:13 aloud. **How did Truett Cathy obey this verse? How do you think
his actions made a difference in other people's lives?** Students tell ideas. **Let's ask
God to help us look for opportunities to be kind and share what we have with
others.** Lead students in prayer.

• •

Discussion Questions

1. *What do you think are some good reasons for obeying Romans 12:13?* (To show
   God's love. To show that we thank God for His love.)

2. *What are some things needed by people you know?*

3. *What can you share with others?* (Clothes. Friendship. Knowledge of God's love.)

Active Game Center: Fish Frenzy

Materials
Bible, goldfish crackers, large bowl, small paper cups.

Sharing what you have can show your love for God and bring kindness to many people. Let's share some fish crackers in our game today!

Prepare the Game
Fill bowl with crackers. Place bowl on one side of the playing area.

Lead the Game

1. Group students in teams of six. Each team lines up in a single-file line across the playing area from the cracker bowl. Give the first student in each line a small paper cup.

2. At your signal, the first student in each line walks quickly over to the bowl, scoops out approximately the same number of crackers as there are students on his or her team and returns to team. Student lets each team member take a cracker from the cup. If student did not get a cracker for each team member, student returns to bowl to get more crackers.

3. Next student in line repeats action, collecting crackers and serving one to each team member. Play continues until all students on each team have had a turn and have served each team member a cracker.

4. Ask one of the Discussion Questions below to a volunteer from the first team to be finished. Continue discussion with remaining questions.

Option
Post a note alerting parents to the use of food in this activity. Also check registration forms for possible food allergies.

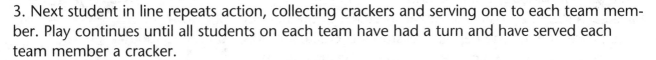

Discussion Questions

1. ***How do you usually feel when someone shares something with you?*** (Thankful. Special. Loved.)

2. ***Sharing what you have is one way to show kindness. What are some of the things you can share with others at home? At school?*** Volunteers respond. ***With whom can you share these things?***

3. ***With whom does Romans 12:13 tell us to share?*** Have a student read the verse aloud. (God's people who are in need.) Tell students a way your church shares resources with people who are in need.

Art Center: The Art of Sharing

Materials

Bibles; a variety of art materials, at least one for each student (crayons, specialty markers, ribbons, yarn, die-cut shapes, chenille wires, sticker sheets, rubber stamps and stamp pads, metallic pens, etc.); construction paper; glue; scissors.

We show God's love and kindness to others by sharing with them. Let's share our abilities as we create art to remind us that sharing is a part of showing kindness.

Lead the Activity

1. Students from groups of six to eight. Distribute one type of art material and a piece of construction paper to each student. **In making today's art project, you can share your abilities and the art materials you have been given.**

2. Allow students several minutes in which to begin creating their pictures. The pictures may be abstract collages, words from Romans 12:13 or pictures of items to share with others. (Note: Glue and scissors may be used as needed.) After three or four minutes, call time and have each student pass his or her art material to the next person. Continue procedure as time permits. As students create pictures, comment about the different ways in which they are using the art materials.

Option

Put all the art materials in a large paper bag. Students take turns pulling items out of the bag to use in creating their pictures. Prepare a separate bag of materials for each group of six to eight students.

• •

Discussion Questions

1. *What are some ways others have shared with you?*

2. *What are some things you could share with others?* (Food. Toys. Books.)

3. *Even if you don't have a lot of things to share with others, what are some other ways you could share with others?* (Let someone else have your turn at a game. Let a brother or sister sit next to you on the couch. Show love and kindness to someone in need. Give encouragement to members on your team.)

Lesson 24

Worship Center

Bible Verse

Share with God's people who are in need. Practice hospitality. Romans 12:13

Materials

Bible; *God's Kids Grow* cassette/CD or music video and player; "Be So Kind" word chart (p. 455 in this book); large sheet of paper on which you have printed Romans 12:13, leaving blank lines for the vowels; masking tape; marker.

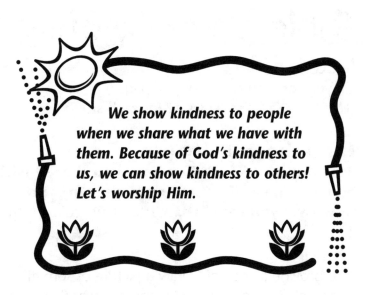

We show kindness to people when we share what we have with them. Because of God's kindness to us, we can show kindness to others! Let's worship Him.

Sing to God

Play "Be So Kind," encouraging students to sing along with the music. **What reason does this song give us for sharing the things we have?** (So that everyone will see God's generosity.)

Hear and Say God's Word

Display paper on which you have printed Romans 12:13. Volunteers take turns guessing the missing vowels and writing them in the blanks. Continue until all words are identified. Then ask students to read the verse aloud. **What does the word "hospitality" mean?** (Being generous and kind to others.) **What are some things you could do this week to show hospitality?** (Share a snack with a brother or sister. Invite a kid who's new to your school to play at your house.)

Pray to God

Who are some people who might need someone to share with them? (People whose house has been destroyed. Homeless people. Someone new to the neighborhood. Younger children.) Students take turns saying short sentence prayers asking God to help them share with others and practice hospitality.

Options

1. Ask an older student to lead the singing of the song.

2. If students usually give an offering during this worship time, explain that giving money to God is one way we can share with others. Describe several ways in which your church family uses the offering to practice hospitality and help others in need.

3. During the verse activity, older students take turns reading ways to show love as described in Romans 12:9-21.

4. Sing "Hear, O Israel" (p. 471 in this book) with students.

Bible Verse Coloring Center

Materials
Crayons or markers, a copy of page 117 or page 118 from *Bible Verse Coloring Pages #2* for each student.

Lead the Activity
Read Romans 12:13. **When have you shared with another person? What are some things you have now that you could share?** Students color picture.

Option
Also provide a copy of "Draw a picture of something you can share" page (p. 215 from *Bible Verse Coloring Pages #2).* Students draw and color pictures.

Service Project Center

Materials
Materials needed for "Meal Add-On" (p. 79 from *The Big Book of Service Projects*).

Lead the Activity
Students complete "Meal Add-On" activity as directed in *The Big Book of Service Projects*. **What are some other ways you or your family have shown kindness to people in need in our community?**

Discipleship Activity Center

Materials
Discussion Cards for Matthew 5:3-9 (pp. 105-110 from *The Big Book of Christian Growth*), materials needed for "Circle Spin" or "Answer Match" (p. 59 or p. 38 from *The Big Book of Christian Growth*).

Lead the Activity
Every day we have opportunities to show kindness. Today we're going to play a game and talk about the words of Matthew 5:3-9. We'll discover ways to show kindness and ways to show our love for God. Students complete activity as directed in *The Big Book of Christian Growth.*

How Goodness Gives

Bible Verse

Let us not love with words or tongue but with actions and in truth. 1 John 3:18

Bible Story Reference

Acts 4:32—5:11

Teacher's Devotional

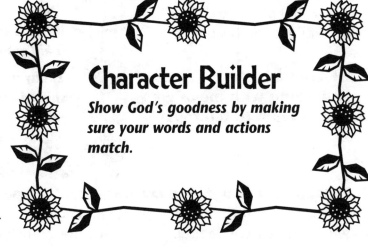

Character Builder

Show God's goodness by making sure your words and actions match.

We've all heard of someone who "talks a good game." The expression refers to attempts to impress others by making our actions and abilities sound better than they really are. The apostle John writes about someone who "talks a good life." He warns us not to confuse empty words with real truth.

Ananias and Sapphira are prime examples of people whose lives did not match their words. They did an excellent job of talking the Christian life, saying all the right things, but their attitudes and actions did not measure up. They were judged, not over the money they held back, but because of the deceit that they allowed to flourish in their hearts.

Teachers in particular must guard against simply talking about God and His Word. It is easy to merely prepare lessons, tell stories, recite verses—all without it penetrating first into the core of who we really are. We must be diligent in striving to live what we teach. As Ananias and Sapphira learned so tragically, we cannot fool God with our nice-sounding words. We aren't likely to fool the children we teach, either, if our words and our lives are not in sync. We are only likely to fool ourselves and miss out on God's true goodness.

Bible Story Center

Materials

Goodness poster from *Poster Pack*; ¼ cup (2 oz.) play dough and plastic knife for each student.

Tell the Story

Follow along with me as we use our dough to tell today's story.

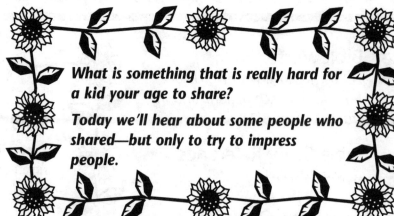

What is something that is really hard for a kid your age to share?

Today we'll hear about some people who shared—but only to try to impress people.

1. **Flatten your dough and cut out a coat shape.** At the time when the first Christians in Jerusalem began to meet together, there were no hospitals or places for homeless people to stay. There were no food pantries where hungry people could get food. Instead, God's family shared everything they had with each other. A man who had two coats gave one to a man who had no coat. A woman who had extra grain shared it with a hungry neighbor. The first Christians were glad to share!

The Bible says that there were NO poor people in this church, simply because everyone shared. Whenever people who owned land sold their land, they brought the money they made to the church leaders. The church leaders gave the money to whomever needed it.

2. **Make the letter *B*.** One member of God's family in Jerusalem was named Joseph. The church leaders nicknamed him "Barnabas," which means "son of encouragement." They called him this because his joyful giving encouraged everyone else! One day Barnabas brought the apostles a large amount of money.

"I sold my field. Here is all the money I got for it. Please, use it to help the others," he may have said.

Everyone must have been quite impressed with such a generous gift. But Barnabas hadn't given the money to impress anyone. He gave it simply because he wanted to show his love for Jesus and help God's family.

3. **Divide your dough in half and flatten one half. Cut 10 flat circles for coins.** Now a husband and wife named Ananias (an-uh-NI-uhs) and Sapphira (suh-FI-ruh) were part of the Jerusalem church, too. Surely they had noticed that Barnabas was very well respected. It might be that Ananias and Sap-

phira wanted to be as well liked and respected as Barnabas. Maybe they were a little jealous of all those thank-yous that Barnabas had gotten. Whatever it was they felt, they decided to copy Barnabas.

Soon Ananias and Sapphira sold a field, too. But instead of giving all the money they had made to the church, they agreed that they'd keep part of the money.

4. From the other half of your dough, make an open bag. Then put eight coins into the bag and close it to make a money bag. When Ananias brought the rest of the money to Peter, one of the church leaders, Ananias acted like he was giving ALL the money he had made. He probably thought Peter would be very impressed. But instead Peter shook his head sadly.

Peter looked at Ananias. "Why did you lie?" he asked. "You could have KEPT all of the money if you wanted. You haven't lied to me. You have lied to GOD!"

When Ananias heard these words, he died right there on the spot! Some young men of the church buried him.

Meanwhile, Sapphira waited and waited for Ananias to return. She finally came looking for her husband.

When Peter saw Sapphira, he asked her if what he'd been given was the full price for the land. Peter wondered, *Would she tell the truth?*

"Oh, yes," Sapphira answered. "That was the price!"

Peter asked. "Why would you agree to lie to God?"

Lie to God? Sapphira must have thought. Then she realized what she had done. Like her husband, she died instantly.

Barnabas gave his generous gift out of love. Ananias and Sapphira gave their money for a selfish reason. It wasn't wrong for them to give only part of the money they made. But it was wrong for them to lie to God and God's family about what they were doing.

• •

Focus on the Fruit

Why were there no poor people in God's family at Jerusalem? (Everyone shared what they had.) **What did Barnabas do? Why?** (Sold land and gave all the money to the church. Gave out of love.) **What was wrong with Ananias and Sapphira's actions?** (They said one thing, but they did something else.)

We can all think of ways to show goodness in our lives. Show the Goodness poster. **But goodness is more than just talking about doing good things. This story helps us know that a big part of goodness is living with God's help so that our actions match our words. That grows the fruit of goodness in our lives!**

Fruitful Lives Object Talk

Bible Verse

Let us not love with words or tongue but with actions and in truth. 1 John 3:18

Materials

Bible with bookmark at 1 John 3:18, world map.

We can show God's goodness by making sure that our words and actions match. Let's find out about a man who became known for loving and obeying God with both his words and actions.

Lead the Activity

1. Show world map. Invite a volunteer to point out the country in which you live. **What other countries have you traveled to or heard of?** Volunteers name countries. Invite volunteers to locate countries on map. Give help as needed. **Today we are going to talk about a man named Billy Graham. He has traveled to over 185 countries!**

2. **In 1934, Billy Graham went to a church meeting and heard a preacher talk about Jesus. Because of what he learned about Jesus at that meeting, Billy decided to love and serve God for his whole life. So after Billy went to college, he started telling people about Jesus' love and how to become a member of God's family.**

   Billy not only told people about Jesus' love, but his actions also showed Jesus' love. Billy traveled to cities all over the world to preach about Jesus. He talked to people who were kings and to people who were members of tribes in Africa. He preached in huge football stadiums and in small villages. Every place that Billy preached, many people decided to become members of God's family. Everyone that met Billy saw that both his actions and words showed Jesus' love.

Conclude

Read 1 John 3:18 aloud. **Billy Graham's words and actions showed that he obeyed this verse. Who are some other people you know who love God and others with their actions as well as with their words?** Volunteers briefly tell about people they know. **Let's ask God to help us show goodness by making sure our words and actions match.** Lead students in prayer.

• •

Discussion Questions

1. *Why is it important for what you do to match what you say you believe?* (Our actions show what we really believe. Our good actions can help others do what is good.)

2. *When are some times it might be hard for a kid your age to act in ways that show goodness? How could you help a friend in a situation like this?*

Active Game Center: Call the Ball

Materials
Bounceable ball best suited for your playing area (playground ball, tennis ball, Ping-Pong ball or small rubber ball).

Prepare the Game
Depending on the type of ball with which you are playing and the ability of your students, choose three actions from the Action List below.

One way to show God's goodness is by making sure our words and actions match. Let's practice matching our words and actions.

Lead the Game

1. Group students into two even teams. (Join one team yourself if needed to even up teams.) Teams line up in single-file lines across the playing area from each other, leaving a wide space between the first player of each team (see sketch).

2. Demonstrate the three actions you chose, identifying each action by name. Give the ball to the first student in one line. Student with ball calls out one of the actions listed below and bounces the ball in that manner to the first student on the other team. First student on the other team catches ball and calls out another action, moving the ball in that manner back to the other team. If the ball does not move in the manner called, student tries again. Game continues until all students have had at least one turn to call out an action and move the ball.

Action List
Single bounce, double bounce or triple bounce: bounce ball the appropriate number of times; **dribble and toss:** dribble ball halfway across playing area and then toss ball; **left-hand bounce or right-hand bounce:** bounce ball with left or right hand; **no bounce:** toss ball with no bounce; **grand slam:** bounce ball very high and hard; **baby bounce:** bounce ball low to the ground.

• •

Discussion Questions
1. *What does it mean to make your words and your actions match?* (Do what you say you are going to do. If you tell someone a good way to act, act that way yourself.)

2. *What are some ways your words and action can match at home? At school?*

3. *Making our words match our actions is one way to show goodness. How does God help us have the fruit of goodness?* (Gives the Bible to help us understand right ways to act. Reminds us of ways to speak and act to show goodness. Answers our prayers for help.)

Art Center: Action Poses

Materials

Bible, butcher paper, scissors, measuring stick, crayons, markers, masking tape, construction paper.

Prepare the Activity

Cut butcher paper into 4- to 5-foot (1.2- to 1.5-m) pieces. Prepare one piece for each student.

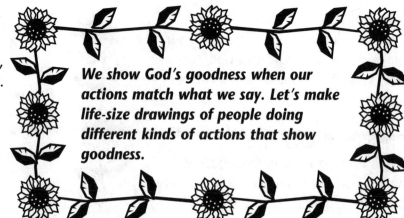

We show God's goodness when our actions match what we say. Let's make life-size drawings of people doing different kinds of actions that show goodness.

Lead the Activity

1. Read 1 John 3:18 aloud. **What are some actions a kid your age could do that would show goodness?** (Pick up trash in the park. Wash the family car. Play a game with a younger brother or sister. Pray for a friend. Open a door. Set the table.)

2. Students pair up. Each student chooses an action that shows kindness. Student lies down on butcher paper, posing as if performing that action. Partner traces body outlines with crayon. Then partners switch roles. Students cut out their body outlines.

3. Students fill in details (hair, faces, clothing, etc.) using markers, and then they tape outlines to walls in classroom or hallway. Students add construction paper objects (ball, door, table, etc.). Conversation balloons may be added to show words that match the actions.

Options

1. If you have mostly younger students, demonstrate activity with one student before forming pairs or lead students to make several outlines for groups of four to five students to color in.

2. Tape a long length of butcher paper to wall, low enough for students to work on. Using a strong light source (film or overhead projector, strong flashlight, halogen lamp, etc.), students cast shadows that are traced onto butcher paper by a partner and then complete activity as described above.

3. Provide additional materials (fabric scraps, wall paper samples, ribbon or yarn, etc.) to be added to outlines.

• •

Discussion Questions

1. *What could happen if your words and actions don't match?* (Others would be confused about what you believe. Other people wouldn't believe what you say.)

2. *What are some actions someone has done to show goodness to you?*

3. *What are some actions you could do this week to show goodness to someone else?* (Play fairly in a game. Carry in the groceries. Let a friend have first choice.)

Worship Center

Bible Verse

Let us not love with words or tongue but with actions and in truth. 1 John 3:18

When we make sure that both our words and actions show goodness to others, we show God's goodness. Let's worship God and praise Him for His goodness.

Materials

Bible, *God's Kids Grow* cassette/CD or music video and player, "Goodness!" word chart (p. 469 in this book), large sheet of paper on which you have printed 1 John 3:18 with five to seven incorrect words in place of correct words, masking tape, marker.

Sing to God

Play "Goodness!" encouraging students to sing along with the music. **What does this song tell us goodness means?** (Showing fairness. Keeping promises. Telling the truth.) **What will make our goodness grow?** (Obeying God.)

Hear and Say God's Word

Read 1 John 3:18 aloud from your Bible. Display paper on which you have printed 1 John 3:18. Ask a volunteer to read the verse aloud. **This verse tells us our actions show our love for others. What are some actions a kid your age could do to show love for God and others?** (Read God's Word. Be kind to brothers and sisters. Share toys with others. Pray to God.) Display paper on which you have printed 1 John 3:18. Ask a volunteer to read the verse aloud from verse paper. **Some of the words on this paper are wrong.** Read the verse aloud and ask a volunteer to cross off one of the incorrect words and write the correct word above it. Repeat until all the words have been corrected.

Pray to God

List students' prayer requests on back of 1 John 3:18 paper. Volunteers each select one item from the list for which to say a sentence prayer. Close by thanking God for His help in showing goodness.

Options

1. Sing "Read All About It" (p. 483 in this book) with students.

2. Provide rhythm instruments for students to play while singing the song(s).

3. Record students' prayer requests and items for which they wish to thank God in a prayer journal to which you can refer each week. Ask students to tell of answers to prior prayer requests.

Bible Verse Coloring Center

Materials

Crayons or markers, a copy of page 209 or page 210 from *Bible Verse Coloring Pages #2* for each student.

Lead the Activity

Read 1 John 3:18. **How might the children in this picture show God's love to each other? What are some other games you play with your friends in which you can show God's love? How?** Students color picture.

Option

Use a paper cutter to cut construction paper into small squares and triangles. Students use glue sticks to glue paper squares and triangles to fill in the picture instead of coloring.

Service Project Center

Materials

Materials needed for "Toy Shine!" (p. 31 from *The Big Book of Service Projects*).

Lead the Activity

Students complete "Toy Shine!" activity as directed in *The Big Book of Service Projects*. **What are some other things we could do in our church to show goodness? What are some actions and words that might show goodness at school?**

Discipleship Activity Center

Materials

Discussion Cards for Galatians 5:22,23 (pp. 147-152 from *The Big Book of Christian Growth*), materials needed for "Knock It Down" or "Discussion Dots" (p. 21 or p. 61 from *The Big Book of Christian Growth*).

Lead the Activity

Today we're going to play a game about the fruit of the Spirit to help us talk about ways of showing goodness in our lives. Students complete activity as directed in *The Big Book of Christian Growth*.

Brave and Faithful

Bible Verse

Even a child is known by his actions, by whether his conduct is pure and right. Proverbs 20:11

Bible Story Reference

Daniel 3

Teacher's Devotional

Character Builder

Acting in ways that demonstrate belief in God shows faithfulness.

If ever young people were known by their actions, they were Hananiah, Mishael and Azariah. True, we also remember them for the uniqueness and rhythm of their Babylonian names: Shadrach, Meshach and Abednego. But as young men, their lives were marked by courageous faithfulness to their convictions. At the time of the famous incident of the fiery furnace, they had been appointed administrators in the Babylonian government on the recommendation of their friend Daniel. After the incident, they were given promotions by King Nebuchadnezzar.

Nebuchadnezzar gave these three a remarkable tribute shortly after being furious with rage at their defiance: "They trusted in [God] and defied the king's command and were willing to give up their lives rather than serve or worship any god except their own God" (Daniel 3:28). It would have been so easy to go along with the crowd and bow down to the king's image. Instead, these young men were faithful when it really counted.

While the three Hebrew youths earned their remarkable reputation through an unusual and dramatic situation, even the youngest child in your class has also earned a reputation by his or her actions. You, too, have come to be known to these same children, as they have formed very real and very strong opinions about the kind of person that you are. Each person's actions are observed by others, and it is these actions that form the basis of judgments that people make. The person who is faithful not only has a good reputation but also a great reward.

Bible Story Center

Materials
Faithfulness poster from *Poster Pack*; ¼ cup (2 oz.) play dough and paper clip for each student.

Tell the Story
Follow along with me as we use our dough to tell today's story.

What's the tallest thing you have ever seen?

Today we'll hear about something very tall that was built for a very interesting reason!

1. **Use part of your dough to make three small figures.** Near the end of Old Testament times, many of God's people were taken to the country of Babylon. Three of these people were young men who were given the Babylonian names of Shadrach (SHAD-rak), Meshach (MEE-shak) and Abednego (uh-BED-nee-goh). These three had been trained to serve King Nebuchadnezzar, and now they were officials in his court.

2. **Make a big figure like a statue and another figure like a king from the rest of your dough. Use a paper clip to make a pattern on the statue.** One day, King Nebuchadnezzar decided to have a statue built. It wasn't any ordinary statue. It was going to be HUGE—90 feet (27 m) high! It was going to be covered with gold; and besides that, it had a very interesting purpose: King Nebuchadnezzar expected everyone to BOW and PRAY to the statue!

When the statue was finished, the king called all the officials of his kingdom to come to see it. Shadrach, Meshach and Abednego were part of the crowd. A royal messenger stood up and told the crowd: "This is what you are commanded to do: As soon as you hear the music, you must bow down and WORSHIP the statue that the king has set up. Whoever does not fall down and worship will be thrown into a blazing furnace!"

WELL! Bow down and worship a statue of gold? Shadrach, Meshach and Abednego could hardly believe their ears! If they obeyed the king and worshiped the statue, they would be disobeying God. God had told His people to worship ONLY Him and NOTHING ELSE! But if they did NOT worship the statue, they would be thrown into the fire.

3. **Use your figures to act out the story.** The music began. Everyone around Shadrach, Meshach and Abednego bowed

low and worshiped the golden statue. But the three friends stood tall. When the king heard that the men had not bowed to his statue, he flew into a rage!

When the three men were brought to the king, he asked angrily, "Is it true you refused to worship the statue? I'll give you one more chance. Bow down before my statue or you will be thrown into the furnace. THEN who can save you?"

Shadrach, Meshach and Abednego looked up at the king. "O king," they said, "if we're thrown into the furnace, our God is able to rescue us. But even if He does not, we want you to know, O king, that we will NOT worship your image of gold!"

4. **Make your statue into a "7."** When King Nebuchadnezzar heard their words, he was FURIOUS! "Make the furnace SEVEN times hotter than normal. Then tie up these three and THROW them in!"

The furnace was SO hot that the soldiers who threw the friends into the furnace DIED just from the heat! Shadrach, Meshach and Abednego fell, tied up, into the flames. The king and his officers watched. Suddenly, the king leaped to his feet. "Didn't we tie up THREE men and throw them into the furnace? Look!" he exclaimed. "I see FOUR. They are not tied. They are walking around! They don't look like they are being burned at all. And the fourth man looks like a . . . a GOD!"

King Nebuchadnezzar called out, "Shadrach, Meshach and Abednego, servants of the true God, come out!"

And out they walked, cool and calm! Not only were they alive and well; but their hair was not burnt, their clothes weren't scorched, and they didn't even SMELL like smoke!

King Nebuchadnezzar praised God and declared, "From this day forward, NO ONE may speak evil about the God of Shadrach, Meshach and Abednego!"

The three friends obeyed God, no matter what! Their faithful actions caused everyone in Babylon to honor God!

. . . .

Focus on the Fruit
Why did the king have the statue made? (For people to bow to it and worship it.)
What did the three friends do? (Stayed standing.) **How would you describe these three men?** (They wanted to love and obey God, no matter what.)

Every day we can make choices that will show how much we love and obey God. When we show our love and obedience to God, it helps others see our belief in Him. Show the Faithfulness poster. **That's a way to grow faithfulness!**

Fruitful Lives Object Talk

Memory Verse

Even a child is known by his actions, by whether his conduct is pure and right.
Proverbs 20:11

Materials

Bible with bookmark at Proverbs 20:11, star cut from yellow construction paper or fabric.

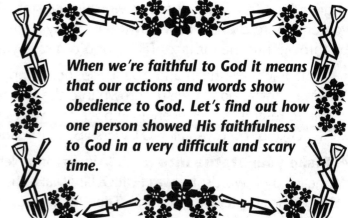

When we're faithful to God it means that our actions and words show obedience to God. Let's find out how one person showed His faithfulness to God in a very difficult and scary time.

Lead the Activity

1. Show yellow star. **When people called Nazis were in control of Germany during World War II, Jewish people were forced to wear stars like this on their clothes. The Nazis wanted everyone to hate Jewish people. Not all of the German people agreed with the Nazis. A German man named Dietrich (DEE-trihk) Bonhoeffer (BAHN-hahf-uhr) dared to help people who wore yellow stars.**

2. **Dietrich Bonhoeffer was a pastor in Germany during World War II. Many other German pastors would not help Jewish people, because they were afraid of Hitler and the Nazi army, but Pastor Bonhoeffer said that this was not right!**

   Pastor Bonhoeffer did more than just say that it was wrong to hate Jewish people; he did what he could to help them. One time Pastor Bonhoeffer helped a group of Jewish people escape from Germany. He had papers that gave him permission to travel in and out of Germany. On one trip, he took some Jews with him. German guards stopped the car, but because of Pastor Bonhoeffer's permission papers, the guards let him leave Germany—along with the Jewish people in his car. Later, the Nazis found out what he was doing and arrested him. While he was in prison, Pastor Bonhoeffer wrote several books about faithfully serving God. Pastor Bonhoeffer was eventually killed because of his actions that showed his belief in God. People today still read the books he wrote and remember how important it is to be faithful to do what is right.

Conclude

Read Proverbs 20:11 aloud. **What are some actions that showed Pastor Bonhoeffer's belief in God? How did this pastor's actions make a difference?** Lead students in prayer, asking God to help them be faithful in showing belief in God.

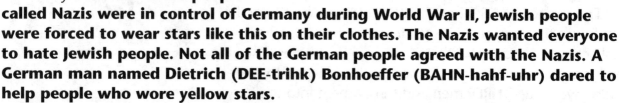

Discussion Questions

1. *How do kids your age show that they believe in God?* (Don't go along with the crowd in doing wrong. Go to church. Read their Bibles. Pray and ask God for help when they have problems. Treat others kindly.)

2. *How do you think your faithfulness to God might help another person?*

Active Game Center: Faithfulness Toss

Materials
Two muffin tins, paper, pencil, coins.

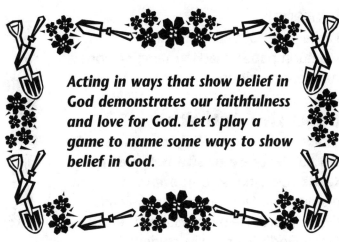

Acting in ways that show belief in God demonstrates our faithfulness and love for God. Let's play a game to name some ways to show belief in God.

Lead the Game

1. Have group line up in two equal teams. Place a muffin tin about 4 feet (1.2 m) from each team. Give one volunteer on each team a sheet of paper and a pencil to record points.

2. Give two coins to the first student in each team's line. Student tosses coins, one at a time, at his or her team's muffin tin. If coin goes into a cup, the team scorekeeper records one point. Continue until each student has had a turn, totaling points after each student's turn.

3. One or two times during the game call "Stop." A volunteer from the team with the most points tells one way to show belief in and faithfulness to God. (Pray to God. Read your Bible. Tell the truth. Tell others about God. Obey God by being kind to others, even when it is hard.) Repeat game as time allows.

Options

1. Instead of using muffin tins, use clean yogurt cups or draw circles on a large sheet of paper.

2. Label small, circular stickers from one to five. Attach a sticker to bottom of each muffin tin cup. Students earn the number of points on sticker.

3. Instead of tossing coins, students place marshmallows or gummy fruits onto plastic spoons and fling them at muffin tins. Score game as above.

Discussion Questions

1. ***How does (praying) show you believe in God?*** (You are trusting God to hear you and answer your prayers.) Repeat question with different actions that show belief in God.

2. ***When are some times you have seen other people show their belief in God?*** Briefly share your own answer before you ask for responses from students.

3. ***How can you show faithfulness to God when you are with your friends? When you are with your family?***

Art Center: Words of Faith

Materials

Large sheet of paper, marker, white construction paper, masking tape, crayons, hole punch, ribbon or yarn.

Lead the Activity

1. **What is something a person can do to show he or she believes in God?** (Do what's right, even when others disobey. Sing praises. Pray. Read God's Word. Help others. Tell the truth. Obey God's Word.) List students' responses on large sheet of paper.

2. Choose one or more responses from list. Assign students one or more letters from the words. Students form their assigned letters by lightly placing strips of masking tape on white construction paper (see sketch a).

3. Using one or more colors of crayons, students draw designs or pictures on the papers, drawing over the masking tape. Students carefully peel off the masking tape to reveal the assigned letters.

We show our faithfulness to God by acting in ways that show we believe in Him. Let's show our faithfulness by making a banner about our belief in God.

4. Students punch holes in the top two corners of their papers. Place papers in order to spell out words, and thread ribbon or yarn through the holes to make a banner (see sketch b). Hang banner(s) in room.

Options

1. Students outline letters using specialty pens (metallic, glitter, neon, etc.).

2. Decorative-edged scissors can be used to trim the edges of the pieces of white paper.

Discussion Questions

1. *What are some other words that mean "faithful"?* ("Trustworthy." "Dependable." "Loyal.")

2. *What are some of the ways you've seen others show their belief in God?*

3. *What are some things you could do this week to show that you believe in God?* (Take time to talk to God at the end of every day. Pray for a friend. Memorize a Bible verse.)

Worship Center

Bible Verse
Even a child is known by his actions, by whether his conduct is pure and right.
Proverbs 20:11

Materials
Bible, *God's Kids Grow* cassette/CD or music video and player, "Good Habits" word chart (p. 467 in this book), large sheet of paper on which you have printed Proverbs 20:11, masking tape.

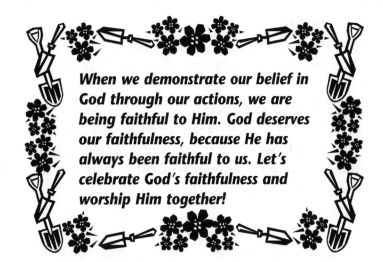

When we demonstrate our belief in God through our actions, we are being faithful to Him. God deserves our faithfulness, because He has always been faithful to us. Let's celebrate God's faithfulness and worship Him together!

Sing to God
Play "Good Habits," encouraging students to sing along with the music. **According to the song, what will practicing good habits do?** (Help us avoid trouble. Please God.)

Hear and Say God's Word
Display paper on which you have printed Proverbs 20:11. Have a volunteer read the verse aloud. **What does it mean for conduct to be "pure and right"?** (Do the right thing. Obey God.) Lead students in reciting the verse together. Then repeat the verse, substituting the name of a student for the words "a child" and "her" for "his" if that student is a girl. The student named then repeats the verse, substituting the name of another student and "her" for "his" if needed. Repeat until every student has had a turn.

Pray to God
Think of something you could do this week that would demonstrate your belief in God. Pray silently to God, asking Him to help you to be faithful in doing that action. End prayer time by thanking God that He is faithful to us and that He will always help us to be faithful to Him.

Options
1. During the verse activity, ask students to list ways of acting that demonstrate a belief in God. Write student responses on the verse paper. Then, before they pray, students may refer to the list for prayer ideas.

2. Invite older students to create their own sign-language motions for the words of Proverbs 20:11. Students demonstrate motions while repeating verse.

3. **The first step in showing faithfulness to God is choosing to believe in Him.** Talk with students about becoming Christians, following the guidelines in the article "Leading a Child to Christ" on page 36.

Lesson 26

Bible Verse Coloring Center

Materials

Crayons or markers, a copy of page 67 or page 68 from *Bible Verse Coloring Pages #2* for each student.

Lead the Activity

Read Proverbs 20:11. **Who is showing God's love in this picture? How? What are some actions you could do to show that you believe in God and want to share His love?** Students color picture.

Option

Students glue completed pictures onto cardstock. Help students cut apart pictures into five or six puzzle pieces. Students put puzzles together. Provide plastic bags in which puzzles may be stored.

Service Project Center

Materials

Materials needed for "Wings of Thanks" (p. 61 from *The Big Book of Service Projects*).

Lead the Activity

Students complete "Wings of Thanks" activity as directed in *The Big Book of Service Projects*. **How do you think this project might show that we believe in God? Why do you think it is good to let other people know what you believe about God? How could knowing what you believe help others? What are some other ways to show that we believe in God?**

Discipleship Activity Center

Materials

Discussion Cards for James 1:22-25 (pp. 165-170 from *The Big Book of Christian Growth*), materials needed for "Musical Chairs" or "What Would You Do?" (p. 64 or p. 53 from *The Big Book of Christian Growth*).

Lead the Activity

We can show the fruit of faithfulness in the ways we talk to others. Today we're going to play a game to help us discover good ways to speak. Students complete activity as directed in *The Big Book of Christian Growth*.

Paul's Gentle Words

Bible Verse

The Lord's servant must not quarrel; instead, he must be kind to everyone, able to teach, not resentful. Those who oppose him he must gently instruct. 2 Timothy 2:24,25

Bible Story Reference

Acts 17:16-34

Character Builder

We can show God's love through attitudes and words that are gentle and respectful.

Teacher's Devotional

Books do not get any more practical and down-to-earth than the Bible. As we read its pages, we do more than gain marvelous glimpses into the nature of God and His glorious purposes for all of creation. Before we have a chance to sit back and admire the heavenly view, the Book brings us back to our present reality.

For example, just a few pen strokes after listing the fruit of the Spirit that God wants to nurture in all of our lives, the apostle Paul jolts us by telling us what to do "if someone is caught in a sin" (Galatians 6:1). The ink was probably not even dry on the words "love, joy, peace" (in Greek of course) when Paul was writing about what to do when one of us is hateful, discontent or causing trouble. Once again, we see that God knows better than we do what real life is like.

It is certainly comforting to notice that the person who fails to show the fruit of the Spirit is not summarily banished from the fellowship. Instead, he or she is to be restored. And notice which of the fruit of the Spirit is to be demonstrated in this restoration: gentleness. Paul writes that "you who are spiritual should restore him gently" (Galatians 6:1).

Paul could have appealed to us to do this lovingly or patiently or kindly. But he chose to remind us of the fruit of gentleness. Gentleness is an inner attitude that results in outward behavior that does not impose on others but accepts them as they are. What could be a more fitting manner in which to help an imperfect person return to spiritual health? And what could be a more fitting fruit to demonstrate to the students in your class? Your sincere acceptance of each child will do more to explain the fruit of gentleness than even the most persuasive words.

Bible Story Center

Materials

Gentleness poster from *Poster Pack*, ¼ cup
(2 oz.) play dough for each student.

*What big cities have you visited?
What kinds of things did you see?*

*Today we'll find out what kinds
of things Paul saw when he
visited a big city!*

Tell the Story

**Follow along with me as we use our
dough to tell today's story.**

1. **Make six fat cylinders for pillars. Place a rectangle
on top.** The city of Athens is a big, important city. It is the cap-
ital of the country of Greece. Athens is also a very, VERY old
city. Even in Bible times, the city was old! Athens was famous
for its big harbor. Many ships came to Athens, bringing things
to sell and bringing people, too. It was famous for its many theaters, temples and statues. Athens was also well known as a city
where people came together to talk about new ideas.

One day Paul, a follower of Jesus, came to Athens. Paul had
never been to this big city before. As he walked through the
streets, he saw beautiful buildings. He saw theaters where plays
were acted out. He saw marketplaces full of colorful things to
buy. But what interested Paul MOST was the fact that there
were so many statues. Most of these statues weren't meant to
be only beautiful decorations. They were meant for people to
PRAY to. These statues were IDOLS—false gods!

Because of all the idols in this city, Paul could see that
these people DIDN'T know about the one true God. They worshiped MANY false gods. Paul felt very sad as he walked
through the streets of the beautiful city. NO one seemed to
have heard about Jesus, who had come to take the punishment
for the sins of ALL people—even the people of Athens!

So what do you think Paul did? He started talking to
EVERYBODY! Everywhere he went, he told anyone who would
listen all about Jesus—about how He is God's Son who died on
the cross and how He rose again so that people could be forgiven for their sins and become part of God's family.

2. **Make one or two things God has created.** Pretty soon, the news had spread all over Athens that there was a man in town who had some NEW IDEAS! A group of men who spent most of their time talking about new ideas came and listened to Paul. After they had heard Paul speak, they asked Paul to come to the Areopagus (ahr-ee-AH-puh-guhs) and talk to everyone in their group. The Areopagus was the place where the leaders of Athens met to make important decisions.

Of course, Paul went! He stood up in the meeting of these men who worshiped so many gods. Now Paul COULD have told the people that their beliefs were all wrong. He COULD have made fun of what they believed. But instead, Paul showed his respect for them by speaking kindly.

"I can see that you are very religious people," Paul said. "As I've walked around your city, I have seen statues and places to worship EVERYWHERE. I even found a place where you worship the god you call 'the unknown god.' I can tell you all about this God you don't know!

"This God made the world and everything in it. He made the trees, the mountains, the rocks and sky. He made all of us! Everything belongs to Him—the one true God.

"The one true God has a message for you: He wants you to stop sinning and do right. He has made a way for you to do this. He sent Jesus, the One He had promised to send. This same Jesus died, but God raised Jesus from the dead!"

Some people didn't want to listen to Paul's words. But when Paul left the meeting, others went with him to learn more about Jesus. It wasn't long before these people believed the good news that Jesus is God's Son who died to pay for everyone's sins and that He lives again. They became part of God's family, too! Because Paul had told the good news of Jesus by speaking gently and respectfully, God's family grew and grew in the huge and ancient city of Athens!

• •

Focus on the Fruit

What did Paul see when he came into Athens? (Places to worship many gods.) **What did Paul do?** (Told many people about the one true God and about Jesus.) **How did Paul act when he told the people of Athens about God?** (Gently. He showed respect for them.)

Every day we meet people we can treat with gentleness and respect. Even when it's hard to show respect to others, God will help us be kind and grow the fruit of gentleness in our lives. Show the Gentleness poster.

Lesson 27
Fruitful Lives Object Talk

Bible Verse
The Lord's servant must not quarrel; instead, he must be kind to everyone, able to teach, not resentful. Those who oppose him he must gently instruct. 2 Timothy 2:24,25

Materials
Bible with bookmark at 2 Timothy 2:24,25; photograph of a newborn baby.

Our gentle and respectful words and attitudes show God's love to others. Let's find out about a woman who was gentle and respectful, even though she didn't agree with what others were doing.

Lead the Activity
1. Show photograph of baby. **How do people usually treat a newborn baby?** Students respond. **Many years ago, people in a village in Africa felt afraid when they saw babies who were twins. These people believed that twin babies were evil and should be killed. The people wouldn't even walk on a road on which a mother of twins had walked!**

2. **In 1876, a woman named Mary Slessor lived near this village. Mary wanted to help the people there learn about God's love. One day, Mary heard that twins had been born in the village. Mary quickly ran through the jungle to the village, hoping to save the lives of the babies. When Mary arrived, one of the babies was already dead, but the other one was alive. Mary gently took the baby and started walking back with the baby's mother to Mary's house.**

   As she was walking on the road, however, Mary realized that if the mother walked on the road, no one in the village would ever come to her house again to hear the good news of God's love. So instead of ignoring the people's beliefs, Mary respected them and had a path cut through the jungle straight to her house. Mary took care of the baby, and soon many people in the village learned to love the baby, too. And best of all, because of Mary's gentle actions, the people kept coming to her house and learned about God's love for them!

Conclude
Read 2 Timothy 2:24,25 aloud. **People who love God are sometimes called servants. What should God's servants be like?** Students respond. **Let's ask God to help us remember to use words and attitudes that are gentle and respectful.** Lead students in prayer.

• •

Discussion Questions
1. *When has someone treated you gently and respectfully? What did they do? What did you do?*

2. *Why do you think God wants us to treat others gently and respectfully?* (Because He loves all people.)

Active Game Center: Human Pretzel

Materials
Bible.

Lead the Game

1. Divide class into groups of six to eight students each. Each group stands shoulder-to-shoulder in a circle, facing inward.

2. Students hold hands and then tangle the circle without letting go of each other's hands. Students may step over hands, move under raised arms, etc.

3. **Now see if you can get untangled without letting go of each other's hands! Remember to work together and use gentle, kind and respectful words while you are untangling!** Students gently untangle themselves. (Note: Students do not need to be facing the same direction after being untangled.)

We can show God's love through attitudes and words that are gentle and respectful. Let's try to use gentle and respectful words to help each other out of a tangled situation!

Options

1. Model conversation by using a kind tone as you walk between the groups and suggest ways for students to get untangled. (For example, "Sam, what if you lift your hand up and over Jill's head?")

2. After older students have completed the activity once, they may regroup and race against each other in the untangling process. Remind students to use gentle and respectful ways of talking about what to do.

● ●

Discussion Questions

1. *What are some gentle and kind words you like to hear?* ("Thank you." "Sorry." "You can have the first turn." Words that are encouraging instead of bossy. Words that show we care about the other person.) *When is it hard to use kind and gentle words?*

2. *Why is it important to have gentle and respectful attitudes when we are trying to show God's love to others?* (Love is gentle and kind. Arguing with people doesn't help them to know about God's love.) Ask an older student to read 2 Timothy 2:24,25 aloud.

3. *Think of one person you would like to have a more gentle and respectful attitude toward. What is a way you can show gentleness to that person this week?*

Art Center: Clip Art

Materials
White paper, markers, scissors, glue, construction paper in a variety of colors.

Lead the Activity

1. Students fold white paper in half lengthwise. **What are some pictures or symbols that remind you of God's love?** (Hearts. Crosses. Bibles.) Students use markers to draw symbols along the fold (see sketch a). Encourage each student to draw at least one open Bible.

2. Students cut along the outer edges of their symbols, leaving at least ¼ inch (.625 cm) of paper above the fold (see sketch b). Students then open the shapes. Students glue cut-out shapes to one side of construction paper and glue cutaway paper to the other side of the construction paper (see sketch c).

When our attitudes and words are gentle and respectful, we are showing God's love. Today we're going to make reminders to show God's love through gentleness and respect.

Options

1. Provide metallic pens, white pens, neon pens or construction-paper crayons to decorate the construction paper.

2. Cover completed designs with clear Con-Tact paper. Punch hole at top of design and insert yarn length. Tie yarn in bow and use to hang design on wall.

3. On open Bible symbols, students write short sentences about showing God's love and gentleness ("Show God's Love," "God's Love Is Gentle," "Have a Gentle Day," etc.).

Discussion Questions

1. **When is a time a kid your age might need to use words that are gentle and respectful?** (When someone else is angry. When someone else is hurt.)

2. **What does a gentle and respectful attitude look like and sound like?** (A smiling face. A quiet voice. Hands at sides or reaching to help. Helpful words. Quietly letting someone else have the first turn. Listening carefully.)

3. **What are some things we can do to help us be gentle and respectful to others and show God's love?** (Ask for God's help. Read His Word. Think before speaking. Think about the other person's feelings. Be a friend to someone who is shy or lonely.)

Worship Center

Bible Verse

The Lord's servant must not quarrel; instead, he must be kind to everyone, able to teach, not resentful. Those who oppose him he must gently instruct.
2 Timothy 2:24,25

Materials

Bible; *God's Kids Grow* cassette/CD or music video and player; "Gentle Servant" word chart (p. 463 in this book); large sheet of paper on which you have printed 2 Timothy 2:24,25, leaving index-card-sized blanks for the words "quarrel," "kind," "teach," "resentful" and "gently"; index cards; marker; masking tape; optional—removable tape.

We can show God's love when our words and actions are gentle and respectful. Let's thank God for His love for us and the ways He helps us show kindness and gentleness to others.

Prepare the Activity

Print on a separate index card each of the words you left off the verse paper.

Sing to God

Play "Gentle Servant," encouraging students to sing along with the music. **What can we do to show God's love with gentle words and actions?** (Love others in the way that Jesus loves them. Say kind words. Treat others better than we want to be treated. Don't argue.)

Hear and Say God's Word

Display paper on which you have printed 2 Timothy 2:24,25. Have a volunteer read the verses aloud, skipping over the blanks. Distribute index cards to several volunteers. One at a time, volunteers hold up their index cards. Students guess where to insert words. Lightly tape each index card to the paper, moving cards as needed until all words are placed correctly. (Optional: Use removable tape.) Lead the group in reading the verses together. **How does 2 Timothy 2:24,25 tell us to act? When is a time you can act in one of these ways?**

Pray to God

Let's ask God for His help in treating others with gentleness and kindness. Students repeat these words after you: **God, please help us to use loving words and show respect to all the people You have made. We love You. Amen.**

Option

At the beginning of this Worship Center, ask a student to read aloud Psalm 28:6,7 as an invitation to worship God.

Bible Verse Coloring Center

Materials

Crayons or markers, a copy of page 197 or page 198 from *Bible Verse Coloring Pages #2* for each student.

Lead the Activity

Read 2 Timothy 2:24,25. **What do these verses tell us to do? How can you obey the instructions in these verses this week?** Students color picture.

Option

Provide blank sheets of paper. Students draw and color their own birdhouses.

Service Project Center

Materials

Materials needed for "New-Kid-at-Church Kit" (p. 24 from *The Big Book of Service Projects*).

Lead the Activity

Students complete "New-Kid-at-Church Kit" activity as directed in *The Big Book of Service Projects*. **Our kind and gentle actions can help people in many different kinds of situations. What are some situations in which your kind and gentle actions can help others older than you? Younger than you?**

Discipleship Activity Center

Materials

Discussion Cards for Matthew 6:9-13 (pp. 117-122 from *The Big Book of Christian Growth*), materials needed for "Candy Toss" or "Count Around" (p. 57 or p. 60 from *The Big Book of Christian Growth*).

Lead the Activity

In Jesus' prayer in Matthew 6:9-13, He teaches us to ask God's help in obeying Him. Today we're going to play a game that will help us think more about this prayer and how to show the fruit of the Spirit. Students complete activity as directed in *The Big Book of Christian Growth*.

The Greatest Love Ever

Bible Verse

This is how we know what love is: Jesus Christ laid down his life for us. And we ought to lay down our lives for our brothers. 1 John 3:16

Bible Story Reference

The Gospels

Teacher's Devotional

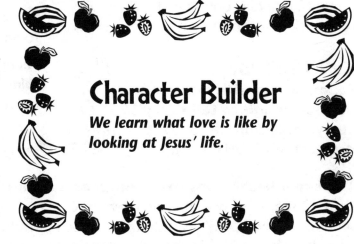

Character Builder

We learn what love is like by looking at Jesus' life.

The writers of Scripture used many devices to emphasize and clarify truths. One of the most commonly used devices was parallelism. The writer would present an important idea twice, giving us parallel statements that either expanded or contrasted with each other. Paul used contrasting parallels in presenting the fruit of the Spirit by first listing for us their opposites, "acts of the sinful nature" (Galatians 5:19). Thus if you are not certain what Paul had in mind by saying that the first fruit of the Spirit is love, you can look back a few verses and see the opposite qualities. Recognizing the opposites of a virtue helps clarify our understanding of that virtue.

Since Paul did not attempt to make a one-to-one connection between each fruit of the Spirit and each act of the flesh, we can find plenty of actions in Paul's list that strike us as obviously being the opposite of love: "hatred, discord, jealousy, fits of rage, selfish ambition, dissensions, factions and envy" (Galatians 5:20,21). Looking over the rest of the list, we can easily see how each of those actions is also unloving, as each is the behavior of someone seeking personal pleasure rather than caring for the needs of others. So since love is the opposite of the actions in that list of negatives, what does the list tell us about love? Would anyone be surprised to know that Paul also wrote the answer to that question in 1 Corinthians 13?

"Love is patient, love is kind. It does not envy, it does not boast, it is not proud. It is not rude, it is not self-seeking, it is not easily angered, it keeps no record of wrongs. Love does not delight in evil but rejoices with the truth. It always protects, always trusts, always hopes, always perseveres. Love never fails" (1 Corinthians 13:4-8).

And if that's not enough, we can look at the best example of what love really is: "Jesus Christ laid down his life for us" (1 John 3:16).

Bible Story Center

Materials

Love poster from *Poster Pack*; ¼ cup (2 oz.) play dough and toothpick for each student.

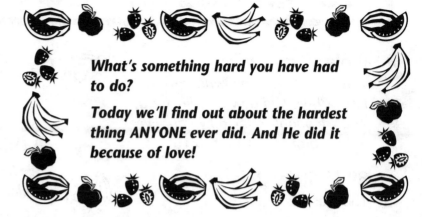

What's something hard you have had to do?

Today we'll find out about the hardest thing ANYONE ever did. And He did it because of love!

Tell the Story

Follow along with me as we use our dough to tell today's story. Invite students to tell details of this familiar story.

1. **Make a heart from your dough as a reminder of God's love.** Jesus was the Savior whom God had promised to send for many, MANY years. Jesus had been born in Bethlehem, but He grew up in the little village of Nazareth. The Bible says that as Jesus grew, God, His Father, loved Him and so did everyone around Him. But God had sent Jesus to do more than be a carpenter. Jesus had come to Earth to show God's great love. He showed this love in many different ways.

When He was around 30 years old, Jesus left Nazareth. He was baptized by John who had been chosen by God to announce Jesus' coming. Soon after that, Jesus began to show His love for people in some AMAZING ways! With 12 men who were His helpers, Jesus traveled around Israel. He began to teach in the synagogues where people met together to pray. He taught out in the fields where great crowds of people followed Him and listened to Him tell about God's kingdom.

2. **Make a hand as a reminder of the ways Jesus helped people.** Another way Jesus showed God's love was by helping and HEALING people—people who had every kind of disease you can think of! He made blind people see again. He made people walk who had never, EVER walked before! He spoke, and people who had horrible skin diseases became WELL! He even made some dead people LIVE again! Jesus did all these things to show His love. But that wasn't all He did. There were other VERY important things He came to do to show His love.

One day, everyone was going to the Passover celebration. People were walking to Jerusalem from all over the country! Jesus and His friends were walking, too. But Jesus sent two of His disciples to find and bring to Him a particular young donkey. This donkey was tied up right where Jesus had said it would be. His friends brought the donkey to Jesus and spread their coats over its back. Jesus sat down and began to ride. His friends walked along beside Him. Soon, the news had passed through the crowd: "Jesus is coming!" One person and then another shouted, "Jesus is coming!" Soon the crowd was buzzing with excitement, eagerly looking down the road.

3. **As a reminder of Jesus' entrance into Jerusalem, make a palm branch and draw leaf details on it.** Some people began to spread their coats across the road like a colorful carpet! Other people cut branches from palm trees and laid them on the road or waved them in the air. Jesus rode through the crowd as the people shouted praises to Him. They welcomed Jesus the way they would welcome a KING!

Some people ran on ahead of Jesus into Jerusalem, shouting, "JESUS is coming!" The crowd of people got even BIGGER, shouting and singing, "Hosanna! Hosanna! God bless the One who comes in the name of the Lord!" ("Hosanna" means "Save us!") Jesus rode the donkey through the big gate into Jerusalem. The children danced around Him, singing and shouting praise to Him. But that was not all Jesus had come to do. Now it was time to show His great love in a special way.

4. **Make a cross as a reminder of how Jesus showed His love for us.** Jesus had His friends get a place ready, so they all could eat the Passover meal together. Jesus took water and a towel and washed His friends' feet. It was the job of a lowly servant. He told His friends He wanted them to be servants like He had shown them how to be. It was a way to show love and the way to be greatest in God's eyes.

During the Passover meal, Jesus told His friends something else: one of them would betray Him and He was going to die, as the prophets had said He would. Jesus was going to die because of His great love. He was willing to take the punishment for all the sins, or wrong things, that people had ever done or would ever do—so we could be forgiven and become members of God's family! That is LOVE!

• •

Focus on the Fruit

In what ways did Jesus show love? (Taught people about God. Healed people. Made dead people alive. Washed friends' feet.) **What was the most important way Jesus showed His love?** (Died on the cross, so our sins could be forgiven.)

Jesus said we should be servants like He was when He washed His friends' feet. Sometimes being a servant and helping others isn't easy to do. Show the Love poster. **But when we are part of God's family, we know God's love. And we can ask God to help us have love and to show love, too!**

Fruitful Lives Object Talk

Bible Verse

This is how we know what love is: Jesus Christ laid down his life for us. And we ought to lay down our lives for our brothers. 1 John 3:16

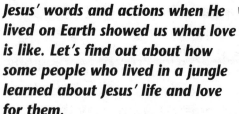

Jesus' words and actions when He lived on Earth showed us what love is like. Let's find out about how some people who lived in a jungle learned about Jesus' life and love for them.

Materials

Bible with bookmark at 1 John 3:16, jungle item (fern, picture of jungle animals from a nature magazine, tape of jungle sounds, rainstick or other artifact, video of jungle scenery, etc.).

Lead the Activity

1. Show and describe the jungle item you brought. **What would you like about living in a jungle? What do you think might be difficult about living there?** Students respond. **One tribe of people who lived in a jungle in New Guinea had a difficult time, because they often fought with another tribe. New Guinea is near Australia.**

2. **A man named Don Richardson, his wife and their little boy went to live in New Guinea and teach these tribes about Jesus. Don learned that one tradition the tribes had for making peace was to give one of their own babies to the tribe with whom they were fighting. That baby was called a peace child. As long as that baby was kept alive and well, the tribes would stay at peace with each other. But if anything happened to the baby, the tribes would be at war again.**

    Don told the people about Jesus by describing Jesus as God's peace child. He told them that God gave Jesus to all people to make peace between God and people forever. After hearing Don's words, the people understood what God's love is like and that Jesus made it possible for sin to be forgiven and for people to live in peace with each other. The people in the village never had to give one of their own children as a peace child again.

Conclude

Read 1 John 3:16 aloud. **How would you describe Jesus' love for us?** Students respond. Lead students in prayer, thanking God for Jesus and for His love for them.

• •

Additional Information for Older Students

Don Richardson has written several books. *Peace Child* tells about the Sawi people and how their lives changed as a result of learning about Jesus. *Eternity in Their Hearts* has many short stories about groups of people from around the world and how they learned about Jesus. (Optional: Bring to class one or more of Don Richardson's books and invite interested students to borrow books for the week.)

Active Game Center: Beat the Ball

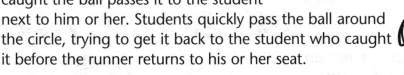

Materials
Foam ball or tennis ball.

Lead the Game

1. Students sit in a circle in the middle of the playing area.

2. Give the ball to one student. Student tosses the ball to any other student in the group. As soon as the student tosses the ball, he or she gets up and begins running around the circle. Student who caught the ball passes it to the student next to him or her. Students quickly pass the ball around the circle, trying to get it back to the student who caught it before the runner returns to his or her seat.

3. Student who gets beaten (either the student who first tossed the ball or the student who first caught the ball) names one thing Jesus did to show love while He was here on Earth. Repeat game as time allows, giving ball to a different student to start each round. Between each round, ask one of the Discussion Questions below.

We learn what love is like by looking at Jesus' life. Let's play a game to think about some of the different ways Jesus showed love.

Options

1. If you have more than 15 students, form two groups to play the game.

2. As a challenge, have older students toss the ball to one another instead of passing it. Each student in the circle must still handle the ball as the runner returns to his or her seat.

• •

Discussion Questions

1. *What are some ways Jesus showed love to people?* (Cared for people's needs. Helped them get well. Gave them food. Was kind to them. Taught them.)

2. *What is one way to show love like Jesus did when you are at school? In your neighborhood?* (Forgive someone when he or she says something rude or mean to you. Invite kids whom other people usually ignore to play with you.)

3. *What might happen if we show love in some of the ways Jesus showed love?*

Lesson 28

Art Center: Palm Prints

Materials

Construction paper, scissors, glue, white paper, crayons.

Lead the Activity

1. **What did people wave in the air and lay on the road to show they were happy when Jesus came into Jerusalem?** (Palm branches.) **Because of this famous event in Jesus' life, what are some of the things palm branches can remind you of?** (Jesus is the King of kings. Jesus loves us so much, He was willing to die for us.)

2. Students cut strips from construction paper and glue them in the shape of a palm branch on another sheet of paper. Placing a sheet of white paper on top of palm branch shape, students rub the long side of a crayon over the white paper. An outline of the palm branch will appear on the paper.

3. Students make several rubbings on the same sheet of paper, trading branch patterns with each other and using different colors of crayon.

When we look at Jesus' life, we learn what love is like. Jesus proved His love when He came to Jerusalem, knowing He would eventually be killed. Let's remember Jesus' arrival in Jerusalem with palm branches like those waved as Jesus rode the donkey into Jerusalem.

Options

1. Students make each palm-branch rubbing on a separate sheet of paper, cut out palm-branch rubbings and tape to walls and/or floor.

2. Students make rubbings by placing large sheets of paper over actual palm branches.

3. Students use palm-branch rubbings to make greeting cards. Students write messages in cards and give cards as a way of showing love for others.

Discussion Questions

1. *What are some examples of love that we see in Jesus' life?* (Jesus loved children and spent time with them. Jesus helped people who were hungry and people who were sick. Jesus died for all people.)

2. *What are some ways we can show God's love to others?* (Be kind to younger kids. Help people who are hungry or sick. Tell others about Jesus and how to become members of God's family. Be kind and show love to brothers and sisters.)

Worship Center

Bible Verse

This is how we know what love is: Jesus Christ laid down his life for us. And we ought to lay down our lives for our brothers. 1 John 3:16

Materials

Bible, *God's Kids Grow* cassette/CD or music video and player, "All My Heart" word chart (p. 453 in this book), large sheet of paper on which you have printed 1 John 3:16, masking tape.

We discover what love is like when we look at Jesus' life. Let's thank Jesus that He gave us such a great example of love!

Sing to God

Play "All My Heart," encouraging students to sing along with the music. **As we learn to love Jesus, what are some of the ways we will treat others?** (Show patience to others. Try to stop arguments. Care about others' feelings.)

Hear and Say God's Word

Display paper on which you have printed 1 John 3:16. Ask a volunteer to read the verse aloud. **What does 1 John 3:16 say is the greatest example of love?** (Jesus' death on the cross.) **What are some ways that we can show love to others?** (Pray for them. Give others first choice. Give up something you want to do so that you can help another person. Be kind even when you feel like being mean to people.) Divide class into three groups. Assign each group a section of the verse. Lead groups in saying the verse in order and standing when it is their turn to say their section of the verse. (Optional: Volunteers choose words in the verse to emphasize by clapping as they say the words.)

Pray to God

What are some of the ways Jesus showed love during His life? Volunteers pray aloud, thanking Jesus for specific times He showed love. End prayer time by thanking Jesus for His example of love and asking for help in showing love to others.

Options

1. Students sing "Read All About It" (p. 483 in this book).

2. Ask an older student to lead the verse activity.

3. To begin the prayer time, ask a volunteer to read 1 Corinthians 13:4-7 aloud. Students name times Jesus showed love in these ways.

Bible Verse Coloring Center

Materials
Crayons or markers, a copy of page 207 or page 208 from *Bible Verse Coloring Pages #2* for each student.

Lead the Activity
Read 1 John 3:16. **How has Jesus shown love for us? How can you show love to people in your family this week?** Students color picture.

Option
Students draw pictures of people to whom they can show love.

Service Project Center

Materials
Materials needed for "Snack Share" (p. 43 from *The Big Book of Service Projects*).

Lead the Activity
Students complete "Snack Share" activity as directed in *The Big Book of Service Projects*. **How did Jesus show love to others? What are some ways we can show love to others?**

Discipleship Activity Center

Materials
Discussion Cards for 1 John 3:16-18 (pp. 171-176 from *The Big Book of Christian Growth*), materials needed for "On-the-Way Relay" or "Draw Straws" (p. 23 or p. 61 from *The Big Book of Christian Growth*).

Lead the Activity
Today we're going to play a game to answer questions about 1 John 3:16-18. We'll learn more about what it means to show God's love. Students complete activity as directed in *The Big Book of Christian Growth*.

Jesus Brings Great Joy!

Bible Verse

Come, let us sing for joy to the Lord; let us shout aloud to the Rock of our salvation. Psalm 95:1

Bible Story Reference

John 18:1—20:20

Teacher's Devotional

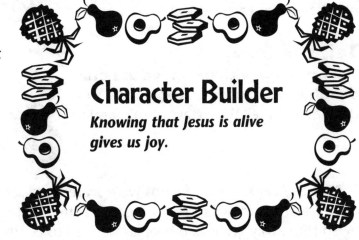

Character Builder

Knowing that Jesus is alive gives us joy.

If given the choice, all of us would probably prefer to sing for joy at times when we feel happy. Joy holds a great attraction for us, because we view it as far preferable to fear or doubt or even amazement. Simple, unadulterated, pure joy seems powerfully appealing.

However, in real life, 100 percent joy is highly unlikely. Such a strong emotion is far too complex to be squeezed into a one-dimensional experience. It is far more likely that we'll experience a mixture of joy and something else, adding a richness that enhances our response to what God has done in our lives.

When Scripture describes times of joy, it goes beyond the simplistic by describing joy as existing together with other emotions, not joy as an idealized state of perfection. As the women left the tomb immediately after meeting the angel, they experienced a strong mix of fear, astonishment and joy. "So the women hurried away from the tomb, afraid yet filled with joy, and ran to tell [Jesus'] disciples" (Matthew 28:8). When the disciples in the locked Upper Room saw the nail prints in Jesus' hands and feet, they were unable to believe that He was alive, not because of stubbornness or resistance, but because of the combination of "joy and amazement." [Jesus] "showed them his hands and feet. . . . [but] they still did not believe it because of joy and amazement" (Luke 24:40,41).

How can it be that a person experiences these very different emotions simultaneously? Perhaps the very paradox of our emotions is God's way of letting us know He is always with us in this far from perfect, very complex world.

Bible Story Center

Materials
Joy poster from *Poster Pack*, ¼ cup (2 oz.) play dough for each student.

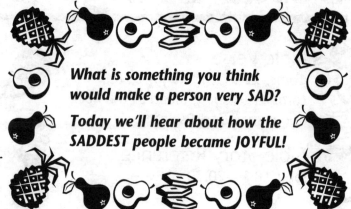

Tell the Story
Follow along with me as we use our dough to tell today's story. Invite students to help tell the details of this familiar story.

What is something you think would make a person very SAD?

Today we'll hear about how the SADDEST people became JOYFUL!

1. **Make a cross.** Jesus' friends were scared and sad. The night before, a crowd of angry men had arrested Jesus and taken Him away. Jesus had been sentenced to death—even though He had done nothing wrong!

   Most of Jesus' friends had run away when Jesus was arrested. But now they stood sadly watching as Jesus died on the cross. *Can't Jesus make this STOP?* they must have wondered. At noon, when the sun should have been brightest, it got dark. Jesus' friends must have felt dark inside, too. They did not understand why Jesus let this horrible thing happen.

2. **Make a hill with a hole in it for a tomb. Cover the hole with a round rock.** After Jesus was dead, two of His friends put His body into a tomb in a little garden. (A tomb was a little room dug into the side of a hill.) A HUGE rock was put in front of the tomb's doorway. Jesus' friends went home feeling VERY sad. Now Jesus was dead. It looked like EVERYTHING had gone wrong. But that wasn't the end. Something more was going to happen!

3. **Move the rock away from the tomb.** On Sunday, the third day after Jesus died, some women who had been Jesus' friends got up at dawn and went to the tomb. When they got there, they could see that the big rock had been rolled away from the tomb's doorway!

One of the women, Mary, didn't know what to think! She ran to get Peter and John, two more of Jesus' friends. Peter and John ran back to the tomb. And when they went inside, they could see that Jesus' body was GONE! The tomb was EMPTY! Peter and John went home wondering what had happened!

4. **Make two angels.** But Mary, who had followed Peter and John back to the garden, stayed there, crying. She stooped down and looked into the tomb again. But NOW it wasn't empty. Now she saw two angels!

One angel asked, "Why are you sad?"

Mary said, "Because Jesus' body is gone. I don't know where He is!"

She turned away from the tomb and almost bumped into someone. *Is this the gardener?* she wondered. But then the person spoke.

5. **Make the letters for the word "joy."** "Mary!" He said. Mary knew that voice—it was Jesus! Jesus was there in front of her, and He was alive! She was so very happy! Jesus said to her, "Go and tell the others."

Mary did! She must have run like the wind! Coming through the door to the house where Jesus' friends were, she said, "Jesus is ALIVE! I've SEEN Him!"

Jesus' friends were amazed! What Jesus had said was true! He DID rise from the dead! He IS alive!

Even though a very SAD thing had happened and Jesus' friends didn't think they would EVER be happy again, God had surprised them! He had made Jesus alive again! God's plan was good! And all of Jesus' friends were filled with JOY!

• •

Focus on the Fruit

Why didn't Jesus stop the people who lied about Him and hurt Him? (He knew it was part of God's plan.) **How did Jesus' friends feel when He died? How did their feelings change?** (SAD when He died. Full of JOY when He was alive again!)

Jesus did the most wonderful thing in all of time for us. He died to take the punishment for our sin. Now He is alive because God raised Him from the dead. When we accept Jesus' love and ask and receive forgiveness for our sins, we become members of God's family. That is good news that fills us with joy! Show the Joy poster. Talk with children about God's gift of salvation, referring to the "Leading a Child to Christ" article on page 36.

Fruitful Lives Object Talk

Bible Verse

Come, let us sing for joy to the Lord; let us shout aloud to the Rock of our salvation.
Psalm 95:1

Materials

Bible with bookmark at Psalm 95:1, keyboard or other musical instrument; optional—CD or cassette of Keith Green's music and player.

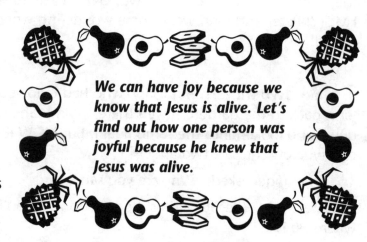

We can have joy because we know that Jesus is alive. Let's find out how one person was joyful because he knew that Jesus was alive.

Lead the Activity

1. Show keyboard or other musical instrument. **What musical instrument do any of you play? How often do you practice your instrument? What do you like most about playing your instrument?** Volunteers answer.

2. **Keith Green started playing instruments when he was only three years old. It didn't take him long to learn to play the piano and write songs. In fact, Keith's songs were recorded and sold when he was still a teenager. He loved music!**

   When Keith grew up, he became a Christian. Knowing about Jesus' love made Keith so joyful that he wanted to love and obey God and to tell everyone he could about Jesus. Keith and his wife, Melody, spent almost every night leading Bible studies for people who had no homes, drug addicts and other people who needed help. But then, because of his love for God, Keith decided to write and sing songs to tell people about Jesus and how to follow Him.

   When Keith was 28 years old, he died in a plane crash. Many of the songs he wrote are still sung today because they tell the truth about what it means to love and obey Jesus. (Optional: Play one or more of Keith Green's songs.) **It's sad to know that Keith Green died, but as Christians we can have joy because we know that Keith is in heaven with a living Jesus.**

Conclude

Read Psalm 95:1 aloud. **When can we do what this verse says? What are some other ways to show that we are joyful because Jesus is alive?** Students respond. **Let's thank God that Jesus is alive.** Lead students in prayer.

● ●

Discussion Questions

1. *Psalm 95:1 tells us to sing for joy to the Lord. When have you sung for joy? How is singing for joy different from singing because you have to?*

2. *What do you know about Jesus that makes you joyful?*

Lesson 29

Active Game Center: Joyful Relay

Materials

God's Kids Grow cassette/CD and player, index cards, marker, two paper bags.

Lead the Game

1. **What are some actions people do to show that they are full of joy?** (Smile. Sing. Jump. Clap. Cheer. High five. Skip.) List each student's idea on two separate index cards to create two identical sets of cards. Put one set in each bag.

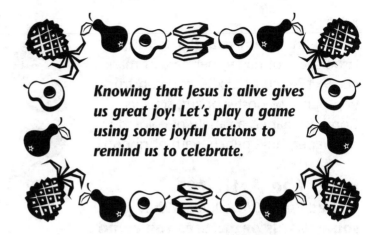

Knowing that Jesus is alive gives us great joy! Let's play a game using some joyful actions to remind us to celebrate.

2. Group students into two equal teams. Teams line up single file on one side of the playing area. Place a bag of cards across playing area from each team.

3. Play "Joy!" from *God's Kids Grow* cassette/CD. When the music begins, the first student on each team runs to the paper bag, takes out an index card, reads action, returns card to bag and performs that action during the entire time it takes to return to his or her team. Student then tags the next student in line. Game continues until each student has had a turn.

Options

1. If you have fewer than eight students, make one set of action cards and one set of directional cards (forward, backward, in a circle, sideways, by the table, etc.). Place each set of cards in a separate bag. Students spread out around the playing area. While you play "Joy!" each student takes a turn picking a card from each bag. The student holds up both cards, so all students can see and perform actions as a group (for example, smile while moving in a circle). Continue until all students have had a turn picking cards.

2. Provide copies of "Joy!" word chart (p. 473 in this book) so that students can sing along with the music as they wait for their turn.

• •

Discussion Questions

1. *What can we do to celebrate the fact that Jesus died for our sins and rose again?* (Sing songs about it. Thank Jesus in our prayers. Accept Jesus' forgiveness and become a member of His family.) Talk with interested students about salvation (see "Leading a Child to Christ" article on p. 36 of this book).

2. *What can we do to share with others the joy that comes from knowing that Jesus is alive?* (Tell them Jesus loves us and rose again because He wants to give us eternal life. Invite them to church on Easter. Ask God to help us show joy to others and explain why we have that joy.)

Art Center: Sun Catchers

Materials

Bible with bookmark at Psalm 95:1, large sheet of paper, permanent markers, 9x12-inch (22.5x30-cm) construction paper or poster board, scissors, Con-Tact paper, a variety of colored tissue paper, hole punch, yarn or ribbon.

Joy comes from knowing that Jesus is alive! Let's make something we can hang in our windows to express our joy that Jesus is our Savior.

Lead the Activity

1. Read Psalm 95:1 aloud. **What are some words or pictures you could make that would remind you that Jesus is alive?** Print student responses on large sheet of paper.

2. Students cut out center of construction paper or poster board to create a frame. Students lay frames on the sticky side of Con-Tact paper, trimming any edges that extend beyond the frame.

3. Students decorate the exposed sticky area with a design of torn tissue paper, covering all exposed adhesive. Then students use permanent markers to decorate the front of the hanging, using words or pictures that remind them that Jesus is alive. Students refer to large paper for ideas as needed. Students punch holes and thread yarn or ribbon through them for hanging.

Options

1. Instead of creating frames, students place objects (tissue-paper pieces, confetti, cut-out letters, etc.) directly on Con-Tact paper and then cover the design with another piece of Con-Tact paper. Students cut the paper into a shape that reminds them that Jesus is alive (heart, cross, etc.).

2. If you have younger students, prepare frames ahead of time.

Discussion Questions

1. *What are some of the ways we can show our joy that Jesus is alive?* (Sing songs of praise. Tell others about Jesus. Pray to Jesus.)

2. *What are some of the reasons we are glad that Jesus is alive?* (Because He died and rose from the dead we can become members of God's family. Now Jesus can always be with us. We know that Jesus will always hear us when we pray to Him.)

3. Read Psalm 95:1 aloud. *Why do you think Jesus is compared to a rock in this verse?* (Because He is powerful enough to be able to help us always.)

Lesson 29

Worship Center

Bible Verse

Come, let us sing for joy to the Lord; let us shout aloud to the Rock of our salvation. Psalm 95:1

Materials

Bible, *God's Kids Grow* cassette/CD or music video and player, "Joy!" word chart (p. 473 in this book), large sheet of paper on which you have printed Psalm 95:1, masking tape.

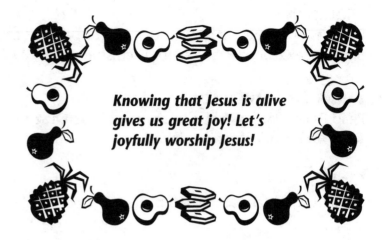

Knowing that Jesus is alive gives us great joy! Let's joyfully worship Jesus!

Sing to God

Play "Joy!" encouraging students to sing along with the music. **What is one reason this song tells us why we can have joy?** (God's love for us. God's gifts to us.)

Hear and Say God's Word

Display paper on which you have printed Psalm 95:1. Ask a volunteer to read the verse aloud. **What does this verse tell us to do?** (Sing and shout aloud to God.) **What reasons do we have today to sing and shout to God?** (Jesus rose from the dead. Jesus loves us. Jesus forgives our sins.) Lead students in suggesting motions for the words of the verse. Lead the group in reciting the verse and performing the motions together.

Pray to God

Print these words on the back of the verse paper: "Thank You, Jesus, that You are alive and have risen from the dead!" Lead students in reciting the prayer together in unison, encouraging students to express the prayer with joyful voices.

Options

1. Bring a portable cassette/CD player with batteries. Lead Worship Center activities outdoors.

2. Teach students the Easter greeting. You (or a volunteer) say "He is risen" and the students reply "He is risen indeed!" Lead students in this several times throughout the worship activities.

3. Provide rhythm instruments for students to use while singing "Joy!"

Bible Verse Coloring Center

Materials
Crayons or markers, a copy of page 37 or page 38 from
Bible Verse Coloring Pages #2 for each student.

Lead the Activity
Read Psalm 95:1. **What are some things that we praise
God for?** Students color picture.

Option
Students glue fabric scraps to picture instead of coloring clothing and puppets.

Service Project Center

Materials
Materials needed for "Easter Celebration" (p. 108 from *The Big Book
of Service Projects*).

Lead the Activity
Students complete "Easter Celebration" activity as directed in *The
Big Book of Service Projects*. **What do you think people who
come to our celebration will learn about Easter? What are
some other ways to help people learn that Jesus is alive?**

Discipleship Activity Center

Materials
Discussion Cards for Psalm 51:1-4,10-12 (pp. 81-86 from *The Big Book of
Christian Growth*); materials needed for "Hopscotch" or "Advice Column"
(p. 63 or p. 37 from *The Big Book of Christian Growth*).

Lead the Activity
**Today we've been talking about showing the fruit of joy. The
game we're going to play will help us discover that we can have joy when we
confess our sins to God and receive His forgiveness.** Students complete activity as
directed in *The Big Book of Christian Growth*.

Isaac Keeps the Peace

Bible Verse

Let the peace of Christ rule in your hearts, since as members of one body you were called to peace. Colossians 3:15

Bible Story Reference

Genesis 26:1-6,12-33

Teacher's Devotional

Character Builder
Working to make peace helps us build friendships.

We often make the mistake of thinking that if we could only remove all the irritants from our lives, we would finally be at peace. However, the much sought-after state of absolute tranquility does not ensure peace. True peace doesn't come from the absence of trouble; rather, it comes from the presence of God.

The Prince of Peace Himself did not live a life free of trouble or conflict. Rather, He triumphed through trouble and conflict to provide for us a right relationship with God, which brings true inner peace.

Long before Jesus demonstrated His rule of peace, the patriarch Isaac showed remarkable strength of character in diffusing a volatile situation. Repeated harassment by Isaac's neighbors seemingly demanded that Isaac stand up for his rights and confront his oppressors. Yet Isaac did not retaliate. Instead, as a man of God who possessed inner peace, Isaac responded in a manner far superior to his neighbors' aggression.

God's Holy Spirit works in our lives to produce peace in even the worst of circumstances. Having called us to peace, God provides the means by which we are able to live up to our calling. Knowing that Jesus has already overcome far worse provocation than we will ever face, we can be confident that His peace will continue to grow in us.

As you teach your students about peace, help them discover not only the practical ways in which our actions can result in peace; but also help them to see that even in situations of seemingly endless conflict with brothers, sisters, friends or classmates, God's offer of peace still stands.

Bible Story Center

Materials
Peace poster from *Poster Pack*, ¼ cup
(2 oz.) play dough for each student.

Tell the Story
**Follow along with me as we use our
dough to tell today's story.**

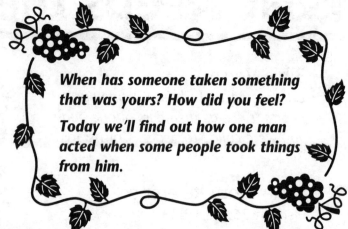

*When has someone taken something
that was yours? How did you feel?*

*Today we'll find out how one man
acted when some people took things
from him.*

1. **Make as many sheep as you can.** One hot and dusty day
in Old Testament times, Isaac, Rebekah, their family and herdsmen trudged along beside their sheep and cattle. There was a
famine where they had been living. A famine is a time when
there isn't enough rain for crops to grow and drinking water
becomes scarce. Isaac and his family were going to the city of
Gerar (JIHR-ahr). Isaac's father, Abraham, had lived there long
before. They hoped that there was still water in the wells Abraham had dug years before.

But Gerar wasn't empty. People called Philistines lived
there. Not long after Isaac and his family arrived, the king of
the Philistines, Abimelech, told his people to leave Isaac's family
alone—and they did, at first. Isaac's family settled down and
planted crops. God blessed their work: They harvested 100
times what they had planted! The number of sheep and cattle
they owned grew and grew!

When the Philistines saw Isaac's BIG harvest and BIG flocks,
they got jealous! Soon they wanted revenge! So they filled with
dirt all the wells Isaac's father had dug! And King Abimelech
told Isaac to move AWAY.

2. **Make a well from small balls.** Even though Isaac, his
family and all his servants had settled in and made themselves
at home, Isaac did what the king asked. He didn't argue; he
didn't try to change Abimelech's mind. He simply moved away
from Gerar and settled in a valley away from the town.

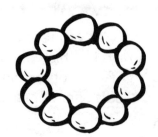

After they looked for a place to set up camp in the valley,
they searched for the most important thing—WATER! Isaac's
men found more old wells that Isaac's father, Abraham, had
dug. After long days of cleaning out the wells, they had water
to drink! They also dug a new well that gave cool, fresh water.

BUT it wasn't long until they had unhappy visitors.

"Didn't we tell you to LEAVE?" the herdsmen from Gerar asked Isaac's men. "THIS is OUR well because this is OUR land," they growled.

The Bible says that Isaac and his people moved on and dug another well in a new place. GUESS who came to take THIS well away? That's right, the herdsmen of Gerar came after them AGAIN and told them to leave!

No doubt some of Isaac's herdsmen grumbled as they packed up to move AGAIN. It wasn't FAIR! They hadn't hurt anybody. But Isaac was determined to keep the peace.

Once again, Isaac and his family, his herdsmen and their families settled at a new place Isaac found. And they began to do the FIRST thing they had to do—dig another WELL. They must have been pretty good at it by now!

But this time, they had moved far enough away. No one came to fight with them over the water! And although Isaac was glad to have some peace, he moved on after a while to a place called Beersheba. There God talked to Isaac and reminded him of His promises to Isaac's father, Abraham. Isaac settled in at Beersheba and guess what they did next? That's right! They dug a WELL!

3. **Make a crown.** Meanwhile, King Abimelech and one of his advisors came to Beersheba. Isaac met them and said, "Why have you come here? You sent me away from your land!"

King Abimelech answered, "We saw clearly that God has helped you. We decided that we should make an agreement with you. Promise us that you will do us no harm because we have never harmed you but only sent you away in peace."

WELL! That wasn't exactly how Isaac remembered it! But he was glad that the king wanted peace. So he made the agreement and made a feast for the visitors. That day, Isaac's servants found water in the newest well they were digging. Now they had water AND peace!

• •

Focus on the Fruit

Why did Isaac's family move? (Famine. No rain. Needed water.) **How did Isaac react when the herdsmen took his wells?** (Didn't fight back. Moved away.) **Why didn't Isaac fight the herdsmen for the wells?** (Wanted to keep peace.) **How did King Abimelech finally treat Isaac?** (With respect. Wanted to make peace.)

Show the Peace poster. **Keeping peace with others isn't always easy, but looking for ways to keep peace often helps us make friends with others. God promises to help us make peace if we ask Him. That's a way to grow the fruit of peace in our lives!**

Lesson 30

Fruitful Lives Object Talk

Bible Verse

Let the peace of Christ rule in your hearts, since as members of one body you were called to peace. Colossians 3:15

Materials

Bible with bookmark at Colossians 3:15, bell or other item used as signal for quiet (whistle, etc.).

When we do our best to make peace, it helps us make friends. Let's find out how one woman worked to make peace and what happened as a result.

Lead the Activity

1. Get students' attention by ringing bell or using other item you brought. **If you were trying to signal a crowd of fighting people to be quiet, what would you do?** Volunteers tell. **In 1932, a woman named Gladys Aylward was asked to quiet down a crowd of fighting prisoners.**

2. **Gladys Aylward had moved from England to China so that she could tell people about Jesus. "People who trust Jesus don't need to be afraid," Gladys said.**

   One day at a nearby prison, a fight among the prisoners was so bad that the soldiers were afraid to go into the prison to stop the fight! The governor of that area remembered what Gladys had said and asked her to make peace among the prisoners.

   Gladys walked into the prison courtyard and shouted for quiet. When the men quieted down, Gladys asked them to tell her why they were fighting.

   "This prison is crowded and the prisoners have nothing to do," the men said. "We fight over food because we don't have enough to eat." As Gladys talked and listened to the men, they agreed to make peace and stop fighting. Then Gladys worked hard to help keep peace among the prisoners. She even found a way for the prisoners to earn money, so they could buy enough food.

Conclude

Read Colossians 3:15 aloud. **When we have Christ's peace in our hearts, it means we do our best to avoid or stop fights and arguments. What can you do to obey this verse at home? At school?** Students tell ideas. **Let's ask God to help us make peace with others.** Lead students in prayer.

• •

Additional Information for Older Students

Before Gladys Aylward went to China, no one thought she would be a good missionary. But Gladys refused to give up her plan to be a missionary. She worked hard and saved money until she was able to buy a ticket to China. In China, God helped Gladys learn to speak the difficult Chinese language and to become a great missionary.

Lesson 30

Active Game Center: Peace Practice

Materials
None.

Lead the Game

1. Students form teams of up to 10 students each. Students on each team form pairs.

2. Assign each pair a letter of the word "PEACE," giving more than one letter to a pair if necessary. Students figure out how to form their letter(s) using their bodies.

3. Pairs on each team line up in correct order to spell "PEACE." At your signal, the first pair of students on each team links arms, moves quickly to the opposite side of the playing area and forms letter. Pair links arms and returns to team.

4. Next pair on team begins as soon as teammates have returned to team. Pairs continue taking turns until each team has spelled the word "PEACE." Ask one of the Discussion Questions below to volunteers from the first team to finish. Continue discussion with other questions. Play game again as time allows, assigning pairs different letters.

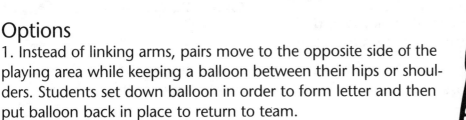

When we work to make peace, we often make new friends. Let's play a game to work together and spell the word "peace."

Options

1. Instead of linking arms, pairs move to the opposite side of the playing area while keeping a balloon between their hips or shoulders. Students set down balloon in order to form letter and then put balloon back in place to return to team.

2. Call out a different way for pairs to move on each turn (back-to-back, hopping on one foot with arms linked, skipping with arms linked, etc.).

• •

Discussion Questions

1. ***When are some times kids your age have to work to make peace at school? At home?*** (When friends are arguing. When brothers or sisters are angry.)

2. ***When have you seen someone else work to make peace? What happened?*** Tell your own example of a situation in which working to make peace resulted in friendship.

3. ***Why might friendships happen when you work to make peace?*** (People like to be around those who are friendly and easy to get along with.)

Art Center: Friendship Square

Materials
Bible with bookmark at Colossians 3:15, large sheet of paper, markers, white paper, scissors, glue, colored construction paper.

Prepare the Activity
Make a sample by following the directions below.

Friendship often results when we work to make peace between people. Let's make and decorate a cut-out of friends to remind us to always try to be peacemakers.

Lead the Activity
1. **What are some ways you could work to make peace between people at school? At home? At the park?** (Stick up for someone being picked on. Help settle an argument between brothers and sisters. Referee a soccer game.) List students' ideas on large sheet of paper.

2. Give each student a sheet of white paper and scissors. Students fold papers diagonally so that edges meet and cut off excess paper to form triangles (see sketch a). Students fold triangles in half. Students draw and cut out figures with legs along unfolded edge (see sketch b).

Cut away shaded areas.

3. Students unfold papers and use markers to draw clothing and features on the four figures (see sketch c).

4. Students glue squares to colored construction paper and print around the outside edges ways they can work to make peace between people, referring to large sheet of paper for ideas as needed.

Options
1. If your students will need help drawing figures, make patterns for them to trace onto folded papers.

2. Play "Peacemaker" from *God's Kids Grow* cassette/CD while students work.

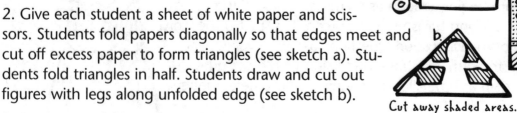

Discussion Questions
1. *When are some times people might need help to make peace?* (When they are too mad to talk to each other. When they don't understand each other.)

2. Read Colossians 3:15 aloud. *According to this verse, from where does peace come?* (Jesus.)

3. *How can we get God's help when we're working to make peace?* (Pray to God. Read His Word. Ask older people who love God for help.)

Lesson 30

Worship Center

Bible Verse
Let the peace of Christ rule in your hearts, since as members of one body you were called to peace. Colossians 3:15

Materials
Bible, *God's Kids Grow* cassette/CD or music video and player, "Peacemaker" word chart (p. 481 in this book), large sheet of paper on which you have printed Colossians 3:15, masking tape.

Let's ask God to show us ways to make peace with others, and let's worship Him for His help and love.

Sing to God
Play "Peacemaker," encouraging students to sing along with the music. **What can you do to be a peacemaker?** (Be kind when someone is arguing with you. Treat others with love and respect. Listen to what people say, even if you don't agree.) **How might these actions help you make friends with others?**

Hear and Say God's Word
What rules do you have to follow at home or at school? What kind of rule does this verse talk about? Display paper on which you have printed Colossians 3:15. Ask a volunteer to read the verse aloud. **God wants the members of His family to follow His rules about living peacefully with others. What can we do to make peace with others?** (Say kind words. Walk away instead of fighting.) Say the verse in short phrases, the students echoing each phrase after you. Invite different students to lead the echo so that students repeat the verse several more times.

Pray to God
Let's ask God's help in making peace with others. Invite students to name people with whom they want to live in peace. Pray, thanking God for His help in making peace.

Options
1. Students sing "Fruit of the Spirit" (p. 459 in this book). Play this theme song every day as students arrive or leave the classroom.

2. During the prayer activity, briefly tell about a time when you made peace with a friend. Invite volunteers to tell examples from their lives.

Bible Verse Coloring Center

Materials
Crayons or markers, a copy of page 185 or page 186 from *Bible Verse Coloring Pages #2* for each student.

Lead the Activity
Read Colossians 3:15. **These children are shaking hands to show that they are friends. What else might kids do to show friendship to others? What actions will help kids make peace?** Students color picture.

Option
Provide sheets of aluminum foil for students to cut or tear and glue onto the mirror in the picture.

Service Project Center

Materials
Materials needed for "Record a Story" (p. 41 from *The Big Book of Service Projects*).

Lead the Activity
Students complete the "Record a Story" activity as directed in *The Big Book of Service Projects*. **How can doing this project be a way to help others discover ways to make peace?** (When people learn about God's Word, they learn ways to show love and live in peace with others.) **What have you learned from God's Word about living in peace with others?**

Discipleship Activity Center

Materials
Discussion Cards for Romans 12:9-14,17-21 (pp. 135-140 from *The Big Book of Christian Growth*); materials needed for "Seat Switch" or "Thumbs Up/Thumbs Down" (p. 69 or p. 70 from *The Big Book of Christian Growth*).

Lead the Activity
Today we're going to play a game to help us discover ways of showing the fruit of peace in our everyday lives. Students complete activity as directed in *The Big Book of Christian Growth*.

The Patient Prophet

Bible Verse

Your hearts must be fully committed to the Lord our God, to live by his decrees and obey his commands.
1 Kings 8:61

Bible Story Reference

Jeremiah 36

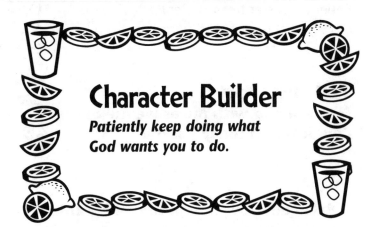

Character Builder

Patiently keep doing what God wants you to do.

Teacher's Devotional

When Solomon led Israel in dedicating the marvelous new Temple, there was an abundance of enthusiasm, eagerness and energy. The event was truly spectacular and stunning. But when Solomon offered a blessing to the people, his focus was not on the beauty of the building, the music or the ceremonies. Instead, he focused everyone's attention on God's patience.

Solomon praised God's patience with His people since the time of Moses (see 1 Kings 8:56,57). Even when the people faltered, God kept on doing what He had promised. Next Solomon prayed for God's patient help in keeping His commands (see verses 57,58). He knew that the people would always need God's help to keep doing what God wanted. Solomon also asked God to attend to the daily needs of His people (see verse 59) as an ongoing testimony to the world (see verse 60). Solomon knew that people were not likely to be impressed with stories of what God had done in the past; they needed continuing evidence that God was with His people. Then came Solomon's final challenge to the people: a full commitment to patiently continue to do what God desires (see verse 61). It is very easy to let our attention jump to the latest fad or eye-catching fashion, so Solomon's call to commit to patient obedience is as timely now as it was then.

Throughout the Bible, we can see one example after another of people who gave their whole lives to God's work in the world. Jeremiah, on whom this lesson focuses, was such a model. Just as Jeremiah patiently reproduced the scrolls that had been destroyed, we must patiently continue to do what is right, not allowing ourselves to succumb to desires for instant fixes to life's problems and challenges.

Bible Story Center

Materials

Patience poster from *Poster Pack*; ¼ cup (2 oz.) play dough and pencil for each student.

Tell the Story

Follow along with me as we use our dough to tell today's story.

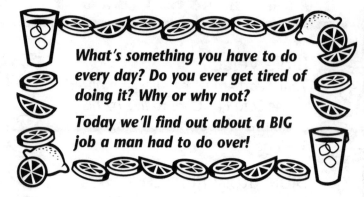

What's something you have to do every day? Do you ever get tired of doing it? Why or why not?

Today we'll find out about a BIG job a man had to do over!

1. **Press out your dough to make a thin rectangle.** The time of the kings ruling over the countries of Israel and Judah was almost over. Because most of the kings had led the people away from obeying God, God had warned that enemies would attack and take the people away. God told a man named Jeremiah to be a prophet and to tell God's messages to the people.

God still loved the people! He wanted to warn them of the terrible things that would happen to them so that they would stop doing what was wrong. God told Jeremiah, "Take a scroll. Write My words on it." Jeremiah sent for his helper, Baruch (BAHR-uhk). Jeremiah spoke the words aloud and Baruch wrote them down.

2. **Roll up both sides to make a scroll.** When the scroll was finally finished, Jeremiah told Baruch to take it to the Temple and read it to the people.

Baruch went to the Temple and read God's words in a loud, clear voice. Some people listened VERY carefully to God's messages. One person who listened was a man who went and told the king about this scroll!

The king ordered one of his leaders to bring the scroll to him. The leader read God's words to the king. The king did not like what he heard. In fact, he was so angry that he grabbed a KNIFE.

3. **Tear pieces off your scroll.** Every time the leader finished reading part of the scroll, the king took his knife and sliced off that part of the scroll. Then he took that piece and threw it into the FIRE! The king watched as each piece burned into ashes. He

didn't care AT ALL about what God said! He wanted to forget all about God's message, and he didn't want anyone ELSE to read God's message! By burning the scroll, he thought he had gotten RID of God's words to His people!

4. **Start over to make a new scroll.** But God's words are important and valuable. God loved these people. He was being patient with them. They needed to know that trouble was coming unless they started obeying Him! So God told Jeremiah to write out the same message again. The new scroll was to have all the words that were on the first scroll—and more besides! What a big job! Jeremiah may have wanted to get angry and quit. But He knew God wanted him to be patient.

Jeremiah and Baruch got a new scroll. Because they wanted to obey God, they patiently followed God's instructions and all the words were written down again!

They also added God's message for the king: God told the king that He knew that the king had cut up the scroll and burnt it piece by piece. But burning the scroll of God's words did NOT mean God's words wouldn't come true! God's message to the angry king told exactly what was going to happen to him and to the people who would not listen.

Jeremiah had patiently done what God wanted him to do, hoping that the king would listen to God. The Bible tells us that the king and the people paid no attention to this message from God.

5. **Roll a ball. Use a pencil to draw a sad face on it.** The sad part of this story is that all the things that God had said would happen DID happen, just like God said they would. The enemies took away most of the people as slaves. Jeremiah had patiently done his job. God had patiently warned His people. But the people had not listened. The trouble that God said would come DID come.

- -

Focus on the Fruit

What did God tell Jeremiah to do? (Write God's words on a scroll.) **What did the king do with the scroll after he listened to its words?** (Cut it apart and burned it.) **How did Jeremiah show patience?** (He did what God wanted him to do, even when it meant repeating a difficult job.)

Show the Patience poster. **To keep doing what God wants can be hard. Sometimes we might even feel like giving up! But when we are patient and keep obeying God, God grows good fruit in us!**

Lesson 31
Fruitful Lives Object Talk

Bible Verse
Your hearts must be fully committed to the Lord our God, to live by his decrees and obey his commands. 1 Kings 8:61

Materials
Bible with bookmark at 1 Kings 8:61, several different versions of the Bible and/or several written in different languages.

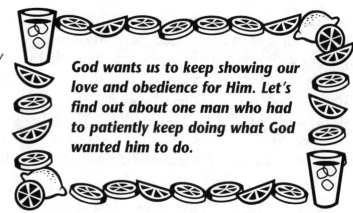

God wants us to keep showing our love and obedience for Him. Let's find out about one man who had to patiently keep doing what God wanted him to do.

Lead the Activity
1. Invite volunteers to examine the Bibles you collected. **In what ways are these books alike? How are they different?** Students respond. **Today the Bible has been written in many different languages so that people all over the world can read God's Word. But a long time ago in the 1500s, the Bible was only written in Latin. Because only a few people could understand Latin, most people couldn't read God's Word for themselves.**

2. **One man, however, named William Tyndale, wanted people to have Bibles they could read. William Tyndale was a teacher who lived in England. But the leaders in England didn't want people to be able to read the Bible for themselves! William didn't let that stop him. He understood Latin, so he carefully translated the New Testament into English. Soon people all over England were buying and reading this English New Testament.**

   The leaders, however, were so angry they bought all the English New Testaments they could find and burned them! William was very discouraged. But then he heard some good news. The money William had earned from selling the English New Testaments to the angry leaders was enough to print even more New Testaments than before! William Tyndale patiently worked to print the English New Testaments over again so that people once again could read God's Word!

Conclude
Read 1 Kings 8:61 aloud. **When we are committed to the Lord, it means we patiently keep doing what's right, even when it's hard. God promises to help us.** Lead students in prayer, asking God to help students patiently continue to obey Him.

• •

Additional Information for Older Students
William Tyndale's first New Testament was printed in 1526. About 10 years later, William was put to death, for his crime of translating the Bible. But within five years of his death, the king of England approved another English Bible (based on William's translation) and required every church to make copies available to the people!

Lesson 31

Active Game Center: Patience Tag

Materials
Masking tape or chalk.

Prepare the Game
Make two parallel masking-tape lines at least 15 to 25 feet (4.5 to 7.5 m) apart and at least 10 feet (3 m) long. (Use chalk if you are playing on asphalt.)

One of the ways we can show the fruit of the Spirit in our lives is to patiently keep doing what God wants us to do. Let's try out our patience during a game of tag.

Lead the Game
1. Choose one volunteer to be "It." "It" stands between the two lines. All other students stand behind one line.

2. At your signal, students run past "It" and across the opposite line, trying not to be tagged by "It." If a student is tagged, that student freezes in place and begins touching his or her head, shoulders, knees and then toes, repeating movements over and over again.

3. At your signal, students who successfully crossed run back to opposite line, tagging any frozen students to unfreeze them. Any new students who are tagged by "It" must freeze in place and repeat the motions until they are freed by another student.

4. Continue giving signal for students to run back and forth between the masking-tape lines. Every few minutes, substitute a new volunteer to be "It." Continue game as time allows.

Options
1. Before beginning the game, give instructions for game, demonstrate the motion that tagged students will repeat and, if time permits, play a sample round.

2. When you choose a new "It," choose a new motion (patting head while rubbing stomach, snapping fingers, marching in place, etc.).

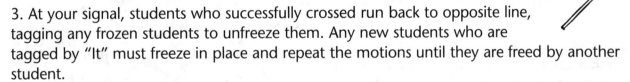

Discussion Questions
1. ***When did you have to be patient while you were playing this game?*** (While repeating the motions and waiting for someone to tag and unfreeze you.)

2. ***What are some of the things we know God wants us to do?*** (Show love to others. Speak kind words to others. Tell the truth. Pray to Him.) ***When would kids your age need patience to keep doing those good things?*** (When they don't feel like being kind. When people aren't being kind to them. When people make fun of them.)

Art Center: Patience Pictures

Materials
Bible with bookmark at 1 Kings 8:61, newspaper, white construction paper, one or more colors of powder tempera paints, ice cubes; optional—paint smocks or adult-sized shirts.

Prepare the Activity
Spread newspaper over work area.

Lead the Activity
Students sprinkle tempera paint on construction paper and use ice cubes as paintbrushes to create abstract drawings or write words that remind them to patiently keep doing what God wants them to do. (Optional: Students wear smocks or adult-sized shirts over their clothing.) **Why do we need patience to paint these pictures?** (Wait for ice cubes to melt.)

We practice patience when we keep doing what God wants us to, no matter what. Let's practice patience as we paint a picture. Our pictures will remind us that we often need patience to keep doing what God wants us to do.

Options
1. Provide craft sticks for students to use instead of their hands to move ice cubes around. (Craft sticks could be frozen into ice cubes ahead of time.)

2. Students work together to create a poster on one large sheet of butcher paper.

3. Students use ice cubes to write and/or draw on sidewalks or outside walls. The words and drawings disappear, and students can recreate them as time allows.

Discussion Questions
1. Read 1 Kings 8:61 aloud. ***What do you think it means to commit our hearts to God?*** (To love God more than anyone or anything.) ***How will this help us to do the right thing?*** (When we are committed to God, we want to please Him in everything we do.)

2. ***What is another word for doing what God wants you to do?*** ("Obeying.") ***When is a time it might be hard to patiently keep obeying God?*** (When friends ask you to do something you know is wrong, or they don't care if you do the right thing or not.)

3. ***What are some things you can do to keep doing what God wants you to do?*** (Pray to God for His help. Talk with others who love God.)

Lesson 31

Worship Center

Bible Verse

Your hearts must be fully committed to the Lord our God, to live by his decrees and obey his commands. 1 Kings 8:61

Materials

Bible, *God's Kids Grow* cassette/CD or music video and player, "Patient Father" word chart (p. 479 in this book), large sheet of paper on which you have printed 1 Kings 8:61, masking tape, blank sheet of paper, marker.

Let's sing to God and thank Him for His help in giving us patience!

Sing to God

Play "Patient Father," encouraging students to sing along with the music. **How does God show His love and patience to us?** (He always forgives us when we ask. He never stops loving us.) **We can ask God for His help in patiently continuing to do what's right.**

Hear and Say God's Word

Display paper on which you have printed 1 Kings 8:61. Have a volunteer read the verse aloud. **How would you say 1 Kings 8:61 so that your friends would understand?** ("Show that you love God more than anything else, always doing what the Bible tells you to do.") Print student paraphrases on blank sheet of paper. Repeat the verse several times, alternating between saying 1 Kings 8:61 and one of the paraphrases students suggested.

Pray to God

When are some times it might be hard for kids your age to patiently keep doing what God wants them to do? (When someone keeps making fun of them. When they're having a hard time at school.) Volunteers pray about situations named, asking God's help to patiently obey Him and love Him. End prayer time by thanking God for His constant love for us and His patience with us.

Options

1. Students sing "Circle of Love" and/or "Just Ask Him" (p. 457 and/or p. 475 in this book).

2. During the verse activity, have an older student find these verses in his or her Bible and read them aloud as examples of God's commands: Micah 6:8; John 15:17; Romans 12:13; Colossians 3:13.

Lesson 31

Bible Verse Coloring Center

FOR YOUNGER CHILDREN

Materials
Crayons or markers, a copy of page 21 or page 22 from *Bible Verse Coloring Pages #2* for each student.

Lead the Activity
Read 1 Kings 8:61. **God helps us to patiently continue obeying His commands. What are some of God's commands that the kids in this picture could obey? What is one command you can obey next time you are playing with other kids?** Students color picture.

Option
Cover tables with newspaper. After coloring picture, students apply glue to playground and then sprinkle sand over glue.

Service Project Center

FOR YOUNGER CHILDREN AND OLDER CHILDREN

Materials
Materials needed for "'Change' a Life" (p. 74 from *The Big Book of Service Projects*).

Lead the Activity
Students complete the "'Change' a Life" activity as directed in *The Big Book of Service Projects*. **Collecting change takes a lot of patience! Sometimes continuing to obey God takes a lot of patience, too. When might doing what God wants us to do take patience?**

Discipleship Activity Center

FOR OLDER CHILDREN

Materials
Discussion Cards for Psalm 146:7-10 (pp. 93-98 from *The Big Book of Christian Growth*), materials needed for "Post-it Pandemonium" or "Go-Fer Game" (p. 24 or p. 43 from *The Big Book of Christian Growth*).

Lead the Activity
Treating others with patience isn't always easy. Today we're going to play a game to help us talk about ways of being patient in hard situations. Students complete activity as directed in *The Big Book of Christian Growth*.

Elisha's Kindness

Bible Verse

Blessed are the merciful, for they will be shown mercy. Matthew 5:7

Bible Story Reference

2 Kings 4:8-37

Teacher's Devotional

We highly esteem, and rightly so, those who respond to someone's needs with acts of kindness. Jesus'

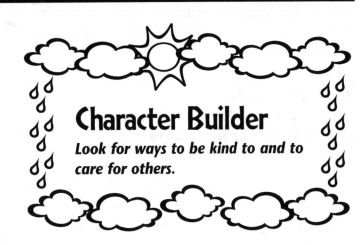

Character Builder

Look for ways to be kind to and to care for others.

story of the good Samaritan is one of the great examples of someone who did not turn away from an opportunity to be a neighbor by showing mercy.

As great as the Samaritan is, however, how much more deserving of honor are those in the Bible who actively sought out a way to be kind to others. King David inquired if there were any surviving relatives of Saul "to whom I can show kindness for Jonathan's sake" (2 Samuel 9:1). A woman of Shunem asked her husband to build a room on the roof of their house for the prophet Elisha (see 2 Kings 4:10). Tabitha (Dorcas) of Joppa "was always doing good and helping the poor" (Acts 9:36). When all seemed comfortable and no urgent concern was at hand, these people went out of their way to look for a kind act they could do to benefit someone else.

The Holy Spirit produces kindness in us—and not just for those moments when we come upon someone with a problem. God also wants to make us people whose nature is marked by kindness. A good test of how we are growing in kindness is whether we are becoming people who seek out others in need. Look for ways you can actively cultivate an awareness of those who need your help, and encourage the students you teach to do the same.

Bible Story Center

Materials
Kindness poster from *Poster Pack;* ¼ cup
(2 oz.) play dough and plastic spoon for
each student.

Tell the Story
**Follow along with me as we use our
dough to tell today's story.**

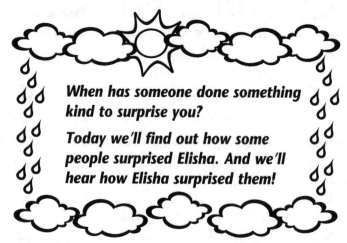

**When has someone done something
kind to surprise you?**

**Today we'll find out how some
people surprised Elisha. And we'll
hear how Elisha surprised them!**

1. **Make a house with a flat roof.** Elisha was a prophet of
God. He traveled from city to city in the country of Israel to
teach people about God and give them God's messages. Elisha
often passed through a town called Shunem (SHOO-nehm).
Whenever he did, a woman who lived there invited Elisha and
his servant, Gehazi (gih-HAY-zi), to eat dinner with her and her
husband.

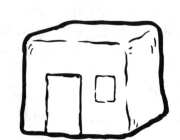

One day the woman said to her husband, "Elisha is a man
of God. Let's build a room on the roof for him. Then he can
stay here whenever he comes."

2. **Make a bed, a table, a chair and a Bible-times lamp.
Use a plastic spoon to shape objects.** The flat roof was a
perfect place to build a guest room for Elisha! His friends put a
bed, a table, a chair and a lamp in the room, so Elisha would be
comfortable. When Elisha came to town, they led him to the
roof and showed him the room they had prepared for him.
Elisha and Gehazi must have been amazed at such kindness!
The room was a wonderful surprise!

As Elisha rested in the room, he asked his servant, "Gehazi,
tell our friend that we're thankful for this wonderful room. Ask
her what we can do for her."

When Gehazi asked her, the woman replied, "Thank you
for asking. But I don't need anything."

Elisha still wanted to show kindness to her somehow. He
asked Gehazi if he had any ideas of ways to do this.

Gehazi said, "She doesn't have a child. Maybe she would
like to have a son to love and care for."

Elisha thought that was a great idea. And God must have,
too! Elisha told the woman that within a year, she and her hus-

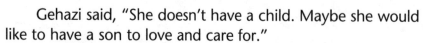

band would have a baby boy. When the baby was born as Elisha had promised, the family was very happy!

3. **Make a little boy, his mom and his dad.** But there was more to this story of kindness! The baby grew into a boy. One day when he was out in the fields with his father, he cried out in pain. "Father!" he said. "My head! My head!" Although a servant quickly carried him to the house, where his mother held him on her lap and rocked him, he soon died.

The boy's mother carried his body to Elisha's room and laid it on the bed. She called for a servant and a donkey and hurried to Elisha's house in the other city as fast as the donkey could go!

Gehazi came out to meet her and asked her if everyone in her house was well. The woman didn't tell him what was wrong. Instead, she hurried into Elisha's house and grabbed his feet. She was VERY upset! She said to Elisha, "You asked God to give me a child," she cried. "Now he is DEAD!"

Elisha gave Gehazi his walking stick and told Gehazi to run back and lay it on the boy. But even after Gehazi left, the woman kept hold of Elisha's feet and said she wouldn't leave without him! So Elisha hurried with her back to her house.

As they traveled, Gehazi came running back to meet them. "I did as you said," he reported, "but he is still dead!"

Elisha hurried to the room where the boy's body lay. He knew only God could make the boy live again. First, Elisha PRAYED! He laid his own body over the boy's until the boy's body grew warm. He did this again, no doubt praying as he lay there! Then the boy SNEEZED seven sneezes! He was ALIVE! The boy's mother came running upstairs. Elisha handed him to his mother. The boy's parents were SO happy!

The couple had shown kindness to Elisha. God had shown kindness to them in return. They must have been glad they had a friend like Elisha, who didn't just talk about God's kindness. He SHOWED it by caring for them and helping them.

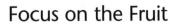

Focus on the Fruit

How did the woman and her husband show kindness to Elisha? (Fed him. Built him a room.) **How did Elisha show them kindness?** (Elisha promised them that God would send them a son. Prayed for God to use His power to bring the son back to life.)

In today's story, people showed kindness in some unusual ways. Show the Kindness poster. **But there are many ordinary ways we can show kindness to each other. Each day we can look for ways to be kind to and care for the needs of others. When we do, we're growing God's good fruit in our lives!**

Fruitful Lives Object Talk

Bible Verse

Blessed are the merciful, for they will be shown mercy. Matthew 5:7

Materials

Bible with bookmark at Matthew 5:7, uniform from a school or sports team.

It is important to always look for opportunities in which we can be kind to and care for others. Let's find out some ways one woman found to be kind to and care for others.

Lead the Activity

1. Show uniform. (Optional: Volunteer wears uniform.) **When do kids your age wear uniforms?** Students tell. **In the early 1900s, school children in China wore uniforms. Schools even had contests to see which school had the best uniform.**

The children in one school, however, were embarrassed because they did not have uniforms like other children. This school was so poor the teachers could hardly buy school supplies. And because the children in the school were orphans (their parents were no longer alive), they couldn't afford to buy uniforms.

2. **Grace Chang was a missionary teacher at this school. She cared for the children at the school so much that she decided to help them get uniforms. Grace planned to use her sewing machine to make the uniforms, but she didn't have any cloth! Grace prayed and asked God to help her.**

God answered Grace's prayer. Soon another missionary gave her some cloth, and Grace started sewing uniforms for the children. Then Grace got women in a nearby village to help make cloth shoes for all the children. (Cloth shoes were typically worn by Chinese children at that time.) Soon the jackets, skirts and shoes were ready. The children excitedly wore their uniforms to school. And when they won the contest for the best uniform, the children were even more pleased!

Conclude

Read Matthew 5:7 aloud. **When we show mercy to others, it means we are kind to them—even when they don't deserve it. What are some ways to show mercy and be kind to others?** Students tell ideas. **Let's ask God to help us find ways to be kind and care for others this week.**

Discussion Questions

1. *Grace Chang used her sewing machine to be kind to others. What could you use to be kind to someone?*

2. *When has someone been kind to you? Why do you think that person chose to be kind? How did you feel as a result of that kindness?*

3. *Who are some people you could be kind to and care for this week?*

 God's Kids Grow Leader's Guide

Active Game Center: Kindness Toss

Materials
Large container, index cards, soft balls or beanbags, marker.

Prepare the Game
Place the container on the floor on one side of the playing area.

With the fruit of the Spirit in our lives, we will look for ways to be kind to others and care for them. Let's try doing that during our game today!

Lead the Game
1. Group the students into teams of six to eight. Teams line up single file about 5 feet (1.5 m) from the container. Give each student an index card. Give the first student on each team a ball or beanbag.

2. Stand near the container with the marker in your hand. Students from each team take turns tossing the ball or beanbag into the container. Each time a student gets the ball or beanbag into the container, print one letter of the word "kindness" on his or her index card.

3. When a student gets all the letters for the word, he or she continues taking turns, giving any letters scored to the next person in line. Continue until all students have "kindness" written on their cards.

Options
1. Adjust according to skill level of the class the distance from which students toss ball.

2. For younger students, play using the word "kind." If time allows, play another round using the word "care."

• •

Discussion Questions
1. *How did we show kindness in this game?* (Gave letters to other people.)

2. *What are some other ways to be kind to and care for others?* (Include everyone in your games. Ask someone to play with you if he or she is looking lonely. Share with others. Help someone or get help for someone who needs it. Use kind words when you speak to others.)

3. *What can you do to discover ways to be kind to others?* (Pray and ask God to help you think of kind things to do. Take more time to notice the people around you instead of just doing your own thing.)

Art Center: Boxed City

Materials

A variety of empty boxes (laundry detergent, shoe, oatmeal, cereal, etc.), colored construction paper, scissors, tape or glue, markers.

Being kind includes looking for ways to care for others. Let's make a model of our town and discuss ways we can show kindness and caring for others.

Lead the Activity

1. **What are some ways to show that we care for others?** Volunteers respond. **What are some places in our town where you could do these things?** (School, church, park, library, store, etc.)

2. Assign pairs of students different buildings in your town or neighborhood. Using empty boxes, students recreate the buildings by covering the boxes with construction paper and decorating them with markers. Students assemble a model of your town or neighborhood with their completed buildings and discuss different ways to show kindness to people in each of the buildings. Ask the Discussion Questions below to extend the conversation.

Options

1. Students use toys and miniatures (furniture, cars, people) to act out ways to show kindness and to care for others.

2. Students use chenille wires to make figures, trees, lampposts and other objects to use in their model town or neighborhood.

3. If you are not able to collect boxes, have students make pencil drawings of their town or neighborhood. Students use markers to color in the places where they would be able to show kindness to others.

• •

Discussion Questions

1. ***What are some ways to show kindness to and care for others at home? At school? At church?*** Repeat question using locations from your model town or neighborhood.

2. ***What are some other ways to care for others?*** (Give first aid or call 9-1-1 when necessary. Give money in the church offering. Help organize and/or donate to a food drive.)

3. ***How can a kid your age look for ways to be kind to and care for others?*** (Pay attention when friends talk about their problems. Get to know your neighbors. Read flyers at school and church to find out about charitable activities. Ask parents or teachers for ideas.)

Lesson 32

Worship Center

Bible Verse
Blessed are the merciful, for they will be shown mercy. Matthew 5:7

Materials
Bible, *God's Kids Grow* cassette/CD or music video and player, "Be So Kind" word chart (p. 455 in this book), large sheet of paper on which you have printed Matthew 5:7, masking tape.

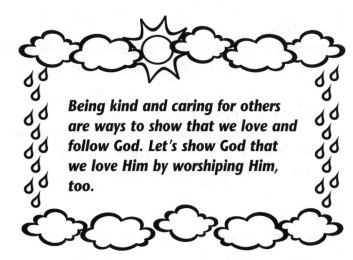

Being kind and caring for others are ways to show that we love and follow God. Let's show God that we love Him by worshiping Him, too.

Sing to God
Play "Be So Kind," encouraging students to sing along with the music. **What does this song suggest as some ways to be kind?** (Give others more than they expect. Put other people first. Be generous.)

Hear and Say God's Word
Display paper on which you have printed Matthew 5:7. Have a volunteer read the verse aloud. **What does it mean to be merciful?** (To show love or forgiveness to someone who has done something wrong. To show more love or kindness than is expected.) Lead students in repeating the verse in this manner: The first time through, clap for each word as you say it. The second time through, say "Blessed" and then clap nine times for the remaining nine words. The third time through, say "Blessed are" and then clap eight times. Continue process until the whole verse has been said.

Pray to God
Let's show kindness to and care for each other by praying. Invite volunteers to tell prayer requests, sharing the ways in which they or their families and friends need God's help. Lead students in prayer, mentioning each request. End prayer time by thanking God that He shows mercy to us and helps us to be kind to others. (Optional: Students form pairs and tell each other a prayer request. Students in pairs pray for each other.)

Options
1. If you have a small group, have students sit in a circle to share prayer requests. Students each pray for the student on their left. If you keep a class prayer journal, record students' requests and any praises or answers to previous prayers.

2. If students give an offering during this worship time, explain that giving an offering is one way to show love for God by caring for those who will receive the offering. Describe several ways in which your church uses the offering to care for others.

Bible Verse Coloring Center

Materials
Crayons or markers, a copy of page 87 or page 88 from *Bible Verse Coloring Pages #2* for each student.

Lead the Activity
Read Matthew 5:7. **Who is showing mercy in this picture? How? What are some ways you can show mercy to others?** Students color picture.

Option
Students glue gauze circles to badminton rackets.

Service Project Center

Materials
Materials needed for "Meals for a Day" (p. 80 from *The Big Book of Service Projects*).

Lead the Activity
Students complete the "Meals for a Day" activity as directed in *The Big Book of Service Projects*. **What else can we do to show mercy to the family we are providing food for? What are some other ways to be kind? What can you do this week to care for people you know?**

Discipleship Activity Center

Materials
Discussion Cards for 1 Corinthians 13:4-8a (pp. 141-146 from *The Big Book of Christian Growth*), materials needed for "Shoe Search Relay" or "Odd or Even" (p. 26 or p. 65 from *The Big Book of Christian Growth*).

Lead the Activity
As we play a game to answer questions about 1 Corinthians 13:4-8a, we'll discover ways to show the fruit of kindness in our lives. Students complete activity as directed in *The Big Book of Christian Growth*.

God's Family Listens

Bible Verse

This is what the Lord Almighty says: "Administer true justice; show mercy and compassion to one another." Zechariah 7:9

Bible Story Reference

Acts 6:1-7

Teacher's Devotional

Anyone who has ever tried to divide a dessert between two children knows that they have a very keen sense of what is fair. Just let one piece be a little bigger than the other, and a child is bound to protest, "That's not fair!" Upon hearing that protest, every adult knows exactly what the next statement will be: "My piece is smaller!"

No one is surprised that the child who complains about unfairness is always the one who feels shortchanged. Why is it that the child with the bigger piece remains silent, not feeling compelled to point out the perceived inequity? Need we even ask that question, since human nature seems so obviously focused on upholding justice and fairness as long as we are the ones benefiting from it?

In contrast, notice God's command to Zechariah in this lesson's Bible verse: "Administer true justice; show mercy and compassion to one another." The Lord makes it very plain what He considers good: true justice linked to mercy and compassion. From God's perspective, goodness is justice that is measured mercifully. Simply distinguishing right from wrong is not enough. Goodness is treating people fairly and compassionately. In other words, we are challenged to seek what is best for the other person and not put ourselves first.

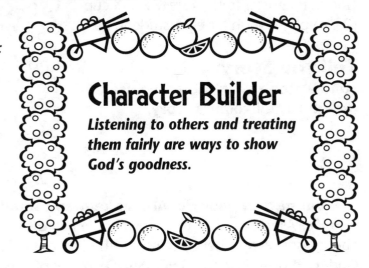

Character Builder

Listening to others and treating them fairly are ways to show God's goodness.

Bible Story Center

Materials
Goodness poster from *Poster Pack,* ¼ cup (2 oz.) play dough for each student.

Tell the Story
Follow along with me as we use our dough to tell today's story.

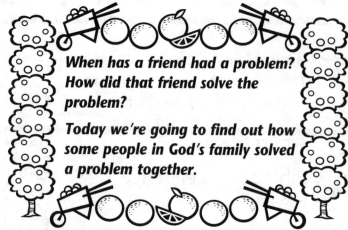

When has a friend had a problem? How did that friend solve the problem?

Today we're going to find out how some people in God's family solved a problem together.

1. **From part of your dough, make many small balls for people.** All over Jerusalem, many people heard the good news about Jesus. People believed Jesus is the Son of God and asked God to forgive their sins. THOUSANDS of people became part of God's family!

These new believers in Jesus loved each other very much. In fact, they cared so much about each other that they didn't want anyone to be hungry or cold or not have the things they needed. All the people in God's church shared the things they owned. Out of the money they had, Jesus' friends, the disciples, bought food and things people needed. Jesus had said that everyone would know members of His family by the way they showed love. That's just what they were doing!

2. **Divide your people into two groups. From the rest of your dough, make some VERY small balls for food.** But in this growing family of God, there were some widows who had a need. (A widow is a woman whose husband has died. In Bible times, widows often had no way to earn money.) These widows needed help to get enough food. They were not from Jerusalem, however; they were from countries where the people spoke Greek.

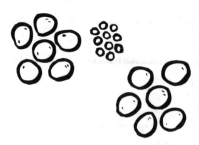

Now the people in the church were already generously giving food and money to anyone who had a need, these widows included. But the problem was this: The Greek widows were not getting as MUCH food as the Hebrew widows—the widows who had always lived in Jerusalem. Maybe it was just because someone forgot. But the Greek widows might have felt it was because they were different. Maybe they felt as if the members of God's family didn't care as MUCH about them as they did about the Hebrew widows.

These Greek widows could have gotten angry. They could have quit meeting with others in their church family. But instead they talked to Jesus' friends about their need.

3. **Divide your very small balls, giving more of them to one group of people than what you give to the other group.** "We're not getting as much food as the other widows," the Greek widows said. "We're not being treated fairly."

Jesus' disciples carefully listened to the women. They talked about this problem and then called everyone together to talk about how to solve the problem.

Jesus' disciples said, "We need to make sure no one goes hungry. We need to be sure everyone is treated fairly. Because we spend a lot of our time preaching and telling others about Jesus, we need helpers. So let's choose some other people who can take over the work of making sure everyone gets enough food."

4. **Collect your very small balls and divide them in half. Give half to each group of people.** Everyone listened carefully. They thought about what the disciples had said. They agreed that having more people to help with the sharing of food was a good way to take care of the problem. They chose seven men for this special job and prayed for them, asking God to help them do this work in a good way.

After that, we never hear again about ANYONE in the first church family who didn't have enough or who felt treated unfairly! God's family listened carefully and cared about the problem of the Greek widows. That's one way they showed they loved Jesus. And it's also a way they showed that the fruit of goodness was growing in their lives!

• •

Focus on the Fruit

What was the problem in this story? (Some widows were not getting as much food as some of the others.) **What was done to solve the problem?** (Widows told disciples. Disciples listened carefully and thought of a way to solve the problem.) **What good thing did the disciples do?** (Chose seven men to help distribute the food evenly.)

When we listen carefully to others, it helps us know good and right things to do. Show the Goodness poster. **Then we know that God's Holy Spirit is helping us grow goodness in our lives!**

Fruitful Lives Object Talk

Bible Verse

This is what the Lord Almighty says:
"Administer true justice; show mercy and
compassion to one another." Zechariah 7:9

Materials

Bible with bookmark at Zechariah 7:9,
can of soup.

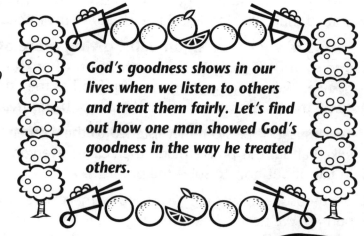

*God's goodness shows in our
lives when we listen to others
and treat them fairly. Let's find
out how one man showed God's
goodness in the way he treated
others.*

Lead the Activity

1. Show can of soup. **When do you like to eat soup? What kinds of soup do you like best?** Volunteers tell. **One man was not happy when he saw some poor-tasting soup that was being served in his city.**

2. **Charles Tindley was born as a slave in 1856, just a few years before Abraham Lincoln set the slaves free. When he grew up, Charles became the pastor of a church in the city of Philadelphia. Charles worried about some poor people who lived on the streets instead of in homes. He wanted to treat them in good ways, and he wanted to teach them about Jesus.**

   One day Charles went to a kitchen where poor people were given soup and bread to eat. But when Charles looked at the food, he saw that the soup was very watery and the bread was stale. Charles felt sorry for the people and wanted them to receive better food.

   The next Sunday, Charles told his congregation that they were going to help the poor people in their city. The church members cooked good, healthy food and welcomed the poor people into their church. Charles often talked to the poor people and showed how much he cared about them. Many of these people considered Charles their own pastor because he cared enough to listen to them and treat them in good ways.

Conclude

Read Zechariah 7:9 aloud. **When we administer true justice, it means we treat others fairly. What else does this verse say God wants us to do?** Students respond. Lead students in prayer, asking God to help them listen to others and treat others fairly.

• •

Discussion Questions

1. *When are some times you want others to listen to you? When can you listen to someone else?*

2. *What are some other ways that your actions can show God's goodness?*

Lesson 33

Active Game Center: Listen Up!

Materials
Bible, large sheet of paper, marker, masking tape.

Prepare the Activity
Print the words of Zechariah 7:9 on a large sheet of paper. Display the paper in your playing area.

Listening to others and treating them fairly show God's goodness. Let's play a game to practice listening to others.

Lead the Game

1. Students form two equal teams. Whisper a number to each student on each team (for example, whisper the numbers one through eight if there are eight students in the team). Do not give out the numbers in order.

2. Students walk around the playing area and clap the number you whispered to them. They may not talk to each other; they must listen to the number of claps to figure out what number each student was given. Students line up in their teams in numerical order.

3. The first team to line up correctly says Zechariah 7:9 in order, each student saying one word at a time, referring to the paper as needed.

4. Begin a new round of the game, whispering a different number to each student. Students play again as above.

Options

1. Print numbers on slips of paper. Give each student a slip of paper. Student secretly looks at number and then places paper facedown on floor before beginning to clap number.

2. If you have mostly younger students, assign the same number to every two students. Students clap and walk around the room to find other students with the same number. The first team to line up answers one of the Discussion Questions below or says Zechariah 7:9.

Discussion Questions

1. ***How does listening to other people help you show God's goodness to them?*** (God listens to and cares for us, so we are showing other people what He is like when we listen to and care for them.)

2. ***What does Zechariah 7:9 tell us to do? How might listening to someone be a way to show mercy and compassion for them?*** (When you listen to people, you can find out what they need or how they are feeling, and then you will know how to best help them.)

3. ***When is it hard for kids your age to treat other people fairly? What can you do in those situations to treat people fairly and show them God's goodness?***

Art Center: Hot Spots

Materials
Colored construction paper, colored chalk.

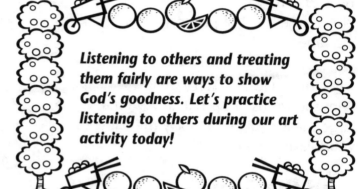

Listening to others and treating them fairly are ways to show God's goodness. Let's practice listening to others during our art activity today!

Lead the Activity

1. Give each student a sheet of colored construction paper and some chalk.

2. Ask one volunteer to think of his or her favorite place to go.

3. Students listen carefully to the answers the volunteer gives to the following questions: **What do you see at your favorite place? What do you do there? What kind of clothes would you wear while you are there? What kinds of animals or other people are there? What time of year or day is it best to go there?** Students draw their ideas of the volunteer's favorite place based on what they have heard. Students show pictures to group, telling what they heard the volunteer say and why they drew what they did. Volunteer then tells which students came closest to guessing his or her favorite place.

4. Choose a new volunteer to describe his or her favorite place to go and repeat activity.

Options

1. Older students form pairs or trios. One student in each group becomes the volunteer and describes his or her favorite place to partner or group. Students in each pair or trio draw picture based upon the volunteer's description.

2. To vary activity, ask additional volunteers to tell about their favorite thing to do, their favorite piece of clothing or their favorite scene from a book or a movie. Adjust questions to fit situation. Students listen to responses and draw pictures according to descriptions.

3. Instead of chalk, use white paper and colored pencils or markers.

Discussion Questions

1. When are some times it might be hard for you to listen to others? Volunteers respond. **How does listening to someone help you know how to best help that person?** (By listening, you can learn what he or she really needs and how to pray for the person.)

2. What does it mean to treat other people fairly? (Respect each person. Care for all people in the same way you care for the people you like most.) **What can you do to treat your brother or sister more fairly? Kids at school?**

3. How can listening to others and treating them fairly help them see God's goodness? (It shows them that God thinks each person is important.)

Worship Center

Bible Verse

This is what the Lord Almighty says:
"Administer true justice; show mercy
and compassion to one another."
Zechariah 7:9

Materials

Bible, *God's Kids Grow* cassette/CD or
music video and player, "Goodness!"
word chart (p. 469 in this book), large
sheet of paper on which you have
printed Zechariah 7:9 with four to six incorrect words, masking tape.

When we listen to others and treat them fairly, we show God's goodness. Let's thank God for His goodness as we worship Him.

Sing to God

Play "Goodness!" encouraging students to sing along with the music. **What actions does this song suggest we do to show God's goodness to others?** (Be fair. Keep promises. Tell the truth. Obey God.)

Hear and Say God's Word

Display paper on which you have printed Zechariah 7:9. **Some of the words on this paper are wrong.** Read Zechariah 7:9 aloud from the Bible. Volunteers take turns crossing off wrong words. Print the correct words on the paper and read the verse together. **The words "administer true justice" mean to treat others fairly and honestly. In what ways does the verse tell us to treat others fairly?** (Show mercy and compassion. Give people more kindness and love than they deserve.) Lead the group in saying Zechariah 7:9 one more time.

Pray to God

Lead students in reciting the following prayer: **Thank You, God, for Your goodness and for showing us more love and kindness than we deserve. Help us to show Your goodness to others. Amen.**

Options

1. During the prayer activity, have one or two volunteers read the definitions of "mercy" and "compassion" from a dictionary. Ask students to think of specific ways to show mercy and compassion, such as sharing a seat on the bus with a younger student or listening to someone who has a problem. Recite the verse together, substituting students' examples for the words "show mercy and compassion."

2. Print the words of the prayer on the back of the verse paper, so students can read the prayer together.

Bible Verse Coloring Center

FOR YOUNGER CHILDREN

Materials

Crayons or markers, a copy of page 81 or page 82 from *Bible Verse Coloring Pages #2* for each student.

Lead the Activity

Read Zechariah 7:9. **Who is showing mercy and compassion in this picture? How? When have you cared for someone who was hurt? When could you care for someone by treating the person fairly?** Students color picture.

Option

Provide watercolor paints and brushes. Students paint pictures instead of coloring.

Service Project Center

Materials

Materials needed for "Canned Food Drive" (p. 71 from *The Big Book of Service Projects*).

FOR YOUNGER CHILDREN AND OLDER CHILDREN

Lead the Activity

Students complete the "Canned Food Drive" activity as directed in *The Big Book of Service Projects*. **How might collecting cans of food show God's goodness to the people who receive them? What else could we do to show God's goodness to the people for whom we are collecting cans of food?** (Collect other items they need. Pray for them.)

Discipleship Activity Center

FOR OLDER CHILDREN

Materials

Discussion Cards for Ephesians 4:29—5:1 (pp. 159-164 from *The Big Book of Christian Growth*), materials needed for "Towel 'n' Ball Toss" or "Family Talk" (p. 32 or p. 42 from *The Big Book of Christian Growth*).

Lead the Activity

Today we're going to play a game to answer questions about Ephesians 4:29—5:1. We'll discover ways to show God's goodness. Students complete activity as directed in *The Big Book of Christian Growth*.

Ruth's Faithfulness

Bible Verse

A friend loves at all times.
Proverbs 17:17

Bible Story Reference

Ruth

Teacher's Devotional

An employer was conducting a personnel review with an employee who lacked many of the skills needed for the job. After detailing a lengthy list of shortcomings, the employer felt obligated to temper

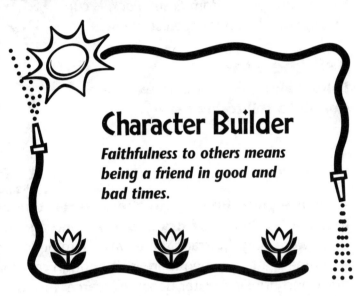

Character Builder

Faithfulness to others means being a friend in good and bad times.

all the criticism with recognition of some positive achievement. "George," the boss said, his mind searching for some good trait, "you're not very good at your job, but you do show up on time every day." This recognition of George's dependability was what we often call a backhanded compliment. Far too often faithfulness is viewed as worth mentioning only when people cannot earn recognition for their talents and achievements.

However, faithfulness is not a secondary virtue to be noted only when everything else is deficient. Faithfulness is one of the most comforting of all God's attributes. His consistent love for us is the ultimate example of faithfulness, especially in light of our inconsistent response to Him.

But is it possible for us to be truly faithful in our friendships, sticking with someone in both good and bad times? The story of Ruth and Naomi gives us a powerful yes in answer to that question. There is hope for all of us. As God grows His own attributes within us—not the least of which is faithfulness—our friendships will endure and flourish.

Bible Story Center

Materials

Faithfulness poster from *Poster Pack*, ¼ cup (2 oz.) play dough for each student.

Tell the Story

Follow along with me as we use our dough to tell today's story.

What are some things you do every day? Is is easy or hard to do them?

Today we'll find out what happened when a woman had to make a hard choice and do a hard job every day.

1. **Divide your dough into three parts. Use one part to make a flat piece of dry ground.** Long ago, even before there were kings in Israel, there was a famine in the country. A famine is a time when there isn't enough rain for crops to grow and drinking water becomes scarce. Because there was not enough food or water, a woman named Naomi and her family left their home in Bethlehem.

With her husband and two sons, Naomi went to Moab to find food. While Naomi's family lived in Moab, her husband died. When her boys grew up, they both married Moabite girls; one son married Orpah and the other married Ruth. Then, about 10 years after moving to Moab, her sons died. Now Naomi and her daughters-in-law were very sad. Without husbands, it would be VERY hard to get enough food. What would they DO?

Naomi had heard that there was food in Bethlehem again. She decided to go back home, where the rest of her family lived. *Maybe I'll find food there,* Naomi thought. Naomi also thought it would be better for Orpah and Ruth if they stayed in Moab. Orpah agreed with Naomi and decided to live with her relatives in Moab. But Ruth said, "Don't tell me to go back, Naomi. I won't leave you! Your people will be my people, and your God will be my God." Ruth stayed with Naomi. Ruth's caring actions showed her faithfulness.

2. **Use another part of your dough to make some tiny balls for grain. Put the grain on the ground.** Ruth and Naomi traveled together back to Israel. They arrived in Bethlehem during the spring barley harvest. Ruth went to the field of

a man named Boaz. She gleaned there. That means she took leftover barley off the ground and put the grain in her basket. It was hard work out in the hot sun. But Ruth was determined to be faithful, helping Naomi no matter what.

3. **Make a small basket from the third part of your dough. Put your grain in it.** Boaz was kind to Ruth. He told her she could come to his field anytime. He told his workers to leave extra grain on the ground for her to pick up. He had heard about Ruth, you see. Boaz was impressed with Ruth's faithfulness and kindness to Naomi.

When Naomi found out that Ruth was working in Boaz's field, she got very excited. Boaz was actually a relative of her husband's! That meant that Naomi and Ruth might be able to convince Boaz to provide a home for Ruth.

Naomi had a plan. She told Ruth to go to Boaz at night when he would be sleeping outdoors to guard his grain. She told Ruth just how to ask Boaz to be her protector. And according to the law, if Boaz would agree, it also meant he would MARRY Ruth!

4. **Use all your dough to make a baby.** Ruth did just what Naomi told her to do. She talked with Boaz, and Boaz was glad to help her and Naomi. He was glad to marry Ruth, too! So Ruth became Boaz's bride. Later, she and Boaz had a baby! They named the baby Obed. Now Naomi had a grandson who would keep her land in the family. Because of Ruth's faithfulness, Naomi was cared for and had a family again!

Best of all, many years later Obed would grow up and become a grandpa himself. He was the grandfather of King David—one of the ancestors of Jesus!

• •

Focus on the Fruit

How did Ruth show faithfulness to Naomi? (Returned to Israel with her. Gleaned in the field to get food.) **Who heard about Ruth's faithful kindness?** (Boaz.) **What were the results of Ruth's faithfulness?** (She and Naomi had food. Boaz married Ruth.)

   Faithfulness sometimes means doing something good, not just once, but over and over. It means always caring for and helping a person. Show the Faithfulness poster. **As we care for others, even when it's not easy, we grow the fruit of faithfulness in our lives. God promises to help us become faithful people if we ask His help!**

Fruitful Lives Object Talk

Bible Verse

A friend loves at all times. Proverbs 17:17

Materials

Bible with bookmark at Proverbs 17:17, sleeping bag or pillow.

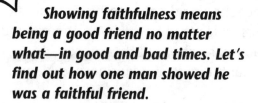

Showing faithfulness means being a good friend no matter what—in good and bad times. Let's find out how one man showed he was a faithful friend.

Lead the Activity

1. Show sleeping bag or pillow. **When do you use this?** (Camping. Sleeping overnight at a friend's house.) **One way to show friendship is to stay overnight at a friend's house. One man showed friendship by doing more than staying overnight with his friends. This man chose to live with the people he wanted to be friends with.**

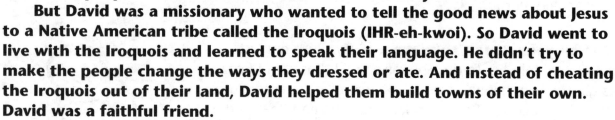

2. **David Zeisberger lived in the 1800s. During that time many Native Americans were being cheated out of the land they lived on. White people and Native Americans weren't usually friends.**

   But David was a missionary who wanted to tell the good news about Jesus to a Native American tribe called the Iroquois (IHR-eh-kwoi). So David went to live with the Iroquois and learned to speak their language. He didn't try to make the people change the ways they dressed or ate. And instead of cheating the Iroquois out of their land, David helped them build towns of their own. David was a faithful friend.

   Later, when the members of David's church wanted to become missionaries to the Iroquois, the tribe didn't want these missionaries to come. They had been cheated by white people too many times! But one of the Iroquois called David a friend and a brother, and others who knew David agreed that David had proven to be a fair and faithful friend by even going to jail instead of giving up his friendship with them. Because of David's friendship, the Iroquois allowed the missionaries to tell them about Jesus.

Conclude

Read Proverbs 17:17 aloud. **Someone who is faithful shows friendship in good and bad times. Let's ask God to help us be faithful friends this week.** Lead students in prayer.

Discussion Questions

1. *Who has been a faithful friend to you? What has this person done to show friendship to you?*

2. *When is it hard to show friendship to others?*

3. *How can you be a good friend to someone who has a hard time learning at school or to someone who has a hard time getting along with others?*

Active Game Center: Stick Together Relay

Materials
Bible, balloons.

Prepare the Game
Inflate one balloon for each team of five students.

Lead the Game
1. Divide students into teams of five. Teams line up on one side of the class-room. Give the first student in each line an inflated balloon.

2. At your signal, the first student in each line taps the balloon up into the air as he or she moves to the other side of the playing area and back. The second student in line then taps the balloon across the playing area and back while holding the wrist of the first student. Game continues until the whole team is holding wrists and moving across the playing area and back as the last student taps the balloon.

3. As teams complete the relay, they sit down. A volunteer from the last team to finish answers one of the Discussion Questions below (or chooses a student from one of the other teams to answer a question). Continue the discussion, asking the remaining questions.

Faithfulness to others means being a friend in good and bad times. Let's practice faithfulness by sticking with each other in our game today.

Options
1. Bounce a basketball, kick a tennis ball or carry a Ping-Pong ball on a spoon instead of tapping a balloon across the room.

2. Students switch teams and play game again if time allows.

3. Younger students complete relay in pairs, instead of whole team holding hands.

• •

Discussion Questions
1. *How does this game show us what faithfulness is?* (Faithfulness is sticking with some-one or something, no matter what.)

2. Read Proverbs 17:17 aloud. *According to Proverbs 17:17, what does a faithful friend do? Would that be hard or easy? Why?*

3. *Why might a kid your age have a hard time continuing to be a faithful friend to someone?* (When that person moves away. When he or she stops being nice. When we find new friends.) *What can we do to remember to be faithful friends, even when it's hard?* (Ask God's help. Remember the words of Proverbs 17:17.)

Art Center: Transfer Prints

Materials

8½x11-inch (21.5x27.5-cm) white paper, crayons, ballpoint pens.

Lead the Activity

1. Give each student a sheet of paper. Students fold paper in half widthwise and then unfold it.

2. Students color heavily with crayons on the top half of the paper, applying as many different colors of crayon as they desire. (Note: Darker colors work best.) Students fold colored half of the paper down on top of the blank half of paper.

3. On the back side of the colored half of the paper, students use ballpoint pens to draw stick-figure pictures of themselves with friends during good or bad times. Students open up paper to reveal multi-colored drawings on the bottom half of the paper. Ask Discussion Questions below as students work on pictures.

Options

1. Students write Proverbs 17:17 above their pictures.

2. If possible, provide jumbo crayons.

3. If time allows, students make more than one picture, each time experimenting with different colors of crayon.

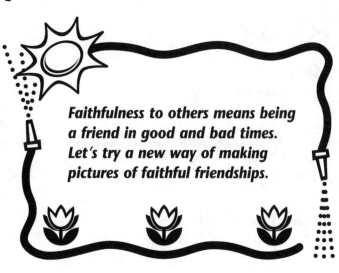

Faithfulness to others means being a friend in good and bad times. Let's try a new way of making pictures of faithful friendships.

Discussion Questions

1. *What does it mean to be faithful?* (Stick with someone or something no matter what happens. Be loyal and trustworthy.)

2. *What are some ways to be a faithful friend?* (Don't argue, but stick up for a friend who is being picked on. Don't stop being a friend, even if you start having other friends, too. Talk to a friend if you see them doing something wrong. Don't listen to gossip about a friend. Pray for your friend.)

3. *Who has been a faithful friend to you? How?*

Worship Center

Bible Verse
A friend loves at all times. Proverbs 17:17

Materials
Bible, *God's Kids Grow* cassette/CD or music video and player, "Good Habits" word chart (p. 467 in this book), large sheet of paper on which you have printed Proverbs 17:17, masking tape.

Faithfulness to others means being a friend in good and bad times. Let's thank God for His faithfulness to us and ask His help in being faithful friends.

Sing to God
Play "Good Habits," encouraging students to sing along with the music. **This song names ways to be faithful. What are they?** (Trust God. Do our best. Pray. Practice helping others.)

Hear and Say God's Word
Display paper on which you have printed Proverbs 17:17. Have a volunteer read the verse aloud. **When does a friend love?** (At all times.) Ask a volunteer to hold up any number of fingers on one hand. Students respond by repeating the verse as many times as the number of fingers held up, each time telling either a time it is easy or hard to love a friend. Repeat the activity several times, having a different volunteer show a different number of fingers each time.

Pray to God
Let's ask God's help in being a friend at all times. Volunteers pray aloud, asking God for His help in showing love, even when it is hard. End prayer time by thanking God that He is always faithful in loving us and asking for His help in faithfully showing love to others.

Options
1. Ask an older student to lead the Bible verse activity.

2. Provide a large sheet of paper and a marker or a white board and erasable marker for students to write prayer requests on. **Praying for other people is one way we can be faithful friends in good and bad times.** Each student takes a turn praying for another student's request. (Optional: Give students large Post-it Notes on which to write their requests. Students trade Post-it Notes before praying silently or aloud for each other.)

Bible Verse Coloring Center

Materials
Crayons or markers, a copy of page 63 or page 64 from *Bible Verse Coloring Pages #2* for each student.

Lead the Activity
Read Proverbs 17:17. **How are the children in this picture showing that they are friends? How can you show that you are a friend to someone?** Students color picture.

Option
Provide leaves and tree bark. Students place leaves and/or bark underneath the paper, positioning leaves and bark under leaves and tree branches in the picture. Students rub over leaves and bark with crayons to create rubbings. (Note: Remove crayon wrapping.)

Service Project Center

Materials
Materials needed for "Snack Sacks" (p. 83 from *The Big Book of Service Projects*).

Lead the Activity
Students complete the "Snack Sacks" activity as directed in *The Big Book of Service Projects*. **When do you usually like to eat a snack? What messages about friendship could you include with the snacks? Besides sharing snacks with someone in need, what are some other ways to be a friend in hard times?**

Discipleship Activity Center

Materials
Discussion Cards for Psalm 23 (pp. 75-80 from *The Big Book of Christian Growth*), materials needed for "Mark the Spot" or "Handy Pileup" (p. 22 or p. 63 from *The Big Book of Christian Growth*).

Lead the Activity
We've been talking today about being faithful friends. Psalm 23 tells us that God is faithful to us. Today we're going to play a game to help us discover ways God's faithfulness can make a difference in our lives. Students complete activity as directed in *The Big Book of Christian Growth*.

Joseph's Forgiveness

Bible Verse

Bear with each other and forgive whatever grievances you may have against one another. Forgive as the Lord forgave you. Colossians 3:13

Bible Story Reference
Genesis 37; 39—45

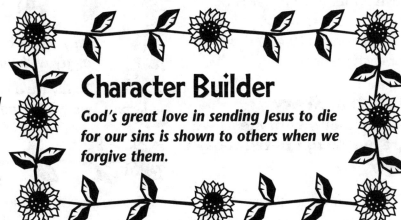

Character Builder
God's great love in sending Jesus to die for our sins is shown to others when we forgive them.

Teacher's Devotional

Agape, the love of which Paul speaks in Galatians 5:22, is love centered in action rather than in emotion. This love sees something infinitely precious in the beloved and does something to show that love. In spite of our unworthiness, God saw something so precious that He GAVE His only Son to take the punishment for our sins. God loved; therefore, He gave. He took action.

As God's children, we are called to love others, even though they may be imperfect or hard to love. While we may not always be able to generate feelings of love toward those who seem to be unlovable, we can always demonstrate our awareness of their eternal worth and value. We can take action to show God's love.

What action can we take to show God's love? Paul calls us to "forgive whatever grievances you may have" (Colossians 3:13). In a culture that encourages us to take our grievances to court and extract the fullest measure of what the law says is due us, is it realistic or even reasonable to advocate forgiveness? What if the wrongs we have endured are truly grievous? What if the other party has truly caused us hurt?

Those are the times when we have the richest opportunity of all, the chance to "forgive as the Lord forgave you" (Colossians 3:13). Have we ever endured even a fraction of the abuse our Lord received? Yet He loved; therefore, He forgave. We are called to take the same action.

Bible Story Center

Materials
Love poster from *Poster Pack*, ¼ cup (2 oz.) play dough and several 4-inch (10-cm) straws for each student.

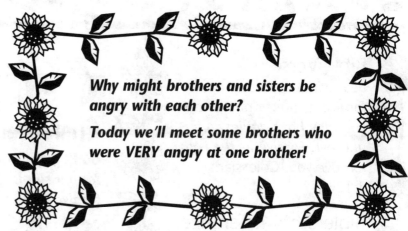

Why might brothers and sisters be angry with each other?

Today we'll meet some brothers who were VERY angry at one brother!

Tell the Story
Follow along with me as we use our dough to tell today's story.

1. **Make a coat.** Four hundred years before God's people were slaves in Egypt, there lived a man named Jacob who had 12 sons. One son, Joseph, was Jacob's FAVORITE son. This made the other brothers jealous!

Joseph also had some dreams when he was young. These dreams seemed to say that his family would one day bow down to him. Well, when he told his family his dreams, his brothers became even more jealous! And if that weren't enough, Jacob made a special coat for Joseph. The special coat showed everyone that Joseph was Jacob's favorite son. Were his brothers ever jealous!

2. **Make a pit—a big hole in the ground.** One day, Jacob sent Joseph to check on his brothers who were taking care of the family's animals far away from home. When the brothers saw Joseph coming, they decided to take his coat from him and throw him into a nearby pit. Soon the brothers sold Joseph to some traders (people who buy and sell things) who were on their way to Egypt.

Joseph's brothers told their father that Joseph was dead. But really, Joseph was now a SLAVE in Egypt. Despite being a slave, Joseph trusted God and did his best. Soon he became his Egyptian owner's most trusted servant.

3. **Roll ropes and use straws to make jail bars.** The wife of the man who owned Joseph lied about Joseph. She got Joseph put into JAIL! But once again, Joseph trusted God. He did his best and helped other prisoners. Soon he was put in charge of the jail! He even helped two prisoners by telling them the meaning of dreams they had.

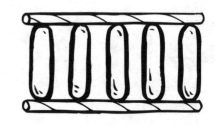

Some time later, Pharaoh, the ruler of all Egypt, had a STRANGE dream. No one could tell him what it meant! But one of the men Joseph had helped in jail told Pharaoh about Joseph. So Pharaoh called for Joseph. Soon Joseph was standing in front of Pharaoh! He told Pharaoh that his dream meant there was going to be a famine—years when there wouldn't be any rain and very little food.

4. Use two ropes to make a ring and a necklace.

Pharaoh thought about what Joseph had told him. He realized that Joseph was a VERY wise man. So he made Joseph second ruler of the whole country of Egypt! He gave Joseph his ring, so Joseph could make laws. He gave Joseph a royal necklace to wear around his neck, so people would know Joseph was a ruler. Joseph had big barns built to store food to eat during the famine. He was in charge of everybody except Pharaoh!

After seven years, the famine DID come, as Joseph had said it would. There was also a famine back where Jacob and all of Joseph's brothers lived. Soon the brothers came to Egypt in search of food. But they didn't recognize Joseph. They bowed low before Joseph, as he had seen in his dream. They BEGGED Joseph to sell them food! Joseph didn't tell them who he was just yet. But he gave them lots of grain and sent them home. He also kept one brother with him, just to be sure they would come back!

5. Make a smile from two other two ropes. Joseph's

brothers DID come back. Finally, Joseph told them who he was! His brothers were afraid. *Would Joseph punish us?* they wondered. Joseph did not. Instead, he FORGAVE them! He loved his brothers, even though they had been so cruel to him. He told them that even though they had meant to hurt him, God had used it for good! Joseph invited them all to come and live in Egypt, where there was plenty of food for all their families! Joseph showed God's love to his family, no matter what!

• •

Focus on the Fruit

Why did Joseph's brothers put him in a pit and sell him? (Jealous. Didn't like his dreams.) **When Joseph was a slave, what did he do? What did he do in jail?** (Did his best. Tried to help.) **What did Joseph's brothers do when they came to ask for food?** (Bowed and begged.) **Why do you think Joseph forgave his brothers?** (God helped him love them. God used their meanness for good.)

Forgiving people is not always easy. Even in our families, people can hurt our feelings. Show the Love poster. **But when we forgive, we show the fruit of God's love!**

Fruitful Lives Object Talk

Bible Verse

Bear with each other and forgive what-ever grievances you may have against one another. Forgive as the Lord forgave you. Colossians 3:13

Materials

Bible with bookmark at Colossians 3:13, laundry basket and/or detergent.

When we have been forgiven by God, we can show His love to other people by forgiving them. Let's find out how a woman helped some people forgive each other and show God's love.

Lead the Activity

1. Show laundry basket and/or detergent. **What are these things used for?** Students respond. **Before washing machines had been invented, it took people many hours to wash and iron their clothes. People often hired others to do their laundry.**

2. **Amanda Smith was a former slave who earned money by doing laundry for others. After her husband died, she had to work hard to earn enough money to care for her family. Amanda also worked hard so that she could spend time telling others about God's love and forgiveness.**

    One day after hearing Amanda speak, a young man asked for help. The man had fought with a friend several years before. Amanda's teaching helped the young man see that he needed to forgive his friend, but he was afraid to speak to him. Amanda prayed for him and said that God would help him.

    The next day, the young man saw the man he had fought with. Even though he was afraid, the young man walked up to him and started to speak. The other man said, "I'm so glad you came to talk to me. I wanted to say something, but I was afraid you wouldn't speak to me!" The two men quickly forgave each other and became good friends again. Amanda felt that seeing those two men forgive each other was worth all the clothes she had to wash in order to have time to tell others about God and His love.

Conclude

Read Colossians 3:13 aloud. **How did Amanda Smith help the two friends obey this verse?** Students respond. **Let's thank God for forgiving us and ask God to help us have courage to obey this verse and forgive others.** Lead students in prayer.

• •

Discussion Questions

1. *When have you needed to forgive a friend? What happened when you forgave your friend?*

2. *Why is forgiveness important? What do you think might happen to friendships if neither friend is willing to forgive the other one?*

3. *How does forgiveness help people get along with each other better?*

Active Game Center: Towel Toss

Materials

Bible, large towels, balls.

Lead the Game

1. Group students into teams of five. Give each team a towel and a ball.

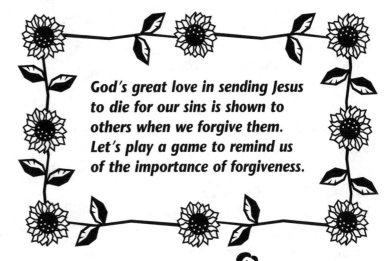

God's great love in sending Jesus to die for our sins is shown to others when we forgive them. Let's play a game to remind us of the importance of forgiveness.

2. Four students on each team hold the towel between them at waist height. The other team member stands across the playing area and throws the ball so that the towel holders can catch it with the towel. If the ball is caught, the thrower runs to the towel and switches places with one of the towel holders. The new thrower takes the ball back across the playing area and throws it for the towel holders to catch.

3. Team members continue rotating between throwing and holding, keeping track of the number of times the team catches the ball on the towel. Teams score one letter of the word "forgiveness" each time the ball is caught. The first team to catch the ball 11 times (completely spelling "forgiveness") calls "Stop." Students from that team answer one of the Discussion Questions below.

Options

1. Play game outdoors if possible.

2. Adjust according to students' ages and abilities the distance from which students toss ball.

3. For teams with more than five players, students form a line behind the thrower and rotate in.

4. Instead of spelling "forgiveness," each team counts how many catches it makes in five minutes. At the end of five minutes, team with the most catches answers a Discussion Question below.

• •

Discussion Questions

1. ***When has someone forgiven you?*** Volunteers respond. ***How did it make you feel?***

2. ***Why is it important to forgive other people?*** (God sent Jesus to Earth to die for us so that our sins could be forgiven. God commands us to forgive people.) Have an older volunteer read Colossians 3:13 aloud.

3. ***What might happen when you forgive someone?*** (You can be friends again. You can show them God's love.)

Art Center: Message Mobiles

Materials
Bibles, paper plates, markers or crayons, scissors, paper clips, curling ribbon.

Prepare the Activity
Make a sample mobile.

We show God's love and forgiveness to others when we forgive them. Other people also show us God's love when they forgive us! Let's make mobiles to help us remember that message!

Lead the Activity

1. Give each student a paper plate. Each student draws a large spiral on his or her plate, starting from the center of the paper plate and leaving at least 1 inch (2.5 cm) between each loop of the spiral (see sketch a).

2. Students draw pictures of or write sentences about forgiveness along the path of the spiral. Suggest the following sentence starters for students to complete: "A time when someone forgave me was . . . " or "I can show forgiveness by . . . " or "People forgive others when . . ." Students may also write the words of Colossians 3:13. Ask Discussion Questions below as students work on their mobiles.

3. Students cut along spiral lines. Students unfold inner loops of paper clips to form S-shaped hooks. Students poke one end of the paper clips through the rounded end of the spirals and tie lengths of curling ribbon to the other end of the hooks to create mobiles (see sketch b).

a.   b.

Options

1. For younger students, draw the spirals on the plates ahead of time.

2. If possible, hang the mobiles in your room or another well-traveled area of the church.

3. Students write across paper plates and then cut spirals to create mystery mobiles. Mobiles can be read only when spiral parts are placed together.

• •

Discussion Questions

1. *What are some of the hardest times to forgive other people?* (When someone is mean more than once. When someone calls you names in front of your friends.)

2. *What good things can come from forgiving others?* (We can help to stop arguments.)

3. *Why does forgiveness show God's love?* (God always forgives us when we ask. God's love includes forgiveness, which He showed us by sending Jesus to die on the cross to provide forgiveness for all people's sins.)

   God's Kids Grow Leader's Guide

Lesson 35

Worship Center

Bible Verse

Bear with each other and forgive whatever grievances you may have against one another. Forgive as the Lord forgave you. Colossians 3:13

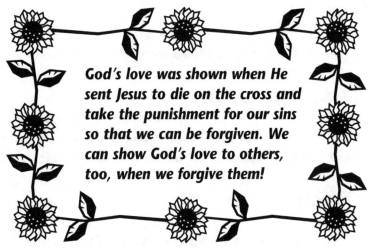

God's love was shown when He sent Jesus to die on the cross and take the punishment for our sins so that we can be forgiven. We can show God's love to others, too, when we forgive them!

Materials

Bible, *God's Kids Grow* cassette/CD or music video and player, "All My Heart" word chart (p. 453 in this book), large sheet of paper on which you have printed Colossians 3:13, masking tape, soft ball.

Sing to God

Play "All My Heart," encouraging students to sing along with the music. **This song talks about loving God and loving others. What are some ways to do that at home? At school?** Volunteers respond.

Hear and Say God's Word

Display paper on which you have printed Colossians 3:13. Volunteer reads the verse aloud. **What does it mean to bear with one another?** (Have patience with each other and not get mad because of the way people act or bother you.) **"Grievances" is another word for complaints we have about someone or some situation. What should we do with our grievances?** (Talk about ways to solve them and forgive the person.) **What reason does the last part of this verse give us to "bear with each other and forgive" each other?** (God forgives us.) (Optional: Talk with students about receiving God's forgiveness for our sins and becoming members of God's family. Follow the guidelines in the "Leading a Child to Christ" article on p. 36.)

Students sit in a circle. Gently toss the ball to a student, saying the first word of the verse as you throw it. Student who catches the ball says second word of verse as he or she tosses the ball to another student in the circle, who then says the third word of the verse. Continue until the entire verse has been said several times.

Pray to God

Lead students in prayer, thanking God for His forgiveness and asking Him to help us show His love by forgiving others.

Options

1. Students sing "Fruit of the Spirit" (p. 459 in this book).

2. Provide Bibles or mark these verses in your Bible for several students to read aloud as reminders of God's forgiveness of us: Psalm 86:5, Daniel 9:9, John 3:16, Ephesians 4:32.

Bible Verse Coloring Center

Materials
Crayons or markers, a copy of page 181 or page 182 from *Bible Verse Coloring Pages #2* for each student.

Lead the Activity
Read Colossians 3:13. **Why might the people in this picture need to forgive each other? How can people show that they forgive each other?** Students color picture.

Option
Also provide a copy of "Draw a picture of your family" page (p. 227 from *Bible Verse Coloring Pages #2*). **Draw a picture of something your family likes to do together.** Students draw and color pictures. **When are some times you need to forgive someone in your family? How can your forgiveness help show God's love to (your brother)?**

Service Project Center

Materials
Materials needed for "Encouraging Flyer" (p. 38 from *The Big Book of Service Projects*).

Lead the Activity
Students complete the "Encouraging Flyer" activity as directed in *The Big Book of Service Projects*. **What are some good things to write on our flyers to help people learn about God's love? What are some actions we can do to help people learn about God's love? How does our forgiveness of others help them learn about God's love?**

Discipleship Activity Center

Materials
Discussion Cards for Romans 8:35,37-39 (pp. 129-134 from *The Big Book of Christian Growth*); materials needed for "Seek 'n' Find" or "The Most" (p. 25 or p. 70 from *The Big Book of Christian Growth*).

Lead the Activity
Romans 8:35,37-39 tells us how great God's love is. Today we're going to play a game to talk about ways God's love helps us. Students complete activity as directed in *The Big Book of Christian Growth*.

Red Sea Celebration

Bible Verse

You make me glad by your deeds, O Lord; I sing for joy at the works of your hands. Psalm 92:4

Bible Story Reference

Exodus 14,15

Teacher's Devotional

When Miriam took a tambourine in her hand and sang about the Lord's greatness (see Exodus 15:20), it was very evident what great works God's hands had accomplished. God had brought plagues on Egypt, secured Israel's release from slavery, parted the waters so that the people could pass through and then "the horse and its rider he has hurled into the sea" (Exodus 15:21). Is it any wonder that the people sang to the Lord and the women danced? Are we at all surprised at the obvious elation expressed in Moses' song? Even thousands of years later we are almost swept up in the powerful emotions of that victorious day.

However, when we look back on events of our own lives, we often fail to notice God's hands at work in our affairs. Granted, day-to-day living is usually a far cry from the spectacular drama of crossing the Red Sea, yet a little reflection usually recalls moments when God's help was present. Thoughtful hindsight often reveals what we missed at the time: God protecting against danger or helping us stay calm under pressure or nudging us to notice what we would otherwise have overlooked.

When we stop and think about His deeds on our behalf, we may not feel comfortable breaking out the tambourines. But Scripture is filled with examples of God's people doing what Miriam and Moses did: singing for joy to celebrate what God has done. Invite the children you teach to join with you in celebration of God's help and protection.

Character Builder

Joyfully celebrate God's help and protection.

Bible Story Center

Materials
Joy poster from *Poster Pack;* ¼ cup (2 oz.) play dough and plastic knife for each student.

Tell the Story
Follow along with me as we use our dough to tell today's story.

What are some reasons people sing songs?

Today we're going to hear about some people who sang a song to praise God.

1. **From most of your dough make a large sea with waves. Save a small part of your dough.** Hundreds and thousands of Israelite people followed Moses away from Egypt. During the day, God sent a big cloud to move across the sky in front of them. At night, God sent a pillar of fire to guide them. The Israelites walked day after day through the desert until they finally set up camp by the edge of a big body of water called the Red Sea.

But soon the ground began to tremble. There was a deep rumbling. It wasn't thunder. It wasn't an earthquake. Out on the horizon, dust rose—not a LITTLE dust, as if a few people were coming. No, there was a LOT of dust. It sounded and looked like an army!

Remember Pharaoh, the king of Egypt? After the Israelites had left, Pharaoh decided he had made a huge mistake in letting the Israelite slaves get away! Hundreds and hundreds of angry Egyptian soldiers were pursuing the Israelites, determined to bring them back to slavery!

"Oh no, Pharaoh has changed his mind!" someone shouted.

The Israelites felt like running, but the sea was in front of them. The whole Egyptian army with its chariots and swift horses was coming! (Chariots are two-wheeled carts pulled by horses.)

The people were angry and afraid. "Why did you bring us here to die?" they shouted at Moses. "We can't go forward because of the sea and we can't go back toward the soldiers!"

"Don't be afraid," Moses said. "You will see how God will bring you out of trouble. He will fight for you!"

And Moses was right! Before Pharaoh and his soldiers could get close to the Israelites, God moved the huge cloud to stand between the Egyptians and the Israelites! The sky over the Egyptians became so dark that the army had to stop. But for the people of Israel, it was still light!

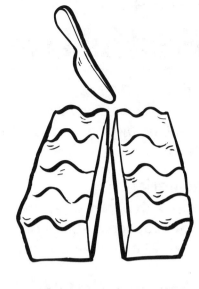

2. **Cut the water in two, making a path down the middle of the water.** God told Moses to hold his staff high in the air over the sea. All night long God sent a strong wind. It blew so hard that it blew a path through the waters of the sea. By morning, the water was stacked up in a wall of water on the right and a wall of water on the left. There was a wide, dry path right through the sea!

3. **From the small part of your dough, make small balls for Moses and the people. Move them from one side of the water to the other.** The people followed Moses over that dry path. Every single person and animal made it safely across. No one even got their feet wet!

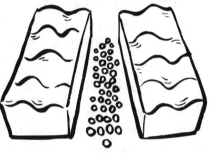

Well, Pharaoh's army wasn't about to let the Israelites get away so easily! The chariots and soldiers rushed down that path to catch the Israelites. But God showed His power and protection once again. God told Moses to stretch out his hand over the sea. When Moses did, those walls of water came CRASHING down! The soldiers and the chariots were all GONE.

4. **Make a musical note.** God's people were so happy they just had to sing and praise God! Moses made up a song, right there on the far shore of the Red Sea! Moses' sister Miriam got the women together to play tambourines and sing.

"Sing to the Lord,
   for He is highly exalted.
The horse and its rider
   He has hurled into the sea."

Everyone sang and danced and played instruments to thank God for His amazing power and help. It was the biggest, noisiest, happiest party ever held in that quiet desert!

• •

Focus on the Fruit

What are some ways God took care of the Israelites? (He rescued them from slavery in Egypt. He made a dry path through the water. He protected them.) **What did the Israelites do when they saw God take care of them?** (They sang songs of praise and thanksgiving to God.) **How would you describe God's actions?**

    God's power is just the same today as it was in Old Testament times, and He is always glad to help us. God shows His love and care in many ways. Show the Joy poster. **We can joyfully celebrate God's help and protection!**

Lesson 36

Fruitful Lives Object Talk

Bible Verse
You make me glad by your deeds, O Lord;
I sing for joy at the works of your hands.
Psalm 92:4

Materials
Bible with bookmark at Psalm 92:4, shovel; optional—*God's Kids Grow* cassette/CD and player.

We can joyfully celebrate God's help and protection! Let's find out about a man who celebrated God at every opportunity he had!

Lead the Activity

1. Ask a volunteer to demonstrate how to use a shovel. **What are some hard jobs people have to do with shovels?** (Dig ditches. Dig in fields. Dig big holes.) **A man named George Chen had to dig with a shovel every day for more than five years doing a job no one else wanted!**

2. **George Chen lived in China and was sent to prison because he was a Christian and came from a wealthy family. In that prison, no one was allowed to talk about God, read a Bible or pray.**

   Each person in the prison had a job to do. George's job was to shovel out the huge hole in the ground where all of the waste from the prison was put. Each day the guards lowered George and his shovel into the pit. All day long George worked hard.

   Most people would have hated such a smelly, dirty job! But George soon discovered that because the pit was so dirty and smelly, no guards came to check on him while he worked. Every day George was free to sing songs of praise to God, to pray out loud and to recite Bible verses he had memorized. If he had worked inside the prison in a cleaner place, he would not have been able to sing and pray aloud! George joyfully thanked God—even when it was hard!

Conclude

Read Psalm 92:4 aloud. **When are some times you can sing to God and tell Him how glad you are for the things He has done?** Lead students in prayer, praising God for specific actions He has done (created the world, forgiven our sins, answered our prayers). (Optional: Lead students in singing "Joy!" from *God's Kids Grow* cassette/CD.)

• •

Additional Information for Older Students

George Chen spent 18 years in the prison. When he was set free, he helped Chinese Christians start new churches and tell people about Jesus. During the years George was in prison, many Chinese Christians who were not in prison were killed by the government. George thanked God that he was in prison for so long because he was kept alive and could continue to obey God after he was set free. Lead students in praying for Christians in China who tell people about Jesus.

Active Game Center: Balloon Blast

Materials

Bible, balloons, permanent markers, Post-it Note.

Lead the Game

1. Give each student a balloon. Students write their first names or initials on balloons.

2. Place the Post-it Note at least 5 feet (1.5 m) away from the students. Students blow up balloons and pinch openings closed so that air does not escape. At your signal, students release balloons toward the Post-it Note.

3. Student whose balloon landed closest to the Post-it Note reads Psalm 92:4 aloud. **This verse gives us an example of praising God. What does the writer of this verse say to praise God?** Volunteers respond. **Now we're going to make up our own sentences to praise God.**

4. Move Post-it Note to another location within the playing area. Students stand 5 feet (1.5 m) away from the Post-it Note and blow up and release balloons again. Student whose balloon lands closest to the Post-it Note completes the sentence "The Lord is . . ." or "I thank God for . . ." Repeat activity as many times as possible so that each student has a chance to say a sentence of praise.

We can joyfully celebrate God's help and protection. Let's play a game to help us praise God!

Option

Provide a large sheet of paper and a marker or a piece of chalk and chalkboard so that students can write their praise sentences.

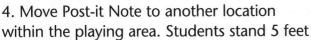

Discussion Questions

1. *When has God helped or protected you or someone you know?* Tell your own answer once students have shared some of their answers.

2. *How can we praise God for His help and protection?* (At church we can worship Him. We can pray and thank Him for His help. We can sing.)

3. *Why do you think praising God brings us joy?* (We are happy that He has cared for us and promises always to care for us. It pleases God when we praise Him. It reminds us of His love and faithfulness. It makes us love Him more.)

Art Center: Miriam's Music

Materials

Materials for the tambourine project you choose.

Lead the Activity

Lead students in making instruments.

Shake It Up

Distribute two paper plates to each student. Students place a small amount of dry beans, pasta shapes or rice in the center of one plate and cover it with the second plate. Students staple, tape or glue edges together.

Because God will always help and protect us, we have good reason to joyfully celebrate! One way to celebrate is to sing songs and play musical instruments. Let's make a musical instrument like the one Miriam used to praise God when He helped the Israelites cross the Red Sea.

Joyful Bells

Distribute a paper plate to each student. Using a hole punch, students punch four or five holes around the edge of the tambourine. For each hole, thread one or two jingle bells onto a piece of chenille wire. Loop the wire through the hole and twist to secure.

Options

1. Provide markers, stickers or rubber stamps and stamp pads for students to use in decorating tambourines.

2. Streamers made from crepe paper, curling ribbon or other fringe material can be attached with stapler, tape or glue to edge of tambourine.

3. Students thread four or five jingle bells onto a length of chenille wire, forming a circle and twisting ends to secure. These tambourines can be held by hand or can be worn as rings, armbands or necklaces.

4. Students play completed tambourines while you play music from *God's Kids Grow* cassette/CD or during singing in this lesson's Worship Center.

• •

Discussion Questions

1. ***When are some times a kid your age might need God's help and protection?*** (During a thunderstorm. When going to a new school. When standing up for what's right.)

2. ***What are some ways God has shown His help and protection to you or other people you know?***

3. ***What are some ways to show your joy and celebrate God's help and protection?*** (Sing songs of praise to God. Pray to God, thanking Him for all He has done to help you. Tell others about how God helps and protects His people.)

Lesson 36

Worship Center

Bible Verse

You make me glad by your deeds, O Lord; I sing for joy at the works of your hands. Psalm 92:4

Materials

Bible, *God's Kids Grow* cassette/CD or music video and player, "Joy!" word chart (p. 473 in this book), large sheet of paper on which you have printed Psalm 92:4, masking tape.

Let's joyfully celebrate God's help and protection by worshiping Him today!

Sing to God

Play "Joy!" encouraging students to sing along with the music. **This song talks about people in the Bible who were joyful because of God's protection. When are some times you might need to ask God for help and protection? What are some ways to celebrate that God always helps us?** (Sing to Him. Thank God in prayer.)

Hear and Say God's Word

Display paper on which you have printed Psalm 92:4. Have a volunteer read the verse aloud. **What is the writer of this psalm glad about?** (God's deeds. What God has done.) **What are some things God has done that make you glad?** Volunteers respond. Lead students in singing the verse to the tune of the chorus for "Jesus Loves Me." Repeat verse several times.

Pray to God

What are some of the ways God has helped and cared for you? Volunteers respond. **Let's joyfully thank God for the help He has given us!** Volunteers pray aloud. End prayer time by thanking God for His help and protection and asking for His help to remember to joyfully celebrate Him.

Options

1. As an invitation to worship, read or ask a volunteer to read Psalm 138:1-5 aloud at the beginning of this Worship Center.

2. Provide a variety of rhythm instruments for students to use while singing the song and completing the verse activity.

3. Invite students to suggest other familiar songs to which they may sing the words of Psalm 92:4 ("Row, Row, Row Your Boat," "Jingle Bells," etc.).

Bible Verse Coloring Center

Materials
Crayons or markers, a copy of page 35 or page 36 from *Bible Verse Coloring Pages #2* for each student.

Lead the Activity
Read Psalm 92:4. **What might the people in this picture be thanking God for? What are some other things God has made?** Students color picture.

Options
1. Play a cassette/CD of children's praise songs as students color. Encourage students to sing along.

2. Provide foil stars for students to stick on their pictures.

Service Project Center

Materials
Materials needed for "Missionary Care Package" (p. 133 from *The Big Book of Service Projects*).

Lead the Activity
Students complete the "Missionary Care Package" activity as directed in *The Big Book of Service Projects*. **What are some ways you like to celebrate God's help and protection? What might help the (name of missionary family) joyfully celebrate God's help and protection? What are the words of some praise songs that we could include with our care package?**

Discipleship Activity Center

Materials
Discussion Cards for Matthew 5:3-9 (pp. 105-110 from *The Big Book of Christian Growth*); materials needed for "Circle Jump-Up" or "Rock, Paper, Scissors" (p. 13 or p. 68 from *The Big Book of Christian Growth*).

Lead the Activity
Today we're going to play a game to answer questions about Matthew 5:3-9. We'll discover what Jesus said to do in order to be blessed, or to have joy. Students complete activity as directed in *The Big Book of Christian Growth*.

Birds and Flowers

Bible Verse

Peace I leave with you; my peace I give you. I do not give to you as the world gives. Do not let your hearts be troubled and do not be afraid. John 14:27

Bible Story Reference
Matthew 6:25-34

Teacher's Devotional

Character Builder

We can have peace because God knows what we need and promises to care for us.

Shalom. This familiar word, meaning "peace," was an everyday greeting and farewell in Bible times, not unlike the Hawaiian *Aloha* and with a depth of meaning beyond our contemporary declaration "Have a nice day!" However, when Jesus used this greeting, He had something in mind far beyond the traditional blessing.

Notice that in this lesson's Bible verse, Jesus said it twice, for emphasis, slightly rephrasing the second statement. Having secured everyone's attention with this common device, He then presented a contrast, distinguishing His blessing from the common experiences people had with the greeting. Jesus explained His peace by saying "I do not give to you as the world gives" (John 14:27). Attaching a new meaning to a long-familiar word is a somewhat risky business, for if people do not pay close attention, they may simply continue to think of the common usage and not the intended new message.

Thus, Jesus inserted a very personal, comforting assurance, telling His followers not to be afraid. And why not? What really is this peace Jesus was offering? What makes it distinct from the way people had been greeting one another for centuries? Jesus explained: His followers can have a deep, lasting peace because Jesus has come from the Father and would return to the Father (see John 14:2-4). Thus, His promise of peace is not just a wish, a hope or even a prayer. It is instead a true reality because He has the authority to produce that peace in our lives.

Bible Story Center

Materials

Peace poster from *Poster Pack; a* variety of small nature objects (twigs, shells, pebbles, etc.) and ¼ cup (2 oz.) play dough for each student.

Tell the Story

Follow along with me as we use our dough to tell today's story.

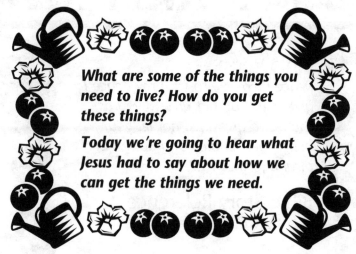

What are some of the things you need to live? How do you get these things?

Today we're going to hear what Jesus had to say about how we can get the things we need.

1. **Make several people.** One day, moms and dads, grandparents, big kids and little kids were all walking out to a hillside where Jesus was going to teach. As the large crowd walked along, they must have talked to each other.

"Did we bring enough food?" one person might have asked. "We may be out here all day long!"

Someone else may have said quietly, "We didn't bring very much food. There wasn't much to eat at our house."

"Should we have brought our warm coats? It might get cold later," some people might have worried. Other people might have wished they even had warm coats at all!

But finally, all the people were out on the hillside where Jesus and His friends were. People were everywhere! They were sitting, standing, bumping and moving, trying to get a better view of Jesus.

Then Jesus began to talk. He told the people things about God. He talked about how God wanted them to live. Everyone listened carefully.

Jesus said, "Don't worry about things. Don't worry about having enough food to eat. And don't worry whether or not you will have enough to drink. Don't worry about what clothes you will wear. There are more important things in life than food and clothes!"

2. **Make one or two birds.** To show the people what He meant about worrying, Jesus talked about things they saw around them. Jesus pointed to the sky where birds were flying. "Look at the birds of the air!" Jesus told the people. "Think about what they do. Birds don't plant seeds to grow crops.

They don't gather up food like farmers do. But God makes SURE they will have enough food to eat. God takes care of them. He loves them. Now think. Aren't you even MORE important to God than birds in the sky? Of course you are! So remember, don't worry. Ask God for help and He will take care of you."

The people looked up to watch the birds for a moment. As they watched and thought about what Jesus said, they must have smiled. God loves the birds and feeds them. And Jesus said God loves us even more than He loves birds!

3. **Divide your dough in half. Make one or two flowers from half the dough. Add nature items to decorate the flowers.** Then Jesus said something else. Perhaps He picked a flower and held it up for everyone to see. He said, "Look at the way the flowers grow. They do not make cloth. They don't sew clothes!"

"But look!" He said. "I'm telling you, even the richest king in the world never had clothes as beautiful as these flowers have."

Jesus went on, "If God gives the flowers such beautiful clothes, don't you think He will take care of you?"

"So," Jesus said, "don't worry! Don't say, 'What are we going to eat?' or 'What are we going to wear?' That's what people who don't know God worry about. But God knows what you need. He will take care of you."

4. **Make a big number one from the other half of your dough.** "Instead of worrying about food or clothes," Jesus said, "the first and most important thing to care about is what God wants you to do. When you put God first and do what's right, all that you need will be given to you."

"And," said Jesus, "don't worry about tomorrow. Don't worry about how long you will live. After all, you won't make your life any longer by worrying about it! Every day has enough things for you to think about. God will take care of you today AND tomorrow!"

Focus on the Fruit

What did Jesus say about birds? (God loves the birds and feeds them.) **About flowers?** (God gives them beautiful clothes.) **What did Jesus say about worrying?** (We do not need to worry about anything.) **What did Jesus want us to know about God's care for us?** (God will take care of us and give us everything we need.)

Because we know that God loves us and will take care of us, we need never worry. We can have peace because God knows what we need and we can depend on God to keep His promises. Show the Peace poster.

Fruitful Lives Object Talk

Bible Verse

Peace I leave with you; my peace I give you. I do not give to you as the world gives. Do not let your hearts be troubled and do not be afraid. John 14:27

Materials

Bible with bookmark at John 14:27, loaf of bread and carton of milk.

God knows just what we need and He promises to take care of us! Because we can depend on God, we can have peace. Let's find out how one man showed that he had peace and trusted God.

Lead the Activity

1. **What is your favorite breakfast food?** Students respond. Show bread and milk. **Let's find out about some children who didn't know if they would have any food to eat for breakfast.**

2. **In the early 1800s, George Muller was a preacher in England. George was also the leader of an orphanage for poor children. One morning the tables in the orphanage dining room were set, but there was no food and no money to buy food. George didn't know where he would get food for breakfast. George and the children prayed, "Dear Father, we thank You for what You are going to give us to eat."**

   As soon as they finished praying, the town baker knocked at the door. He had loaves of fresh bread! The baker had gotten up early to make bread because he felt that God wanted him to give this gift to the children at the orphanage. A moment later, there was another knock at the door. The milkman's cart had broken down outside of the orphanage, and he needed to empty the cart before he could repair it. The milk would be wasted, so he offered to give the milk to the children. Time after time, God answered George's prayers just like this! George and the orphans had peace because they trusted God's care.

Conclude

Read John 14:27 aloud. **How did God care for George Muller and the orphans?** Students respond. **What are some other ways God cares for people?** Lead students in prayer, thanking God for taking care of us, so we can have peace and depend on Him.

• •

Discussion Questions

1. *What are some reasons we have for not being afraid or concerned about the future?*

2. *How can we show that we trust God's care?*

3. *What could you say to encourage a friend to have peace and trust God's care?*

Active Game Center: Cereal Spell-Off

Materials
Bible, bowls, alphabet-shaped cereal.

Prepare the Game
Pour a large amount of cereal into two bowls. Place bowls on the far side of the playing area.

We can have peace because God knows what we need and promises to care for us. Let's find a reminder of that during our game today.

Lead the Game
1. Divide group into two teams. Students line up in the playing area, across from the bowls of cereal letters.

2. At your signal, the first student on each team moves quickly to his or her team's bowl of cereal letters and digs through it to find a *P*. Student returns to team with letter. The next student moves to the bowl and searches for an *E*. Relay continues in this manner with each student finding the next letter of the word "PEACE." Continue playing until all students have had a turn and each team has formed the word "PEACE" as many times as possible.

3. Students from the team that formed "PEACE" the most times answer one of the Discussion Questions below. Continue discussion with other questions.

Options
1. Cut out at least 50 small slips of paper. Print a letter on each slip of paper, making sure to include several papers with the letters from the word "Peace" printed on them. Substitute paper slips for cereal letters in game.

2. At the bottom of each bowl of letters, bury a small slip of paper with John 14:27 written on it. Student who finds that slip of paper collects it and reads it aloud at the end of the game.

3. Letter "PEACE" on large sheet of paper for younger students to refer to.

• •

Discussion Questions
1. ***God knows what we need and promises to care for us. Why can we depend on God's help?*** (God always keeps His promises. God promises to answer our prayers. God's love for us never changes or fails.)

2. ***What does John 14:27 tell us about peace from God?*** (He gives us peace so that we do not need to be worried or afraid.)

3. ***How can we get the peace that Jesus said He left with us?*** (Ask Jesus to forgive our sins and tell Him that we want to be members of God's family. Keep trusting God, even when we're worried.) Talk to interested students about salvation (see "Leading a Child to Christ" article on p. 36 in this book).

Lesson 37

Art Center: Peaceful Pasta

Materials
Chenille wires, one or more kinds of pasta shapes (large elbow, mostaccioli, wheel, etc.), scissors.

Lead the Activity
Students thread pasta shapes onto chenille wires, forming birds or flowers as reminders that God provides all we need.

We can have peace because God knows what we need and promises to care for us, just like He cares for the birds and flowers. Let's make birds and flowers to remind us that we never need worry.

chenille wire

rigatoni

elbow macaroni

chenille wire

Option
Instead of using chenille wires, students form objects by gluing varieties of pasta to a sheet of construction paper.

Discussion Questions
1. *What are some things a kid your age might worry about?* (A test in school. A sick parent or grandparent. Being liked by others.)

2. *What does Jesus tell us about worrying?* (There is no need to worry, because God knows what we need and will provide for us.)

3. *What is something a kid can do if he or she is feeling worried about something?* (Remember God's promise to care for us. Talk to a teacher, parent or older sibling. Tell God what he or she is worried about. Read in God's Word about how He takes care of His family.)

Lesson 37

Worship Center

Bible Verse

Peace I leave with you; my peace I give you. I do not give to you as the world gives. Do not let your hearts be troubled and do not be afraid. John 14:27

Materials

Bible, *God's Kids Grow* cassette/CD or music video and player, "You Promised!" word chart (p. 487 in this book), large sheet of paper on which you have printed John 14:27, masking tape, marker.

Let's thank God for the peace we can have because He knows what we need and promises to care for us.

Sing to God

Play "You Promised!" encouraging students to sing along with the music. **We can have peace because we know God keeps His promises to care for us. What are some of the ways God cares for us?** (Answers our prayers. Helps us learn more about Him. Gives us family and friends. Helps us know how to live. Provides for all our needs.) **Why can we trust God's promises?** (His Word is true. He loves us. He always keeps His promises.)

Hear and Say God's Word

Display paper on which you have printed John 14:27. Have a volunteer read the verse aloud. **Jesus said these words when He was talking to His disciples. Why does He say not to be afraid or worried?** (He gives us peace.) Students stand in a circle. One student begins saying the verse through the first "you." As the word "you" is spoken, he or she points to another student to continue the verse. Continue this pattern, with students saying words of verse and pointing to new students each time the word "you" or "your" is spoken. Repeat until all students have had a turn and/or the verse has been repeated several times.

Pray to God

On the back of the Bible-verse paper, print "God, please help (Amy) to have Your peace and not be afraid. Thank You that You care for (Amy) and know everything she needs. In Jesus' name, amen." Ask a volunteer to read the words of the prayer aloud. **Let's pray this prayer for each other.** Students form pairs. Partners take turns praying the prayer for each other.

Options

1. Students sing "Read All About It" (p. 483 in this book).

2. Invite a musician from your church to play on a guitar, flute, trumpet, etc. one or both of the suggested songs for this lesson.

Bible Verse Coloring Center

Materials
Crayons or markers, a copy of page 109 or page 110 from *Bible Verse Coloring Pages #2* for each student.

Lead the Activity
Read John 14:27. **What does this verse say we don't have to do? Why? How has God shown His care for the kids in this picture? How does God show His care for you?** Students color picture.

Option
Provide fruit-scented markers for students to use to color picture.

Service Project Center

Materials
Materials needed for "Prayer Magnets" (p. 90 from *The Big Book of Service Projects*).

Lead the Activity
Students complete the "Prayer Magnets" activity as directed in *The Big Book of Service Projects*. **How can we help missionaries have peace?** (Pray that they will have peace and trust that God will provide for their needs and care for them.)

Discipleship Activity Center

Materials
Discussion Cards for Psalm 139:1-3,13-16 (pp. 87-92 from *The Big Book of Christian Growth*); materials needed for "Water-Pass Relay" or "Sentence Connections" (p. 33 or p. 49 from *The Big Book of Christian Growth*.

Lead the Activity
Because God made us and loves us, we can have peace as we depend on Him to care for us. Today we're going to play a game using Psalm 139:1-1,13-16 to discuss the special way in which God made us. Students complete activity as directed in *The Big Book of Christian Growth*.

God Talks to Job

Bible Verse

Trust in the Lord with all your heart and lean not on your own understanding. Proverbs 3:5

Bible Story Reference

Job 1—2:10; 42

Teacher's Devotional

Certain Bible characters are almost synonymous with certain character traits. When we think of Abraham,

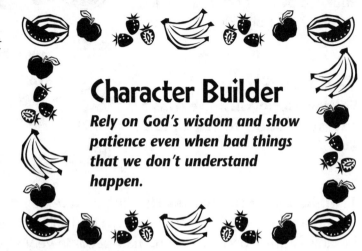

Character Builder

Rely on God's wisdom and show patience even when bad things that we don't understand happen.

we think of faith. When we think of Esther, we think of courage. And when we think of Job, we think of patience. "The patience of Job" is a common expression that refers to someone who demonstrates more than the average amount of this virtue.

Job's patience is remarkable, for he endured great suffering without resorting to anger or bitterness. His patient trust in God enabled him to endure the lack of faith of friends and family. Everyone else in the book of Job came to totally wrong conclusions because they depended on their ability to reason their way to understanding Job's disaster. Job alone held fast to his trust in God, even though he could not possibly comprehend any explanation for his troubles.

How was Job able to be so patient? How did he maintain his trust in God? A major clue is seen in his initial response to the news of his great calamity: Job got up and tore his robe and shaved his head (Biblical signs of mourning). Then he "fell to the ground in worship" (Job 1:20). Right from the start, Job looked to God and acknowledged that his life was in God's hands.

Again and again as Job responded to the accusations of his friends, even in moments of anguish and despair, he spoke to God. The heart-rending honesty of his prayers reveals trust in God that far surpassed his human understanding. When we truly place our trust in God, then "the patience of Job" can become a reality in our lives.

Bible Story Center

Materials
Patience poster from *Poster Pack*, ¼ cup (2 oz.) play dough for each student.

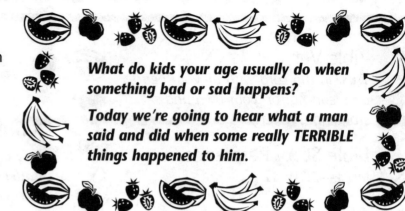

What do kids your age usually do when something bad or sad happens?

Today we're going to hear what a man said and did when some really TERRIBLE things happened to him.

Tell the Story
Follow along with me as we use our dough to tell today's story.

1. **Make a ball for the earth.** Things were going very badly for a man named Job. A terrible storm had killed his children; his animals had been stolen; he had become very sick. And he wondered why. In fact, Job wondered if God had forgotten all about him.

God had not forgotten about Job. Even though sad, terrible things had happened to Job, God still loved and cared for him. So God talked to Job to help him understand how great God is and how much He cared for Job.

"Tell me, Job, do you know how I made the earth? And do you know how I control the oceans and keep their waters from washing all over the land?"

Job must have thought about the beautiful world. He knew that God made the sweet-smelling flowers and the roaring waterfalls, the puffy clouds and the blue sky. Job KNEW God made the earth and everything in it.

2. **Pinch out rays on the earth to turn it into the sun.**  God wasn't finished asking Job questions. "Job, can you make the sun rise? Or can you make the rain fall and the grass grow?"

Job didn't know HOW God made the clouds or the rain. He didn't know exactly what God did to make it possible for the little grass seeds to sprout and grow. But there was one thing Job did know for sure—he didn't make the sun and he couldn't make it rain and he couldn't make the grass grow. Only God can do that!

3. **Make a star.** God had MORE questions to ask Job. "Do you know how to control the stars?" Job couldn't even count all the stars, much less control them!

"And Job, can you give food to the birds and the lions? Can you help the mother deer teach their babies to live on their own in the forests? Do you make horses to run SO FAST that the ground flashes by underneath them?"

Job knew God had made all the stars, created all the animals and made many of them strong and fast.

4. **Make a bird's nest.** "And Job," God continued, "does the eagle fly at your command? Are you the one who tells him to build his nest on rocky ledges high above the ground?"

Job must have thought of the strong eagles he had seen. He remembered how an eagle perched on the edge of its nest, carefully watching for food. Then the eagle flew off the nest, swooped down and caught the food. That's the way God planned for an eagle to get the food it needs. Job knew that God made eagles able to do all those things.

5. **Make a heart for love and a lightning bolt for power.** Job must have thought some more about his troubles. Then he must have thought about God's love and power.

Job said to God, "Now I know that you can do all things. All that you have planned will happen. Before I had heard of You, but I did not understand Your power or Your love. Now I know all that You can do. I'm sorry that I did not trust You."

Even though Job still had all of his troubles, he now trusted God to do what was best. Later, God gave Job twice as many sheep and cows and donkeys as he had ever had before. God also gave Job seven sons and three daughters. Job lived for a long, long time, enjoying all that God had given him.

Most important of all, God taught Job about His greatness. And Job learned that he could trust God's love and power when things were going well AND when things were going badly. Job waited patiently for God to answer him. God helped Job learn that people can depend on Him ALL the time.

● ●

Focus on the Fruit

What are some of the things God reminded Job He had made? (The whole earth. The sun and stars. Deer. Horses. Eagles.) **When bad things happened to him, what did Job do?** (He talked to God.) **What did Job learn?** (That he could always depend on God's love and power.) **God gave Job the patience he needed to wait for good things to happen again.**

When we're members of God's family, God doesn't promise that nothing bad will ever happen to us. But He does promise us that we can always trust in His love, power and wisdom. Show the Patience poster. **When we depend on God, He helps us grow patience.**

Lesson 38
Fruitful Lives Object Talk

Bible Verse
Trust in the Lord with all your heart and lean not on your own understanding.
Proverbs 3:5

Materials
Bible with bookmark at Proverbs 3:5, sheet of paper, pencil; optional—hymnbook with "It is Well with My Soul," a musician to lead students in singing the hymn.

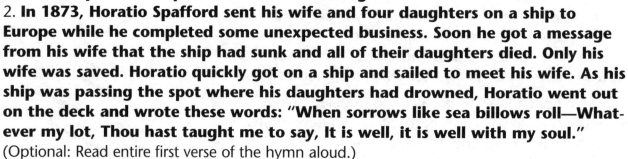

When bad things happen that we don't understand, sometimes the hardest thing to do is trust God's wisdom and show patience. But that is actually the best thing to do! Let's find out how one man trusted God's wisdom when something terrible happened to his family.

Lead the Activity
1. Hold up paper and pencil. **What do you usually do with these two objects?** Students respond. **A man named Horatio Spafford used a pencil and paper to write a poem to express how he was feeling.**

2. **In 1873, Horatio Spafford sent his wife and four daughters on a ship to Europe while he completed some unexpected business. Soon he got a message from his wife that the ship had sunk and all of their daughters died. Only his wife was saved. Horatio quickly got on a ship and sailed to meet his wife. As his ship was passing the spot where his daughters had drowned, Horatio went out on the deck and wrote these words: "When sorrows like sea billows roll—Whatever my lot, Thou hast taught me to say, It is well, it is well with my soul."** (Optional: Read entire first verse of the hymn aloud.)

3. **What do you think he meant by writing "it is well with my soul"?** Students respond. **Horatio wrote that whether he felt peace or sorrow, he was truly okay because he trusted God. People were so impressed with the words of Horatio's poem that they put the poem to music and it became a popular hymn which people still sing today.** (Optional: Musician leads students in singing hymn.)

Conclude
Read Proverbs 3:5 aloud. **What are some ways to show that you trust in God, even when bad things happen?** Lead students in prayer, thanking God that we can trust Him with our problems, no matter how bad the situation.

• •

Additional Information for Older Students
When they were reunited, Horatio Spafford and his wife moved to Israel and had more children. One day a Muslim man came and asked Mrs. Spafford to raise his newborn baby. His wife had died giving birth to the baby, and he thought that if he took the baby back to the desert where he lived, the baby would die, too. Mrs. Spafford agreed because after her daughters drowned, she decided that she would do everything she could to save other children. Soon many people were bringing her children whose parents had left them, and the Spafford's Children's Home began. God helped the Spaffords raise as many as 60 children at a time!

Active Game Center: String Search

Materials
Scissors, string, measuring stick or ruler.

Prepare the Game
Cut at least 30 lengths of string or 3 lengths for each student, each length varying between 8 inches (20 cm) and 3 feet (90 cm). Hide lengths of string around the playing area.

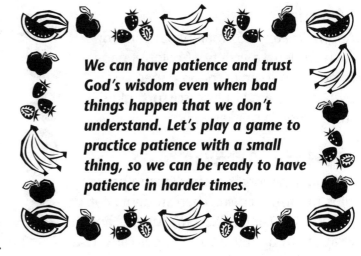

We can have patience and trust God's wisdom even when bad things happen that we don't understand. Let's play a game to practice patience with a small thing, so we can be ready to have patience in harder times.

Lead the Game
1. Group students in three or four teams.

2. At your signal, students begin searching around the playing area for lengths of string. As students find strings, team members tie them together to form one long string.

3. After all strings have been found, teams compare the length of their strings. A volunteer from the team with the longest string answers one of the Discussion Questions below.

Options
1. If possible, play this game outside or in a large room with many hiding places.

2. Advise each team to choose two team members to tie the strings together. All other team members look for the strings.

3. Challenge teams to form the word "trust" or "patience" with their long strings.

Discussion Questions
1. **When did you have to practice patience during this game?** (Searching for the strings. Tying the lengths of string together. When someone took a string you saw.)

2. **When are some times kids your age might need to show patience and trust God?** Volunteers respond. Share your own age-appropriate example or that of a child you know. **Why can we trust God, even in hard times?** (He loves us and promises to help and protect us. He made us and knows what is best for us.)

3. **What might help you show patience during hard times?** (Talking to God about your situation. Praying and asking God for patience. Reading the Bible to find out how God helped people in all kinds of hard situations.)

Art Center: Clip-On Chain

Materials

Approximately 25 small paper clips for each student, a variety of colorful paper (magazines, comics, neon paper, wrapping paper, etc.), rulers, scissors, glue sticks, fine-tip markers.

Lead the Activity

Even when bad things that we don't understand happen, we can show patience by trusting in God's wisdom. Let's patiently work together to make a chain of colorful links.

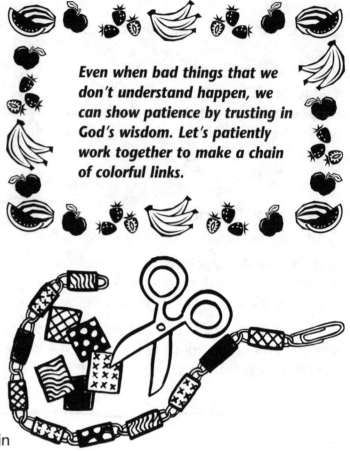

1. Students work together linking paper clips to form a chain. Then students cut papers into 1-inch (2.5-cm) squares and wrap them tightly around paper clips. Use glue sticks to seal the ends, and create colorful paper beads. Students use markers to write on beads words that remind them to be patient and trust in God's wisdom.

2. Display chain by hanging it from ceiling or stringing it along walls. At the end of the session, separate chain into sections for students to take home. Students may form armbands or necklaces by closing chain with another paper clip.

Options

1. Provide colorful vinyl-coated paper clips for students to use in making chains.

2. Use jumbo-size paper clips and 1½-inch (3.75-cm) square pieces of paper.

3. Students write the words of Proverbs 3:5, one word per paper bead, to make a verse chain.

4. If using glue instead of glue sticks, allow time for glue to dry before displaying chains.

Discussion Questions

1. *When are some times kids your age might need wisdom from God to show patience?* (When bad things happen. When they are hurt or angry or afraid.)

2. *How does knowing that God is wise make it easier to be patient in hard times?* (God knows what we need and will give it to us at just the right time. He plans everything for our good. He has a reason for everything.)

3. *What are some things you can do to remember God's wisdom in order to help you show patience?* (Talk to God like Job did. Read about how God helped people in the Bible. Talk to others about times they relied on God's wisdom.)

Lesson 38

Worship Center

Bible Verse

Trust in the Lord with all your heart and lean not on your own understanding. Proverbs 3:5

Materials

Bible, *God's Kids Grow* cassette/CD or music video and player, "Patient Father" word chart (p. 479 in this book), large sheet of paper on which you have printed all but four words of Proverbs 3:5 (leave blank space for "Trust," "Lord," "heart" and "lean"), masking tape.

Let's thank God and worship Him for His great wisdom that allows us to have patience, even when bad things happen.

Sing to God

Play "Patient Father," encouraging students to sing along with the music. **What are some ways this song describes God?** (Patient. Merciful. Forgiving. Wise.)

Hear and Say God's Word

Display paper on which you have printed Proverbs 3:5. Help students guess the missing words by pointing to the first blank and giving a clue such as, "This is a word that means to depend on someone." When students guess the word "Trust," print it in the blank space. Repeat for the other three words. Students recite completed verse together. **What does it mean to do something with all your heart?** (To do something as best you can.) **Why can we trust in God?** (God knows all that has happened in the past and all that will happen in the future. God is more powerful than anything. God's love for us is so great.)

Pray to God

Let's pray to God and tell Him we trust in Him. Students repeat this prayer after you, one phrase at a time: **God, please help us to trust in You. Thank You that Your wisdom is so great we can trust You and have patience, even when we don't understand why bad things happen. In Jesus' name, amen.**

Options

1. Ask an older student to read Job 12:13 aloud as an invitation to worship.

2. Invite students to think of motions illustrating the words of Proverbs 3:5. Students do motions while reciting the verse.

Bible Verse Coloring Center

Materials

Crayons or markers, a copy of page 59 or page 60 from *Bible Verse Coloring Pages #2* for each student.

Lead the Activity

Read Proverbs 3:5. **How are the kids in this picture showing they are trusting in God and His wisdom? What are some of the stories in the Bible that help us know we can trust in God and His plan for us?** Students color picture.

Option

Also provide a copy of "Draw a picture of a place where you can pray" page (p. 220 from *Bible Verse Coloring Pages #2*). Students draw and color pictures. **When you pray to God, you can ask Him to help you trust in Him and depend on His wisdom.**

Service Project Center

Materials

Materials needed for "Doorknob Hangers" (p. 36 from *The Big Book of Service Projects*).

Lead the Activity

Students complete the "Doorknob Hangers" activity as directed in *The Big Book of Service Projects*. **What can we write on our doorknob hangers to remind others and ourselves to trust patiently in God? Why can we trust in God?**

Discipleship Activity Center

Materials

Discussion Cards for Proverbs 3:3-6 (pp. 99-104 from *The Big Book of Christian Growth*), materials needed for "Chair Share" or "Coin Cups" (p. 11 or p. 59 from *The Big Book of Christian Growth*).

Lead the Activity

When we trust in God and His wisdom, it helps us show the fruit of patience in our lives. Today we're going to play a game to help us discover ways of trusting in God. Students complete activity as directed in *The Big Book of Christian Growth*.

The Lame Man

Bible Verse

As God's chosen people, holy and dearly loved, clothe yourselves with compassion, kindness, humility, gentleness and patience. Colossians 3:12

Bible Story Reference

Acts 3

Teacher's Devotional

Character Builder

Our kind actions demonstrate God's love.

For the lame man sitting beside the Temple gate, kindness came in an unexpected way. He asked passersby for money, hoping that among the crowds would be people kind enough to give him enough money to live on. Then he received an act of kindness that far exceeded what he had asked. Instead of receiving just enough, he received an abundant gift that resulted in his "walking and jumping, and praising God" (Acts 3:8).

Kindness is a virtue that goes beyond the minimum. There was nothing mean-spirited or grudging about Peter's response to the beggar's plea. Instead, we can easily see Peter smiling with pleasure as he reached out his hand and pulled the man to his feet. Somehow we often find ourselves so overcome with busyness that we overlook the opportunity to extend ourselves in kindness. Kindness opens our eyes so that, rather than seeing the person in need as an interruption to our plans, we see the potential impact of concerned words and actions.

Kindness is also a virtue to open the way for people to meet Jesus for themselves. Not only did the man who was healed find himself praising God, but also the people who saw what had happened "were filled with wonder and amazement" (Acts 3:10). Being generous with acts of kindness helps people become receptive to hearing the truth about God's great love for them. This principle can be illustrated in your class as you show God's kindness in practical ways to each student.

Bible Story Center

Materials
Kindness poster from *Poster Pack*; ¼ cup (2 oz.) play dough and coin for each student.

Tell the Story
Follow along with me as we use our dough to tell today's story.

What are some of the ways you've learned about God's love for you?

Today we're going to hear how a whole crowd of people heard the good news of God's love!

1. **Make one big square between two flat small rectangles for the Temple.** After Jesus died on the cross and rose from the grave, His followers started telling more and more people about Him. People from many different countries heard about Jesus and became members of God's family. One group of believers lived in Jerusalem and met together every day in the Temple in Jerusalem to worship God.

Every day, there was a 40-year-old man who was brought to the Beautiful Gate of the Temple to beg. The man had been born crippled; he'd never walked a step in his life! So every day, he was brought to this gate through which many people had to walk on their way to worship God. The Temple was a good place for begging, since many people felt that giving money to a poor, crippled man would please God.

2. **Make a bowl and several coins to put in it. Press a coin onto each coin shape.** On one particular day, two men came up to the gate on their way to pray.

"Please help me!" the crippled man called out as he held up a bowl for coins.

The two men turned and looked the crippled man straight in the eyes. This action surprised him. Usually people just ignored him, or they put coins in his bowl without looking at him and hurried on. But these men were different! They were Jesus' disciples Peter and John.

Although Peter and John might have wanted to put money into the man's bowl, they didn't have any. "But what I have I will give to you," Peter said.

3. **Make a stick-figure man. Bend the man's legs to show that he is walking or jumping.** Peter took the lame man by the hand, pulled him to his feet and said, "In the name of Jesus, WALK!" And the man did!

Suddenly the man's feet and legs became strong! He was so excited and happy that he went into the Temple with Peter and John, jumping and walking and praising God!

Since this happened at one of the regular times for people to meet at the Temple and pray, there were many other people at the Temple, too. All these people were amazed at what they had seen!

They all knew this man. For a long time, he'd spent every day at the Temple, begging. Now he was walking and jumping and praising God! Of course the people wanted to know how this wonderful thing had happened. A large crowd gathered around Peter and John.

This was too good an opportunity to miss! Peter's act of faith and kindness had given him a chance to tell about Jesus. Peter didn't want people to think he had some sort of magical power, so the first thing he said was, "Why are you surprised? Do you think we healed this man with our own powers? It was God, who raised Jesus from the dead, who did this miracle!"

4. **Make a cross.** Peter told the crowd who Jesus was. "Do you remember Jesus? The One that you convinced Pilate to put to death on the cross?" asked Peter. "Well, I am here to tell you that God has raised Jesus from the dead."

Peter told the people to repent—to turn away from sin and start obeying God. The crowd was excited about Peter's message. The Bible tells us thousands of people came to accept God's love and believe in Jesus as the promised Messiah sent from God.

• •

Focus on the Fruit
Why was the lame man brought to the gates of the Temple? (To beg for money.)
What did Peter do instead of giving the lame man money? (Peter healed him in Jesus' name, so he could walk.) **What did the people in the Temple learn from Peter's kind actions?** (They learned about God's love. They learned about Jesus.)

People can learn about God's love in many ways. One important way is through our kind actions and kind words. Show the Kindness poster. **As we experience God's love for us, we grow kindness in our lives so that we can help others experience God's love, too!**

Fruitful Lives Object Talk

Bible Verse

As God's chosen people, holy and dearly loved, clothe yourselves with compassion, kindness, humility, gentleness and patience. Colossians 3:12

Our kind actions demonstrate God's love. Let's learn about a woman whose kind actions helped people around the world experience God's love.

Materials

Bible with bookmark at Colossians 3:12, one or more objects with slogans (T-shirt, bumper sticker, poster, ads, etc.); optional—photo of Mother Teresa.

Lead the Activity

1. Show object(s) and ask volunteers to read the slogans aloud. **When people want others to know important things they believe, they often write slogans.**

2. **In 1910 a special girl was born in Macedonia, a country in Eastern Europe. During her teenage years, this girl joined a group of young people who raised money for the poor and learned about missionaries in foreign lands. The motto of this group was "What have I done for Christ? What am I doing for Christ? What will I do for Christ?" This motto showed how important these teenagers thought it was to love and obey Jesus.**

   When this young lady was 18, she decided to serve Christ by becoming a missionary in India. For the rest of her life, she lived among the poorest people in India. She taught street children and comforted the sick and dying. She became known as Mother Teresa. Other women joined her, forming a group called the Missionaries of Charity. "Charity" is another word for "love." Today this group has more than 500 centers around the world where the hungry, the sick and the dying are cared for. (Optional: Show photo of Mother Teresa.)

Conclude

Read Colossians 3:12 aloud. **How did Mother Teresa obey this verse?** Volunteers tell. Lead students in prayer, asking for God's help serving those who are in need so that others can learn more about God's love.

• •

Additional Information for Older Students

The Missionaries of Charity spend their whole lives cleaning people's wounds, feeding dying people and rocking abandoned babies. When one missionary was asked if she got tired of doing this difficult work, she said that she could never get tired because she loves and cares for each person as if he or she were Jesus Himself (see Matthew 25:40).

Active Game Center: Circle Ball

Materials
Large sheet of paper, marker, playground ball or tennis ball.

Our kind actions demonstrate God's love. In our game today we'll show some kind actions.

Lead the Game

1. **What are some kind actions we can do?** (Listen to someone who is upset. Give someone flowers. Call someone who is sick. Rake leaves for a grandparent.) List students' ideas on large sheet of paper.

2. Choose one volunteer. Other students stand in a large circle, spreading their legs so that each student's right foot is touching the left foot of the student next to him or her. Volunteer stands in the middle of the circle. Give ball to the volunteer.

3. Volunteer rolls the ball toward a student in the circle, trying to get the ball between the student's legs. Students in circle may use hands to bat away the ball, but they cannot move their feet. If volunteer gets the ball past a student, that student goes to the middle of the circle and pantomimes a kind action from the list on the large sheet of paper. Students guess kind action being pantomimed. First student to guess pantomimed action takes a turn rolling the ball. If volunteer does not get the ball past any student, volunteer rolls ball again. After three unsuccessful tries, volunteer pantomimes a kind action before a new student is chosen to roll the ball. Continue playing game as time allows.

Option
Challenge older students by allowing students to pantomime kind actions that are not listed on the large sheet of paper.

• •

Discussion Questions

1. *What are some kind actions you can do at home? At school? In your neighborhood?* (Let your brother or sister choose which video to watch. Help your parents empty the dishwasher. Invite a new kid to play a game at school. Carry groceries for a neighbor.)

2. *Why do your kind actions help other people learn about God's love?* (They can see some of the ways God cares for them. They might ask why you are being kind, and you can tell them about God's love.)

3. *What is one kind action you can do this week? For whom?* Volunteers respond.

Lesson 39

Art Center: Kindness Clothing

Materials
White construction paper, markers, one or more T-shirts with slogans printed on them, large sheet of paper, scissors.

Prepare the Activity
Draw the outline of a T-shirt on construction paper, making one for each student (see sketch).

We show God's love when we demonstrate kindness to others. Let's make shirts to remind us of ways to be kind.

Lead the Activity
1. Show T-shirt(s). **What does this T-shirt tell or show you? What does this T-shirt remind you of?** Volunteers answer.

2. Invite students to tell words or pictures which remind them of ways to show kindness. List students' responses on large sheet of paper.

3. Each student cuts out a T-shirt outline from construction paper and draws pictures or write words on the outline as a reminder of ways to show kindness, referring to list as needed. Ask the Discussion Questions below as students work.

Options
1. Older students may draw their own T-shirt outlines.

2. Purchase (or ask students to bring) white fabric T-shirts. Students draw pictures and write words on the T-shirts with fabric markers.

3. Display completed T-shirts in your classroom or along a wall in a public area of your church.

• •

Discussion Questions
1. *What are some ways people have shown kindness to you or someone you know?*

2. *What are some ways you could show kindness at home? At school? While playing with your friends?* (Pray for someone who has a problem. Help someone who has tripped and fallen. Invite a kid who may be feeling lonely to play.)

3. *How does being kind show God's love to others?* (When we show kindness, we are showing that God loves everyone and wants us to love each other.)

Lesson 39

Worship Center

Bible Verse

As God's chosen people, holy and dearly loved, clothe yourselves with compassion, kindness, humility, gentleness and patience. Colossians 3:12

Materials

Bible; *God's Kids Grow* cassette/CD or music video and player; "Be So Kind" word chart (p. 455 in this book); large sheet of paper on which you have printed Colossians 3:12; five index cards on which you have printed the following words, one word per card: "compassion," "kindness," "humility," "gentleness," "patience"; masking tape.

We can demonstrate God's love through our kind actions. Let's worship God for His great love and ask His help in being kind to others!

Sing to God

Play "Be So Kind," encouraging students to sing along with the music and do the actions shown on the word chart or music video. **What does this song tell us about God?** (He is generous.) **How can kids your age show God's love and generosity to others?**

Hear and Say God's Word

Display paper on which you have printed Colossians 3:12. Give index cards to volunteers. Say the word on each card as you hand it to each volunteer. **As I read Colossians 3:12, listen for the word on your card. When you hear it, stand up and hold up your card. The rest of us will echo the word as you hold up your card.** Say verse, pausing for volunteers to hold up cards and for students to echo the words. Collect cards and give to different volunteers. Say verse again, allowing volunteers with cards to pop up and say words. Repeat as time allows, with different students holding the cards each time. **What does it mean to clothe yourself with something?** (Wear something so that people see what you've chosen to wear.) **What would someone do who was clothed with kindness?** (Choose to act kindly each day.)

Pray to God

What are some words you can use to describe God's love? ("Great." "Patient." "Always the same." "Kind." "Caring.") Volunteers pray, completing sentence "God, Your love is . . ." End prayer by thanking God for His love and asking for His help in being kind.

Options

1. Students sing "Good Fruit" and/or "Circle of Love" (p. 465 and/or p. 457 in this book).

2. Older students look up the definitions of "compassion" and "humility" in a children's Bible dictionary and tell the definitions to other students during the verse discussion.

Lesson 39

Bible Verse Coloring Center

Materials
Crayons or markers, a copy of page 179 or page 180 from *Bible Verse Coloring Pages #2* for each student.

Lead the Activity
Read Colossians 3:12. **What does this verse say we are to clothe ourselves with or put on? To "wear" kindness means to treat others in a kind way. What can you do to show kindness? Patience?** Students color picture.

Option
Provide felt or fabric scraps for students to glue onto clothing in picture.

Service Project Center

Materials
Materials needed for "Puppet Fun" (p. 99 from *The Big Book of Service Projects*).

Lead the Activity
Students complete the "Puppet Fun" activity as directed in *The Big Book of Service Projects*. **For whom could we do a puppet skit? What can we do with our puppets to help other people learn about Jesus? What are some other ways that we can be kind and show God's love?**

Discipleship Activity Center

Materials
Discussion Cards for Galatians 5:22,23 (pp. 147-152 from *The Big Book of Christian Growth*); materials needed for "Sticky Ball" or "Telephone" (p. 27 or p. 69 from *The Big Book of Christian Growth*).

Lead the Activity
There are lots of ways to show kindness. Today we're going to play a game to answer questions about the fruit of the Spirit, so we can grow the fruit of kindness in our lives. Students complete activity as directed in *The Big Book of Christian Growth*.

Cheerful Giving

Bible Verse
Each one should use whatever gift he has received to serve others. 1 Peter 4:10

Bible Story Reference
Acts 11:19-30; 2 Corinthians 8; 9

Character Builder
Goodness includes using what God gives you to help others.

Teacher's Devotional
"Good, Better, Best." We've all seen those three words attached to products, services and experiences. These familiar comparisons express the common understanding that there are degrees of goodness. Brand A may well be recognized as being good, but Brand B has features that make it even better. But why settle for either of those when you can buy Brand C, which surpasses the other two?

The apostle Paul used a similar approach in his appeal that Corinthian believers do their best in giving money to aid fellow Christians who were facing severe troubles. Paul commended the Corinthians for having made a good beginning in their fund-raising efforts. But he did not want them to settle for just having done something good. Instead, he urged them to "see that you also excel in this grace of giving" (2 Corinthians 8:7).

To make sure the Corinthians did not look at what they had already done and simply say "That's the best we can do," Paul presented the example of the Macedonian churches who "gave as much as they were able, and even beyond their ability" (2 Corinthians 8:3).

Nowhere in his letter does Paul cite the dollar (denarii) amount the Macedonians had given or suggest a goal for the Corinthians to meet. Excelling in the grace of giving is not determined by some financial measurement. Excelling is to give freely of what God has given us. After all, "God is able to make all grace abound to you, so that in all things at all times, having all that you need, you will abound in every good work" (2 Corinthians 9:8).

Bible Story Center

Materials

Goodness poster from *Poster Pack*, ¼ cup
(2 oz.) play dough for each student.

Tell the Story

**Follow along with me as we use our
dough to tell today's story.**

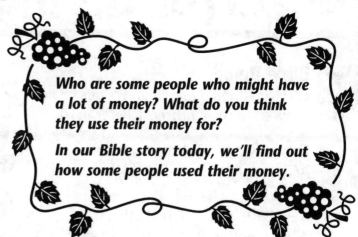

*Who are some people who might have
a lot of money? What do you think
they use their money for?*

*In our Bible story today, we'll find out
how some people used their money.*

1. **Make several long ropes from your dough. Then use
the ropes to make a face with a talking mouth.** It had
not been very long since Jesus had died, risen and gone back to
heaven. Jesus' followers were busy telling EVERYONE the good
news about Jesus! This good news about Jesus was being
spread as far away as Antioch, a city hundreds of miles (kilome-
ters) from Jerusalem. And not just Jewish people were becoming members of God's family. Many others were believing, too.

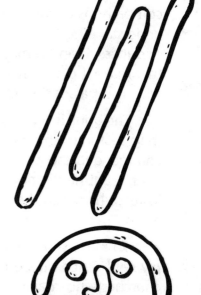

Two of Jesus' followers, Paul and Barnabas, were living and
working in Antioch, teaching the believers and telling others
about Jesus. Then one day, some men from Jerusalem came to
visit them. One of the men, Agabus, said that a severe famine
would soon spread through the land. The people in Jerusalem,
including all of Jesus' followers who lived there, would not have
enough to eat!

The people in Antioch could have said, "Why should we
help THOSE people? They're too far away!"

But they DIDN'T say those things. Instead, they were glad
to help their Christian brothers and sisters who were going to
be having trouble getting food. After all, they were all part of
God's family, no matter how far away from each other they
lived!

2. **Turn face into a smiling face.** So the believers in Antioch
gave as much money as they could to help the believers in
Jerusalem. Paul and Barnabas returned to Jerusalem with the
gift of money from the believers in Antioch. Later they continued their travels, going to many other cities and telling people
about Jesus. Sometimes as he traveled, Paul would stop and
stay in a particular city for a while to teach the people more
about Jesus.

One place Paul stopped and stayed for a while was the city of Corinth, which was very far away from Jerusalem. He lived there for about a year and a half. Eventually, Paul traveled on, but he sent letters back to the people of Corinth. He wrote letters that helped them know how God wanted them to live.

3. **Make many small coins.** In the first letter that Paul wrote to his friends at Corinth, he asked them to save some money every week for the Christians in the city of Jerusalem. These Christians still needed help from believers in other parts of the world.

Just like the people of Antioch, the Corinthians began to save money to send to the believers in Jerusalem. They knew it pleased God for them to give what they had to help others who were in need.

Because traveling in those days took lots of time, weeks and months went by before the Corinthians got another letter from Paul. "I'm coming to Corinth on my way to Jerusalem," Paul wrote. He was going to take the money they had saved and give it to their brothers and sisters who were in need.

4. **With a friend, make the word "GIVE" from coins.** Paul wrote, "I know you are very willing to take care of your brothers and sisters in God's family. I've told other people about your giving and it's made them want to give, too!"

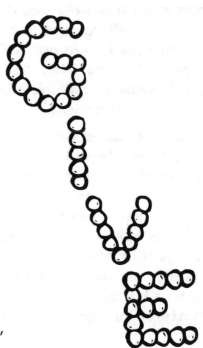

Then Paul wrote an example to help the Corinthians understand more about giving. He wrote, "Giving to help others in God's family is a lot like a farmer planting seeds. If he only plants a few seeds, he'll only grow a few plants. But if the farmer plants a lot of seeds, he grows a lot of plants and has a BIG harvest! God will always give you everything you need, so you can give generously.

"This giving does more than just help to take care of the needs of your brothers and sisters in Jerusalem. It will also make everyone who hears about it glad. They will praise God! And it will show them that you are obeying and trusting God."

• •

Focus on the Fruit
How did people in our Bible story show that they thought giving to others was really important? (They gave whatever they could to help people they didn't even know.) **Why do you think they wanted to give to others?** (God had been good to them by giving to them, so they wanted to be good to others. They wanted to please God, because they loved Him.)

Paul took that money to the poor people in Jerusalem a long time ago. But the very same kind of giving still happens today. Helping others by sharing what God gives us is one way to show God's goodness. Show the Goodness poster.

Fruitful Lives Object Talk

Bible Verse
Each one should use whatever gift he has received to serve others. 1 Peter 4:10

Materials
Bible with bookmark at 1 Peter 4:10, peanuts.

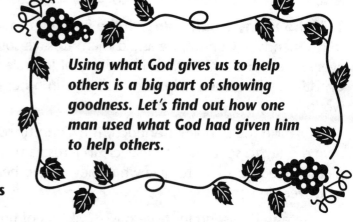

Using what God gives us to help others is a big part of showing goodness. Let's find out how one man used what God had given him to help others.

Lead the Activity

1. Show peanuts. **What are some things that people use peanuts for?** (To eat. To make peanut butter.) **Before the early 1900s, few people grew peanuts because they didn't know how to use the peanuts. But a man named George Washington Carver believed that God had given him a brain to help him discover how the peanut could be used. Dr. Carver discovered over 300 things that could be made from peanuts, including printer's ink, a milk substitute, face powder, soap and candy.** (Note: If student indicates he or she is allergic to peanuts, comment, **While some people are allergic to peanuts, there are other good uses for them besides eating them.**)

2. **George Carver also discovered many things about the best ways to grow plants. And he didn't keep what he learned to himself! Dr. Carver used what he had learned about plants to help others.**

    Dr. Carver and a friend got a horse and wagon and set up a portable school. They traveled to poor farms all over their county to teach African-American farmers better ways to grow plants. He also taught them new ways to use the things they grew so that they could make money selling new products. Some people complained that Dr. Carver should make people pay to learn the things he was teaching. But Dr. Carver insisted that money was not important. All that mattered to him was helping people.

Conclude

Read 1 Peter 4:10 aloud. **How did George Washington Carver show goodness and obey 1 Peter 4:10?** Lead students in prayer, asking God to help them find good ways to help others.

• •

Discussion Questions

1. *Who is someone you know that shows goodness? What does he or she do?*

2. *What are some things you enjoy doing or are good at doing? How can you use these things to help others?*

3. *Who are some people you can help or serve this week?*

Lesson 40

Active Game Center: Helpful Actions

Materials
Slips of paper, marker, paper bags, paper plates.

Prepare the Game
Print the following words on slips of paper, one word on each paper: "head," "shoulder," "hand," "elbow," "knees" (see sketch a). Prepare two sets of papers and put each set in a separate paper bag.

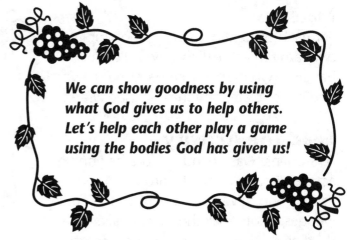

We can show goodness by using what God gives us to help others. Let's help each other play a game using the bodies God has given us!

Lead the Game
1. Group students into teams of no more than eight. Students within teams form pairs. Teams line up in pairs on one side of the room.

2. Give one bag of papers and one paper plate to each team. Volunteer on each team chooses two slips of paper from his or her team's bag. Students read papers aloud. The first pair of students on each team places the paper plate between the two body parts listed on the chosen slips of paper (see sketch).

3. At your signal, the first pair of students on each team walks to the other side of the room and back, keeping the paper plate in position. As pairs return to teams, the next pairs position the plates in the same way and walk across the room. Relay continues until all pairs have had a turn with the plates in that position. Ask a volunteer from the team that finished first to answer one of the Discussion Questions below. Begin a new round of the game with new pairs choosing slips of paper for their teams.

Option
With older students, group them into teams of boys and girls. Also, to challenge older students, have each pair of students choose new slips of paper from the bag so that each pair completes the relay with the plate in a different position.

Discussion Questions
1. *What parts of your body can you use to help other people?* (Arms. Legs. Mouth. Mind.) *What skills?* (Skill at drawing. Skill at taking care of other kids.)

2. *What are some ways to help other people using (your arms)?* (Carry groceries into the house. Fold laundry. Hold a crying baby.) Repeat question with other skills.

3. *What are some ways you can use the money or possessions God has given you and your family to help other people?* (Give money to organizations that help other people. Give offering at church. Share clothes or food with others.) Tell students some of the ways your church uses its money to help others.

Art Center: Fruit Skewers

Materials

For each student: two wedges of apple, two large marshmallows, two slices of banana, two grapes, one bamboo skewer, one paper plate; optional—plastic wrap.

Lead the Activity

1. Students wash hands before beginning activity. Divide class into groups of four. In each group, give one student all the apple wedges, another all the marshmallows, a third all the banana slices and the fourth all the grapes. Give the four bamboo skewers and four paper plates to one student in each group who will be the Snack Master.

When we use what God gives us to help others, we show the fruit of goodness. Let's give what we have to help others create a fruity snack!

2. In each group, the Snack Master puts one of his or her ingredients on a skewer, places skewer on a plate and passes plate to the next student. Snack Master repeats process with each skewer. Plates and skewers are passed around the circle twice, with students placing one of their ingredients on the skewer at each turn.

3. Ask Discussion Questions below as students work. Students give fruit skewers to another class. (Optional: Wrap skewers with plastic wrap.)

Options

1. Students thread breakfast cereal pieces shaped like Os onto string or fishing line to make necklaces or bracelets.

2. Instead of making skewers, students use plastic knives to cut apples and bananas and mix all ingredients together for a fruit salad. Drizzle salad with orange juice and serve (with forks) in paper cups.

3. Post a note alerting parents to the use of food in this activity. Also check registration forms for possible food allergies.

• •

Discussion Questions

1. *What are some of the good things God has given to you?*

2. *How could you use these good things to help someone in need?* Tell of a time you or someone you know was helped by someone using his or her gift from God.

3. *Besides money and things, what are some abilities God has given to you? How can you use (the ability to read) to help others?*

Lesson 40

Worship Center

Bible Verse
Each one should use whatever gift he has received to serve others. 1 Peter 4:10

Materials
Bible, *God's Kids Grow* cassette/CD or music video and player, "Goodness!" word chart (p. 469 in this book), large sheet of paper on which you have printed 1 Peter 4:10, masking tape, marker.

We can show goodness by using what God gives us to help others. Let's thank God for all that He has given us!

Sing to God
Play "Goodness!" encouraging students to sing along with the music. **In what ways does this song suggest to show goodness?** (Be fair. Keep promises. Tell the truth. Do what is right by obeying God.) **What has God given you to help you show goodness in these ways?** (Gives us courage to obey Him. Gives us a mouth to use to tell the truth.)

Hear and Say God's Word
Display paper on which you have printed 1 Peter 4:10. Have a volunteer read the verse aloud. **What kinds of gifts is this verse talking about?** (Money. Talents. Abilities.) **What does 1 Peter 4:10 say we should do with the gifts God has given us?** (Use them to serve others.) Students stand or sit in a circle. In clockwise order around the circle, students repeat words of 1 Peter 4:10. When you clap your hands, the students repeat the words in a counterclockwise order around the circle. Continue, with students reversing the order in which they are repeating the verse each time you clap your hands.

Pray to God
Cross off words on verse paper and print this prayer: "God, help each one of us use whatever gift we have received to serve others." Lead students in reciting the prayer together aloud. **When are some times we can serve others at home? At school?**

Options
1. If you take an offering during this Worship Center, remind students that giving an offering is one way to help others by sharing what God has given us. Tell specific ways your church shows goodness in how they use the offering money to help others.

2. Before the prayer, students brainstorm a list of items God has given them. Challenge students to think of one gift for each letter of the alphabet. During the prayer, students thank God for items on list.

3. Ask an older student to find and read 2 Thessalonians 2:16,17. **What has God given us?** (His love. Encouragement. Hope.) **What can God's love and hope encourage and strengthen us to do?** (Do good deeds. Show caring actions. Speak kind words to others.)

Lesson 40

Bible Verse Coloring Center

Materials
Crayons or markers, a copy of page 205 or page 206 from *Bible Verse Coloring Pages #2* for each student.

Lead the Activity
Read 1 Peter 4:10. **Who is serving or helping someone in this picture? What are some ways you can serve or care for people at home? At church?** Students color picture.

Option
Bring bread, peanut butter, jelly and plastic knives. Students make sandwiches for each other. (Note: Some children are allergic to peanuts. Outside classroom door, post a notice about the use of food in this activity so that parents may alert you about food allergies their children have.)

Service Project Center

Materials
Materials needed for "Seasonal Service" (p. 92 from *The Big Book of Service Projects*).

Lead the Activity
Students complete the "Seasonal Service" activity as directed in *The Big Book of Service Projects*. **How do you think this project might help someone? What are some other ways you could help people this week?**

Discipleship Activity Center

Materials
Discussion Cards for Romans 12:9-14,17-21 (pp. 135-140 from *The Big Book of Christian Growth*); materials needed for "C.H.O.I.C.E." or "Guest Talk" (p. 12 or p. 44 from *The Big Book of Christian Growth*).

Lead the Activity
Today we're going to play a game to help us think about ways to show goodness toward others. Students complete activity as directed in *The Big Book of Christian Growth*.

Noah Is Faithful

Bible Verse

Let us not become weary in doing good, for at the proper time we will reap a harvest if we do not give up.
Galatians 6:9

Bible Story Reference

Genesis 6—9

Teacher's Devotional

Everyone at some time or another faces physical and emotional weariness.

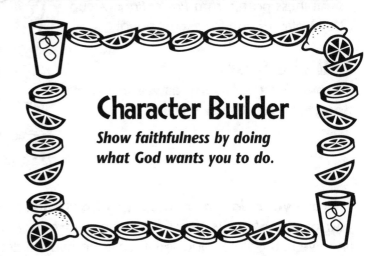

Character Builder

Show faithfulness by doing what God wants you to do.

That very human condition is the reason why Paul raised the issue in his letter to the Galatians (see Galatians 6:9). For the same reason, he also wrote almost the same exact words to the Christians in Thessalonica: "Never tire of doing what is right" (2 Thessalonians 3:13).

Lest you start feeling guilty about occasionally running out of energy and enthusiasm, consider that the Greek word translated in the above verses as "become weary" or "tire" is also translated "lose heart" (2 Corinthians 4:1,16) or "be discouraged" (Ephesians 3:13) in other letters from Paul. Paul's point is not to tell us we should always be full of energy but rather that we should not let our weaknesses take over and squeeze out our determination to do what is right.

So what will keep us going in the right direction when we face wearisome problems? Paul encourages us to think of the great reward that comes to those who do not give up. It's one thing to get tired, but it's a very different thing to let tiredness become an excuse to quit. When Paul wrote to the Corinthians about his own struggles to be faithful, he shared the same key to success in the face of difficult challenges: "Our light and momentary troubles are achieving for us an eternal glory that far outweighs them all. So we fix our eyes not on what is seen, but on what is unseen. For what is seen is temporary, but what is unseen is eternal" (2 Corinthians 4:17,18).

Bible Story Center

Materials
Faithfulness poster from *Poster Pack,* ¼ cup (2 oz.) play dough for each student.

Tell the Story
Follow along with me as we use our dough to tell today's story.

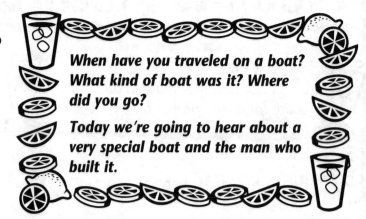

When have you traveled on a boat? What kind of boat was it? Where did you go?

Today we're going to hear about a very special boat and the man who built it.

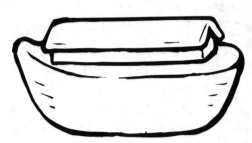

1. **From your dough, make a big boat that reminds you of Noah's ark.** After God made the world, Adam and Eve had children and THEIR children had children, until finally, there were more people than anyone could count! But the Bible says that all those people became so wicked that all they thought about was doing evil. They were cruel and selfish. They lied to each other. They stole from each other. They even killed each other.

God was sad that He'd ever created people. He decided to put an end to the people who were so mean and who kept on disobeying God and doing all kinds of evil things. There was only one person who really loved and obeyed God—Noah. So God planned for Noah and his family to be safe. God said, "Noah, I want you to build a big boat, an ark. I'm going to send a lot of rain until the whole earth is COVERED with water. But you and your family will be safe in the ark."

God told Noah EXACTLY how to build the ark. The ark was to be made from certain kinds of wood. And it was going to be BIG! When it was finished, it was going to be as long as one and a half football fields! Once again, Noah did just what God told him to do.

Noah must have looked pretty silly to his neighbors—especially since this boat wasn't near the sea, and people had never heard of a great flood before!

We don't know what Noah said to people about the ark, but in 2 Peter 2:5 Noah is called "a preacher of righteousness." All during the time Noah worked on the ark, he must have told people what was going to happen, and he may have tried to get them to change their ways. But people didn't listen to him.

2. **Make one or two animals of your choice.** After the ark was built, God said, "Noah, take your family and some of EVERY kind of animal and bird with you."

Again, Noah did what God told him to do! He loaded food for his family and for ALL those animals into the ark. Then God sent the animals to Noah. Rhinoceroses, elephants and lightning bugs—animals of every kind and size came to Noah! Rabbits and hippos, lions and mice, sparrows and eagles—all these and more found places in the ark.

Noah obeyed God, even though it hadn't rained at all yet. For all we know, there wasn't even a cloud in the sky. When his family and all the animals were finally in the ark, Noah went inside. And God closed the door.

Then it started to rain. And it rained. And it rained. For 40 days and 40 nights the rain fell hard and fast. Outside the ark, the water got DEEPER and DEEPER until even the tallest mountain on Earth was COVERED with water. But inside the ark, Noah and his family and all the animals were snug and dry.

3. **Roll three ropes and make a rainbow.** One day, it got very quiet. The rain had stopped! But it was a LONG time before the water dried up. Noah, his family and the animals lived on the ark for almost a YEAR. Then one day God said, "Noah, come out of the ark. Bring your family. And bring out all those animals and birds from the ark, too." Noah and his family and ALL the animals they'd been taking care of could leave the ark!

The first thing Noah did was to thank God for keeping him and his family safe during the flood. God made a special promise. "I will NEVER again destroy the whole earth with a flood." Then to remind everyone of His promise, God put a beautiful rainbow in the sky. Even today, whenever we see a rainbow, we remember that God promised NEVER again to destroy the earth by covering it with water. And we know that God is faithful—He always does what He promised.

• •

Focus on the Fruit

What made Noah different from all the other people? (Noah was faithful to God. He loved and obeyed God.) **How did Noah show his faithfulness to God? What did God promise after the flood was over?** (He would never destroy the whole earth with a flood.)

Because God loves us so much, He wants us to do what's right. It can be hard to obey Him when others are doing wrong, but God will help us be faithful and do what He wants us to do—just like He helped Noah! Show the Faithfulness poster.

Fruitful Lives Object Talk

Bible Verse

Let us not become weary in doing good, for at the proper time we will reap a harvest if we do not give up. Galatians 6:9

Materials

Bible with bookmark at Galatians 6:9, tablecloth, place setting (plate, utensils, glass or cup).

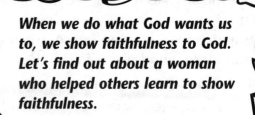

When we do what God wants us to, we show faithfulness to God. Let's find out about a woman who helped others learn to show faithfulness.

Lead the Activity

1. Invite volunteers to use items you brought to show how to set a table. **For what kinds of jobs would you need to know how to set a table?** (Waiter.) **What are some other jobs you know of?** Volunteers answer. **In the early 1900s many African-Americans had a hard time finding good jobs. Mary McLeod Bethune was an African-American school teacher who wanted her students to be able to get good jobs.**

2. **Mary started a school for African-American children. She taught her students how to read, how to study Bible stories and how to speak a language called Latin. She also taught practical skills like setting tables, cooking, gardening, sewing and cleaning. Mary wanted her students to learn these things so that they could get good jobs.**

   One day some of the students had to wash white linen tablecloths. Mary told the girls to boil the tablecloths to get the tablecloths clean. But the girls didn't want to make a fire and wait for the water in the large kettle to boil before they could finish the job! Not much later, Mary saw the girls hanging up the tablecloths to dry. When Mary asked if the girls had boiled the tablecloths, they admitted that they had not. Mary insisted that the girls do the job again—the right way. Mary wanted her students to understand that being faithful and not giving up was important in every job they did, even washing tablecloths. Mary McLeod Bethune faithfully served God.

Conclude

Read Galatians 6:9 aloud. **When might kids today show faithfulness?** (Caring for a younger brother or sister. Doing a chore without being reminded.) **Let's ask God to help us show faithfulness by doing what He wants.** Lead students in prayer.

Discussion Questions

1. *What does it mean to be faithful?* (To do what God wants consistently.)

2. *What are some things that God wants us to do faithfully?* (Be fair. Tell the truth.)

3. *Read Galatians 6:9. When might kids your age get tired, or grow weary, of obeying God?*

Lesson 41

Active Game Center: Repetition Relay

Materials
Bible.

Lead the Game
1. Students form two equal teams. Teams line up on one side of the playing area.

2. At your signal, the first student on each team runs to the other side of the playing area, does 10 jumping jacks and runs back to his or her team. The next student in line repeats the action.

3. Students continue until everyone has completed the relay. Have a volunteer from the first team to complete the relay answer one of the Discussion Questions below.

4. Repeat relay with a new action such as clapping 10 times, touching toes or hopping on one foot.

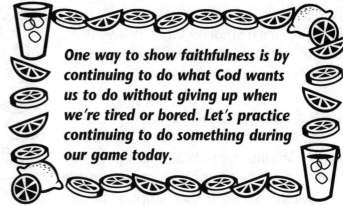

One way to show faithfulness is by continuing to do what God wants us to do without giving up when we're tired or bored. Let's practice continuing to do something during our game today.

Options
1. Bring two basketballs, paddleballs, jump ropes and/or hula hoops. Students bounce the ball, hit the paddleball, jump rope or spin the hula hoop 10 times as the relay actions.

2. For older students, play this game with two hula hoops: each team stands in a circle and holds hands. One pair of students on each team holds hands through the hula hoop. At your signal, one of the students from each pair begins moving the hula hoop around the circle without unclasping hands—each student slides hula hoop over his or her head, steps through and slides it along arms and over the next person's head. Teams race to move hula hoop around the circle three times.

Discussion Questions
1. Have a student read Galatians 6:9 aloud. *What does Galatians 6:9 say that we should continue doing?* (Good.)

2. *We can do good by obeying what God wants us to do. How do we find out what God wants us to do?* (Read the Bible. Listen to our pastors and teachers. Ask our parents or other people who love God.)

3. *What are some of the things you already know that God wants you to do?* (Show love to God and others. Be kind. Treat others as you want to be treated. Forgive others.) *When can you (be kind) to others at home? At school?*

Art Center: Waiting for the Harvest

Materials

Bible; for each student: white or sweet potato, three or four toothpicks, wide-mouthed jar or clear plastic cup, water.

Lead the Activity

1. Students insert toothpicks in a circle evenly around the potato, making sure at least half of the toothpick remains outside the potato. Students then suspend potato from jar or cup, adjusting placement of the toothpicks as needed.

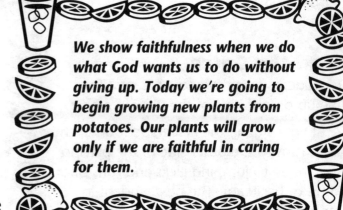

We show faithfulness when we do what God wants us to do without giving up. Today we're going to begin growing new plants from potatoes. Our plants will grow only if we are faithful in caring for them.

2. Students add water to cover the bottom inch (2.5 cm) or so of potato. Potatoes may be placed in a sunny spot in the classroom, or students may take them home to care for them. **How will we continue to care for our potatoes so that they will grow into new plants?** (Add water. Make sure potato has sunlight.) (Note: Once the plants begin to develop and the roots grow long, guide students in adjusting the water level so that only the roots are submerged. This will help prevent rotting of the potato.)

Options

1. Instead of piercing potato with toothpicks, place several rocks in jar or drinking cup and place potato so that the lower part of the potato is submerged.

2. Students may grow carrots, turnips or pineapples using the same technique.

3. Add a lump of charcoal to the water to help prevent odors and rotting of the developing plant.

• •

Discussion Questions

1. *How can a kid your age learn what God wants him or her to do?* (Read God's Word. Talk to God. Ask a parent, teacher or older kid who loves and obeys God.)

2. *What are some of the good things you know God wants us to do?* (Love Him and love others. Be kind to one another. Read and obey God's Word. Tell others about Jesus.)

3. Read Galatians 6:9 aloud. *The Bible says that being faithful brings good things into our lives.* Describe a time you showed faithfulness in doing what God wanted you to do and tell what the result was. *When can you be faithful in obeying God so that something good results?*

Lesson 41

Worship Center

Bible Verse

Let us not become weary in doing good, for at the proper time we will reap a harvest if we do not give up. Galatians 6:9

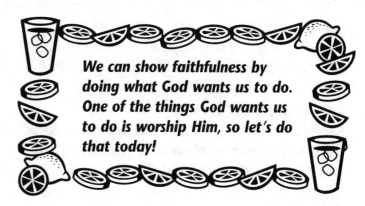

We can show faithfulness by doing what God wants us to do. One of the things God wants us to do is worship Him, so let's do that today!

Materials

Bible, *God's Kids Grow* cassette/CD or music video and player, "Good Habits" word chart (p. 467 in this book), large sheet of paper on which you have printed Galatians 6:9, masking tape.

Sing to God

Play "Good Habits," encouraging students to sing along with the music. **What fruit of the Spirit does this song describe?** (Faithfulness.) **How does God help the fruit of the Spirit to grow in us?** (He loves us. He helps us love Him and others.)

Hear and Say God's Word

Display paper on which you have printed Galatians 6:9. Have a volunteer read the verse aloud. **Reaping a harvest describes the time when a farmer picks the fruit from the trees or gathers all the wheat or vegetables that have grown in the fields. When might we get to see the reward of what we have worked for?** (Getting a good grade on a test. Playing well at a piano recital. Winning a soccer game.) Replace "reap a harvest" with times students suggest and lead students in repeating verse, inserting suggestions.

When we work hard at obeying God and doing good things for others, what results might we see? (We might see that our care for others has helped them. We might see that our kindness to someone has helped that person be kind to others.) Lead students in reciting Galatians 6:9 correctly.

Pray to God

What are some of the good things God wants us to do? (Help poor people. Love Him. Forgive others. Tell God how much we love Him.) Lead students in prayer, mentioning actions described by students and asking His help in faithfully doing what He wants us to do.

Options

1. Sing "Galatians 5:22,23" and/or "Hear, O Israel" (p. 461 and/or p. 471 in this book) with students.

2. Students make up motions for the verse instead of substituting phrases. Students recite verse while performing motions.

Lesson 41
Bible Verse Coloring Center

Materials
Crayons or markers, a copy of page 163 or page 164 from *Bible Verse Coloring Pages #2* for each student.

Lead the Activity
Read Galatians 6:9. **When is it hard for kids your age to do what is good? How can you encourage someone to not give up doing good things?** Students color picture.

Option
Cover a table with newspaper and provide watercolor paints, small paintbrushes and small bowls of water. Instead of coloring the picture, students paint the picture.

Service Project Center

Materials
Materials needed for "Calendar Encouragement" (p. 15 from *The Big Book of Service Projects*).

Lead the Activity
Students complete the "Calendar Encouragement" activity as directed in *The Big Book of Service Projects*. **How will this activity require us to be faithful in doing good? What are some other things we can do to faithfully show God's love to other people?**

Discipleship Activity Center

Materials
Discussion Cards for James 1:22-25 (pp. 165-170 from *The Big Book of Christian Growth*), materials needed for "Three-Ball Toss" or "Spin the Light" (p. 31 or p. 50 from *The Big Book of Christian Growth*).

Lead the Activity
James 1:22-25 tells about some ways to obey God. Let's play a game to help us talk about these verses and how we can faithfully obey them. Students complete activity as directed in *The Big Book of Christian Growth*.

Like a Forest Fire

Bible Verse

Everyone should be quick to listen, slow to speak and slow to become angry. James 1:19

Bible Story Reference

James 3

Teacher's Devotional

James wrote very bluntly about one area of life that everyone struggles to control. His brutally honest conclusion was that "no man can tame the tongue. It is a restless evil, full of deadly poison" (James 3:8). James was addressing the age-old problem of people claiming to have a measure of spiritual maturity but allowing their tongues to run wild.

Character Builder

Being careful in what you say shows self-control.

How, James wants to know, can a person speak and sing praises to God and then use the same mouth to stir up trouble? How can a person go from saying prayers to whispering gossip? James's explanation is simple: The words we speak when we are under pressure are a reflection of the true condition of our inner being. Words that sting or offend do not just pop out of nowhere, James tells us; they come from harboring "bitter envy and selfish ambition in your hearts" (James 3:14).

So how can the tongue be brought under control? Certainly it won't happen just by using simple tricks such as counting to 10 before spouting off or by resolving that "if you can't say something nice about someone, don't say anything at all." Control of the tongue, or of any other parts of our being, comes from God's Spirit building His character into the total fabric of our lives. True self-control is an outgrowth of God's Spirit transforming us into new creatures (see 2 Corinthians 5:17).

In the varied activities of your sessions, you and the children you teach will have many opportunities to put into practice James's advice in this lesson's Bible verse. Help your students identify practical ways to show self-control in their speech. Model these actions yourself. Listening to others, thinking before speaking and demonstrating patience instead of anger are significant ways your teaching can truly make a difference in the relationships built within your class.

Bible Story Center

Materials
Self-Control poster from *Poster Pack;* ¼ cup (2 oz.) play dough and paper clip for each student.

Tell the Story
Follow along with me as we use our dough to tell today's story.

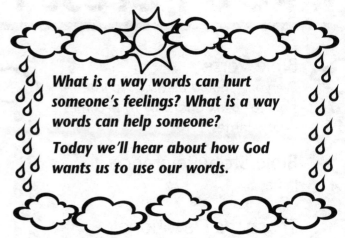

What is a way words can hurt someone's feelings? What is a way words can help someone?

Today we'll hear about how God wants us to use our words.

1. **Make the letter J from your dough.** James was one of the first church leaders, and many people who study the Bible believe he was a younger brother of Jesus. He wrote the book of James in the Bible. This book was written as a letter to Jews who had become Christians.

These Jewish Christians lived in many different countries and were often treated unkindly by people who did not love Jesus. They needed lots of help in knowing how to love and obey God in everyday life. James's letter can help us know how God wants us to live, too.

2. **Make a horse.** James tried to help the readers of his letter understand how important it is to control the things we say. He wrote about some things the people were familiar with. The first was a horse's bit. A bit is a small piece of metal about as thick as two pencils. The bit is put into a horse's mouth and attached to the horse's reins. The direction the horse travels is controlled by the way the rider moves the reins and the bit.

3. **Make a ship.** Next, James compares the tongue to the rudder of a ship. A ship moves through the water like a knife slicing the water. The rudder is at the back of the boat. When the rudder is held straight, the boat pushes through the water in a straight line. But when the rudder is turned to one side or the other, the boat moves in a different direction. A very small rudder can change the direction of a very big boat.

The bit and rudder are very small, but the ways in which

they are used make a BIG difference! The tongue is just a small part of our bodies, but the things we say with it can make BIG differences, too.

4. **Make a large flame. Use a paper clip to draw details on the flame.** The tongue has so much power that the words we say with it affect the whole body. James compares the tongue to a small spark that can set an entire forest on fire. Just as a little spark can cause a huge, uncontrollable fire, just a few words can cause a lot of trouble! Words can be used to persuade others to do good or bad things. There have been times when people have done some extremely bad things because someone convinced them those things were okay to do. What people have said has led to anger, unfairness, prejudice, murder and even war.

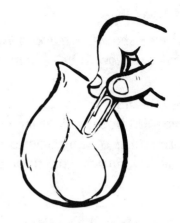

5. **Make the letters of a word God wants us to use.** James tells us that even though all kinds of animals, birds, reptiles and sea creatures can be tamed and controlled by people, we still can't control our own tongues! In fact, James says that we even use the same mouth to praise God and to say bad things to other people.

"This should not be!" says James. "We should use our tongues only to say good things." James wanted us to realize that we need God's power and love to help us control what we say. We can always count on God to help us in controlling our tongues and using our words in good ways.

• •

Focus on the Fruit

What things does James compare the tongue to? (A horse's bit. A ship's rudder. A spark that can start a forest fire.) **What do we need in order to learn to control our tongues and say things that are pleasing to God?** (We need to become members of God's family and ask for His help.) Be aware of students who may wish to learn more about becoming Christians. Refer to the guidelines given in the "Leading a Child to Christ" article on page 36.

James was using his words to help others. But after reading James's instructions, it might seem like it's better not to talk at all so that we won't be tempted to say wrong things! But James believed that with God's help we can control what we say and our words can do a lot of good. Show the Self-Control poster.

Lesson 42
Fruitful Lives Object Talk

Bible Verse
Everyone should be quick to listen, slow to speak and slow to become angry. James 1:19

Materials
Bible with bookmark at James 1:19, one or more copies of Chronicles of Narnia books (available in most church and public libraries).

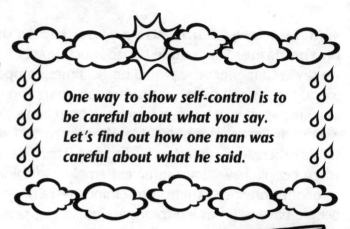

One way to show self-control is to be careful about what you say. Let's find out how one man was careful about what he said.

Lead the Activity
1. Show book(s) you brought. **The Chronicles of Narnia is a series of books written by a man named C. S. Lewis. What do you know about these books?** Volunteers tell about stories they know. **C. S. Lewis wrote these books to help children learn about loving and obeying God. But Mr. Lewis also did many other things in his life.**

2. **Clive Staples Lewis was born in Ireland in 1898. He joined the army to fight for England during World War I and was a brave army officer. But during World War II, C. S. Lewis helped people in another way in England.**

   During the war, while cities in England were being bombed by the Nazis, many people listened to C. S. Lewis talk on the radio about what it meant to be a Christian. C. S. Lewis carefully chose what to say so that all kinds of people could understand God's love for them, even when bad things, like a war, happened. The talks helped people see that loving and obeying God was the most important thing to do. So many people were helped by the radio talks that later some of the talks were written down in a book now called *Mere Christianity*. Even today people learn about being part of God's family from this book.

Conclude
Read James 1:19 aloud. **Why do you think it is good to be careful about what we say? When are some times that kids your age need to listen more?** Students respond. **Let's ask God to help us listen to each other and use self-control in what we say.** Lead students in prayer.

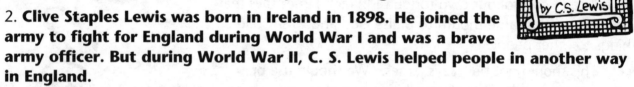

Additional Information for Older Students
Many people wrote letters to C. S. Lewis, and he spent a lot of time answering the letters, many of them from children who read the Chronicles of Narnia. Some of the letters he wrote back to these children were published in a book called *Letters to Children*. Invite students to tell what they would write in letters to C. S. Lewis. (Optional: Read aloud some of the letters from *Letters to Children* by C. S. Lewis.)

Active Game Center: Quick-Slow Switch

Materials
Bible, masking tape.

Prepare the Game
On the floor, use masking tape to form at least three large squares.

Lead the Game
1. Ask a volunteer to be "It." Form three groups from remaining students. Each group stands in a separate square.

2. Call out either "Quick" or "Slow" and a description such as "kids wearing green" or "kids with brown hair." Students who fit that description move at the called speed to a new square, while "It" moves at same speed to tag students before they reach a new square. Any student who is tagged outside a square becomes "It" also.

3. Continue play, periodically calling out "Quick switcheroo" or "Slow switcheroo," at which time all students must move to a new square at the designated speed. When only a few students have not been tagged, begin a new round of the game with a new "It."

Being careful about what we say shows self-control. James 1:19 tells us to be "quick to listen, slow to speak and slow to become angry." Let's practice being quick and slow in our game today.

Options
1. Before playing game, have students demonstrate appropriate quick- and slow-motion movements.

2. To challenge older students, review James 1:19 and then say "Listen" to indicate quick movement and "Speak" to indicate slow motion during the game.

3. Increase the number of squares and add additional "Its" for classes having more than 15 students.

Discussion Questions
1. When might it be hard to show self-control when you talk to others? (When you're angry. When you feel like saying something unkind. When you don't like what someone is saying.)

2. What can you do when you need help showing self-control in your speech? (Follow James 1:19 and be quick to listen and slow to speak. Pray and ask God for His help. Count to 10 before you speak when you feel upset. Walk away before you say something you shouldn't say.)

3. How would your (school) be a better place if kids were careful about what they say?

Art Center: Communication Collage

Materials
Bible, large sheets of paper, markers, glue, scissors, a variety of collage materials (magazine photographs, yarn, toothpicks, straws, pasta, twigs, construction paper, chenille wires, rickrack, ribbon, etc.).

When we are careful about what we say, we show self-control. Let's make collages to remind us of what God says about controlling our words.

Lead the Activity
1. Read James 1:19 aloud. **What are we to be quick to do? Slow to do?** Volunteers respond. **What does it look like when someone is listening? How can we practice being better listeners?** (Don't answer back right away. Take a moment to think about what the person said before saying anything in return.)

2. Lead students in using materials to make individual collages of the words "Quick to listen, slow to speak" (see sketch). Ask Discussion Questions below to promote discussion as students work.

Options
1. Students may wish to form mouths and ears with collage materials or cut out mouths and ears from magazines to use in decorating their collages.

2. Display completed collages on a bulletin board or in a hallway.

3. Invite older students to write James 1:19 on their papers, replacing as many words as possible with pictures or symbols to make rebuses.

4. Create a class collage. Assign each student a letter or each group a word. When finished, place letters or words in order on a piece of butcher paper or on the wall.

•••

Discussion Questions
1. *When are some times it might be difficult for kids your age to listen?* (They're tired. They're hungry. Someone is taking a long time to speak.)

2. *When are some times it might be hard for kids your age to control what they say?* (They're angry. They don't think before they speak.)

3. *What should we do when we make mistakes and say things we shouldn't?* (Ask for God's forgiveness and apologize to the people we were talking to.)

4. *What can you do that will help you listen better and control what you say?* (Ask God for help. Practice listening without speaking. Count to 10 before speaking when angry.)

Lesson 42

Worship Center

Bible Verse
Everyone should be quick to listen, slow to speak and slow to become angry.
James 1:19

Materials
Bible, *God's Kids Grow* cassette/CD or music video and player, "Self-Control" word chart (p. 485 in this book), large sheet of paper on which you have printed James 1:19, masking tape.

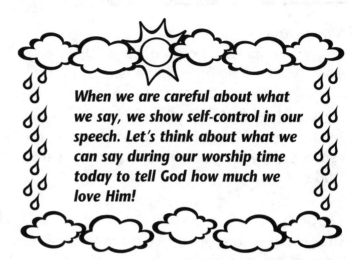

When we are careful about what we say, we show self-control in our speech. Let's think about what we can say during our worship time today to tell God how much we love Him!

Sing to God
Play "Self-Control," encouraging students to sing along with the music. **What does this song suggest we do when we need self-control?** (Pray to God and ask Him for help.)

Hear and Say God's Word
Display paper on which you have printed James 1:19. Have a volunteer read the verse aloud. **What does James 1:19 tell us to do quickly?** (Listen.) **Slowly?** (Speak. Become angry.) Lead students in saying the verse aloud, speaking quickly for the first part of the verse (up through "listen") and slowly for the second part of the verse. Lead the group in reciting the verse together in this manner several times. **When is it hard to listen? When might kids your age talk without thinking? Why is it best to be quick to listen and slow to speak?** (It is a way to show that you care about the other person. Keeps you from saying things you should not say. Shows self-control in your speech.)

Pray to God
What are some of the things you can say to God to tell Him how much you love Him? Students respond. Lead students in prayer, inviting volunteers to express their love to God. End prayer by thanking God that we can use our mouths to tell others we care about them and asking for His help in showing self-control in our speech.

Options
1. Students sing "Circle of Love" and/or "Just Ask Him" (p. 457 and/or p. 475 in this book).

2. Ask an older student to lead the verse activity, modeling how to say the verse quickly and slowly.

3. As part of the prayer activity, students write letters to God, telling Him how much they love Him. Encourage students to take letters home, find a quiet place and read the letters aloud to God.

Bible Verse Coloring Center

Materials
Crayons or markers, a copy of page 199 or page 200 from *Bible Verse Coloring Pages #2* for each student.

Lead the Activity
Read James 1:19. **Who are some people you like to listen to? Why do you think listening is important?** Students color picture.

Option
Students glue completed pictures onto large sheets of construction paper and then draw pictures on the paper of what the children on the coloring page might be listening to (cat meowing, ice-cream truck, friend, etc.).

Service Project Center

Materials
Materials needed for "Thank-You Cards" (p. 19 from *The Big Book of Service Projects*).

Lead the Activity
Students complete the "Thank-You Cards" activity as directed in *The Big Book of Service Projects*. **How might remembering to be thankful help you use self-control in the things you say?**

Discipleship Activity Center

Materials
Discussion Cards for Ephesians 4:29—5:1 (pp. 159-164 from *The Big Book of Christian Growth*, materials needed for "Group and Regroup" or "What's the Question?" (p. 62 or p. 52 from *The Big Book of Christian Growth*).

Lead the Activity
Ephesians 4:29—5:1 tells us some good ways to show the fruit of self-control in our lives. Let's play a game to talk about these verses. Students complete activity as directed in *The Big Book of Christian Growth*.

Caring for Naaman

Bible Verse

Each of you should look not only to your own interests, but also to the interests of others. Philippians 2:4

Bible Story Reference

2 Kings 5:1-18

Teacher's Devotional

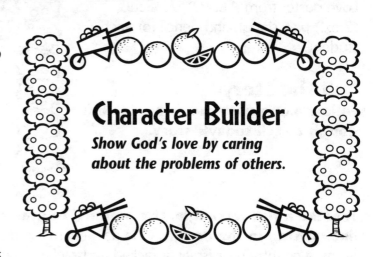

Character Builder

Show God's love by caring about the problems of others.

We live in a world of special interests and niche marketing. Our political system is driven by groups that promote or oppose a particular cause. Merchants target specific age groups, ethnic groups and socio-economic groups. The proliferation of cable television channels caters to people's particular interests, with channels that show only fishing, only golf, only news, only shopping, etc. The very clear message is "Pursue your own interests and ignore whatever doesn't interest you."

While the ways in which people choose to indulge their interests may be new with each generation, the basic message of selfishness has been part of human experience from the beginning. Why else would Scripture, so many times and in one form or another, have to remind people to "look not only to your own interests" (Philippians 2:4)? Obviously, people have a problem loving and caring for others. Therefore we must often be told:

- "Love your neighbor as yourself" (Leviticus 19:18; Mark 12:31).

- "Each of us should please his neighbor for his good, to build him up" (Romans 15:2).

- "Nobody should seek his own good, but the good of others" (1 Corinthians 10:24).

- "Love . . . is not self-seeking" (1 Corinthians 13:4,5).

- "If you really keep the royal law found in Scripture, 'Love your neighbor as yourself,' you are doing right" (James 2:8).

As you tell this lesson's Bible story about the slave girl's concern for her master, pray that her example will encourage children to show concern for the needs and interests of people they meet. Your students will learn this even more thoroughly by your own example. Listen to your students, respond to them with genuine interest and watch to see the fruit of God's love grow in their lives!

Bible Story Center

Materials
Love poster from *Poster Pack;* ¼ cup
(2 oz.) play dough and pencil for each
student.

Tell the Story
**Follow along with me as we use our
dough to tell today's story.**

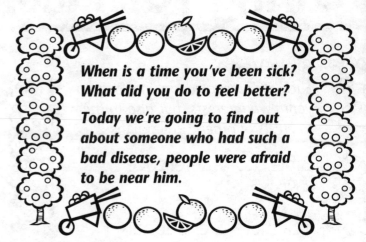

*When is a time you've been sick?
What did you do to feel better?*

*Today we're going to find out
about someone who had such a
bad disease, people were afraid
to be near him.*

1. **Make a flat rectangle. Use a pencil to make marks
like writing in the dough.** One day, enemy soldiers from
Aram, a country near Israel, attacked an Israelite town and captured a young girl. The Israelite girl began to work for the
wife of a captain in Aram's army. This captain, named Naaman, was a brave leader and famous war hero.

But Naaman had a problem—he had leprosy. Leprosy is
a skin disease that causes sores all over a person's body. In Bible
times, there was no medicine and no cure for leprosy. People
were terrified to go near anyone who had this disease because
they were afraid they would get sick, too. When Naaman found
out he had leprosy, he didn't think he would EVER be well
again.

The Israelite slave girl knew that Naaman had this terrible
disease. AND she knew of a man in Israel who could help. That
man was God's prophet Elisha.

Perhaps the slave girl thought to herself, *I could help Captain Naaman if I told him about the prophet, BUT he made me a
slave! Why should I care about Captain Naaman's problems?* The
girl probably wondered about what she should do.

The girl finally decided to tell Naaman's wife about the
prophet. And the wife told her husband.

"I must go to Israel to see this man!" said Naaman. And he
hurried off to ask the king to let him go.

"Go and see this man right away," encouraged the king. "I
will send a letter with you that will tell the king of Israel to cure
you of your leprosy."

2. **Roll up rectangle like a scroll.** Armed with a letter for
the king of Israel and lots of silver and gold, Naaman went to

see Joram, the king of Israel. Of course, Naaman thought that everyone in Israel—including the prophet Elisha—would obey King Joram! That's why the letter was written to Joram and not to Elisha. But when Naaman gave Joram the letter, Joram thought Naaman was just trying to cause problems!

"Do I have power over life and death?" Joram fumed. "Why would the king of Aram expect me to cure this man's leprosy? This king is trying to start a war with me!"

Elisha heard about what happened and sent a message to Joram: "I've heard about Naaman's visit. Don't worry. Have Naaman come to me, and he'll learn who God's prophet is."

Naaman drove his chariots filled with gifts to Elisha's house. He waited for Elisha to come outside and cure him.

3. **Make the number seven.** But Elisha didn't come! Instead, he sent a messenger. The messenger told Naaman to wash himself seven times in the Jordan River, and he would be healed.

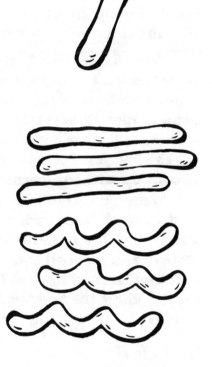

Naaman was furious! "If washing myself could have gotten rid of my leprosy, I could have done that at home!"

4. **Roll several ropes and use them to make a river.** "Look," Naaman's servants said, "if the prophet had asked you to do something hard, you would have done it! So why not do something simple?"

Fortunately, Naaman realized his servants were right. Naaman went to the Jordan River and dipped himself in it seven times, just as Elisha had instructed. To his amazement, Naaman was cured! His skin was completely free of leprosy!

He hurried back to Elisha's house to try to pay Elisha for healing him. But Elisha refused the gifts. "I am here to serve God," Elisha told Naaman. "I won't accept gifts for doing what He asks of me."

Naaman promised to always remember and worship the one true God. How glad Naaman was that Elisha and the slave girl cared for him and helped him!

● ●

Focus on the Fruit

Despite how she must have felt about being a slave, how did the slave girl help Naaman? (She told him about Elisha, who could heal him.) **How would you describe the slave girl?** (Caring. Kind to others, even her enemies.)

When you show God's love by helping someone who is hurt or by being friendly to someone who is lonely, you're helping that person learn about God's love. And you're growing God's fruit in your life! Show the Love poster.

Fruitful Lives Object Talk

Bible Verse

Each of you should look not only to your own interests, but also to the interests of others. Philippians 2:4

Materials

Bible with bookmark at Philippians 2:4, newspaper.

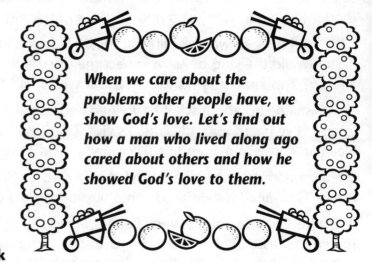

When we care about the problems other people have, we show God's love. Let's find out how a man who lived along ago cared about others and how he showed God's love to them.

Lead the Activity

1. Invite a volunteer to look through the newspaper to find names of people who write for the paper. **What do you think would be fun about working for a newspaper? What might be hard? Let's find out about a newspaper editor from a long time ago.**

2. **Robert Raikes was born in England in 1736. Robert was the editor of a newspaper called the *Gloucester* (GLAHS-tuhr) *Journal*. But Robert was more than just a newspaper editor. He cared about the problems of the people who lived around him. Robert wrote stories in the newspaper about problems in prisons. He wanted other people to know about the problems, so they would help to make changes. Robert realized that the prisons were full of people who had grown up without learning about God's love.**

   Many poor children at that time didn't go to school or church. Instead they had to work from early morning to late at night in dark and dirty factories, even on Saturdays! The only day on which they didn't have to work was Sunday. Robert and a friend started a school for those children—a Sunday School. The children learned to read the Bible and heard stories about God's love. Robert wrote about the Sunday School in his newspaper. Soon churches all over the country were starting Sunday Schools to show God's love to poor children.

Conclude

Read Philippians 2:4 aloud. **This verse uses the word "interests" to describe problems, or things that a person worries about. How can you show your friends that you care about their worries and needs?** Lead students in prayer, asking God to help them find ways to care about other people.

Discussion Questions

1. *What are some problems that people you know have? How can you show that you care about these problems?*

2. *Why do you think God wants us to care about problems other people have? What might happen if we didn't care about other people's problems?*

3. *When has someone cared about a worry or need you had?*

Lesson 43

Active Game Center: Secret Pass

Materials
Bible, *God's Kids Grow* cassette/CD and player, small index card with a star on it.

Lead the Game

1. Students stand in a circle (shoulder-to-shoulder if possible) to play a game similar to Button, Button, Who's Got the Button?

2. Choose one student to be "It." "It" stands in the middle of the circle and closes eyes. Give the index card to a student in the circle. "It" opens eyes.

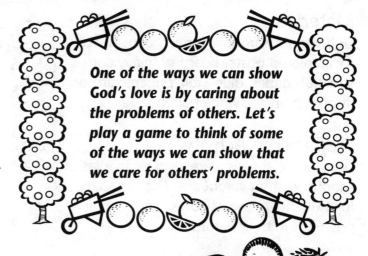

One of the ways we can show God's love is by caring about the problems of others. Let's play a game to think of some of the ways we can show that we care for others' problems.

3. Play "Circle of Love" from *God's Kids Grow* cassette/CD. As music plays, students pass card around the circle behind their backs, trying to keep "It" from seeing who has the card.

4. When you stop the music, "It" tries to identify who has the card by asking a student "How can you care for someone else's problem?" If the student does not have the card, he or she answers "Keep asking," and "It" asks another student. If the student does have the card, he or she answers by telling one way to care for other peoples' problems. (Listen to them. Pray for them. Help them with something they need to get done.) Continue game as time permits, asking Discussion Questions below.

Options

1. If you have a large group of students, give students more than one index card to pass.

2. Print Philippians 2:4 on the index card. When "It" guesses who has the card, student with card reads verse aloud and tells one way to obey the verse.

3. If students have difficulty secretly passing the card, "It" keeps eyes closed until the music stops.

• •

Discussion Questions

1. ***What are some of the problems kids your age might have?*** Students respond. ***What could you do to help someone who (is mad at his or her brother)?***

2. ***When has someone helped you with a problem? What did he or she do to help? When could you help another person in that way?***

3. ***What can you do when someone needs to talk about a problem?*** (Listen. Be friendly. Ask how you can help.) ***What are some of the ways you can help someone when you know about his or her problem?*** (Pray. Help with something he or she needs to do. Write a note.)

Art Center: Pictures of Caring

Materials
Lightweight cardboard, ruler, pencils, scissors, colored poster board or heavy construction paper, glue, hole punch, yarn or ribbon, markers, white paper, tape.

We show God's love for everyone when we care about the problems of others. Let's make something to remind us of some people we care about.

Prepare the Activity
Use ruler to draw squares and rectangles of various sizes on cardboard. Cut out shapes for students to use as patterns for creating openings in their frames.

Lead the Activity
1. Students use patterns to draw several shapes on colored poster board or construction paper and then cut out the shapes. (Note: To help younger students, you or an older student may have to start cutting each opening.)

2. Students punch holes in the top two corners of their frames and thread yarn or ribbon through them. Tie knots in the ends to make a hanger.

3. Tape white paper on the back of the frame behind each opening. Students use markers to draw pictures of people they care about in each opening. Students decorate their frames with words or other designs.

Options
1. Provide a variety of material (colored pasta, seashells, glitter, stickers, rubber stamps and stamp pad, etc.) for students to use in decorating their frames.

2. Have students take home frames and insert pictures of family members and/or friends, or in class take instant pictures of classmates for students to insert in their frames.

Discussion Questions
1. ***What are some problems kids your age sometimes face?*** (Moving to a new neighborhood. Getting along with an older brother or sister. Trying out for a baseball team.)

2. ***What are some ways you can help someone who is having a problem?*** (Pray for him or her. Listen when he or she wants to talk. Get others to help solve the problem.)

3. ***Why should we care about the problems of others?*** (God cares about everyone and their problems. God wants us to show His love by caring for and helping others. We all need help at one time or another.)

Lesson 43
Worship Center

Bible Verse
Each of you should look not only to your own interests, but also to the interests of others. Philippians 2:4

Materials
Bible, *God's Kids Grow* cassette/CD or music video and player, "All My Heart" word chart (p. 453 in this book), large sheet of paper on which you have printed Philippians 2:4, masking tape, marker.

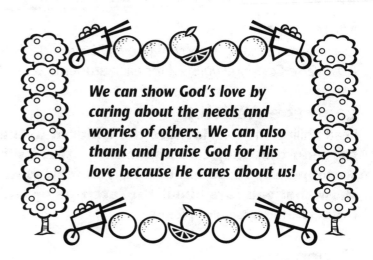

We can show God's love by caring about the needs and worries of others. We can also thank and praise God for His love because He cares about us!

Sing to God
Play "All My Heart," encouraging students to sing along with the music. **According to this song, how should we show love to others?** (With all our heart, strength, soul and mind.) **What is one way you can obey the words of this song?** Volunteers respond.

Hear and Say God's Word
Display paper on which you have printed Philippians 2:4. Have a volunteer read the verse aloud. **How would you say Philippians 2:4 in your own words?** (Care for other people's problems, not just your own. Think about other people, not just yourself. Help other people with what they want to do, instead of only doing what you want to do.) List students' suggestions below the verse. Repeat the verse several times, alternating between saying Philippians 2:4 and one of the paraphrases the students suggested. **What are some ways to follow this verse at home? At school?**

Pray to God
When is a time God has cared for you or for someone you know? How? Volunteers answer. Lead students in prayer, having volunteers thank God for times He has cared for them. End prayer time by asking God to help you and your students show His love to others by caring for them.

Options
1. If you are keeping a prayer journal with the students, ask volunteers to read past prayer requests and talk about ways God has answered the prayers. Ask a volunteer to pray, thanking God for showing His love by caring for our needs.

2. Before the prayer, students draw pictures of times God has cared for them. During the prayer time, students refer to pictures when they pray.

Lesson 43

Bible Verse Coloring Center

Materials
Crayons or markers, a copy of page 175 or page 176 from *Bible Verse Coloring Pages #2* for each student.

Lead the Activity
Read Philippians 2:4. **How are the children in this picture showing that they care about each other? When has someone else cared about how you feel? How can you show that you care about the interests or feelings of others?** Students color picture.

Option
Students draw their favorite foods on the back of the pictures.

Service Project Center

Materials
Materials needed for "Birthday Box" (p. 52 from *The Big Book of Service Projects*).

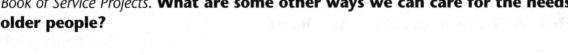

Lead the Activity
Students complete the "Birthday Box" activity as directed in *The Big Book of Service Projects*. **What are some other ways we can care for the needs of older people?**

Discipleship Activity Center

Materials
Discussion Cards for 1 John 3:16-18 (pp. 171-176 from *The Big Book of Christian Growth*), materials needed for "Hopscotch Rocks" or "Partner Concentration" (p. 18 or p. 46 from *The Big Book of Christian Growth*).

Lead the Activity
Today we're going to play a game to talk about ways to show the fruit of love in our lives. Students complete activity as directed in *The Big Book of Christian Growth*.

Dedicated to God

Bible Verse
Worship the Lord with gladness; come before him with joyful songs.
Psalm 100:2

Bible Story Reference
2 Chronicles 5—7

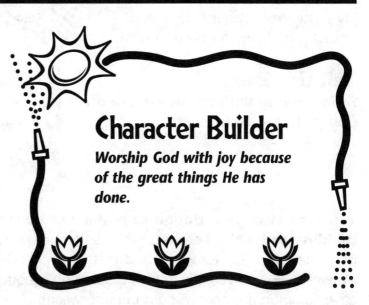

Character Builder
Worship God with joy because of the great things He has done.

Teacher's Devotional
"Go-o-o-o-o-a-a-a-l!" When sports announcer Andres Cantor launches his trademark cheer, millions of soccer fans burst into joyous celebration. (Of course, at the same moment, similar numbers of fans are plunged into despair because the team they support was just scored upon.) Non-soccer fans who have heard Cantor's glorious bellow during a soccer telecast usually have two immediate questions: How long can he stretch out that one word? and How can anyone get so excited about a game?

To the person who is not caught up in the excitement of an athletic contest, the fanaticism of the rabid fan seems truly odd. Similarly, many people find joyful worship of God to be somewhat peculiar. Praise only becomes reasonable and meaningful when a person comes to grips with two remarkable and related truths: (1) God is great— "Know that the Lord is God. It is he who made us" (Psalm 100:3); and (2) we belong to Him—"We are his; we are his people, the sheep of his pasture" (Psalm 100:3).

Euphoria over a goal is a transitory emotion. But knowing that the God of the universe cares for us as gently and intimately as a shepherd cares for his sheep brings a kind of joy that lasts forever.

Bible Story Center

Materials
Joy poster from *Poster Pack*, ¼ cup (2 oz.) play dough for each student.

Tell the Story
Follow along with me as we use our dough to tell today's story.

What is something you have built? Did anyone help you?

Today we're going to hear about what King Solomon built to show God how much he love Him.

1. **Use most of your dough to make a large rectangular building to be the Temple.** When Solomon became king of Israel, he asked God for wisdom so that he could rule the people well. God was very pleased with Solomon's request. He gave Solomon not only wisdom but also wealth. That meant Solomon was a very rich man. As the king, he could do anything he wanted with all his money, food, gold and silver.

Solomon loved God very much, and he was grateful for all the gifts God had given him. Solomon wanted to give a gift to God. His gift was to lead the people in constructing a beautiful building where they could worship God. This building was called the Temple.

2. **Make two pillars from a small piece of dough and place in front of the Temple.** It took seven years for Solomon's workers to build the Temple. It took a long time to build because it was so beautiful! The Temple was built on a hill, so everyone could see it. There were two tall bronze pillars in front of it. The white stones of its walls sparkled in the sunlight. Much of the inside was covered with gold.

King Solomon led a joyful parade to bring the Ark of the Covenant to its permanent home in the Temple. The Ark was the box where God had told Moses to place the stone tablets of the Law. The Ark was special to the Israelites because it reminded them that God was always with them. As the parade traveled the streets of Jerusalem, people came out to join in the celebration. Everyone wanted to see the beautiful new Temple!

The Ark of the Covenant was put in a special room called the Most Holy Place. Great statues of angels with gold wings that reminded people of God's power stood guard on either side of the Ark of the Covenant.

3. Make one or two trumpets. The priests gathered together to begin the first worship service in the new Temple. The celebration began with priests playing cymbals, harps and lyres (Bible-times instruments like small harps). There also were 120 priests playing trumpets! All the musicians and singers joined together to give praise and thanks to God. They sang, "He is good; His love endures forever." The people were very happy to have such a beautiful place to worship God.

As the priests were singing, an amazing thing happened. The whole Temple was filled with a beautiful cloud. By this cloud, God showed that He was very pleased with this Temple Solomon had built. Now God's people could come together to worship Him in a special place.

Solomon stood in front of the Temple. He spoke to the people who had come to worship God. He praised God and told the people the story of how the Temple had been built. He reminded the people of the ways God had used His power to protect them over the years, rescuing them from Egypt, keeping His promises and forgiving their sins. Then Solomon prayed. Solomon asked God to take care of His people forever and to help people everywhere come to know Him.

4. Make several music notes. The people listening to Solomon had come from all over the kingdom. Some were from very far away. They were so full of joy to be able to worship God at the beautiful Temple that when the week of celebration had ended, they all stayed for another week! The Temple stood for many, many years. The people of Israel were filled with joy because they had a Temple in which they could worship God for all the great things He has done.

. . . .

Focus on the Fruit

Why did Solomon want to build a Temple? (He loved God. He was thankful to God.)
What did the priests and people do to show their joy that the Temple was built? (Sang songs of praise. Played musical instruments.) **What did Solomon do to worship God at the Temple?** (Prayed to God. Praised God with all the other Israelites.)

Solomon built the Temple because He loved God and wanted to give the Israelites a place to worship God. Just like the Israelites, we can joyfully worship God for all the wonderful, mighty things He has done. Show the Joy poster.

Lesson 44
Fruitful Lives Object Talk

Bible Verse
Worship the Lord with gladness; come before him with joyful songs. Psalm 100:2

Materials
Bible with bookmark at Psalm 100:2, cassette/CD recording of "Hark! the Herald Angels Sing" and player or photocopies of words and music, large sheet of paper, marker.

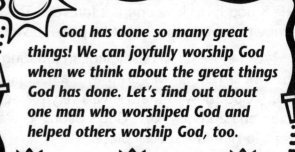

God has done so many great things! We can joyfully worship God when we think about the great things God has done. Let's find out about one man who worshiped God and helped others worship God, too.

Lead the Activity

1. Invite students to sing "Hark! the Herald Angels Sing" or listen to song on cassette/CD. **When do we usually sing this song? What does this song say about Jesus?** Students respond. **A man named Charles Wesley wrote this song and many other songs about Jesus.**

2. **Charles Wesley grew up in a very big family in England in the 1700s. He went to church and did many good things all his life, but he didn't really understand what it meant to be a Christian or how much God loved him.**

     When Charles was a grown-up, he lived with some Christians in London. While he was there, Charles saw how kind and gentle they were, and he heard them talk about how they lived as part of God's family. Those Christians helped Charles understand God's love for him.

     Charles was so glad to know of God's love that he began to write songs about God's love and forgiveness. For many years Charles and his brother, John, preached and sang about God's love and forgiveness to people all over England. Charles eventually wrote 6,000 hymns! Many people learned to love and worship God because of Charles's music and preaching.

Conclude

Read Psalm 100:2 aloud. **What are some reasons for doing what this verse says?** Students tell things God has done for which they are thankful. List ideas on a large sheet of paper. Lead students in prayer, thanking God for items students listed.

● ●

Discussion Questions

1. *How do people often show that they are joyful or happy?* (Smiling. Singing.)

2. *How can we show joy when we worship God?* (Sing songs that tell of God's greatness. Tell others about the ways in which God helps us. Thank God in prayer for the good things He gives us.)

3. *What is one way we have worshiped God today?*

Lesson 44

Active Game Center: Praise Toss

Materials
Beach ball or other soft ball.

Lead the Game
1. Students stand in a large circle. Assign each student a number.

2. Stand in the center of the circle with the ball. Call out one of the numbers you assigned as you toss the ball into the air. Student whose number you called catches the ball and names one reason to thank God or one thing that God has done or made.

God has done so many great things for which we can worship Him! Let's play a game to joyfully name some of the great things God has done.

3. After naming reason or thing, student tosses ball into the air and calls out another number. Student whose number is called catches ball and names a reason to thank God or one thing that God has done or made. Game continues as time allows.

Options
1. During the game, list the reasons or things the students name. After playing the game for a while, gather together for a prayer time. Students thank God and celebrate the great things He has done, referring to list.

2. If you have more than 20 students, bring another ball and form two circles to play game.

3. To add variety, call out "Circle switch" several times during the game. At that signal, all students must move to new positions in the circle but keep their same numbers.

4. Play *God's Kids Grow* cassette/CD or other children's praise music as students play game.

• •

Discussion Questions
1. *What are your favorite parts of God's creation?*

2. *What are some things you have learned about God from the Bible? What are some of the great things God has done for you or people you know?* Share your own answer after students tell ideas.

3. *What are some ways you can worship God and thank Him for all these wonderful things?* (Sing to Him. Pray to Him. Write Him a letter or draw a picture to express your thanks. Make up a song to tell Him how much you love Him and appreciate what He has done.)

Art Center: Art Walk

Materials

Sidewalk chalk, bucket of soapy water, paper towels.

Because of the great things God has done, we can joyfully worship Him! Today we're going to draw chalk pictures to show how great God is.

Lead the Activity

1. Lead students outdoors to a sidewalk or asphalt area. Assign each student a section in which to draw. (Optional: Draw lines to designate drawing areas.)

2. Students use chalk to draw pictures of great things God has done or things that make them feel joyful. Encourage students to include words or prayers with their pictures. Each student may draw one large picture or several smaller pictures in his or her section.

3. When pictures are completed, students wash hands in soapy water and then walk around the chalk drawings to see what others have created. Invite volunteers to describe their pictures to the group.

Options

1. If sidewalk chalk is not available, spread out a length of butcher paper on sidewalk (or on classroom or hallway floor). Tape edges firmly in place. Students draw with markers.

2. Invite others in your church to see the chalk drawings.

3. Before students draw with chalk, wet the sidewalk with water to create brighter images.

• •

Discussion Questions

1. *What has God made that shows how great He is?* (Mountains. People. The ocean.)

2. *What are some of the great things that God has done for you or people you know?*

3. *What are some of the ways you can joyfully worship God for all the great things He has done?* (Sing songs of praise to God. Read in the Bible about some of the great things He has done. Give offerings to show thankfulness.)

Lesson 44

Worship Center

Bible Verse

Worship the Lord with gladness; come before him with joyful songs. Psalm 100:2

Materials

Bible, *God's Kids Grow* cassette/CD or music video and player, "Joy!" word chart (p. 473 in this book), large sheet of paper on which you have printed Psalm 100:2, masking tape, marker.

We can worship God with joy because of the great things He has done!

Sing to God

Play "Joy!" encouraging students to sing along with the music. **How did the people named in this song show joy and worship God?** (Paul and Silas sang to God while they were in prison. The man that was healed ran back and thanked Jesus.) **What can we do to show joy because of the great things God has done?**

Hear and Say God's Word

Display paper on which you have printed Psalm 100:2. Have a volunteer read the verse aloud. **In what ways does this verse say we should worship the Lord?** (With gladness. With joyful songs.) **What are some things you usually do "with gladness"?** Students respond. **Let's practice worshiping the Lord with gladness by saying this verse a few different ways.** Lead students in reciting the verse in a variety of ways: say the words quickly and/or slowly, say the words with an echo, say the words while clapping hands, etc.

Pray to God

What are some of the great things God has done for which we can worship Him? List students' responses on the back of the Bible verse paper. Students sit in a large circle. Lead students to pray, in turn around the circle, by completing one of the following sentences: **Thank You, God, for . . .** or **I worship You, God, for . . .** Students refer to the list as needed.

Options

1. Ask a student to read aloud Psalm 77:11-13 as a call to worship.

2. During the prayer time, ask students to name words which describe God. ("Loving." "Forgiving." "Powerful." "Holy." "Kind." "Good.") Students complete the sentence, **We worship You, God, because You are . . .**

Bible Verse Coloring Center

Materials
Crayons or markers, a copy of page 41 or page 42 from *Bible Verse Coloring Pages #2* for each student.

Lead the Activity
Read Psalm 100:2. **When is a good time to do what this verse says?** Students color picture.

Option
Also provide copies of "Draw a picture of a way to praise God" page (p. 222 from *Bible Verse Coloring Pages #2)*. Students draw and color pictures.

Service Project Center

Materials
Materials needed for "Verse Commercials" (p. 48 from *The Big Book of Service Projects*).

Lead the Activity
Students complete the "Verse Commercials" activity as directed in *The Big Book of Service Projects*. **Why do you think it is good to praise God? How can our commercials help other people praise and worship God?**

Discipleship Activity Center

Materials
Discussion Cards for Romans 8:35,37-39 (pp. 129-134 from *The Big Book of Christian Growth*); materials needed for "Crazy Relay" or "Cartoon Creations" (p. 15 or p. 40 from *The Big Book of Christian Growth*).

Lead the Activity
God's love is so great that it gives us joy. Today we're going to play a game to help us talk about ways to remember God's love and have joy in our everyday lives. Students complete activity as directed in *The Big Book of Christian Growth*.

Paul Keeps the Peace

Bible Verse

Live in harmony with one another; be sympathetic, love as brothers, be compassionate and humble. 1 Peter 3:8

Bible Story Reference

Philemon

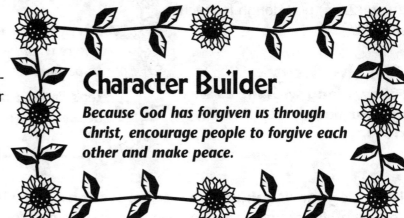

Character Builder

Because God has forgiven us through Christ, encourage people to forgive each other and make peace.

Teacher's Devotional

A runaway slave is hardly the image most people would use to illustrate the idea of peace. Slavery in New Testament times was anything but a peaceful state; in fact, it was usually forced on people through the violence of war. A slave who ran away faced the brutal force of Roman law and thus lived in constant fear of discovery. The slave owner, fearing that other slaves might follow suit, engaged in every method possible to regain this lost property. Angry, often hateful emotions were strong on both sides. This is hardly a peaceful image.

How then did Paul's meeting with Onesimus, the runaway slave, turn this volatile situation into an example of making peace through forgiveness? How did the former runaway slave end up returning to his owner? How did this fugitive become a traveling companion of Tychicus, helping to deliver Paul's letters? How could Paul refer to Onesimus as "our faithful and dear brother" (Colossians 4:9) and "my son" (Philemon 10)?

As with the growth of any other fruit of the Spirit, peace grows to replace conflict as a result of God's working in a person's life. Onesimus had previously rebelled against being forced to serve in his master's house. God's Spirit transformed him into a man who willingly served Paul, a prisoner in a Roman jail. Once he had hated his lot as a slave. Now he returned in voluntary submission. Onesimus had allowed God's Spirit to bring peace into his life in place of fear, distrust and resentment. In addition, Paul was confident that Onesimus's former master would welcome the returning slave as a brother in Christ, rather than as a piece of property.

If God's Spirit can allow peace to grow between master and slave, is there any relationship where resentment is so deep that God's peace cannot bring healing? Hardly. God's peace that passes understanding (see Philippians 4:7) will guard the hearts and minds of those who trust in Him.

Bible Story Center

Materials
Peace poster from *Poster Pack*,
¼ cup (2 oz.) play dough for each student.

Tell the Story
Follow along with me as we use our dough to tell today's story.

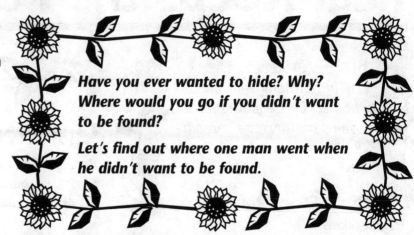

Have you ever wanted to hide? Why? Where would you go if you didn't want to be found?

Let's find out where one man went when he didn't want to be found.

1. **Divide your dough into five equal sections.** In the New Testament, we can read about a slave named Onesimus (oh-NEHS-uh-muhs). Onesimus was the slave of a man named Philemon (fi-LEE-muhn) who lived in the city of Colosse. But Onesimus escaped from Philemon—maybe even stealing some of Philemon's money—and ran away to the big city of Rome!

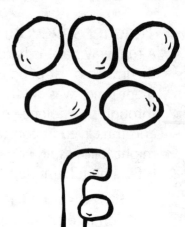

2. **Make the letter *E* for the words "escape" and "empire."** Rome was the biggest city in the empire; it was a place where anyone could hide! And it was an exciting city—especially if you were a slave who was finally free to go where you wanted to go and do what you wanted to do.

But Onesimus must have felt scared. He probably didn't know anyone in the city. And if he DID see someone he knew, Onesimus would have hidden! If anyone who knew Onesimus saw him, that person might tell the soldiers that they'd seen a runaway slave! Then Onesimus would be captured and sent back to his master, Philemon. Onesimus would have been severely punished. He could be sent to work in a mine, beaten, tortured or even killed!

3. **Make the letter *P* for the words "Paul" and "Philemon."** Somehow, Onesimus heard that Paul—the man who loved Jesus—was in Rome! Onesimus may have heard his master, Philemon, talk about Paul or Jesus, for Philemon was a follower of Jesus. No one knows exactly how Onesimus and Paul met. We only know that the two men became friends. Eventually, Onesimus told Paul what he had done.

Paul told Onesimus about Jesus. He probably told Onesimus that God loved him so much that He sent His Son, Jesus, to die to take the punishment for the wrong things he had done. Paul must have told Onesimus that if he believed in what Jesus did for him, he could trust God to forgive him.

4. **Make the letter _A_ for the word "ask."** Onesimus asked God to forgive him, and Onesimus became a member of God's family.

The next days were wonderful. Onesimus helped Paul by doing whatever Paul asked. And all the time, Onesimus was learning more and more about God and His Son, Jesus.

Then one day Paul called Onesimus to him. "Onesimus," Paul said, "I have an idea. My friend Tychicus (TIHK-ih-cuhs) is going on a trip. He's taking a letter from me to the Christians at Colosse. And I want you to go with him."

5. **Make the letter _C_ for the word "Colosse."** COLOSSE! Onesimus's heart jumped! A shiver of fear ran through him. Colosse was the town where Philemon, his master, lived. Paul wanted him to go back to his master!

It would be hard for Onesimus to go back to Philemon. So because Paul loved Onesimus as if he were his own son, Paul wrote a letter to Philemon. "My friend, do me a favor," Paul wrote. "Welcome Onesimus back home the same way you would welcome me." Paul even said he was willing to pay back whatever money Onesimus owed Philemon!

6. **Make another letter _E_ for the word "encourage."** When it was time to leave, Paul handed Onesimus the letter he had written. "Don't be frightened," Paul encouraged Onesimus. "In this letter I've asked Philemon to forgive you and treat you kindly as a brother in God's family."

7. **Arrange letters to form the word "peace."** Paul's words and actions made all the difference in Onesimus's life. He helped Onesimus learn that Jesus would forgive his sins, so he could become a member of God's family. And Paul's letter helped Onesimus return home to receive forgiveness from his master, and it encouraged Philemon to forgive Onesimus so that they could live together in peace.

• •

Focus on the Fruit

What did Paul do for Onesimus? (Told Him about Jesus. Wrote a letter to Philemon.) **How would you describe Paul's actions?** (Paul tried to make peace between Philemon and Onesimus.) **What did Paul do to help Onesimus and Philemon learn to forgive each other?** (Paul offered to pay whatever money Onesimus owed Philemon.)

Paul reminded Philemon of Jesus' great love and asked Philemon to treat Onesimus as a member of God's family, not as his slave. When we remember Jesus' love for all people, it helps us remember to forgive each other, grow the fruit of peace in our lives and encourage others to do the same! Show the Peace poster.

Fruitful Lives Object Talk

Bible Verse

Live in harmony with one another; be sympathetic, love as brothers, be compassionate and humble.
1 Peter 3:8

Materials

Bible with bookmark at 1 Peter 3:8, world map.

> **We can encourage people to forgive each other and make peace, because God has forgiven us. Let's find out about one man who worked hard to help people and make peace.**

Lead the Activity

1. Show students the map. **Where is the country in which we live?** Volunteer locates country on map. Show students or ask an older student to find the country of the Democratic Republic of the Congo (formerly Zaire). **William Sheppard was an African-American missionary to the Congo in 1890. He went to this country because many of the tribes of people who lived there did not know about Jesus.**

2. **William learned the different languages the people in the Congo spoke and helped the people build churches, schools and homes for children. William even became friends with a tribe of people who had always killed any outsiders who came to their area. William's work with these people made him so famous that he was invited three times to the White House, home of the president of the United States.**

   William could have felt like he had done enough to help the people in the Congo, but he knew there was a lot more important work left to do. At that time, the king of Belgium was in control of the Congo. His soldiers forced many people in the Congo to work under terrible conditions. William began to write about the problems he saw. Soon people all around the world learned about these problems and convinced the king of Belgium to treat the people in the Congo in better ways.

Conclude

Read 1 Peter 3:8 aloud. **Which instructions in this verse tell ways to make peace?** ("Live in harmony with one another." "Be sympathetic.") **How did William Sheppard obey this verse? How can you make peace with others? Let's ask God to help us encourage people to forgive each other and make peace.** Lead students in prayer.

• •

Discussion Questions

1. *People can live in harmony with each other when they choose to respect each other. What can you do to show more respect and kindness to your friends? Your family?*

2. *How do you think living in harmony or respecting each other can make peace?*

3. *How can you live in harmony with someone you know?*

Active Game Center: Find and Tag

Materials
Blindfold.

Lead the Game

1. Lead students in playing a game like Marco Polo. Blindfold a volunteer to be "It."

2. "It" begins moving around the playing area calling out "God forgives us." Students respond by saying "We forgive others" as they walk around the playing area. "It" moves toward the students by listening to their voices, continuing to say "God forgives us" to hear students respond.

3. When "It" tags another student, that student becomes "It" and game begins again.

Because God has forgiven us, we can encourage people to forgive each other and make peace. Let's play a game with messages about forgiveness!

Options

1. Play the game outdoors, using traffic cones or masking tape to mark the boundaries of the playing area.

2. Instead of a blindfold, place a large paper grocery bag over the head of "It."

3. After several rounds, ask students to think of a new phrase and response about forgiveness (for example, "Forgiveness from God" and "helps us forgive others"; or "We are forgiven" and "so make peace with others").

4. Students stand still while "It" walks around trying to tag them.

• •

Discussion Questions

1. ***How do we know that God forgives us?*** (The Bible tells us that God forgives us when we ask for forgiveness and believe Jesus died on the cross to pay for our sins. God always keeps His promises.)

2. ***Because God forgives us, we should forgive others and encourage people to forgive each other. What are some ways to encourage people to forgive each other?*** (Be an example of forgiving others. Remind them of God's forgiveness.)

3. ***How does forgiveness help us make peace?*** (When we forgive, we can stop being angry. We can start doing the right things.) ***What might your family be like if no one forgave each other? What might your school be like if everyone worked at making peace?***

Art Center: Peace Pinwheels

Materials

Bible; a variety of colored paper, 6-inches (15-cm) square; scissors; tape; ½-inch (1.25-cm) paper fasteners; drinking straws.

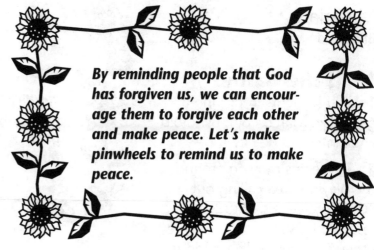

By reminding people that God has forgiven us, we can encourage them to forgive each other and make peace. Let's make pinwheels to remind us to make peace.

Lead the Activity

1. Students fold 6-inch (15-cm) paper squares in half diagonally two times and then snip off the tip of the triangle, at the center of the paper (sketch a).

2. Students open papers and cut halfway from each corner to center. Then students fold in every other corner to meet near the center hole (sketch b) and use a small piece of tape to hold corners in place.

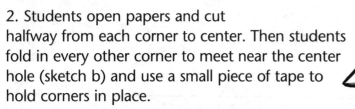

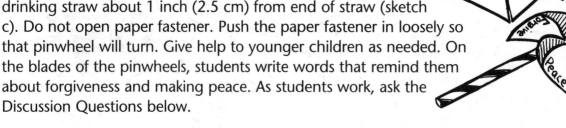

3. Students poke a paper fastener through tape and into a drinking straw about 1 inch (2.5 cm) from end of straw (sketch c). Do not open paper fastener. Push the paper fastener in loosely so that pinwheel will turn. Give help to younger children as needed. On the blades of the pinwheels, students write words that remind them about forgiveness and making peace. As students work, ask the Discussion Questions below.

Options

1. Use wrapping paper, paper with a different color on each side or origami paper for colorful pinwheels.

2. Provide stickers for students to use to decorate the blades and/or handle of their pinwheels.

• •

Discussion Questions

1. ***What are some words that would help you remember to forgive each other and live in peace?*** ("Peace," "love," "Jesus," "forgive," etc.)

2. ***What can a kid your age do when it seems difficult to forgive others?*** (Ask for God's help. Read about God's forgiveness in the Bible. Think about how much God has forgiven us. Forgive, even when it's hard.)

3. Read 1 Peter 3:8 aloud. ***What does it mean to "live in harmony"?*** (Get along with others. Refuse to fight with each other. Help each other with problems and needs.)

Worship Center

Bible Verse

Live in harmony with one another; be sympathetic, love as brothers, be compassionate and humble. 1 Peter 3:8

Materials

Bible, *God's Kids Grow* cassette/CD or music video and player, "Peacemaker" word chart (p. 481 in this book), large sheet of paper on which you have printed 1 Peter 3:8, masking tape, marker.

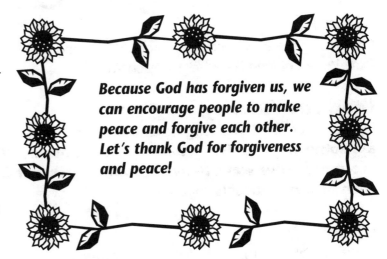

Because God has forgiven us, we can encourage people to make peace and forgive each other. Let's thank God for forgiveness and peace!

Sing to God

Play "Peacemaker," encouraging students to sing along with the music. **What can kids your age do to be peacemakers and help people forgive each other?**

Hear and Say God's Word

Display paper on which you have printed 1 Peter 3:8. Have a volunteer read the verse aloud. **To "live in harmony with one another" means to live peacefully and not have arguments with others. The rest of the verse tells us how to treat others in order to live peacefully with them.** Draw lines to divide the verse into four sections. Divide the class into two groups. Groups alternate reading sections of the verse in order. **How does loving each other as brothers help people to forgive each other and make peace? How does being compassionate (caring for other peoples' problems) help people to forgive each other and make peace?**

Pray to God

Think of some friends you know whom you could help to forgive each other and make peace. Lead students in silently praying for these people. End prayer by thanking God for His forgiveness of us and asking for His help to be peacemakers.

Options

1. Ask several volunteers to read aloud these verses about God's forgiveness: Psalms 103:2,3; 130:3,4; 1 John 1:9.

2. During the verse activity, divide the class in a different way for each repetition of the verse: boys and girls, grade levels, teacher(s) and students, etc.

3. **When we receive God's forgiveness for our sin, it helps us want to forgive others.** Talk with children about becoming members of God's family. Follow suggestions in the "Leading a Child to Christ" article on page 36.

Bible Verse Coloring Center

Materials
Crayons or markers, a copy of page 203 or page 204 from *Bible Verse Coloring Pages #2* for each student.

Lead the Activity
Read 1 Peter 3:8. **Forgiving each other and making peace are some ways to live in harmony with others. What are some other ways to live in harmony or get along with others?** Students color picture.

Option
Students color picture with fruit-scented markers.

Service Project Center

Materials
Materials needed for "Mail Service" (p. 97 from *The Big Book of Service Projects*).

Lead the Activity
Students complete the "Mail Service" activity as directed in *The Big Book of Service Projects*. **How do you think getting mail will encourage the people we send these to? What are some other ways to encourage people?**

Discipleship Activity Center

Materials
Discussion Cards for Psalm 51:1-4,10-12 (pp. 81-86 from *The Big Book of Christian Growth*); materials needed for "Foiled Juggling" or "Match Up" (p. 17 or p. 45 from *The Big Book of Christian Growth*).

Lead the Activity
God's Word helps us learn how to make peace with God when we've sinned and how to make peace with others. Today we're going to play a game about the ways in which God's forgiveness can help us live in peace. Students complete activity as directed in *The Big Book of Christian Growth*.

Four Patient Friends

Bible Verse

Blessed are they who maintain justice, who constantly do what is right.
Psalm 106:3

Bible Story Reference

Mark 2:1-12

Teacher's Devotional

The benediction of Psalm 106:3 is the answer to a question posed in Psalm 106:2: "Who can proclaim the mighty acts of the Lord or fully declare his praise?"

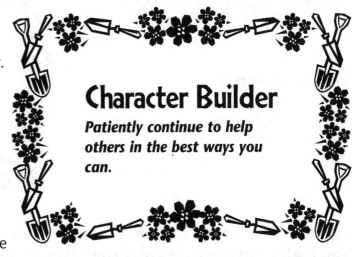

Character Builder

Patiently continue to help others in the best ways you can.

The question in Psalm 106:2 is the response to the challenge in Psalm 106:1: "Praise the Lord. Give thanks to the Lord, for he is good; his love endures forever."

Therefore, in order to fully appreciate the blessing in verse 3, we need to consider the question in verse 2, which, of course, leads us to think about the challenge, the call to praise God, in verse 1. When the psalms issue a call to praise God, the intent is not to elicit a private, inner reflection of praise. Instead, the purpose is to produce a public declaration of God's greatness.

But can just anyone proclaim praise to God? Is a particular type of person required to effectively lead the people in giving thanks for God's goodness and love? Verse 3 tells us that the people who can declare praise to God are those who "maintain justice, who constantly do what is right." Notice the repetitive nature of these actions. The psalmist is not pronouncing a blessing on those who occasionally do the right thing or those whose right actions outweigh their wrong behaviors. The psalmist is stressing the need to patiently, consistently do what is good for others. Because God is patient and consistent in doing good for us, those who would truly praise Him must seek to show that same patience and consistency toward those who need our help. What better opportunity than in our classrooms do we have to offer the patience and consistency that only God can give through us?

Bible Story Center

Materials

Patience poster from *Poster Pack;* ¼ cup
(2 oz.) play dough and two craft sticks for
each student.

Tell the Story

**Follow along with me as we use our
dough to tell today's story.**

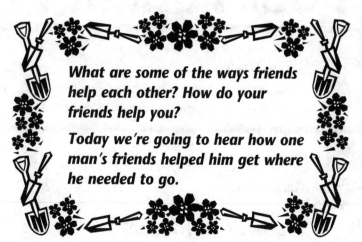

*What are some of the ways friends
help each other? How do your
friends help you?*

*Today we're going to hear how one
man's friends helped him get where
he needed to go.*

1. **Divide your dough into three sections. From one sec-
tion make a house with a flat roof.** When Jesus lived on
Earth, He went from town to town, teaching people about
God. Besides teaching, He also healed people. If they were sick,
He made them well again. If they couldn't walk or hear or see,
He made their feet or ears or eyes work the way they should.

One day, Jesus was in the town of Capernaum. Crowds of
people gathered around Him. They filled the house where He
was, and they filled the front yard and the backyard, too! People stood in the doorways, leaned through the windows and sat
or stood on almost every inch of the floor. Many of these people had probably come to see Jesus perform the miracles that
they had seen or heard about when He was in town before.

Nearby, there lived a man who was paralyzed. His legs did
not work at all. But this man had some wonderful friends. His
friends decided, "We'll take our paralyzed friend to Jesus. Jesus
can make his legs well!"

2. **From another section of your dough make a flat rectangle for a mat. Add two craft sticks, one on either
side of the mat.** Each of the four friends took a corner of the
man's sleeping mat. They lifted the paralyzed man and his mat
right up off the ground and started walking. It didn't matter
how heavy he seemed or how tired they got. They were going
to make SURE that their paralyzed friend got to Jesus. They had
heard about Jesus and knew He could help their friend!

Finally, they came to the house where Jesus was. Well, they
were ALMOST to the house. There were so many people, it was
even hard to see the house! And the crowd certainly didn't
make room for them to get through. How could they carry

their friend on his mat through ALL these PEOPLE and into the house to see Jesus?

3. Use your third section of dough to make stairs on the side of the house. The four friends looked at each other and wondered, *How can we get our friend to Jesus?!* Then one of them had an idea that he quickly told the others. The friends carried the man on his mat to the side of the house where there were stairs that led to the roof of the house. The friends carefully carried the paralyzed man up the stairs and onto the roof where they gently laid down their friend.

The roof was made of mats of woven branches plastered with clay. And what do you think those friends did? They pulled up some of these mats and laid them aside. Soon they had made a HOLE in the roof! They made the hole bigger and BIGGER, until it was SO big they could lower their friend's mat right down through it!

4. Use all of your dough to spell "JESUS." The friends slid ropes under the mat and lowered the paralyzed man down through that hole until he was right in front of Jesus! Jesus looked down at the paralyzed man. He knew the man needed two things: his sins forgiven and healing. So Jesus said to him, "Your sins are forgiven. And so that everyone will know I have the power to forgive sins, pick up your mat. You can walk!"

Right there, in the middle of that crowd, the man stood. He picked up his mat. And he walked right out of that crowded house! His friends must have been VERY happy! They had known Jesus would be able to make their friend able to walk. And Jesus did! Even better, because He is God's Son, Jesus forgave the man's sins!

• •

Focus on the Fruit
What did the four men do to help their paralyzed friend? (Took him to see Jesus.)
What made it difficult for the four men to take their friend to Jesus? (He was paralyzed, so they had to carry him. Huge crowds kept them from going through the door.)
Even though it was hard work to carry their friend, the four men didn't give up. They did their best to help their friend.

We can patiently keep on helping others in the very best ways we can, too. Show the Patience poster. **When we show the fruit of patience in our lives, our actions and words make a difference in the lives of those around us!**

Lesson 46
Fruitful Lives Object Talk

Bible Verse
Blessed are they who maintain justice, who constantly do what is right. Psalm 106:3

Materials
Bible with bookmark at Psalm 106:3, book of rules (game rule book, driver's manual, etc.).

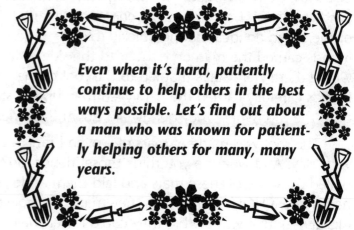

Even when it's hard, patiently continue to help others in the best ways possible. Let's find out about a man who was known for patiently helping others for many, many years.

Lead the Activity

1. Show book you brought. **What does this book tell about?** (Rules for [playing chess].) **Why do you think rules are important?** Students tell ideas. **William Wilberforce's job was making rules. He was a member of Parliament in England from 1780 to 1825. (That's like being a member of Congress in the United States.)**

2. **After William became a member of God's family, he realized that he could serve God and show his love for Him by doing his best to help others through his job in Parliament. Let's find out what he did.**

   In 1788, William made a long speech in Parliament. He asked the other people in Parliament to make a new law to end slavery. Many people didn't want to hear that slavery was wrong because they made a lot of money from selling slaves and from the work slaves did. Parliament voted down William's idea, but William didn't give up. Every year for 18 years, William tried to convince people to end slavery.

   Finally, Parliament decided to pass a law that made it illegal to force people to be slaves. But there were still many people who were already slaves, and the new law didn't set them free. So William's job wasn't over! He patiently kept working to free slaves until the end of his life. Just four days before William died, Parliament passed a law saying that ALL slavery was illegal in England and in all the British colonies.

Conclude

Read Psalm 106:3 aloud. **This verse says that God is pleased when people do what is right to help others. What are some right things you can do to help others this week?** Lead students in prayer, asking God to help them do their best in helping others.

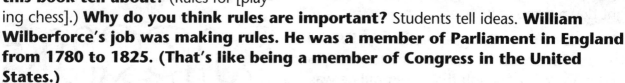

Discussion Questions

1. ***When might it be hard to help others?*** (When you're tired. When you have your own jobs to do.)

2. ***How can you remember to patiently do your best to help others?*** (Ask God's help. Remember God's patience with us.)

Lesson 46

Active Game Center: Towel Travel

Materials

Two of each of the following: towels, stuffed animals, balloons.

Lead the Game

1. **In today's Bible story, four friends were so convinced that Jesus could help their paralyzed friend get better, they carried him on a mat all the way to the house where Jesus was.**

One of the ways we can show the fruit of the Spirit is to patiently continue to help people in the best ways we can. Let's play a game to imitate how four friends in Bible times helped someone in the best way they knew.

2. Students form two teams. Teams line up in single-file lines on one side of the playing area. Give a towel and a stuffed animal to each team.

3. At your signal, the first four students on each team grasp the corners of the towel and place the stuffed animal in the center. Students walk together, carrying the animal across the playing area and back. If the stuffed animal falls off, students return to the starting point and try again.

4. When first group of students is finished, the next foursome carries the stuffed animal on the towel across the room and back. Relay continues until all students have had a turn. (Note: Some students may need to take more than one turn to provide a foursome for each turn.) Ask one of the Discussion Questions below to a volunteer from the first team to finish.

5. **Now let's try to carry something a little bit tougher.** Give each team a balloon. One student on each team inflates balloon. Students repeat relay, carrying a balloon instead of a stuffed animal on the towel.

Options

1. Invite students to tell other Bible story details if they have already heard the story.

2. If you have fewer than 20 students, students may work in pairs instead of foursomes to carry the towel.

• •

Discussion Questions

1. *What are some of the ways you can help people in your family? People at school? People in your neighborhood?*

2. *What are some of the ways people have helped you at home or school?*

3. *Why might you need patience when you try to help other people?* (Might have to help someone more than once. Others may not seem grateful.) *What might help you continue helping others, even when you don't feel like it?* (Praying to God and asking for patience. Remembering how God and others have helped you.)

Art Center: Circles of Patience

Materials

Large sheets of paper, a variety of circular shapes (margarine lid, potato chip can lid, pot lid, jar lid, cookie cutter, plate, etc.), markers.

Lead the Activity

1. Students trace around a variety of circular shapes to cover paper with at least eight overlapping circles. Then they fill in each circle or section with a different repeating pattern (dots, squares, flowers, squiggles, etc.). Encourage students to use a variety of patterns and colors.

2. Printing large, thick letters, students write one letter from the word "patience" in each of eight consecutive sections. Ask Discussion Questions below as students work.

Options

1. Students work together to form a large banner of many overlapping circles on butcher paper.

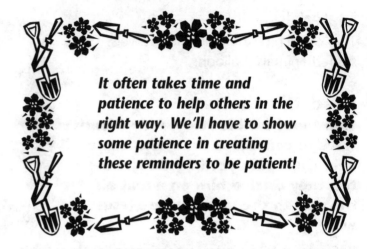

It often takes time and patience to help others in the right way. We'll have to show some patience in creating these reminders to be patient!

2. Students fill in some circles or sections with pasta shapes, glitter, seeds or confetti.

Discussion Questions

1. ***Who are some people kids your age can help?*** (Family members. Kids new to school. Kids who are hurt or crying. Friends.)

2. ***How can we know the right way to help others?*** (Ask the person we are helping. Ask a parent or teacher. Read God's Word and know His commands. Watch others who are good helpers.)

3. ***What can a kid your age do to become more patient?*** (Ask God for His help. Talk to a parent, teacher or coach. Remember how God has shown patience to us. Read about people in the Bible—Noah, Job, etc.—who showed patience.)

Lesson 46

Worship Center

Bible Verse

Blessed are they who maintain justice, who constantly do what is right. Psalm 106:3

Materials

Bible, *God's Kids Grow* cassette/CD or music video and player, "Patient Father" word chart (p. 479 in this book), large sheet of paper on which you have printed Psalm 106:3, masking tape, marker.

Let's thank God that He helps us patiently continue to help others in the best ways we can.

Sing to God

Play "Patient Father," encouraging students to sing along with the music. **What does this song tell us about God's patience and love?** Volunteers respond. **What are some ways the song suggests that we can be patient?** (Ask for God's help. Be kind. Be slow to get mad.)

Hear and Say God's Word

Display paper on which you have printed Psalm 106:3. Have a volunteer read the verse aloud. **When people "maintain justice," it means that they keep doing what is right and fair. What are some of the right things we can do to help people?** (Be kind. Tell the truth. Be patient. Serve others. Share what we have.) List students' ideas on paper under Psalm 106:3. Repeat the verse together several times, each time substituting one of the phrases suggested by students for "do what is right."

Pray to God

Who is someone you know who patiently helps others in a good way? How? Ask volunteers to pray, thanking God for people they mentioned. End prayer by thanking God for His patience and love and asking for His help to patiently care for others.

Options

1. Students sing "You Promised!" and/or "Just Like You" (p. 487 and/or p. 477 in this book).

2. If you collect offering during this time, talk with students about the money they give as one good way to help people. Explain how some people patiently continue to give money each month to help a child in another country have food and clothes, or tell about a missionary that your church sends money to each month so that the missionary can help people learn about Jesus.

Bible Verse Coloring Center

Materials
Crayons or markers, a copy of page 43 or page 44 from
Bible Verse Coloring Pages #2 for each student.

Lead the Activity
Read Psalm 106:3. **When is it hard to do what is right?
What can you do to remember to keep on doing what
is right in situations like this?** Students color picture.

Option
Each student begins coloring his or her own page. After several minutes, each student signs
name on page and trades page with another student. Repeat trading several times until all
pages are colored.

Service Project Center

Materials
Materials needed for "Prayer Baskets" (p. 134 from *The Big Book of
Service Projects*).

Lead the Activity
Students complete the "Prayer Baskets" activity as directed in *The
Big Book of Service Projects*. **Regularly praying for missionaries is a way to keep doing
what's right. What are some other ways to keep doing what's right and grow
the fruit of patience in our lives?**

Discipleship Activity Center

Materials
Discussion Cards for Psalm 146:7-10 (pp. 93-98 from *The Big Book of Chris-
tian Growth*), materials needed for "Behind-the-Back Toss" or "Add-On
Answers" (p. 56 or p. 36 from *The Big Book of Christian Growth*).

Lead the Activity
**Psalm 146:7-10 talks about some of the people whom God patiently loves and
helps. Today we're going to play a game to talk about ways we can help these
people, too.** Students complete activity as directed in *The Big Book of Christian Growth*.

Moses in the Nile

Bible Verse

Serve wholeheartedly, as if you were serving the Lord, not men.
Ephesians 6:7

Bible Story Reference

Exodus 2:1-10

Teacher's Devotional

Dictionaries can only take us so far in understanding the meanings of certain words. Besides the problem of definitions sometimes creating

Character Builder

Use your abilities to show kindness to others.

more confusion than clarity, dictionaries tend to focus on the obvious, surface meanings of the words they define.

For example, a typical dictionary (*Merriam-Webster's Collegiate Dictionary*, 10th ed.) defines kindness as "the quality or state of being kind." Obviously, this definition forces us to see how the word "kind" is explained. We usually discover synonyms such as "humane, considerate, tolerant, generous," and definitions such as "showing sympathy or understanding; charitable" or "persons and their actions when they show evidence of concern or sympathy for others."

These definitions are fine, as far as they go. What they do not do is push us to a deeper understanding of kindness the way the Bible does. In the pages of Scripture, we find that God does not only value kind behavior, actions that are humane and evidence of sympathy but also that God cares at least as much about the attitude of the one engaging in the behavior. He pays particular attention to the motives for human actions.

Paul's instruction in Ephesians 6:7 to "serve wholeheartedly, as if you were serving the Lord" calls us to go beyond half-hearted, perfunctory service for others. Instead, we are to employ all of our energy, enthusiasm and abilities. And if we find that hard to do, we just need to remind ourselves to show kindness as we would for the Lord Himself. And suddenly, we are far, far beyond the scope of a dictionary definition.

Bible Story Center

Materials
Kindness poster from *Poster Pack,* ¼ cup (2 oz.) play dough for each student.

Tell the Story
Follow along with me as we use our dough to tell today's story.

Have you ever helped care for a baby? What are some of the things you did for the baby?

Today we'll hear about the unusual way one baby was cared for.

1. **Make at least six bricks from your dough.** For 400 years, the Israelites (also called the Hebrews) lived in Egypt. During those years, the number of Israelites grew and grew and GREW! Pharaoh, the ruler of Egypt, was worried that the Israelites might become more powerful than the Egyptians!

"Those Hebrews will become my slaves," the Pharaoh decided. "They will work in the hot sun from morning to night making bricks."

The taskmasters used whips to make the Hebrews work very hard. The Hebrew slaves built two large cities. But the harder the Israelites worked, the more of them there seemed to be. Pharaoh was hoping to DECREASE the number of Hebrews, but instead their numbers INCREASED.

2. **Make a baby from one brick.** Soon Pharaoh thought of another plan. He sent for the Hebrew midwives, women who helped the Hebrew mothers when they were having babies. Pharaoh told the midwives to KILL any baby boys that were born. These women knew God would not want them to obey Pharaoh's order, so they protected the baby boys instead.

Then Pharaoh gave a terrible order. "Drown all the Hebrew baby boys," he said. "Throw them into the Nile River!"

3. **Make a basket from two bricks. Put the baby in the basket.** One Hebrew family was determined they would NOT let Pharaoh kill their baby boy. For three months the family kept their baby a secret. Soon the baby's mother, Jochebed (JAHK-eh-behd), had a new idea about how to keep the baby safe. She smeared some gooey, sticky tar all over the outside of a basket and lined the inside of the basket with soft blankets. Then Jochebed gently laid her baby inside the basket.

4. **Make lid from a brick to cover basket.** Jochebed put a lid on the basket, picked it up and carried it all the way to the Nile River. Miriam, the baby's big sister, followed. She watched as Jochebed carefully set the basket in the water. The basket floated right on top of the river. The baby was safe and dry.

5. **Roll out remaining dough as ropes to make a river.** Miriam hid in the tall plants (called reeds) beside the river and watched as the basket floated on the water. *What if soldiers see the basket? What if there is a crocodile nearby?* she might have wondered. Then she heard voices. Some women were coming down to the river to bathe. Miriam peeked through the reeds. Miriam could hardly believe her eyes! It was the PRINCESS—the Pharaoh's own daughter and her servants! *Would they see the basket? Would they call Pharaoh's soldiers?*

"That looks like a basket over there," the princess said. "Go and get it," the princess told her maid. When the the basket was opened, the baby was crying. The princess felt sorry for him. "This is one of the Hebrew babies," the princess said.

Miriam left her hiding place and ran over to the princess. "Would you like me to get one of the Hebrew women to help you take care of this baby?" Miriam asked politely.

"Yes," answered the princess, "go and do that." So Miriam ran all the way home to get her mother.

When Miriam introduced Jochebed to the princess, the princess said, "I'll pay you to take care of this baby for me." Now the baby was safe! No one would try to hurt a baby that belonged to the princess—and the baby still got to live with his own family while he was little!

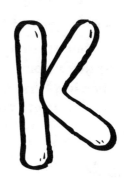

6. **Make a *K* for the word "kindness."** The baby grew to be a little boy. Finally the time came when he was old enough to live in the palace with the princess. The princess named the baby Moses and treated him as kindly as if he were her very own son.

• •

Focus on the Fruit

How did the Hebrew midwives show kindness? How did Jochebed show kindness? Miriam? The princess? (The midwives protected the baby boys. Jochebed made a warm, dry basket for Moses and put it where someone would find it. Miriam watched over Moses when he was in the basket. The princess treated Moses like her own son.)

Each of the people who helped Moses used the abilities God had given them to show kindness. In the same way, we can use whatever abilities we have to show kindness to others. Show the Kindness poster.

Lesson 47

Fruitful Lives Object Talk

Bible Verse

Serve wholeheartedly, as if you were serving the Lord, not men. Ephesians 6:7

Materials

Bible with bookmark at Ephesians 6:7, long strips of cloth or an elastic bandage.

We can use our abilities to show kindness to other people. Let's find out how one woman's actions helped others learn to be kind.

Lead the Activity

1. Invite a volunteer to wrap his or her arm or ankle in cloths or bandage.

When are some times people wrap their arms or ankles like this? (When they've sprained or broken their arm or ankle.) **A long time ago in China, people wrapped the feet of girls for a very different reason. At that time in China, people thought that small feet were beautiful! Parents tightly wrapped their daughters' feet with the small toes bent under. The bones in the feet would break and then heal into tiny twisted feet that were very painful to walk on.**

2. **In 1873, a woman named Lottie Moon went to China as a missionary. She wanted to help people learn about Jesus. Lottie started a school for girls. But Lottie soon found that her students had a hard time learning. The girls were in constant pain because their feet were bound so tightly!**

Lottie felt so sorry for her students that she even convinced one girl's family to let the girl unbind her feet. It wasn't easy for Lottie Moon to convince others to stop hurting girls by binding their feet. But in time, Lottie's actions convinced many people to treat girls kindly; and eventually, foot binding became illegal.

Conclude

Read Ephesians 6:7 aloud. **What reason does this verse give for using your abilities in the best way possible? How can you use the things you do well to show kindness to others? Let's ask God to help us use our abilities to show kindness to others.** Lead students in prayer.

Discussion Questions

1. *What are some things you do well? When could you use these things to help someone else?*

2. *What are some kind things someone else has done for you? When have you done something kind for someone else?*

408

Active Game Center: Cookie Caper

Materials

Sugar cookies (at least one for each student), frosting, plastic knives, sugar sprinkles, paper plates, napkins.

Prepare the Game

Set up two cookie-frosting stations on one side of the playing area (see sketch). Put half of the cookies at each station. Make sure students wash their hands before playing this game.

We can use the abilities God has given us to show kindness to others. Let's play a game and show kindness to others by making snacks for each other.

Lead the Game

1. Divide class into two equal teams. Teams line up on one side of the playing area, across from the cookie-frosting stations.

2. At your signal, the first student on each team quickly walks heel-to-toe to team's cookie-frosting station, puts a cookie on a paper plate, frosts it, puts sprinkles on it and places plate on table. Student returns to team and next student in line takes a turn. Game continues until all students have frosted a cookie. Ask a volunteer from the first team to finish to answer one of the Discussion Questions below. Students from each team give cookies their team frosted to the members of the opposite team. As students eat cookies, continue discussion.

Options

1. Instead of frosting cookies, students spread peanut butter on celery sticks and add raisins, or they spread soft cheese spread on crackers or apple slices.

2. Post a note alerting parents to the use of food in this activity. Also check registration forms for possible food allergies.

• •

Discussion Questions

1. ***What are some things kids your age have the ability to do?*** (Prepare food. Play sports. Read. Make things. Care for animals. Write.)

2. ***How might kids use (reading) to show kindness to others?*** (Read a book to a younger brother or sister. Read a road sign to help a parent figure out where to go.) Repeat question with other abilities students mention.

3. ***When has someone showed kindness to you?*** Volunteers respond. ***What ability did he or she use?***

Art Center: Basket Blessings

Materials

Bible, a variety of colored paper cut in 3x9-inch (7.5x22.5-cm) rectangles, scissors, stapler and staples, paper, pens, small flowers or treats.

Lead the Activity

1. Students select two different colors of rectangles. After folding each rectangle in half lengthwise, students cut to round the unfolded ends. Then they cut two slits, each 3 inches (7.5 cm) long, from each folded edge (see sketch a).

2. Baskets are woven by alternately slipping the strips from one folded rectangle through or around the strips of the second one (see sketch b). Actions are repeated for each of the three strips on each rectangle, alternating whether the strip goes through or around the strip from the other rectangle.

3. Students cut a strip of paper from colored paper for a strap and attach it to basket using stapler (see sketch c). Students fill baskets with notes of kindness, promises to do something kind, small flowers or treats (gum, individually wrapped candy, etc.). Baskets may be exchanged in class or taken home to be given to a friend or family member.

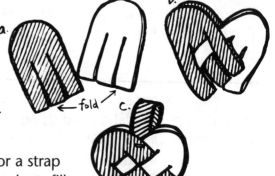

We can use all the different abilities God has given us to show kindness to others. Let's use our artistic abilities to make baskets that we can use to show kindness to others.

Options

1. Students make baskets from felt or wrapping paper.

2. Provide glue, ribbons, yarn, buttons, beads, rickrack, narrow laces and/or other trims for students to use in decorating their baskets.

Discussion Questions

1. ***What are some of the abilities God has given you?*** Volunteers respond. Guide students in discussing all kinds of abilities (reading well, playing soccer, being a good friend, singing, cooking, fixing things, painting, etc.).

2. ***What are some ways you can use these abilities to show kindness to others?***

3. Read Ephesians 6:7 aloud. ***According to this verse, what are the ways we are supposed to serve others?*** (With our whole hearts. As if we were serving God.)

© 2001 Gospel Light. Permission to photocopy granted. *God's Kids Grow Leader's Guide*

Lesson 47

Worship Center

Bible Verse

Serve wholeheartedly, as if you were serving the Lord, not men. Ephesians 6:7

Materials

Bible, *God's Kids Grow* cassette/CD or music video and player, "Be So Kind" word chart (p. 455 in this book), large sheet of paper on which you have printed Ephesians 6:7, masking tape.

We can use the abilities God has given us to show kindness to others and to worship God. Let's worship God and thank Him for the abilities He has given us.

Sing to God

Play "Be So Kind," encouraging students to sing along with the music. **When can you show kindness and put others first when you are at soccer practice? How can you show kindness while you are taking care of a younger child?** Volunteers respond.

Hear and Say God's Word

Display paper on which you have printed Ephesians 6:7. Have a volunteer read the verse aloud. Lead students in saying the verse, clapping once for each syllable of the verse. Repeat verse several times. If time permits, invite students to suggest other rhythmic motions (snap fingers, stamp feet, etc.). **What does it mean to do something wholeheartedly?** (To do it in the best way you can and do it with a good attitude.) **What should we do wholeheartedly?** (Show kindness to others with our God-given abilities!)

Pray to God

What abilities has God given you that you can use to worship Him? (Remember all the great things God has done and praise Him for those things. Tell other people why you love God and why He is so amazing. Sing songs of worship to God.) **Let's use the voices God has given us to thank Him for all the abilities He has given us.** Lead students in saying "Thank You, God" in unison. End prayer time by thanking God for our abilities and asking for His help to use them to show kindness to others.

Options

1. Students sing "Good Fruit" and/or "Just Ask Him" (p. 465 and/or p. 475 in this book).

2. During the verse activity, older students find these verses in their Bibles and read them aloud as examples of ways to use our abilities to show kindness to others: Romans 12:13; Galatians 5:14; Colossians 3:12.

Lesson 47

Bible Verse Coloring Center

Materials
Crayons or markers, a copy of page 169 or page 170 from *Bible Verse Coloring Pages #2* for each student.

Lead the Activity
Read Ephesians 6:7. **When are some times you can serve others? What are some good attitudes to have when you serve others?** Students color picture.

Option
Students draw and color pictures of ways their family members can serve or help each other.

Service Project Center

Materials
Materials needed for "Terrific Toys" (p. 88 from *The Big Book of Service Projects*).

Lead the Activity
Students complete the "Terrific Toys" activity as directed in *The Big Book of Service Projects*. **What else can you do to show kindness to younger children? To kids your age? To adults?**

Discipleship Activity Center

Materials
Discussion Cards for 1 Corinthians 13:4-8a (pp. 141-146 from *The Big Book of Christian Growth*), materials needed for "Determination Squares" or "You Blew It!" (p. 16 or p. 54 from *The Big Book of Christian Growth*).

Lead the Activity
When we show God's love to others, we're growing the fruit of kindness in our lives. Today we're going to play a game to talk about ways to show God's love. Students complete activity as directed in *The Big Book of Christian Growth*.

Esther Saves God's People

Bible Verse

As we have opportunity, let us do good to all people, especially to those who belong to the family of believers. Galatians 6:10

Bible Story Reference

Esther

Teacher's Devotional

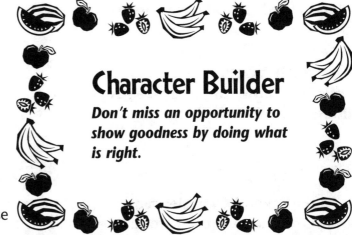

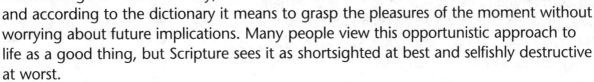

Character Builder

Don't miss an opportunity to show goodness by doing what is right.

Carpe diem! This familiar Latin phrase is a challenge to "Seize the day," and according to the dictionary it means to grasp the pleasures of the moment without worrying about future implications. Many people view this opportunistic approach to life as a good thing, but Scripture sees it as shortsighted at best and selfishly destructive at worst.

Scripture does advocate taking advantage of opportunities but of a different kind and for a higher purpose. Instead of seeking transitory pleasure, we are called to grasp hold of chances to do good. And sometimes this may entail a risk.

Queen Esther had everything going her way when she became aware of her unique opportunity to attempt to rescue her people from slaughter. However, there was the very real possibility that her effort would fail, and she would suffer the same fate, losing not only her exalted position but her life as well. With the encouragement of Mordecai, Esther chose to seize her opportunity and preserve her people.

Few of us encounter such dramatic opportunities to do good to others, but we do frequently face the choice of either providing for our own pleasures or extending ourselves on someone else's behalf. As God's Holy Spirit continues to nourish His nature within us, we will be able to choose the path of goodness instead of settling for momentary pleasures.

Bible Story Center

Materials
Goodness poster from *Poster Pack;* ¼ cup (2 oz.) play dough and pencil for each child.

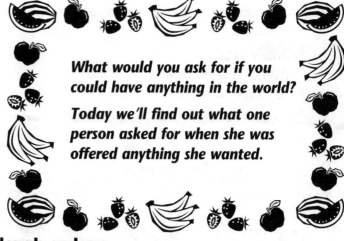

What would you ask for if you could have anything in the world?

Today we'll find out what one person asked for when she was offered anything she wanted.

Tell the Story
Follow along with me as we use our dough to tell today's story.

1. **Make several triangles from your dough and use them to make a crown.** Toward the end of Old Testament times, many Jews had returned to Israel; but many Jews still lived in Persia, too. One was a man named Mordecai (MOHRD-ih-ki). His cousin, Esther, was an orphan, so he raised Esther as his own daughter.

When Esther was grown, Xerxes (ZUHRK-seez), the king of Persia, wanted a new queen. He sent officers through the land to find beautiful young women, who were then taken to the palace. The king would choose one of them as his new queen. Esther was one of the girls chosen. But because many Persians didn't like the Jews, Mordecai told Esther, "Tell no one that you are a Jew. Then you will be safe."

The day came for Esther to appear before the king. She was so lovely, he chose HER to be his queen! God was preparing Esther to take part in some very big plans! Now Esther had beautiful clothes, a sparkling crown and servants all around; BUT she couldn't leave the palace! And Mordecai was not allowed to visit her. So each day, Mordecai walked near the palace gates to get news of Esther. When Mordecai was around the palace, Haman, the chief official of the kingdom, often passed by.

Haman was next to the king in power. And everyone in Persia BOWED before him—everyone except Mordecai! Mordecai bowed only before God. This made Haman ANGRY. He hated Mordecai and all the Jews. Haman came up with a terrible plan to punish Mordecai and every Jew in Persia! Haman told the king how much trouble all the Jews were. He asked the king to make a law that all the Jews should be KILLED!

2. **Make a ring and draw the first letter of your name on it.** The king didn't KNOW Esther was a Jew (she'd kept her secret very well), so he AGREED to let Haman write the law! And he gave Haman his signet ring to seal it. Haman's law ordered that all the Jews be killed on a certain day. With the king's seal on it, the law could never be changed! What an uproar! The Jews asked each other, "What have WE ever done to deserve THIS?"

Mordecai was VERY sad. When Esther heard that he was upset, she sent servants to find out why. Mordecai told Esther about the law. Esther would not escape being killed just because she was the queen. Mordecai told her she HAD to talk to the king about this terrible law!

BUT there was a problem: If a person went into the throne room without being invited and the king didn't hold out his scepter to that person, it meant DEATH! This at first made Esther afraid to go to the king. But Mordecai was sure she had become queen for this very reason! Only someone the king liked more than Haman could plead for the Jews!

3. **Make a scepter, a short rod held by a king to show his power.** Esther was willing to trust God, even if it meant she had to die. Esther fasted for three days—instead of eating she spent time praying to God. Then Esther dressed up— maybe for the last time. She walked into the throne room, her heart pounding. *Will the king hold out his scepter to me?* Her life and the lives of her people depended on his next move!

The king held out his scepter! She touched it and invited the king and Haman to two feasts. At the second feast, Esther told the king that an enemy wanted to kill her and her people. Esther pointed to Haman and said, "The enemy is Haman!" So the king got rid of Haman and put Mordecai in his place. The king made a new law saying that on the day the Jews were to be killed, they could defend themselves! The Jews' enemies were quickly defeated, and the Jews living in Persia were saved—because Esther did what was right for God's people!

• •

Focus on the Fruit

What did Esther do to save her people? (Asked Xerxes to protect her people and told him how Haman had tricked him.) **What happened because Esther did the right thing?** (God's people were saved.) **What did Esther do to help her have the courage she needed?** (She fasted and prayed.)

Esther's goodness and her right actions made a huge difference to her people. Show the Goodness poster. **God uses our right actions to make a difference, too! Just like Esther, we can take every opportunity we are given to show goodness and do the right thing.**

Fruitful Lives Object Talk

Bible Verse

As we have opportunity, let us do good to all people, especially to those who belong to the family of believers. Galatians 6:10

Materials

Bible with bookmark at Galatians 6:10, item typically given to a teacher as a gift (bell; apple; sign saying "Thank you, teacher!"; etc.).

We should use every chance we have to show goodness by doing what is right. Let's find out about someone who showed goodness and helped others because she did what was right.

Lead the Activity

1. Hold up teacher gift. **Have you ever given something like this to one of your teachers or seen anything like this on one of your teachers' desks? What other kinds of gifts might make a teacher feel special?** Volunteers respond. **A long time ago, a teacher named Prudence Crandall got the opposite of a thank-you gift from the people who lived around her school.**

2. **In the early 1800s, when people were still fighting about slavery, Prudence Crandall started a school for teenage girls in Connecticut. All the girls attending the school were white. At that time, some people did not want to be friends with African-Americans. So when Prudence welcomed an African-American girl to attend the school, people in her town got angry. They took their daughters out of the school. But Prudence loved all of God's people and wanted to give African-American students a chance to learn. She invited more African-American girls to the school to take the place of the students who had left.**

   Now the townspeople became very upset! When a group of angry townspeople attacked her school, Prudence closed the school because she was afraid the girls would get hurt. It seemed like anger and hatred had won. But when some of her students grew up, they helped other African-American girls get an education. The good choices Prudence Crandall made caused many people to be able to learn. That was even better than receiving a thank-you gift!

Conclude

Read Galatians 6:10 aloud. **What does this verse tell us to do for all people?** Thank God for the opportunity to do good and ask for His help in choosing to do what is right.

• •

Discussion Questions

1. *When might a kid your age be able to show goodness by choosing to do what is right?* (Choosing to say something nice to a kid who is being teased. Let your brother or sister have the first turn, instead of fighting about whose turn it is.)

2. *When has someone shown goodness to you by doing what was right? How did that make you feel?* Volunteers respond. Tell your own answer as well.

Lesson 48

Active Game Center: Target Relay

Materials
Masking tape or yarn, several Frisbees.

Prepare the Game
For every four to six students, make a 2-foot (.6-m) masking-tape or yarn square on one side of the playing area.

Lead the Game

We can show the fruit of goodness by using every opportunity we have to do what is right. Let's practice doing what is right in our game today.

1. Group students in teams of four to six. Teams line up across the playing area from the targets. Give the first person on each team a Frisbee. **For each round of the game, we'll have a different way to "do what is right," or correctly get the Frisbee onto the target. The first way is to hang the Frisbee by its rim on your fingertip and toss it onto the target.** Demonstrate the motion.

2. At your signal, the first student on each team hangs the Frisbee by its rim on his or her fingertip, runs across the room and tosses the Frisbee onto the team's target. Whether or not the Frisbee lands on the target, student retrieves the Frisbee and runs back to line. The next student in line repeats the action.

3. When all students have completed the relay in this manner, announce a new way to get the Frisbee onto the target and begin game again. Continue as time allows, announcing a new way to "do right" each round (for example, rolling Frisbee onto the target, tossing Frisbee from a standing position, tossing Frisbee back over the shoulder, rolling the Frisbee between the legs, etc.).

Options
1. Play this game outdoors on asphalt or blacktop and use chalk to make the targets.

2. Use paper plates or cups instead of Frisbees, adjusting actions as needed.

Discussion Questions

1. *What are some ways to learn the right things to do?* (Read the Bible. Listen to parents or teachers. Watch older people who love Jesus.)

2. *What are some ways to show goodness by doing what is right at home? At school?* Volunteers tell ideas.

3. *What are some ways you can remember to do what is right when you have the opportunity?* (Pray and ask God to help you remember. Think of a slogan or a question to ask yourself when you have to make a choice.)

Lesson 48

Art Center: Magnetic Goodness

Materials
Bible with bookmark at Galatians 6:10, large sheet of paper, markers, colored file folders, scissors, a variety of art materials (colored construction paper, white paper, tissue paper, glitter, metallic markers, etc.), glue, small bar magnets.

Prepare the Activity
Print the words of Galatians 6:10 on large sheet of paper.

Whenever we take the opportunity to do the right thing, we show God's goodness to others. Let's make reminders to help us do good to others, especially other members of God's family.

Lead the Activity
1. Students cut out shapes from file folders. Shapes should be approximately 3 to 5 inches (7.5 to 12.5 cm) in size. Read, or ask a volunteer to read, verse from large sheet of paper. **What are some slogans that would remind you to do good to others?** (It's good to do good. Don't miss a chance to do good! Be good to the family! Just do good!) Each student chooses a phrase and prints it on a shape.

2. Students use art materials to decorate shapes. When finished, students glue bar magnets to the back of their shapes. Ask the Discussion Questions below to help students talk about ways to show goodness.

Options
1. Photocopy the words "Let us do good to all people" onto paper for younger students to cut out and use to create magnets.

2. Provide small beads, lace, puffy paint and other materials for students to use in decorating shapes.

• •

Discussion Questions
1. *According to Galatians 6:10, for whom are we supposed to do good?* (All people, especially members of God's family.)

2. *What are some ways others have shown goodness to you?* Tell students about a personal, age-appropriate experience of your own.

3. *What can you do to be ready to take advantage of every opportunity to do good for others?* (Read God's Word to know what is good. Talk with others about ways to help people. Pray to God for courage or wisdom. Ask God to show you opportunities to do good for others.)

Lesson 48
Worship Center

Bible Verse
As we have opportunity, let us do good to all people, especially to those who belong to the family of believers.
Galatians 6:10

Materials
Bible, *God's Kids Grow* cassette/CD or music video and player, "Goodness!" word chart (p. 469 in this book), large sheet of paper on which you have printed Galatians 6:10, masking tape.

We shouldn't miss an opportunity to show goodness by doing what is right, so let's use this opportunity to sing and pray to God!

Sing to God
Play "Goodness!" encouraging students to sing along with the music. **What are some ways to show our goodness by doing what is right?** (Obey God. Tell the truth. Be fair. Show God and others our love for them.)

Hear and Say God's Word
Display paper on which you have printed Galatians 6:10. Have a volunteer read the verse aloud. Then mark lines on the paper to divide the verse into four phrases. Divide group into two teams. Lead one team in saying the verse one phrase at a time, stopping after each phrase to let the other team echo the phrase. Rotate which group leads and which group echoes. **For whom does Galatians 6:10 tell us to do good? What are some of the ways to do good for people at school? At church? At home?** (Treat others as you want to be treated. Share generously. Pray for people you know.)

Pray to God
The reason we can show goodness to others is because God has shown His love and goodness to us! What are some of the ways God has shown His love and goodness to you and people you know? (Hears our prayers. Sent Jesus to make it possible for our sins to be forgiven.) Invite volunteers to pray aloud, thanking God for His love and goodness.

Options
1. Ask an older student to lead the Bible verse activity.

2. After the prayer time, invite younger students to draw pictures of ways God has shown His goodness. Students may also include themselves in the picture showing goodness to others.

3. If you take an offering during this worship time, explain to students that giving an offering is one way to obey Galatians 6:10. Tell a way your church uses its offering to help members of your church or other believers (missionaries, local charities, etc.).

Lesson 48

Bible Verse Coloring Center

FOR
YOUNGER
CHILDREN

Materials
Crayons or markers, a copy of page 165 or page 166 from *Bible Verse Coloring Pages #2* for each student.

Lead the Activity
Read Galatians 6:10. **According to this verse, when can we do good things for people? When can you do something good for your family this week?** Students color picture.

Option
Provide copies of page 218 from *Bible Verse Coloring Pages #2*. Students color picture.

Service Project Center

Materials
Materials needed for "Age-Old Funds" (p. 66 from *The Big Book of Service Projects*).

FOR
YOUNGER
CHILDREN
AND
OLDER
CHILDREN

Lead the Activity
Students complete the "Age-Old Funds" activity as directed in *The Big Book of Service Projects*. **We have an opportunity to do good by collecting money to help other people. What are some other opportunities you might have this week to show goodness?**

Discipleship Activity Center

Materials
Discussion Cards for Psalm 23 (pp. 75-80 from *The Big Book of Christian Growth*), materials needed for "Human Tic-Tac-Toe" or "Pass and Switch" (p. 19 or p. 47 from *The Big Book of Christian Growth*).

FOR
OLDER
CHILDREN

Lead the Activity
In our Bible story today, Esther needed to remember that God was always with her, helping her do right even in difficult times. Today we're going to play a game that reminds us of some of the ways God is with us, helping us do right and show goodness in our lives. Students complete activity as directed in *The Big Book of Christian Growth*.

Parable of the Talents

Bible Verse

Whatever you do, work at it with all your heart, as working for the Lord, not for men. Colossians 3:23

Bible Story Reference

Matthew 25:14-30

Teacher's Devotional

If you have been involved throughout the past year in teaching this course on the fruit of the Spirit, you have noticed that the fruit are not nine separate and distinct virtues. There is a great deal about love that sounds a great deal like kindness, which is very similar to goodness, which reminds one of patience, which is a lot like faithfulness, and so on.

You might even have wondered if the similarities and overlap among the virtues have made the emphases of some of the lessons seem remarkably familiar. Perhaps you've asked yourself whether there is anything at all left to say to children about the fruit of the Spirit that has not been thoroughly covered at least several times in this course.

Before you jump to the conclusion that you have "squeezed all the juice possible" from the fruit, ask yourself these questions:

1. Does your life always demonstrate the fruit of the Spirit as fully and consistently as possible? Or is there still a need for further growth of some of these godly virtues?

2. Do the children you teach always demonstrate the fruit of the Spirit as fully and consistently as possible? Or do they still need to experience further growth of some of these godly virtues?

Answer: Since there is still room for growth, now is a great time to focus on the fruit of faithfulness! Now is not the time to give up; instead, keep at it by seeking to nurture the Holy Spirit's active role in your own life and in the lives of the children you teach.

Character Builder

God gives us abilities and wants us to be faithful in using them.

Bible Story Center

Materials
Faithfulness poster from *Poster Pack*; ¼ cup (2 oz.) play dough and coin for each student.

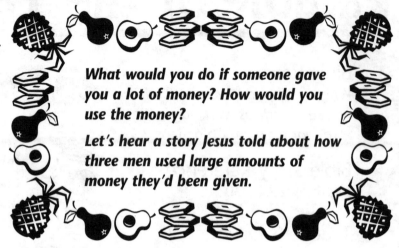

What would you do if someone gave you a lot of money? How would you use the money?

Let's hear a story Jesus told about how three men used large amounts of money they'd been given.

Tell the Story
Follow along with me as we use our dough to tell today's story.

1. **Pinch off eight small pieces of your dough, leaving some dough for later. Use a coin to make coin shape in each piece of dough.** Once there was a man who had three servants that he really trusted. The master had to go on a long trip. While he was gone, he wanted his servants to use his money to make more money for him. They could use the money to buy a piece of cloth and then sew it into clothes and sell them. They could buy and plant vegetable seeds and sell the vegetables for money.

2. **Separate coins into three piles: five coins, two coins, one coin.** The master went to his servants and gave each of them some of his money to use. He gave the first servant five talents. In those days, the word "talent" did not mean an ability. It meant a huge amount of money. The master gave the second servant two talents. And he gave the third servant one talent. Then the master left on his trip.

3. **Make five more coins and add to pile of five coins.** At once the servant with five talents went to work. He used the money to make more money. While his master was gone, this hardworking servant earned five MORE talents. He had been given five talents to begin with, and now he had 10! His hard work had certainly paid off!

4. **Make two more coins and add to pile of two coins.** The servant with two talents also got right to work. He took his master's money and increased it as well. Perhaps he bought and sold some animals. Whatever he did certainly increased his money. Now he had four talents, twice what he had started with!

5. **Make a shovel with remaining dough.** The third servant could have taken his one talent and bought and sold some sheep. But he was afraid. The money might get lost or stolen. So instead of using it to make more money for his master, he dug a hole in the ground and buried the money, hiding it in the dirt!

After a time the master returned. He called the servants together to see what they had done with his money. The servant who had earned five more talents gave the 10 talents to his master and said, "You gave me five talents and see—I have earned five more for you!"

"Good work!" the master told him. "You were faithful to use what I gave you! Now I will give you MUCH MORE to take care of. I'm happy with what you have done for me."

6. **Add pile of four coins to pile of ten coins.** The second servant gave the money he had earned to his master and said, "Master, you gave me two talents. Now here are two more talents for you."

"You have been faithful and did what I said to do!" the master smiled. "I will put you in charge of more, too. You've pleased me!"

7. **Add single coin to large pile of coins.** Then the third servant who had buried his money said, "I knew you would be angry if I lost your money. I was afraid! So I hid your money in the ground. Here is the one talent you gave me."

"WHAT?" roared the master. "You did NOTHING with my money? At least you could have put it in the bank! It would have earned interest there." (Interest is the money a bank pays for being able to use the money stored there.)

The master said, "I'll give your money to my servant who earned the most money!" The master had wanted his money to be USED, not hidden away. Jesus told this story so that we would all know that God expects us to USE the abilities and gifts He has given us. It doesn't matter how much we have to start with. What's important to God is that we are faithful to use what He gives us to help others. That pleases Him!

- -

Focus on the Fruit

Why was the master angry with the servant he'd given one talent? (The servant did nothing to earn more money for the master.) **What do you think Jesus wanted people to learn from this story?** (To use the gifts God gives us. To be faithful and dependable. To do our best.)

God has made each of us with special gifts, or abilities. We need never feel afraid or nervous about using a gift from God. And by using these gifts, we show God and others that we are growing the fruit of faithfulness! Show the Faithfulness poster.

Fruitful Lives Object Talk

Bible Verse
Whatever you do, work at it with all your heart, as working for the Lord, not for men. Colossians 3:23

Materials
Bible with bookmark at Colossians 3:23, marker, paper.

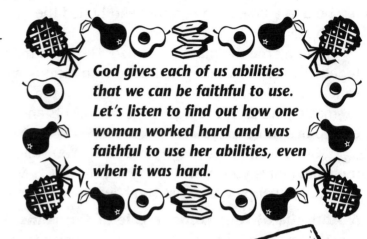

God gives each of us abilities that we can be faithful to use. Let's listen to find out how one woman worked hard and was faithful to use her abilities, even when it was hard.

Lead the Activity
1. Ask a volunteer to put the marker in his or her mouth and try to draw a picture of a tree. **It's pretty hard to draw this way, but this is how a woman named Joni (JAHN-ee) Eareckson Tada draws all her pictures!**

2. **Joni didn't always draw this way. When Joni was a teenager, she had an accident. She dove into a lake at a place where the water was too shallow, and she broke her neck and became paralyzed. Joni could no longer use her hands or legs. But Joni was determined to be able to learn to do things again using her body parts that did work—like her mouth.**

For two years, Joni worked hard to learn to draw by holding things like pencils and paintbrushes between her teeth. She began to draw beautiful pictures. Joni signed her pictures "PTL" for "Praise the Lord," reminding herself that God cared for her and thanking God for her ability to draw, even when most of her body no longer worked. Her pictures were put onto cards and sold and displayed around the world. The pictures and the "PTL" reminded people to use whatever abilities they had to give praise to God. Joni and Friends is the name of an organization Joni started to give special encouragement to people with disabilities.

Conclude
Read Colossians 3:23 aloud. **What did Joni Eareckson Tada do to obey this verse? How did she show that she was working to please God?** (Signed her pictures "Praise the Lord.") **What are some of the abilities you have? What can you do to use them like you are working for God?** Lead students in prayer, thanking God for the abilities He has given us.

● ●

Additional Information for Older Students
People were so amazed at Joni's story that they encouraged her to write a book about her life. Joni wrote an autobiography, and a movie was also made about her life. Now Joni has used her abilities to illustrate and write more books.

Active Game Center: Ability Blast

Materials
Bible, *God's Kids Grow* cassette/CD and player, index cards, marker, tape.

Prepare the Game
Print one of the following abilities on each index card: play baseball, play piano, math skills, spell, compete in gymnastics, write, read, play soccer, draw, sing, act, run.

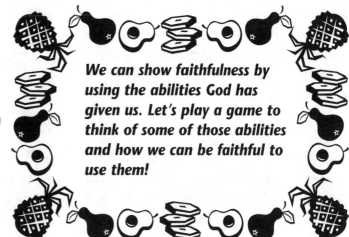

We can show faithfulness by using the abilities God has given us. Let's play a game to think of some of those abilities and how we can be faithful to use them!

Lead the Game
1. Play "Good Habits" song from *God's Kids Grow* cassette/CD as students walk around the room. When you stop music, each student quickly moves to a corner of the room, making sure there is approximately the same number of students in each corner.

2. Tape an index card in each corner. Students in each corner read card and plan a way to pantomime the ability. Groups take turns pantomiming abilities for the other groups to guess. Ask a Discussion Question from below after abilities have been guessed.

3. At the end of each round of play, collect cards and repeat entire game as time allows, distributing a new set of ability cards each round.

Options
1. Bring additional index cards to class and ask students to suggest abilities they have. Print one ability on each card and use cards during the game.

2. At the end of each round, when all four abilities have been guessed, call out "Find your ability." Each student runs to the corner representing his or her greatest ability.

● ●

Discussion Questions
1. **What does it mean to be faithful?** (To keep doing something you said you would do. To keep your promises.)

2. **How does Colossians 3:23 describe being faithful?** Ask an older student to read the verse aloud. (Doing something with your whole heart. Doing something to please God, not just to please the people around you.)

3. **What are some ways to be faithful to using the abilities God has given you?** (Practice using the abilities. Keep using them to help others. Have a good attitude while using your abilities. Use your abilities to please God, doing the best you can do.)

Art Center: Ability Book

Materials
Bible, a variety of 9x12-inch (22.5x30-cm) colored construction paper, scissors, ruler, markers, white paper, stapler and staples, glue.

Prepare the Activity
Cut strips of construction paper 1½x12 inches (3.75x30 cm), to create binding strips—one for each student. Make a sample book.

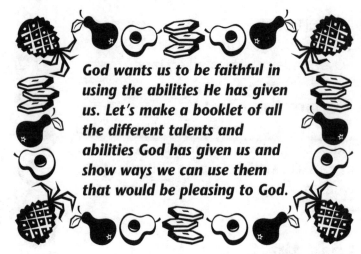

God wants us to be faithful in using the abilities He has given us. Let's make a booklet of all the different talents and abilities God has given us and show ways we can use them that would be pleasing to God.

Lead the Activity

1. Students select several sheets of white paper and two pieces of colored construction paper. Sandwiching white paper between construction paper covers, students place a binding strip flush along the left edge of the top cover. Holding the papers carefully, students staple three or four times down the length of the paper approximately ½ inch (1.25 cm) from the left edge (see sketch a).

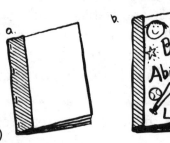

2. Students fold the binding strip back over the staples and around left edge to the back and glue binding to back cover to secure.

3. Students complete the book by drawing pictures or describing in words the different talents and abilities God has given them and showing how those abilities can be used in ways that would be pleasing to God. Ask the Discussion Questions below to guide students as they complete their books. Encourage students to title their books and decorate the covers (see sketch b).

Options
1. Older students may measure and cut out their own binding strips.

2. Provide poster board or card stock for covers.

• •

Discussion Questions

1. ***What are some of the things you like to do or are good at doing?*** Encourage students to think beyond obvious talents such as reading well or playing sports, to abilities such as being a good friend or listening well.

2. ***How can you use those abilities to serve God or help others?*** Answer this question with an example from your own life before asking students to respond.

3. Read Colossians 3:23 aloud. ***According to this verse, how are we supposed to do things?*** (Do our best as if we were obeying God, not other people.)

Worship Center

Bible Verse

Whatever you do, work at it with all your heart, as working for the Lord, not for men. Colossians 3:23

Materials

Bible, *God's Kids Grow* cassette/CD or music video and player, "Good Habits" word chart (p. 467 in this book), large sheet of paper on which you have printed Colossians 3:23, masking tape.

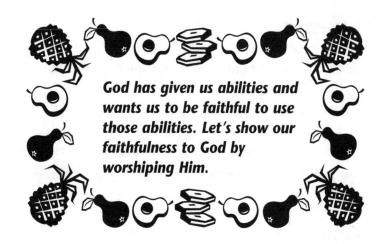

God has given us abilities and wants us to be faithful to use those abilities. Let's show our faithfulness to God by worshiping Him.

Sing to God

Play "Good Habits," encouraging students to sing along with the music. **When might kids your age practice some of the habits described in this song?** (Pray every night before bed. Help neighbor bag papers every week.)

Hear and Say God's Word

Display paper on which you have printed Colossians 3:23. Have a volunteer read the verse aloud. **How does this verse tell you to work or use your abilities?** Volunteers respond. **When we are working for the Lord, it means we are trying to do our best work.** Suggest that each student think of a type of work for which to do a motion (hammer nails, sweep floor, wash dishes, make a bed, etc.). Students say the verse and do motions. Repeat verse several times with students doing different motions each time.

Pray to God

Think of an ability God has given you. Students pray silently, thanking God for the ability and asking for His help to faithfully keep using that ability. End prayer time by thanking God that He has given us such wonderful abilities and that we can worship Him by using those abilities well.

Options

1. Ask an older student to read a definition of the word "faithful" from a children's Bible dictionary. Brainstorm with students and list on a large sheet of paper ways God is faithful to us and ways we can be faithful to God.

2. During the Bible verse activity, discuss the abilities the students have been given. Each student makes a motion for an ability he or she has. **What might you do to be faithful at using your (good math skills)?** (Keep working hard at math. Help other people who have a hard time understanding math.)

Bible Verse Coloring Center

Materials

Crayons or markers, a copy of page 187 or page 188 from *Bible Verse Coloring Pages #2* for each student.

Lead the Activity

Read Colossians 3:23. **How might the children in this picture do their best work? When have you done your very best or worked on something with all your heart?** Students color picture.

Option

Use a paper cutter to cut construction paper into small squares and triangles. Students use glue sticks to glue paper squares and triangles to fill in the picture instead of coloring.

Service Project Center

Materials

Materials needed for "Scent-sational Thanks" (p. 59 from *The Big Book of Service Projects*).

Lead the Activity

Students complete the "Scent-sational Thanks" activity as directed in *The Big Book of Service Projects*. **How do you think doing this project can help us remember to be faithful in using our abilities?**

Discipleship Activity Center

Materials

Discussion Cards for Psalm 139:1-3,13-16 (pp. 87-92 from *The Big Book of Christian Growth*); materials needed for "Keep It Moving!" or "Penny Pass" (p. 20 or p. 48 from *The Big Book of Christian Growth*).

Lead the Activity

Psalm 139:1-3,13-16 tells us about the wonderful way in which God made each of us, giving us abilities to faithfully use. Today we're going to play a game using what we've learned in these verses. Students complete activity as directed in *The Big Book of Christian Growth*.

Mary's Wise Choice

Bible Verse

Listen to advice and accept instruction, and in the end you will be wise. Proverbs 19:20

Bible Story Reference

Luke 10:38-42

Teacher's Devotional

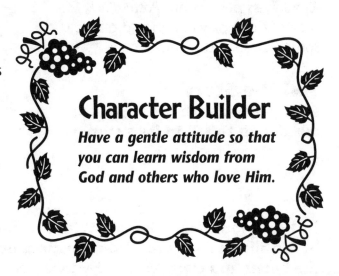

Character Builder

Have a gentle attitude so that you can learn wisdom from God and others who love Him.

Love and marriage, potatoes and gravy, Mom and apple pie, birds and bees— there are certain pairs of words that are commonly linked in our language and our memories. They just naturally go together, and thinking of one tends to recall the other and vice versa.

Two words in Scripture seem to fit that pattern: "gentleness" (or "meekness") and "humility."

• "I will leave within you the meek and humble, who trust in the name of the Lord" (Zephaniah 3:12).

• "I am gentle and humble in heart" (Matthew 11:29).

• "Be completely humble and gentle" (Ephesians 4:2).

• "Clothe yourselves with . . . humility, gentleness" (Colossians 3:12).

As we look at these quotes, it becomes clear that the writers were not really linking two different or even related concepts. Instead, they were strengthening our understanding of one concept by using two very similar words. The person who is humble is gentle (meek). And the gentle person is humble.

We see an example of these words in Mary's actions when Jesus visited Bethany. While her sister, Martha, bustled about the house with last-minute preparations, Mary "sat at the Lord's feet listening to what he said" (Luke 10:39). Mary was not trying to impress Jesus. Nor was she even trying to serve Him. On that occasion, she humbly listened to Him.

Reading this story, we find it easy to empathize with Martha's frustration over Mary's not helping with the work. However, Jesus clearly wanted to make the point that there are times we must cease from busily doing good things. Then humbly, meekly and gently, we put aside our egos and ambitions so that we can listen and learn. After all, a gentle spirit is a teachable spirit.

Bible Story Center

Materials
Gentleness poster from *Poster Pack*;
¼ cup (2 oz.) play dough and plastic
spoon for each student.

Tell the Story
**Follow along with me as we use
our dough to tell today's story.**

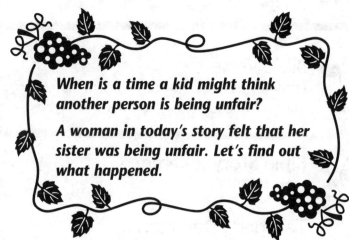

*When is a time a kid might think
another person is being unfair?*

*A woman in today's story felt that her
sister was being unfair. Let's find out
what happened.*

1. **Divide your dough in half. With one half make
bowls, plates and cups. Use a plastic spoon to shape
the bowls and cups.** Mary and Martha were sisters who lived
in Bethany with their brother, Lazarus. They were friends of
Jesus, and they loved to have Him visit their home! Today Jesus
was coming to visit. There were so many things to do to get
ready—many of the same things your family does when company is coming. There were bowls and plates and cups to wash.
There were floors to be scrubbed, meat to be roasted and vegetables to be picked from the garden.

"Hurry, Mary!" Martha might have said. "I've swept the
floor, but everything needs dusting. Oh, and where are the
spices for the fish?"

Mary and Martha must have made sure the house was
spotless. But there was still work left to do. They probably had
to fetch the water, bake the bread and wash the grapes! They
hustled and bustled and hurried all over the house to finish the
work before Jesus arrived.

Soon they saw a little cloud of dust rising over the horizon.
Jesus and His friends were walking down the road! Mary probably shouted, "Jesus is here! He's here!" and ran out to meet
Him. Martha probably stayed in the house because she saw
that there still was work to be done. She wanted this dinner
with Jesus to be PERFECT!

2. **Make a table with the other half of the dough.** As
Jesus and the other guests came in, Martha continued to hurry
around, making sure that everyone's feet were washed and that
everyone was comfortable. She ran back and forth with bowls
of water and plates of grapes and olives.

Suddenly Martha stopped and looked around. *Where is Mary?* she wondered. *Why isn't she helping me?*

Mary was sitting on the floor at Jesus' feet. She was watching Him and listening closely to every word He said. She didn't want to miss one second of Jesus' visit!

In Bible times, women were not usually in the room where a group of men sat. They usually came in and out with food and drink for the men, perhaps listening while they worked. But Mary stayed in the room with the men, as if she belonged there! It was so wonderful to her just to be near Jesus. She had forgotten EVERYTHING else but listening to Him.

3. **Set table with bowls, plates, cups.** Martha saw Mary sitting by Jesus—not working, not helping out, just sitting and listening to Jesus with a big smile on her face. Martha grumbled and complained to herself as she worked to finish getting dinner ready. Finally, Martha couldn't stand it any longer. She walked up to Jesus.

"Lord, don't You care that my sister has left me to do the work by myself? Tell her to help me!" Martha insisted.

Martha was thinking so much about the work and the fact that Mary wasn't helping that she couldn't enjoy being with Jesus—even though HE was the reason she was working so hard to make everything wonderful.

Jesus understood how Martha felt. "Martha, Martha," Jesus said. "You are worried and upset about many things, but only one thing is needed. Mary has chosen what is better, and it will not be taken away from her."

Martha had hurried and worked so hard to help make Jesus and the other guests comfortable. She was doing a very good, kind thing. The only problem was that Martha had forgotten that the BEST thing was that Jesus had come to talk with them and teach them. That's why Jesus said that Mary had chosen what was better—the wisdom she learned from Jesus was something that could never be taken away from her.

● ●

Focus on the Fruit

How were Mary and Martha the same? Different? (Mary and Martha both loved Jesus. Mary wanted to listen to Jesus. Martha wanted to make a good dinner for Him.) **What did Jesus say about the choices Mary and Martha made?** (Mary had made a better choice than Martha because Mary would not lose the wisdom she learned from Jesus.)

People who take the time to listen to God and others and learn from them show the fruit of gentleness in their lives. Mary's gentle attitude caused her to want to spend time listening to Jesus. Show the Gentleness poster. **By having a gentle attitude, we can learn wisdom from God and others who love Him.**

Fruitful Lives Object Talk

Bible Verse

Listen to advice and accept instruction, and in the end you will be wise. Proverbs 19:20

Materials

Bible with bookmark at Proverbs 19:20; object representing something a friend has taught you or helped you with (golf club, crocheted blanket, paintbrush, pie tin, etc.).

Having a gentle attitude helps us learn wisdom from God and others who love Him. Let's listen to find out how one man's gentle attitude helped him learn something that helped people all over the world.

Lead the Activity

1. Show and describe object. **I brought this (golf club) because my friend (Sam) helped me learn how to (play golf). What is something a friend has helped you learn?** Students respond. **A man named Cameron Townsend went to Guatemala as a missionary. He was very glad to find a friend there to help him out!**

2. **When Cameron first went to Guatemala, whenever he met people with whom he wanted to talk about God, he'd ask, "Do you know the Lord Jesus?" But when he asked this question in Spanish, it translated as, "Do you know Mr. Jesus (hay-SOOS)?" Because Jesus is a common Hispanic name, the people he was talking to did not know Cameron was talking about Jesus the Son of God. He also discovered that many of the people he talked to did not even know Spanish but spoke other languages. There were hundreds of different languages in that area!**

   Cameron wondered how he would be able to talk to these people about Jesus, so he prayed for God's help. Soon Cameron met an Indian man named Francisco Diaz (FRAHN-cees-coh DEE-ahz) who loved God, too. Francisco taught Cameron his language and helped him translate the New Testament into that language. Cameron was so excited about this idea of translating the Scriptures into everyone's own language that he began an organization called Wycliffe Bible Translators. Today Wycliffe missionaries help people all over the world learn about God in their own language, all because of God's help and Cameron Townsend's willingness to learn from Francisco Diaz.

Conclude

Read Proverbs 19:20 aloud. **This verse describes what someone who has a gentle attitude is like. What advice have you learned from people who love Jesus?** Students tell. Lead students in prayer, asking God's help in learning from others.

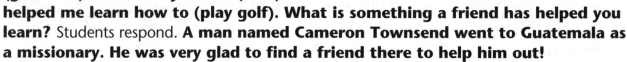

Additional Information for Older Students

Wycliffe Bible missionaries have translated the New Testament into over 500 languages, and they work in over 70 countries. The average translation job takes 10 to 20 years! (Optional: Invite someone who has served with Wycliffe to talk to your students, or find additional information at www.wycliffe.org.)

Active Game Center: Hop Up

Materials
Bible, masking tape, black and red markers, index cards.

Prepare the Game
Use masking tape to make two Hopscotch grids on the floor. Using the black marker, print "gentle" on six index cards, one letter on each card. On the back of each of those cards, use red marker to print one letter of "wisdom" in mixed-up order. Prepare two sets of cards. Place one set of shuffled cards at the end of each Hopscotch grid.

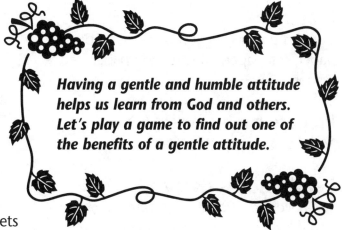

Having a gentle and humble attitude helps us learn from God and others. Let's play a game to find out one of the benefits of a gentle attitude.

Lead the Game
1. Group students in two teams of no more than six. Each team lines up at the start of one of the Hopscotch grids. At your signal, students on each team take turns hopping through team's grid and collecting a card from the stack at the end of the grid. Students carry cards as they hop back to teams. (If there are fewer than six students on a team, one or more students may take two turns.)

2. Teams order cards to determine word written in black ("gentle"). Volunteer from first team finished reads word aloud. **The Bible tells us that being gentle will help us find something very important. Flip your cards over to see what results from gentleness.** Students flip cards over and put them in order to reveal the word "wisdom." Ask Discussion Questions below.

Options
1. Play this game outside on an asphalt playing area. Use chalk to draw the hopscotch grids.

2. If you have more than 12 students, make additional grids and sets of cards as needed.

3. Make additional cards for the words "humble," "listen" or "advice." Repeat game with teams collecting cards to find words that help describe a gentle attitude.

● ●

Discussion Questions
1. *What other words can you use to describe someone who has a gentle attitude?* ("Listens." "Humble." "Peaceful." "Respectful." "Unselfish.")

2. *Why does having a gentle attitude lead to wisdom?* (When you listen to others, you can learn from them. When you put other people first, you can learn their ideas, instead of just telling your own.) Ask a volunteer to read Proverbs 19:20 aloud.

Art Center: Get the Picture?

Materials
Colored paper (origami paper, wrapping paper, foil paper, construction paper, etc.), scissors.

Prepare the Activity
Make a sample picture frame.

Lead the Activity
1. Challenge students to create a picture frame by folding a piece of paper.

2. After several minutes, lead students in following the directions below to create an origami picture frame.

People with gentle attitudes are glad to listen and learn from God and others who love Him. Let's listen to these instructions and make something that is useful and fun to look at!

a) Make a square by folding paper diagonally from one corner and cutting off excess (see sketch a).

b) Open paper and fold four corners to center. Use diagonal fold line as guide (see sketch b).

c) Turn paper over and fold four corners to center again.

d) Turn paper over and fold points outward from center.

e) Open folds in back to stand up picture frame (see sketch c).

Options
1. Use paper with different colors on each side.

2. Provide stickers, markers, glitter, craft jewels and other art materials for students to use in decorating their picture frames.

3. Use an instant camera to take pictures of students to place inside their picture frames.

Discussion Questions
1. **Which way was the best way to make a picture frame—by trying it on your own or by listening to instructions?**

2. **What are some other things that are easier to do when you have instructions to follow?** (Bake a cake. Play soccer. Learn to play a guitar.)

3. **What are some ways you can get instructions from God?** (Read God's Word. Pray to Him. Talk to other people who love God.)

Lesson 50

Worship Center

Bible Verse
Listen to advice and accept instruction, and in the end you will be wise. Proverbs 19:20

Materials
Bible, *God's Kids Grow* cassette/CD or music video and player, "Gentle Servant" word chart (p. 463 in this book), large sheet of paper on which you have printed Proverbs 19:20, masking tape.

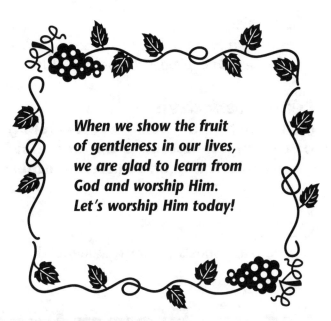

When we show the fruit of gentleness in our lives, we are glad to learn from God and worship Him. Let's worship Him today!

Sing to God
Play "Gentle Servant," encouraging students to sing along with the music. **According to this song, what are three questions we can ask to find ways of showing the fruit of gentleness?** (What can I do to make things better? What can I do to help you out? What can I do to make you happy?)

Hear and Say God's Word
Display paper on which you have printed Proverbs 19:20. Have a volunteer read the verse aloud. **What does Proverbs 19:20 tell us to do so that we can be wise?** (Listen to advice and accept instruction.) **What do you need to do in order to listen to other people's advice and accept instruction?** (Listen to the other person without thinking only of your own response. Be humble. Be willing to do something someone else's way.) Lead students in saying the verse, inserting a different student's name for "you" each time the verse is said. Let named student choose next name to insert. Continue until all students have been named.

Pray to God
When are some times it is hard to listen to advice or instruction? Volunteers respond. Invite an older student to pray for the class, asking for God's help to have a gentle attitude and learn from God and others in the times students mentioned.

Options
1. If you have been keeping a prayer journal during these worship times, ask a volunteer to read several of the entries. Students report how prayers have been answered. Invite students to name and record more requests. During the prayer time, students thank God for answering their prayers.

2. Invite an older Christian from your church to briefly share some practical advice or instruction about a way to learn from God.

Bible Verse Coloring Center

Materials

Crayons or markers, a copy of page 65 or page 66 from *Bible Verse Coloring Pages #2* for each student.

Lead the Activity

Read Proverbs 19:20. **What will the young boy in this picture learn if he listens to the older boy? When are some times it is good to listen to others?** Students color picture.

Option

Provide blank sheets of paper. Students draw and color pictures of people they can listen to.

Service Project Center

Materials

Materials needed for "Bible Balloons" (p. 51 from *The Big Book of Service Projects*).

Lead the Activity

Students complete "Bible Balloons" activity as directed in *The Big Book of Service Projects*. **Older people who love God can help us be wise when we listen to their advice. Let's make these balloon gifts as a way to thank and encourage older people in our church.**

Discipleship Activity Center

Materials

Discussion Cards for Proverbs 3:3-6 (pp. 99-104 from *The Big Book of Christian Growth*), materials needed for "Active Alphabet" or "Calendar Toss" (p. 56 or p. 39 from *The Big Book of Christian Growth*).

Lead the Activity

Today we're going to play a game to talk about ways to obey the instructions in Proverbs 3:3-6. These verses will help us discover ways to learn from God and others. When we're willing to learn from God, it shows we're growing the fruit of gentleness in our lives. Students complete activity as directed in *The Big Book of Christian Growth*.

Solomon's Wisdom

Bible Verse

Direct my footsteps according to your word; let no sin rule over me.
Psalm 119:133

Bible Story Reference

1 Kings 2:1-12; 3:1-15; 4:29-34; 10:1-13; 11:1-13

Teacher's Devotional

Self-control is a virtue that involves strength. It does not take any great insight to realize that the person who says no to an impulse is stronger than the person who gives in. Resisting peer pressure, media influences, physical urges and appealing temptations is no job for a weakling. Our language is full of descriptions of the person who lacks inner strength: spineless, weak-willed, foolish, easily swayed, pushover, patsy, soft touch, etc. The list goes on and on, because lack of self-control is such a common failing. We all know people who at some time or the other lacked the strength to control themselves. And we all know that at times, we have been just as weak.

Compare this rather depressing state of affairs with Paul's encouragement to the Christians in Thessalonica: "It is God's will that . . . each of you should learn to control his own body in a way that is holy and honorable" (1 Thessalonians 4:3,4). Imagine: it is God's will that we not be spineless, weak-willed pushovers who are ruled by our appetites or the influences of others.

As you imagine that, keep in mind that when God wills something, He always provides a way for His will to be done. His Spirit works within us, building us up and strengthening us. He gives us His Word as a source of wisdom. When have you seen evidence of greater self-control in your own life? Keep asking God to continue growing His character within you. He will make a big difference in the kind of person you become.

Character Builder

God's Word helps us learn how to have self-control and live wisely.

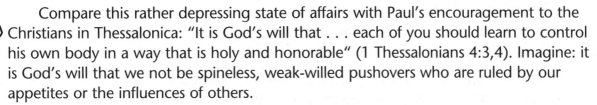

Bible Story Center

Materials

Self-Control poster from *Poster Pack,* ¼ cup (2 oz.) play dough for each student.

Tell the Story

Follow along with me as we use our dough to tell today's story.

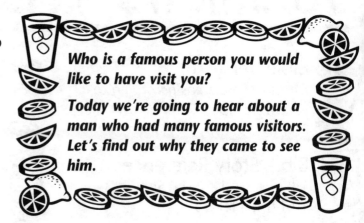

Who is a famous person you would like to have visit you?

Today we're going to hear about a man who had many famous visitors. Let's find out why they came to see him.

1. **With your dough, make an *S* for Solomon.** Solomon was still a young man when his father, King David, made him the new king of Israel. Shortly before King David died, he gave Solomon some advice. "Be strong and always obey God," David told his son. "Follow God's laws and commands, and you will prosper in everything you do and everywhere you go."

2. **Make a crown.** Solomon had older brothers who might have been expected to take David's place as king. After all, they had much more experience and knowledge than a young man of 20! But unlike his brothers, Solomon loved and trusted God and followed God's ways. So Solomon was chosen by God to be the next king of Israel.

   After David died and Solomon was proclaimed king, he went to a city called Gibeon to worship God.

   While Solomon was at Gibeon, God appeared to him in a dream. "Solomon," God said, "ask Me for anything and I will give it to you."

3. **Make a *W* for wisdom.** Solomon could have asked for great wealth so that he could live in luxury. Or he could have asked for great power to keep himself safe from his enemies. He could have asked to be very popular or to have a long life. But instead Solomon asked for wisdom. "I am so young to be king," Solomon said, "I need Your wisdom in order to know right from wrong so that I can lead Your people well."

   God was very pleased with Solomon's request. He gave Solomon the wisdom he wanted. In fact, God told Solomon that he would be the wisest man ever! In addition, God gave Solomon what he didn't ask for: riches and honor so that there wouldn't be another king like him anywhere on Earth! God made one more, very special promise. "As long as you obey my

438

commands as David your father did, I will give you a long life as well!"

4. **Make a book like a Bible.** Solomon studied plants, animals, birds, reptiles and fish. The Bible tells us that Solomon also wrote 1,005 songs and 3,000 proverbs! Most of the book of Proverbs in the Bible was written by Solomon. Proverbs are wise sayings that help people know the right way to live. Because God had given him such great wisdom, Solomon had a lot to say about living life wisely!

For many years, Solomon ruled God's people wisely. The news of his wisdom traveled around the world. Leaders from all over the world traveled to see King Solomon and ask for his advice.

5. **Make a question mark.** One of Solomon's most famous visitors was the queen of Sheba. The Bible tells us that when she heard about Solomon, she couldn't believe such a great king existed! So she came to Jerusalem to talk with Solomon. She asked him very hard questions to see if he really was the wisest man on Earth. When Solomon was able to answer all of her questions, she realized what a great king he was. She saw the food, the clothes and everything else Solomon had.

"I did not believe what I'd heard about you until I could see for myself, but in wisdom and wealth you are even richer than I'd heard! Praise the Lord God, for He has shown His great love for Israel by making you a great king!" she said.

As long as Solomon followed God's laws and instructions, he was a wise, wealthy and powerful king. But later in his life, Solomon stopped listening to God and started listening to his wives instead. Solomon had wives who worshiped false gods. Instead of doing what was right, Solomon built temples for those false gods. And then he made an even BIGGER mistake and worshiped those false gods! Since Solomon did not obey God, he didn't get to live a long life like his father, David.

• •

Focus on the Fruit

What did Solomon ask God for? Why did he want that? (Wisdom. In order to do a good job leading God's people.) **What did God give Solomon?** (Wisdom, wealth and honor. God promised Solomon a long life if Solomon would obey His commands.) **Why did Solomon end up not living a long life?** (Solomon disobeyed God.)

Every day we can make choices that show self-control. Show the Self-Control poster. **We show self-control when we do what is right and obey God. God's Word, including the books written by Solomon, show us how to have self-control and live wisely.**

Fruitful Lives Object Talk

Bible Verse

Direct my footsteps according to your word; let no sin rule over me. Psalm 119:133

Materials

Bible with bookmark at Psalm 119:133, umbrella.

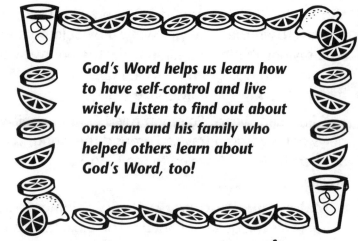

God's Word helps us learn how to have self-control and live wisely. Listen to find out about one man and his family who helped others learn about God's Word, too!

Lead the Activity

1. Show umbrella. **When do people use this? Why?** Students respond. **People use an umbrella for shelter from rain and snow. A man named Francis Schaeffer and his family named their home in Switzerland** *L'Abri,* **the French word for "shelter." Why might you call a home a shelter?** (Keeps you safe.)

2. **Francis Schaeffer and his family moved from America to Switzerland because they wanted to help people in Europe learn about God. They knew that many Europeans had questions about God and the Bible. Francis and his family wanted to help people discover the answers to their questions by teaching them about God's Word.**

The Schaeffer family made their house, L'Abri, a place where people from around the world could come and study God's Word. They prayed that God would send to L'Abri people who had questions about God. While the Schaeffers' guests lived at L'Abri, they saw how people who loved God lived each day. The Schaeffers helped their guests learn wisdom from the Bible. Many of these guests became convinced that God is real and that His Word tells the best way to live.

Conclude

Read Psalm 119:133 aloud. **What does it mean for God to "direct [your] footsteps according to [His] word"?** (He will help you obey the Bible.) **God's Word teaches us wise ways to live, and as we follow these wise ways, we learn to have self-control.** Lead students in prayer, thanking God for His Word that tells us wise ways to live.

Discussion Questions

1. *What are some of the ways God's Word tells us to live?* (Love and forgive others. Ask Jesus to forgive our sins. Pray to God and ask for help with our problems. Tell the good news about Jesus to other people.)

2. *What is one way you can obey God's Word this week?* Students respond. Share your own answer with your students.

Lesson 51

Active Game Center: Path Shuffle

Materials
Bible, yarn, paper or plastic plates.

Prepare the Game
Use the yarn to form a random path that begins and ends at the same place. Prepare one path for every 10 students.

Lead the Game
1. Students line up in groups of no more than 10 at the beginning of each path. Give the first students in each line two plates. Students stand on plates.

2. At your signal, the first student in each line begins shuffling alongside the path, keeping the plates underfoot at all times. When student returns to group, next student in line begins. Play continues until everyone has had a turn.

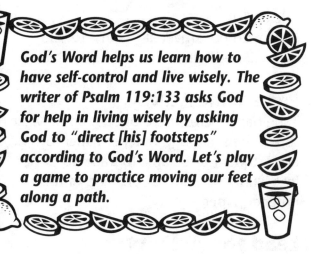

God's Word helps us learn how to have self-control and live wisely. The writer of Psalm 119:133 asks God for help in living wisely by asking God to "direct [his] footsteps" according to God's Word. Let's play a game to practice moving our feet along a path.

Options
1. Change the yarn path after every few students have had a turn.

2. Replace torn or bent plates during the relay.

3. Use Frisbees instead of paper or plastic plates.

4. Print each word of Psalm 119:133 on a separate index card. Place cards in mixed-up order along path. As students move along the path, they collect the verse cards and then put the cards in order.

• •

Discussion Questions
1. Ask a student to read Psalm 119:133 aloud. ***What does it mean for God to "direct [our] footsteps according to His Word"?*** (God helps us talk and act in ways that show obedience to Bible commands.)

2. ***What are some of the actions you will do when God is directing your footsteps?*** (Tell the truth. Show love and kindness. Share with others. Have self-control. Pray and sing to God.)

3. ***What might be different about your (school) if kids obeyed God's Word and showed self-control?*** Students respond.

Art Center: Wisdom Walk

Materials

Bible with bookmark at Psalm 119:133, dark-colored butcher paper, tape, chalk.

Prepare the Activity

Tape paper across floor of classroom. Make sure there is enough butcher paper for each student to be able to trace his or her feet. Print "wisdom" at one end of the butcher paper.

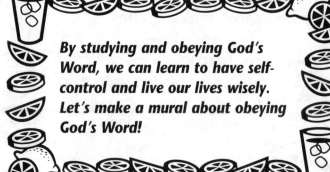

By studying and obeying God's Word, we can learn to have self-control and live our lives wisely. Let's make a mural about obeying God's Word!

Lead the Activity

1. Read Psalm 119:133 aloud. **What does the psalmist want God to help him do?** (Walk according to God's Word.) **The Bible tells us that walking according to God's Word will lead us to wisdom. In other words, if we live our lives obeying God's Word, we will be wise!**

2. Students form pairs. Students take turns standing on butcher paper facing the word "wisdom" while their partners trace around their feet. (Note: You may wish to have students remove their shoes and socks before beginning activity.) Students write their names in their footprints and decorate the mural with the words of the verse, drawings, etc.

3. Display mural on classroom wall, hallway or other public area at your church.

Options

1. Instead of laying paper on the floor, tape it to a wall at ground level. Students stand next to paper and trace each other's legs and feet.

2. Use colored chalk. Students dip chalk into water for brighter artwork. Provide disposable wipes for students to use in cleaning hands.

3. Use light-colored butcher paper and markers.

• •

Discussion Questions

1. *According to Psalm 119:133, what can we avoid by following God's Word?* (Doing wrong things. Sin.)

2. *What are some of the things God's Word tells us to do?* (Love God and love others. Be kind and gentle to others. Help people in need.)

3. *What are some things a kid your age can do to help him or her follow God's Word?* (Look for one new way to obey God every day. Choose one Bible command and try to obey it every day for a week. Memorize God's commands to know what to do. Put up reminders of God's Word in your room and on your notebooks.)

Lesson 51

Worship Center

Bible Verse
Direct my footsteps according to your word; let no sin rule over me. Psalm 119:133

Materials
Bible, *God's Kids Grow* cassette/CD or music video and player, "Self-Control" word chart (p. 485 in this book), large sheet of paper on which you have printed Psalm 119:133, masking tape.

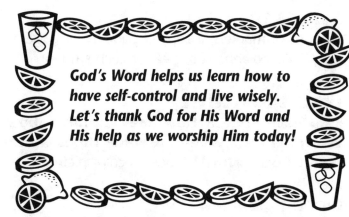

God's Word helps us learn how to have self-control and live wisely. Let's thank God for His Word and His help as we worship Him today!

Sing to God
Play "Self-Control," encouraging students to sing along with the music. **One of the ways we learn self-control is by reading God's Word, the Bible. When do you like to read God's Word? When is a time God's Word helps you?** Tell your own answer before asking volunteers to respond.

Hear and Say God's Word
Display paper on which you have printed Psalm 119:133. Have a volunteer read the verse aloud. **What does it mean for God to direct our footsteps according to His Word?** (He will help us obey His commands in the Bible.) **Instead of sin, what should "rule over," or be in charge of, how we live?** (God.) Students form a single-file line and walk around the room as they say the verse. (Optional: As students walk around the room, students each say one word of the verse, starting with the first student in line. Students continue until every student has had a turn to say a word of the verse or until the verse has been repeated several times.)

Pray to God
Psalm 119:133 was written as a prayer to God. Let's pray it together today. Lead students in praying by reciting the verse together. End prayer by thanking God for His Word and His help in following His Word.

Options
1. Students sing "Read All About It" (p. 483 in this book).

2. During the verse or prayer activity, older students find these verses in their Bibles and read them aloud as examples of God's Word guiding us and helping us to live wisely: Psalm 119:9-11,29,35,59,68,72,93,97-101. Add one or more of these verses to the prayer, printing the words below Psalm 119:133.

Bible Verse Coloring Center

FOR
YOUNGER
CHILDREN

Materials
Crayons or markers, a copy of page 49 or page 50 from
Bible Verse Coloring Pages #2 for each student.

Lead the Activity
Read Psalm 119:133. **How does learning about God's
Word help us? When are some times we can learn
about God's Word?** Students color picture.

Option
Students add drawings of themselves to picture.

Service Project Center

Materials
Materials needed for "Reminder Bands" (p. 42 from *The Big Book of
Service Projects*).

FOR
YOUNGER
CHILDREN
AND
OLDER
CHILDREN

Lead the Activity
Students complete the "Reminder Bands" activity as directed in *The
Big Book of Service Projects*. **What can you write on your bands
that will remind others to obey God's Word and learn to
live wisely?**

Discipleship Activity Center

Materials
Discussion Cards for Matthew 6:9-13 (pp. 117-122 from *The Big Book of
Christian Growth*), materials needed for "Straw Relay" or "This Is a Fish"
(p. 28 or p. 51 from *The Big Book of Christian Growth*).

FOR
OLDER
CHILDREN

Lead the Activity
**God's Word helps us learn how to have self-control and live wisely. Let's play a
game to help us learn about a wise prayer Jesus taught us to pray.** Students complete activity as directed in *The Big Book of Christian Growth*.

A Man After God's Own Heart

Bible Verse

Over all these virtues put on love, which binds them all together in perfect unity. Colossians 3:14

Bible Story Reference

1, 2 Samuel; 1 Chronicles

Teacher's Devotional

David was a shepherd, musician, poet, soldier and king. His life shows the heights of spiritual devotion, courage, leadership and integrity. His life also shows the depths of human sin and the pain and destruction that sin brings. David was called a man after God's own heart (see 1 Samuel 13:14), but he sinned horrendously. God's love and forgiveness for David extended through the centuries until the sinless Son of David died so that the breach caused by sin could be restored. Therefore, in David's life we also see the hope of restoration.

God's great love, far from causing Him to overlook the sins of His people, drove Him to make the ultimate sacrifice to overcome sin and death. God offers to meet all of our failures and disobedience with His boundless love and grace, grace that cost the life of His only Son.

The story of David provides an opportunity to help children begin to understand how to choose between the attractive but deadly fruit of this world and the life-giving fruit of the Spirit. This story can help children to know how deeply God loves them and how much He wants them to experience His love in their lives. Ask God to make this final session of *God's Kids Grow* the beginning of new and wonderful things for the children you teach.

Character Builder

The fruit of the Spirit is shown through our love for God and others.

Bible Story Center

Materials
Love poster from *Poster Pack;* ¼ cup (2 oz.) play dough and toothpicks for each student.

Tell the Story
Follow along with me as we use our dough to tell today's story.

What kinds of animals have you taken care of?

In today's story, we'll hear about a boy who took care of his father's sheep and grew up to be a mighty king!

1. **Roll four ropes from your dough and use them to spell "KING."** In the Old Testament, we read about King Saul. Saul was the first king of the Israelites. But there was a problem: King Saul seemed to want to do everything his own way, instead of God's way. God was patient with him, but Saul kept disobeying God and making excuses. Finally, God's prophet Samuel had to tell Saul, "Because you no longer obey God, your sons will not be kings. The Lord wants a man who loves and obeys Him to be king!"

Although Saul was still the king, God chose someone else to be the new king. God sent Samuel to Bethlehem to the home of a man named Jesse so that God could show Samuel the next king. Samuel met seven fine-looking sons of Jesse, but God said NONE of them was the one He had chosen.

2. **Use your dough and several toothpicks to make a harp.** Jesse had one more son—his youngest son, David, who was out watching the sheep. When Samuel met him, God told Samuel, "HE is the one!" Samuel poured olive oil on David's head to show that God had chosen David as king.

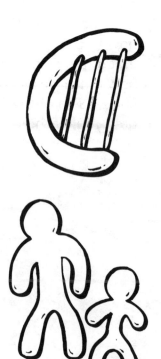

Some time later, King Saul was often upset and needed a person to play soothing music to help him calm down. Someone told the king about this young man named David who played the harp and who sang and wrote songs. So David was brought to the palace, not to be the new king, but to play his harp and make music for Saul.

3. **Make two figures, one much taller than the other.** One day, enemies called Philistines came to fight Israel. The Israelites were afraid! Among the Philistines was a giant named Goliath who was over 9 feet (2.7 m) tall! NOBODY could fight him! Day after day, Goliath made fun of the Israelites because

no one would fight him. Goliath would yell out to the Israelites, "Send me someone to fight! If he wins, we will become your servants. But if I win, all of Israel will serve the Philistines!"

One day David came to bring food to his brothers who were in the Israelite army. When David heard Goliath making fun of the Israelites, he WANTED to fight Goliath. Even though he was younger and smaller than many of the men in the army, David was the only one who was not afraid.

4. **Make five small stones.** David took five stones from the stream. He told Goliath, "You have a spear, but I have the Lord God with me! God doesn't need a sword or a spear. The battle is His!" David whipped his sling around his head and then let go. WHAP! The stone hit Goliath squarely between his eyes, and he fell to the ground! The Philistines ran! David became a hero!

David married King Saul's daughter and lived in the palace. But Saul was jealous because everyone in Israel loved David. Saul even tried to KILL David. David ran from Saul, but he never tried to hurt Saul. David trusted God to keep him safe and make him king at just the right time. After Saul died, the people came to David and made him their king.

5. **Make musical notes.** Now that David was the king, he didn't want to be like Saul, doing things his own way. Instead, David wanted to love and obey God. David helped his people worship God. David wrote many songs, called psalms, to help the people worship God. The book of Psalms in the Bible has many of these songs David wrote.

David did many other things, too. He fought many battles so that there would be peace in his country. Sometimes, David did wrong things. But David always talked to God. He asked God for help with his hard choices and asked for God's forgiveness when he had done wrong. David showed his love for God by praying whether he was glad or sad. Throughout his life, David showed his love for God and others.

• •

Focus on the Fruit
What are some of the things David did to show his love for God and others?
(Obeyed God. Wrote songs of praise to God. Prayed to God for help and forgiveness.)

David was called a man after God's own heart because he loved and obeyed God all of his life. David made mistakes and sometimes sinned, but he always asked forgiveness because he loved God so much. Show the Love poster. **Just like David's actions showed his love for God, the fruit of the Spirit growing in our lives will show our love for God and others.**

Fruitful Lives Object Talk

Bible Verse

Over all these virtues put on love, which binds them all together in perfect unity.
Colossians 3:14

Materials

Bible with bookmark at Colossians 3:14; optional—words to the hymn "Take My Life, and Let It Be" by Frances Havergal.

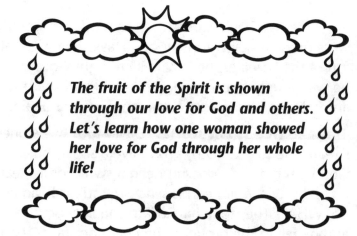

The fruit of the Spirit is shown through our love for God and others. Let's learn how one woman showed her love for God through her whole life!

Lead the Activity

1. Hold out your hand. **What do you use your hands to do?** Repeat question with feet and voice. **Frances Havergal is a woman who wrote a song about how she wanted to use her hands, her mouth, her money—her whole life! Frances said she wanted to use everything in her life to show her love for God and obedience to Him.** (Optional: Read entire hymn or sing hymn together.)

2. **The words that Frances wrote were not just nice-sounding words to her. She actually gave away most of her money to help others. And she studied the Bible often. Frances memorized the entire New Testament and several books in the Old Testament.**

   Frances spent her whole life loving God. She started writing poems about her love for God when she was only seven years old. Before she would do anything or write any songs or poems, Frances would pray. In fact, the words of "Take My Life, and Let It Be" are a prayer to God. Frances only lived to be 42 years old, but she wrote many books and poems, including over 60 songs that still help people tell about their love for God.

Conclude

Read Colossians 3:14 aloud. **What does this verse say we are to "put on," or show? How did Frances Havergal show her love for God?** Students respond. Lead students in prayer, expressing their love for God. (Optional: Read or sing hymn again as a prayer.)

• •

Discussion Questions

1. ***How can you show love for God with your hands? Your feet? Your voice?*** Students respond.

2. ***How does showing love for God and others also show the other fruit of the Spirit?***
   (When we show love, we also have the attitudes of joy, kindness, patience, etc.)

Active Game Center: Fruit Basket Upset

Materials
None.

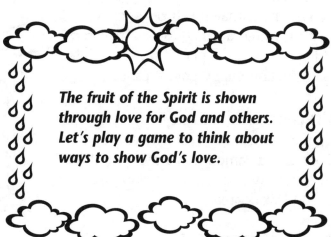

The fruit of the Spirit is shown through love for God and others. Let's play a game to think about ways to show God's love.

Lead the Game

1. Students sit in a circle. One volunteer is selected to be the Farmer and stands in the middle of the circle. Assign each student a fruit (banana, strawberry, peach, grape, pineapple, orange, etc.), making sure to assign each fruit to more than one student.

2. The Farmer calls out the name of a fruit. Students with that fruit jump up to trade places in the circle before the Farmer can take one of the places. If the Farmer calls out "Fruit Basket Upset!" all students must change places.

Blueberries

3. The student left without a place becomes the new Farmer. Before calling out a fruit name, the Farmer tells one way to show love for God or others. Ask Discussion Questions below to guide student as needed. Repeat play as above. Game continues as time allows or until all students have had a chance to be the Farmer.

Options

1. Students sit in chairs instead of on the floor.

2. Play another round of the game using the names of the fruit of the Spirit from Galatians 5:22,23 instead of using the names of actual fruits. Ask students to name the fruit of the Spirit as a review before assigning them to each student. You may want to list the fruit of the Spirit on a large sheet of paper for students to refer to during the game and discussion.

• •

Discussion Questions

1. ***What can you do to show (patience) to someone you know?*** Repeat question with other fruit of the Spirit. ***Practicing the fruit of the Spirit is a way to show love for others.***

2. ***What are some ways to show love for God?*** (Obey Him. Sing songs of praise to Him. Thank Him in your prayers. Tell others about Him.) ***How can you show your (faithfulness) to God? How does showing (self-control) demonstrate love for God?***

3. ***Who is someone you know who shows love for God and others? How does he or she show that love? What can you do to show love for God or others in that way?***

Art Center: Fruit-Flavored Art

Materials
Newspaper, small bowls or other containers, water, a variety of fruit-flavored drink mix packets, plastic spoons, white construction paper, paintbrushes.

Prepare the Activity
Spread newspaper over the work area. Pour a small amount of water into three or four bowls or containers and place around work area.

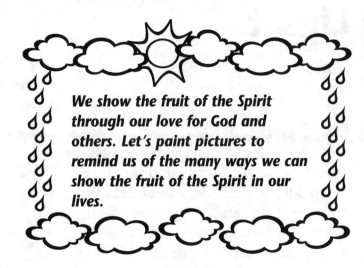

We show the fruit of the Spirit through our love for God and others. Let's paint pictures to remind us of the many ways we can show the fruit of the Spirit in our lives.

Lead the Activity
1. Students pour contents of fruit-flavored drink mix packets into empty bowls or other containers. Adding water one spoonful at a time, students stir to create a paint.

2. Ask the Discussion Questions below to help students think of actions that show love for God and others. Each student paints a scene showing an action that demonstrates love for God and/or others. Remind students to rinse their brushes in the bowls of water before switching colors.

Options
1. Older students may wish to combine fruit-flavored drink packets to create different colors.

2. Provide discarded men's shirts (T-shirts or dress shirts) or paint smocks for students to wear to protect clothing.

3. If time is limited, mix paints before class.

• •

Discussion Questions
1. *What are some actions that show love for God?* (Singing songs of praise to God. Telling others about Jesus. Praying. Helping someone in need. Obeying God's commands. Giving an offering.)

2. *What are some actions that show love for others?* (Helping someone who is hurt. Being honest. Saying kind words.)

3. *What is a way you can show love for God this week? Show love for others?*

Lesson 52

Worship Center

Bible Verse
Over all these virtues put on love, which binds them all together in perfect unity.
Colossians 3:14

Materials
Bible, *God's Kids Grow* cassette/CD or music video and player, "Fruit of the Spirit" word chart (p. 459 in this book), large sheet of paper on which you have printed Colossians 3:14, masking tape.

The fruit of the Spirit is shown through our love for God and others. Let's show God how much we love Him as we worship Him.

Sing to God
Play "Fruit of the Spirit," encouraging students to sing along with the music. **What are the fruit of the Spirit with which we can show God our love for Him?** (Love. Joy. Peace. Patience. Kindness. Goodness. Self-control. Faithfulness. Gentleness.) **God helps the members of His family grow these good characteristics that we call fruit.** Talk with children about becoming Christians, following the guidelines in the "Leading a Child to Christ" article on page 36.

Hear and Say God's Word
Display paper on which you have printed Colossians 3:14. Have a volunteer read the verse aloud. **What quality does this verse say to put on that helps us show all the fruit of the Spirit?** (Love.) **Our love for God and others helps all the other fruit, or virtues, to be shown.** Lead students in saying Colossians 3:14 together. Then have different groups of students say the verse together. **Stand up and say the verse if you (have brown hair).** Repeat as time allows, using other descriptions (like to play games, like to read, have a brother, have a sister, etc.).

Pray to God
Let's tell God that we love Him! Students pray aloud, telling God why they love Him and thanking Him for His love. End prayer by thanking God for His love and for helping the fruit of the Spirit to be shown in your life and in the lives of your students.

Options
1. At the beginning of this Worship Center, ask an older student to read aloud Psalm 89:1,2 aloud as an invitation to worship.

2. Students sing "All My Heart" and/or "Galatians 5:22,23" (p. 453 and/or p. 461 in this book).

3. During the verse activity, lead students in saying one or two of the fruit of the Spirit instead of "virtues" each time the verse is repeated.

Lesson 52

Bible Verse Coloring Center

FOR **YOUNGER** CHILDREN

Materials
Crayons or markers, a copy of page 183 or page 184 from *Bible Verse Coloring Pages #2* for each student.

Lead the Activity
Read Colossians 3:14. **How can you show love for others in your family? How can you show love for your friends and neighbors?** Students color picture.

Option
Also provide a copy of "Draw a picture of your family" page (p. 227 from *Bible Verse Coloring Pages #2)*. Students draw and color pictures and then tell ways to show love to each person in their families.

Service Project Center

FOR **YOUNGER** CHILDREN AND **OLDER** CHILDREN

Materials
Materials needed for "Early Morning Entertainment" (p. 77 from *The Big Book of Service Projects*).

Lead the Activity
Students complete the "Early Morning Entertainment" activity as directed in *The Big Book of Service Projects*. **What do you think the children we help in this project might learn about God's love? What are some other ways we can show love for God and others this week?**

Discipleship Activity Center

FOR **OLDER** CHILDREN

Materials
Discussion Cards for Galatians 5:22,23 (pp. 147-152 from *The Big Book of Christian Growth*); materials needed for "Knock It Down" or "Coin Cups" (p. 21 or p. 59 from *The Big Book of Christian Growth*).

Lead the Activity
Today we're going to play a game to help us discover ways of showing the fruit of the Spirit in our lives. Students complete activity as directed in *The Big Book of Christian Growth*.

452

All My Heart

How can I love the Lord with all my heart?

Lord, help me learn to love You from the start.

Lord (as a royal sash)

I want to love the Lord,

Love Him all the time

With all my heart, strength, soul and mind.

love

Even when it's hard to do what's right,

Help me show Your love with all my might.

Help me love You, Lord,

Love You all the time

With all my heart, strength, soul and mind.

time

God's Word can help us learn to do what's good,

And God can help us love Him as we should.

I'll show I love You, Lord,

Love You all the time,

With all my heart, strength, soul and mind.

With all my heart, strength, soul and mind.

With all my heart, strength, soul and mind.

heart

Words and Music: Gary Pailer. © 2001 Gospel Light. Permission to photocopy granted. *God's Kids Grow Leader's Guide*

All My Heart

      D
How can I love the Lord with all my heart?
      D
Lord, help me learn to love You from the start.

  G   **D**   **Em**   **G**   **D**   **Em**
I want to love the Lord,   love Him all the time
  G   **D**   **Em**   **A**   **D**
With all my heart, strength, soul and mind.

  D
Even when it's hard to do what's right,
  D
Help me show Your love with all my might.

G   **D**   **Em**   **G**   **D**   **Em**
Help me love You, Lord,   love You all the time
    G   **D**   **Em**   **A**   **D**
With all my heart, strength, soul and mind.

    D
God's Word can help us learn to do what's good,
    D
And God can help us love Him as we should.

  G   **D**   **Em**   **G**   **D**   **Em**
I'll show I love You, Lord,   love You all the time,
    G   **D**   **Em**   **A**   **D**
With all my heart, strength, soul and mind.   (2x)
    G   **D**   **Em**   **A**   **D**
With all my heart, strength, soul / / / / and mind.

Words and Music: Gary Pailer. © 2001 Gospel Light. Permission to photocopy granted. *God's Kids Grow Leader's Guide*

Be So Kind

Would you give someone more
Than what they're looking for?
Is that the kind of love you have?
Will everybody see your generosity?
Here is the question to be asked:

Would you be so kind
To put others first and you behind?
Could you share good things you find?
Would you be so kind?

Yes, I'll give someone more
Than what they're looking for;
That's the kind of love I want to have.
I want everyone one to see God's generosity,
So I will share the things I have.

Yes, I will be so kind
To put others first and myself behind.
Lord, help me share good things I find.
I will be so kind.

Would you be so kind
To put others first and you behind?
Could you share good things you find?
Would you be so kind?
I will be so kind.
I will be so kind.

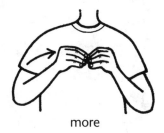

more

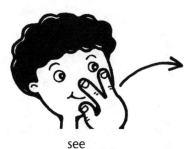

see

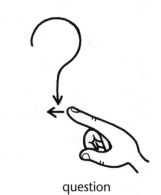

question

kind

share

Be So Kind

Intro: **D G** **D G**

D G   **D G**   **D G**
     Would you give someone more   than what they're looking for?

                       D   **C**
Is that the kind of love you have?

D G   **D G**   **D G**
     Will everybody see   your generosity?

                      D   **C**
Here is the question to be asked:

D   **C**   **G**   **C**   **D**
Would you be so kind to put others first and you behind?

D   **C**   **G**   **D**
Could you share good things you find? Would you be so kind?

D G   **D G**   **D G**
     Yes, I'll give someone more   than what they're looking for;

                 D   **C**
That's the kind of love I want to have.

D G   **D G**
     I want everyone one to see   God's generosity,

D G   **D**   **C**
So I will share the things I have.

D   **C**   **G**   **C**   **D**
Yes, I will be so kind to put others first and myself behind.

D   **C**   **G**   **D**
Lord, help me share good things I find. I will be so kind.

D   **C**   **G**   **C**   **D**
Would you be so kind to put others first and you behind?

D   **C**   **G**   **D**
Could you share good things you find? Would you be so kind?

C **G**   **D** **C** **G**   **D**
I will be so kind. I will be so kind.

Circle of Love

Jesus, I give thanks to You;
You loved me even before I knew You.
You loved me first, and now
I wanna show my love to You somehow.

Because You've shown Your love, Your love,
    Your love for me,
I can be a part of Your own family!

Jesus I pray to You;
Please help me do the things You want me to do.
When I am kind and share and say what's true,
It's a way to circle my love back to You!

I want to show my love, my love, my love for You
Every day, every way, in everything I do!

I want to show my love, my love, my love for You
Every day, every way, in everything I do!

I want to show my love, my love, my love for You
Every day, every way, in everything I do!

I want to show my love, my love, my love for You.

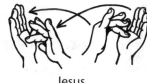

Jesus

thanks

love

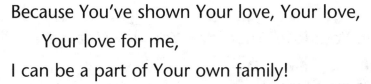

family

pray

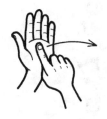

show

Circle of Love

Intro: F#m Em D (2x)

F#m   Em   D   F#m   Em   D
Jesus, I give thanks to You; You loved me even before I knew You.

F#m   Em   D   F#m   Em   D
You loved me first, and now   I wanna show my love to You somehow.

                        G   D   Em   D   Em   D
Because You've shown Your love, Your love, Your love for me,

        G   D   Em   G   Em   D
I can be a part of Your own family!

F#m   Em   D   F#m   Em   D
Jesus I pray to You;   Please help me do the things You want me to do.

                F#m   Em   D
When I am kind and share and say what's true,

                F#m   Em   D
It's a way to circle my love back to You!

                G   D   Em   D   Em   D
I want to show my love, my love, my love for You

                G   D   Em   G   Em   D
Every day, every way, in everything I do! (3x)

                G   D   Em   D   Em   D
I want to show my love, my love, my love for You.

Fruit of the Spirit

I love You, Lord. I see Your love and mirror it;

I'm growin' in the fruit of the Spirit!

I praise You, Lord; I'm glad You see and hear it.

I'm growin' in the fruit of the Spirit!

The fruit of the Spirit, the fruit of the Spirit—

I'm growin' in the fruit of the Spirit!

In Your Word I can read and hear it;

I'm growing in the fruit of the Spirit!

I learn Your way and bring others near it;

I'm growing in the fruit of the Spirit!

The fruit of the Spirit, the fruit of the Spirit—

I'm growin' in the fruit of the Spirit! (3x)

Lord (as a royal sash)

love

grow

hear

learn

Words and Music: Gary Pailer. © 2001 Gospel Light. Permission to photocopy granted. *God's Kids Grow Leader's Guide*

Fruit of the Spirit

Intro: D C G C G D

D   C
I love You, Lord. I see Your love and mirror it;

G C   G   D
I'm growin' in the fruit of the Spirit!

D   C
I praise You, Lord; I'm glad You see and hear it.

G C   G   D
I'm growin' in the fruit of the Spirit!

C   C#   D   C   C#   D
The fruit of the Spirit, the fruit of the Spirit—

C   G   D   B
I'm growin' in the fruit of the Spirit!

E   D   A
In Your Word I can read and hear it;

D   A   E
I'm growing in the fruit of the Spirit!

 E   D   A
I learn Your way and bring others near it;

D   A   E
I'm growing in the fruit of the Spirit!

        D   D#   E   D   D#   E
The fruit of the Spirit, the fruit of the Spirit—

D   A   E
I'm growin' in the fruit of the Spirit! (3x)

Galatians 5:22,23

The fruit of the Spirit is love,

joy, peace, patience, kindness,

goodness, faithfulness, gentleness and self-control.

Against such things there is no law.

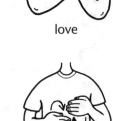

love

joy

The fruit of the Spirit is love,

joy, peace, patience, kindness,

goodness, faithfulness, gentleness and self-control.

Against such things there is no law.

peace

Against such things there is no law.

patient

Against such things there is no law.

kind

good

Words and Music: Gary Pailer. © 2001 Gospel Light. Permission to photocopy granted. *God's Kids Grow Leader's Guide*

Galatians 5:22,23

Intro: C# B F#

      F#   C#   B   F#   C#
The fruit of the Spirit is love, joy, peace, patience, kindness,

      B   F#   C#
goodness, faithfulness, gentleness and self-control.

      B   C#   F# D#m
Against such things there is no law.

      B   C#   F#
Against such things there is no law.

      F#   C#   B   F#   C#
The fruit of the Spirit is love, joy, peace, patience, kindness,

      B   F#   C#
goodness, faithfulness, gentleness and self-control.

      B   C#   F#   D#m
Against such things there is no law (no,no,no,no). *This line 2x third time through*

      B   C#   F#
Against such things there is no law.

Repeat second verse

Gentle Servant

Chorus:

I'm ready to serve you like Jesus wants me to;

I'm ready to serve you like Jesus would do.

What did He do to be a servant?

What did He teach His friends to do?

I want to follow His example;

He served with a gentle attitude.

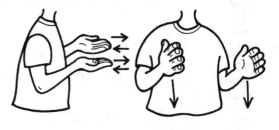

servant

Chorus

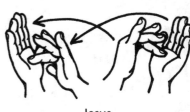

Jesus

What can I do to make things better?

What can I do to help you out?

What can I do to make you happy—

To show you what gentleness is about?

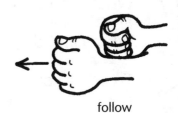

follow

I'm ready to serve you with a gentle attitude;

I'm ready to serve you like Jesus would do.

Chorus twice

Words and Music: Gary Pailer. © 2001 Gospel Light. Permission to photocopy granted. *God's Kids Grow Leader's Guide*

Gentle Servant

Intro: **E F#m A E**

Chorus:

    E   **F#**   **A**   **E**
I'm ready to serve you like Jesus wants me to;
    E   **F#**   **A**   **E**
I'm ready to serve you like Jesus would do.

E   **D**   **A**   **E**
What did He do to be a servant?
E   **D**   **A**   **E**
What did He teach His friends to do?
E   **D**   **A** **E**
I want to follow His example;
E   **D**   **A**   **E**
He served with a gentle attitude.

Chorus

E   **D**   **A**   **E**
What can I do to make things better?
E   **D**   **A**   **E**
What can I do to help you out?
E   **D**   **A**   **E**
What can I do to make you happy—
    E   **D**   **A**   **E**
To show you what gentleness is about?

    E   **F#**   **A**   **E**
I'm ready to serve you with a gentle attitude;
    E   **F#**   **A**   **E**
I'm ready to serve you like Jesus would do.

Chorus twice

Good Fruit

love

Love, joy, peace, patience and kindness,

Goodness and self-control,

Faithfulness and gentleness—

My fruit is gonna grow!

kind

Chorus:

Lord, because I know You love me,

It's like I've got strong roots;

Like an orange, banana or apple tree,

I'm gonna grow good fruit!

good

So when I'm growing this good fruit,

I will live in peace;

I'll be kind and faithful—patient, too.

Lord, help my fruit increase!

grow

Chorus

Tag:

I'm gonna grow, I'm gonna grow,

    I'm gonna grow good fruit!

peace

Good Fruit

Intro: G D C D F D   G D C D F D G

   C   D   Bm   Em
Love, joy, peace, patience and kindness,
   C   D   G
Goodness and self-control,
   C   D   Bm   Em
Faithfulness and gentleness—
     A7   D
My fruit is gonna grow!

Chorus:
                G   D   C   D
Lord, because I know You love me,
      F   D
It's like I've got strong roots;
             G   D   C   D
Like an orange, banana or apple tree,
      F   D   G   D C D G
I'm gonna grow good fruit!

      C   D   Bm   Em
So when I'm growing this good fruit,
C   D   G
I will live in peace;
      C   D   Bm   Em
I'll be kind and faithful—patient, too.
        A7   D
Lord, help my fruit increase!

Chorus

Tag:
F   F
I'm gonna grow, I'm gonna grow,
      F   D   G   D C D F D G
I'm gonna grow /// good fruit!

Note: To play song to match recording (G#), place capo on first fret.

 Words and Music: Gary Pailer. © 2001 Gospel Light. Permission to photocopy granted. *God's Kids Grow Leader's Guide*

Good Habits

Uh-oh! Here comes trouble again!

It's up to me if it will lose or win.

Trouble won't stand a chance,

    even from the start,

If I've grown faithful habits

    that help to make me smart!

good

Good habits! Good habits!

Bit by bit by bit, I'm forming good habits!

habits

Most habits we hear about are bad;

Those are the ones that make God sad.

When we trust God every day

    and do our very best,

We practice praying and helping,

    so we pass that trouble test!

sad

Good habits! Good habits!

Day by day by day,

Help me form good habits!

Good habits!

Day by day by day, day by day by day,

    day by day by day,

Help me form good habits! Good habits!

trust

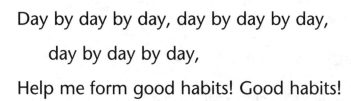

Words and Music: Gary Pailer. © 2001 Gospel Light. Permission to photocopy granted. *God's Kids Grow Leader's Guide*

Good Habits

Intro: **slide into G7 (10th fret; 11th with capo)**

D   A7   G7
Uh-oh! Here comes trouble again!
           D   A7   G7
It's up to me if it will lose or win.
D   A7   G7
Trouble won't stand a chance, even from the start,
                 D   A7   D   D7
If I've grown faithful habits that help to make me smart!

G7   D7
Good habits! Good habits!
G   G#   A   G7
Bit by bit by bit, I'm forming good habits!

D   A7   G7
Most habits we hear about are bad;
D   A7   G7
Those are the ones that make God sad.
                 D   A7   G7
When we trust God every day and do our very best,
                 D   A7   D   D7
We practice praying and helping, so we pass that trouble test!

G7   D7
Good habits! Good habits!
G   G#   A   G7
Day by day by day, help me form good habits!
D7
Good habits!

G   G#   A   G   G#   A   G   G#   A
Day by day by day, day by day by day, day by day by day,
                              G7   G7   D7
Help me form good habits! Good habits!

Note: To play song to match recording (Eb), place capo on first fret.

Goodness!

Every day people tell me I've got to be good.
Just what are they saying? If I knew that, maybe I could!

Goodness! How do I let it show?
I want to show goodness,
Even when nobody knows.

good

It means showing fairness in the things I say and do.
It means keeping my promise; it means telling the truth.

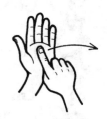

show

Goodness! How do I let it show?
I want to show goodness,
Even when nobody knows.

Every day we make choices; some are easy, some hard.
We will always show goodness when we obey the Lord.

promise

Bridge:

It's like being pure chocolate—
    just sweet all the way through!

telling

Goodness! I know how to let it show.
I'm gonna show goodness, goodness.
Obeying God makes goodness grow.

Repeat last chorus

obey

Goodness!

Intro: **Cm7 Dm (2x)**

Cm7   **Dm**   **Cm7**   **Dm**   **G**
   Every day people tell me   I've got to be good.

Cm7   **Dm**   **Cm7**   **Dm**   **G**
   Just what are they saying?   If I knew that, maybe I could!

Cm7   **Dm**   **G**   **Cm7**   **Dm**   **G**
Goodness! How do I let it show?

      Cm7   **Dm**   **G**   **Cm7**   **Dm**   **G**
I want to show goodness,   Even when nobody knows.

Cm7   **Dm**   **Cm7**   **Dm**
   It means showing fairness in the things I say and do.

Cm7   **Dm**   **Cm7**   **Dm**   **G**
   It means keeping my promise;   it means telling the truth.

Cm7   **Dm**   **G**   **Cm7**   **Dm**   **G**
Goodness! How do I let it show?

      Cm7   **Dm**   **G**   **Cm7**   **Dm**   **G**
I want to show goodness,   Even when nobody knows.

Cm7   **Dm**   **Cm7**   **Dm**   **G**
   Every day we make choices;   some are easy, some hard.

Cm7   **Dm**   **Cm7**   **Dm**   **G**
   We will always show goodness   when we obey the Lord.

Bridge:

Dm   **Cm7**   **Dm**   **G**
It's like being pure chocolate—just sweet all the way through!

Cm7   **Dm**   **G**   **Cm7**   **Dm**   **G**
   Goodness!   I know how to let it show.

        Cm7
I'm gonna show goodness, goodness.

Dm   **G**   **Cm7**   **Cm7 Bb Cm7**
Obeying God makes goodness grow.

Repeat last chorus

Words and Music: Gary Pailer. © 2001 Gospel Light. Permission to photocopy granted. *God's Kids Grow Leader's Guide*

Hear, O Israel

(Mark 12:28-31)

command

"Of all the commandments, which is the most important?"

"The most important one is this," answered Jesus;

important

" 'Hear, O Israel, the Lord our God, the Lord is One;

Love the Lord your God with all your heart

hear

And with all your soul and with all your mind

And with all your strength.'

God

The second is this: 'Love your neighbor as yourself.'

There is no commandment greater than these."

strength

Words and Music: Darla Plice. © 1996 Gospel Light. Permission to photocopy granted. *God's Kids Grow Leader's Guide*

Hear, O Israel

(Mark 12:28-31)

Intro: **C**

             C   **F**
"Of all the commandments, which is the most important?"

                C   **G**
"The most important one is this," answered Jesus;

   C   **F**
" 'Hear, O Israel, the Lord our God, the Lord is One;

C   **G**
Love the Lord your God with all your heart

         C   **G**
And with all your soul and with all your mind

         C
And with all your strength.'

   Bb   **G**   **C**
The second is this: 'Love your neighbor as yourself.'

     F   **G**   **C**
There is no commandment   greater than these."

Joy!

Paul and Silas were inside prison walls
For loving the Lord with all their might;
They started praying and singing songs of joy,
    'round about midnight.
God shook the ground so hard, it opened all the prison doors!
Their joy amazed the jailer and helped him know the Lord!

praying

Joy, joy! You don't have to wear a frown!
Joy, joy beats anything around!
Joy, joy is from the Lord—that's for sure.
Joy, joy shakes things up and opens doors.

When ten men were sick by the side of the road,
They called to Jesus, "Won't You help us, Lord?"
Jesus healed them all, but one man stopped and stared;
He could see that he was cured!
When he realized what had happened, his joy just overflowed;
He was so very grateful, he ran back to thank the Lord!

shaken

Joy, joy! You don't have to wear a frown!
Joy, joy beats anything around!
Joy, joy! Look at what God's given you.
Joy, joy! You'll praise Him the whole day through!

Remember, if you're feeling down, sad or even mad,
God knows how you feel.
Think about His loving you, about how much He cares;
His love for you is real.
Soon joy will fill your sadness; praise will fill your prayers;
Your face will break into a smile that reaches to your ears!

thank

Joy, joy! You don't have to wear a frown!
Joy, joy beats anything around!
Joy, joy is from the Lord—that's for sure;
Joy, joy gives us His strength forevermore.

Words: Gary Pailer, Mary Gross, Wes Haystead. Music: Gary Pailer. © 2001 Gospel Light. Permission to photocopy granted. *God's Kids Grow Leader's Guide*

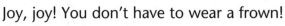
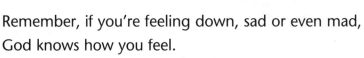

Joy!

Intro: C F Dm G (2x)

C   F   Dm   G   C   F   Dm   G
Paul and Silas were inside prison walls for loving the Lord with all their might;

         C   F   Dm   G   C   F   Dm G
They started praying and singing songs of joy, 'round about midnight.

      Am   G
God shook the ground so hard, it opened all the prison doors!

      Bb   F   G
Their joy amazed the jailer and helped him know the Lord!

C F Dm   G   C F Dm   G
Joy, joy! You don't have to wear a frown! Joy, joy beats anything around!

C F   Dm   G   C F Dm   F G C
Joy, joy is from the Lord—that's for sure. Joy, joy shakes things up and opens doors.

        C   F   Dm   G
When ten men were sick by the side of the road,

         C   F   Dm G
They called to Jesus, "Won't You help us, Lord?"

       C   F   Dm   G
Jesus healed them all, but one man stopped and stared;

C   F   Dm G
He could see that he was cured!

      Am   G
When he realized what had happened, his joy just overflowed;

     Bb   F   G
He was so very grateful, he ran back to thank the Lord!

C F Dm   G   C F Dm   G
Joy, joy! You don't have to wear a frown! Joy, joy beats anything around!

C F Dm   G
Joy, joy! Look at what God's given you.

C F Dm   F G C
Joy, joy! You'll praise Him the whole day through!

      C   F   Dm   G C   F   Dm G
Remember, if you're feeling down, sad or even mad, God knows how you feel.

C   F   Dm   G   C   F   Dm G
Think about His loving you, about how much He cares; His love for you is real.

      Am   G
Soon joy will fill your sadness; praise will fill your prayers;

     Bb   F   G
Your face will break into a smile that reaches to your ears!

C F Dm   G   C F Dm   G
Joy, joy! You don't have to wear a frown! Joy, joy beats anything around!

C F Dm   G   C F   Dm   F G C
Joy, joy is from the Lord—that's for sure; Joy, joy gives us His strength forevermore.

Just Ask Him

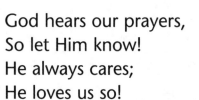

God will help us when we pray
    (just ask Him, just ask Him);
We all can use help every day
    (just ask Him, just ask Him).

God hears our prayers,
So let Him know!
He always cares;
He loves us so!

pray

If we ask God's help, He'll help us grow
    (just ask Him, just ask Him);
We'll have more good fruit to show
    (just ask Him, just ask Him).

Love, joy, peace, patience and kindness
    (just ask Him, just ask Him);
Goodness, faithfulness, gentleness, self-control.

help

God hears our prayers,
So let Him know!
He always cares;
He loves us so!

Love, joy, peace, patience and kindness
    (just ask Him, just ask Him);
Goodness, faithfulness, gentleness, self-control.

hear

Ooh, ooh, ooh (just ask Him);
Ooh, ooh, ooh (just ask Him);
Ooh, ooh, ooh (just ask Him);
Ooh, ooh, ooh.

loves

Words and Music: Gary Pailer. © 2001 Gospel Light. Permission to photocopy granted. *God's Kids Grow Leader's Guide*

Just Ask Him

Intro: **Bb F C (2x)**

F   **C**
God will help us when we pray (just ask Him, just ask Him);
F   **C**
We all can use help every day (just ask Him, just ask Him).

     Bb **F** **C**   **Bb** **F** **C**
God hears our prayers, So let Him know!
     Bb F C   **Bb** **F C**
He always cares; He loves us so!

         F   **C**
If we ask God's help, He'll help us grow (just ask Him, just ask Him);
F   **C**
We'll have more good fruit to show (just ask Him, just ask Him).
F   **C**
Love, joy, peace, patience and kindness (just ask Him, just ask Him);
F   **C**
Goodness, faithfulness, gentleness, self-control.

     Bb   **F** **C**   **Bb** **F** **C**
God hears our prayers, So let Him know!
     Bb F C   **Bb**   **F C**
He always cares; He loves us so!

F   **C**
Love, joy, peace, patience and kindness (just ask Him, just ask Him);
F   **C**
Goodness, faithfulness, gentleness, self-control.

 Bb   **F**   **C**
Ooh, ooh, ooh (just ask Him);
 Bb   **F**   **C**
Ooh, ooh, ooh (just ask Him);
 Bb   **F**   **C**
Ooh, ooh, ooh (just ask Him);
 Bb   **F**   **C**
Ooh, ooh, ooh.

Just Like You

Teach me to be like You, Lord Jesus;

I want to live like You, Lord Jesus.

Teach me to be like You, Lord Jesus;

I want to love like You, Lord Jesus.

I will learn to live my life

In ways that please You.

I will learn to do what's right

By loving like You do.

I want to be like You.

Repeat song

Tag:

Teach me to be like You.

Teach me to be like You.

Teach me to be like You,

Lord Jesus.

teach

Jesus

love

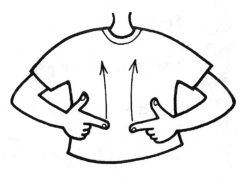

life

Just Like You

F#   B   F#
Teach me to be like You, Lord Jesus;
F#   C#   F#
I want to live like You, Lord Jesus.
F#   B   F#
Teach me to be like You, Lord Jesus;
F#   C#   F#
I want to love like You, Lord Jesus.

C# F#   B   F#
I will learn to live my life
  C# F# B
In ways that please You.
C# F#   B   F#
I will learn to do what's right
  C# F# B
By loving like You do.
B   C#
I want to be like You.

Repeat song

Tag:
F#   B
Teach me to be like You.
F#   B
Teach me to be like You.
F#   C#   F#
Teach me to be like You, Lord Jesus.

Patient Father

Oh, patient Father, Your mercy has no end.
Your love is like no other;
You always reach out to welcome me in.
I know You are forgiving; that's how I want to live;
Whatever comes, please help me to forgive!

patient

Oh, patient Father, help me be more like You.
While I am waiting, help me to trust in You.
I know You keep your promises;
    please help me to keep mine.
Whatever comes, please help me to be kind!

wait

Bridge:
I'll ask You for Your wisdom. I'll keep on trying,
Even when I might want to stop.
I'll try to show Your mercy
    and be slow to get mad.
If someone calls me names, I'll let it drop.

mercy

Oh, patient Father, Your mercy has no end.
Your love is like no other; You always reach
    out to welcome me in.

promises

Tag:
You always reach out to welcome me in.
You always reach out to welcome me in.
Thanks for reaching out to welcome me in.

kind

Words and Music: Gary Pailer and Mary Gross. © 2001 Gospel Light. Permission to photocopy granted. *God's Kids Grow Leader's Guide*

Patient Father

Intro: A E D A (2x)

```
A    E       D       A    E      D      A
```
Oh, patient Father, Your mercy has no end.
```
       A     E      D A   A       E       D         A
```
Your love is like no other; You always reach out to welcome me in.
```
      D              E              F#m             C#m
```
I know You are forgiving; that's how I want to live;
```
          D             E        A      E D A A E D A
```
Whatever comes, please help me to forgive!

```
A    E       D       A    E      D        A
```
Oh, patient Father, help me be more like You.
```
A    E       D       A    E      D    A
```
While I am waiting, help me to trust in You.
```
      D              E                F#m                C#m
```
I know You keep your promises; please help me to keep mine.
```
           D              E            A       E D A
```
Whatever comes, please help me to be kind!

Bridge:
```
   G                     D         G      D
```
I'll ask You for Your wisdom. I'll keep on trying,
```
G              D           A
```
Even when I might want to stop.
```
      G            D            G          D
```
I'll try to show Your mercy and be slow to get mad.
```
      G                D  E          A E D A   A E D A
```
If someone calls me names, I'll let it drop.

```
A    E       D       A    E      D      A
```
Oh, patient Father, Your mercy has no end.
```
       A     E      D A   A       E       D         A
```
Your love is like no other; You always reach out to welcome me in.

Tag:
```
       A         E      D          A
```
You always reach out to welcome me in.
```
       A         E      D          A
```
You always reach out to welcome me in.
```
A               E       D          A
```
Thanks for reaching out to welcome me in.

Words and Music: Gary Pailer and Mary Gross. © 2001 Gospel Light. Permission to photocopy granted. *God's Kids Grow Leader's Guide*

Peacemaker

I'm gonna honor you my friend
    and put my love to the test;
I'll try to put you first
    and treat you like you're the best.
If we start to argue,
    I'll do my best to be kind;
Lord, help me find a way
    to keep my goal in mind

To be a peacemaker, a peacemaker.

I'm gonna do what it takes to live
    in peace with everyone;
With my God's help
    I know it can be done.
I'm gonna treat you with a lot of respect;
I'm gonna say good things about you;
    I'm gonna do my best

To be a peacemaker, a peacemaker—
    I want to be a peacemaker.

I'm gonna be a peacemaker,
    a world shaker.
I want to be a peacemaker.

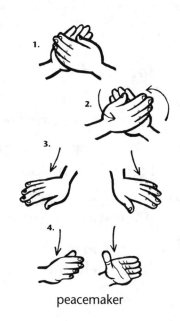

peacemaker

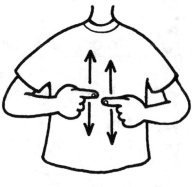

argue

Peacemaker

Intro: **F7**

         F   **Bb**   **F**   **Bb**   **F7**
I'm gonna honor you my friend and put my love to the test;

      F   **Bb**   **F**   **Bb**   **F7**
I'll try to put you first and treat you like you're the best.

     Gm   **C**   **Bb**   **F**
If we start to argue, I'll do my best to be kind;

     Gm   **C**   **Bb**
Lord, help me find a way to keep my goal in mind

        F7   **F7**
To be a peacemaker, a peacemaker.

        F   **Bb**   **F**   **Bb**   **F7**
I'm gonna do what it takes to live in peace with everyone;

     F   **Bb**   **F**   **Bb**   **F7**
With my God's help I know it can be done.

Gm   **C**   **Bb**   **F**
I'm gonna treat you with a lot of respect;

     Gm   **C**   **Bb**
I'm gonna say good things about you; I'm gonna do my best

     F7   **F7**   **F7**
To be a peacemaker, a peacemaker—I want to be a peacemaker.

        F7   **F7**   **F7**
I'm gonna be a peacemaker, a world shaker. I want to be a peacemaker.

Hint: **Play F7 at 8th fret with index finger on 2nd and 1st strings at 6th fret.**

Read All About It

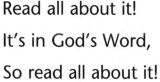

Hey, what's in that book?
God's story of love to us,
  if we'll just look!
Hey, have you heard the good news?
Jesus died and rose to bring forgiveness
    and new life, too.

Read all about it!
It's in God's Word,
So read all about it!

Hey, have you heard the good news?
We can learn how to grow good fruit
    like God wants us to do.
Hey, I bet you already knew it:
God's Word tells us what to do
    and He'll help us do it.

Read all about it!
It's in God's Word,
So read all about it!
Read all about it!
So read all about it!
So read all about it!

God

good

grow

help

Words and Music: Gary Pailer. © 2001 Gospel Light. Permission to photocopy granted. *God's Kids Grow Leader's Guide*

Read All About It

E7
Hey, what's in that book? God's story of love to us, if we'll just look!
E7
Hey, have you heard the good news?
    E7
Jesus died and rose to bring forgiveness and new life, too.

C#m7 B7   E7   C#m7 C#m7   C#m7   B7
Read all about it! It's in God's Word,
            E7
So read all about it!

E7
Hey, have you heard the good news?
    E7
We can learn how to grow good fruit like God wants us to do.
E7
Hey, I bet you already knew it:
    E7
God's Word tells us what to do and He'll help us do it.

C#m7 B7   E7   C#m7 C#m7   C#m7   B7
Read all about it! It's in God's Word,
         E7   A7   E7
So read all about it! Read all about it!
   A7   E7   A7   E7
So read all about it! So read all about it!

Self-Control

Don't want to fly off the handle;

Help me see a better angle.

Don't wanna fight; don't wanna tangle.

Give me self-control, self-control!

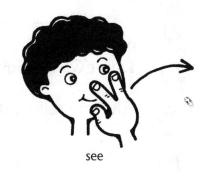

see

Don't wanna say bad things to you;

I want to say what God wants me to.

I'm praying hard His love will come through

To give me self-control, self-control!

Bridge:

Lord, help me take it slow;

    teach me self-control.

Lord, help me take it slow;

    teach me self-control.

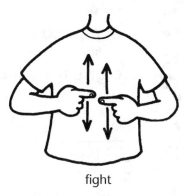

fight

I'm awake; I am ready.

I'm alert; I am steady.

I'm not gonna pop my cork—

He gives me self-control, self-control!

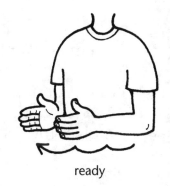

ready

Tag:

Self-control! Self-control! Self-control!

Self-Control

Intro: D G D G D **(4x)**

D   G7   D   G7

      Don't want to fly off the handle; help me see a better angle.

D   G7

Don't wanna fight; don't wanna tangle.

Bb   A   D G D G D **(2x)**

Give me self-control, self-control!

D   G7

Don't wanna say bad things to you;

D   G7

I want to say what God wants me to.

     D   G7

I'm praying hard His love will come through

     Bb   A   D G D G D **(2x)**

To give me self-control, self-control!

Bridge:

G   F   D G D G D

Lord, help me take it slow; teach me self-control.

G   F   D G D G D **(2x)**

Lord, help me take it slow; teach me self-control.

D   G7   D   G7

      I'm awake; I am ready. I'm alert; I am steady.

D   G7

I'm not gonna pop my cork—

     Bb   A   D G D G D **(2x)**

He gives me self-control, self-control!

Tag:

G7   D   G7   D   G7   D

Self-control! Self-control! Self-control!

Note: **To play song to match recording (Eb), place capo on first fret.**
Hint: **Try playing a bar chord "G" on third fret with the first string open.**

Words: Gary Pailer, Wes Haystead. Music: Gary Pailer. © 2001 Gospel Light. Permission to photocopy granted. *God's Kids Grow Leader's Guide*

You Promised!

You help me to know (every day);
You help me to grow (in every way);
You help me to see (what to do);
You help me to be more like You.

know

Chorus:

You promised (Lord, I love You),
You promised (You always come through),
You promised; Your word is true.
You promised (Lord, I love You),
You promised (You always come through),
You promised; I can count on You.

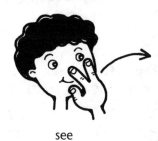

grow

Please help me to care (lend a hand);
Please help me to share (all I can);
Please help me to give (like You give);
Please help me to live more like You.

see

Chorus

I can count on You; I can count on You.
   (You promised!)
I can count on You; I can count on You.
   (You promised!)

promised

You Promised!

Intro: **G A D (2x)**

G   A   D   G   A   D
You help me to know (every day); You help me to grow (in every way);
G   A   D   G   A   D   G A D
You help me to see (what to do); You help me to be more like You.

Chorus:

    Bm
You promised (Lord, I love You),
    D   **Bm**
You promised (You always come through),
    G   A   D
You promised; Your word is true.

    Bm
You promised (Lord, I love You),
    D   **Bm**
You promised (You always come through),
    G   A   G A D   G A D
You promised; I can count on You.

G   A   D   G   A   D
Please help me to care (lend a hand); Please help me to share (all I can);
G   A   D
Please help me to give (like You give);
G   A   D   G A D
Please help me to live more like You.

Chorus

G   A   G   D
I can count on You. (You promised!) (8x)
G   A   D
    I can count on You.

Note: **To play song to match recording (Eb), place capo on first fret.**

 Words and Music: Gary Pailer. © 2001 Gospel Light. Permission to photocopy granted. *God's Kids Grow Leader's Guide*